SOCIETY OF BIBLICAL LITERATURE
1979 SEMINAR PAPERS
VOL. I

SOCIETY OF BIBLICAL LITERATURE
SEMINAR PAPERS SERIES
Edited by
Paul J. Achtemeier

Number 16

Society of Biblical Literature
1979 Seminar Papers
Vol. I
Edited by
Paul J. Achtemeier

SCHOLARS PRESS
Missoula, Montana

SOCIETY OF BIBLICAL LITERATURE
1979 SEMINAR PAPERS
VOL. I

Edited by
Paul J. Achtemeier

One Hundred Fifteenth Annual Meeting
15–18 November 1979
Statler-Hilton Hotel, New York, New York

Published by
SCHOLARS PRESS
for
The Society of Biblical Literature

Distributed by
SCHOLARS PRESS
PO Box 5207
Missoula, Montana 59806

SOCIETY OF BIBLICAL LITERATURE
1979 SEMINAR PAPERS
VOL. I

Edited by
Paul J. Achtemeier

ISBN: 0-89130-357-x pbk
ISSN: 0145-2711

Printed in the United States of America

Printing Department
University of Montana
Missoula, Montana 59812

7999—UM Printing Services

TABLE OF CONTENTS

Introductory Note. . . . .*vii*

S 20   *The* Kareth *Penalty in P: Rational and Cases*
    Donald J. Wold 1

S 31   *Windows and Mirrors: Literary Criticism and Luke's Sitz im Leben**
    Robert J. Karris 47

S 32   *Luke, Josephus and Rome: A Comparative Approach to the Lukan* Sitz im Leben
    Benjamin J. Hubbard. 59

S 33   *The Problem of Food in Acts: A Study of Literary Patterns with Particular Reference to Acts 6:1-7*
    Joseph B. Tyson. 69

S 34   *On Finding the Lukan Community: A Cautious Cautionary Essay*
    Luke T. Johnson. 87

S 35   *The Feeding of the Five Thousand: A Markan Composition*
    Robert M. Fowler 101

S 36   *Collected Fragments: On the Priority of John 6 to Mark 6-8*
    Mahlon H. Smith III. 105

S 37   *Peter's Denial Reexamined: John's Knowledge of Mark's Gospel*
    Kim E. Dewey 109

S 38   *The Cleansing of the Temple and the Anointing at Bethany: The Order of Events in Mark 11/John 11-12*
    Edward F. Glusman, Jr. 113

S 39   *Evidence from Jn. 12 that the Author of John Knew the Gospel of Mark*
    Lloyd R. Kittlaus. 119

S 40   *Two Changing Patterns! Conflicts and the Necessity of Death: John 2 and 12 and Markan Parallels*
    Anitra Bingham Kolenkow. 123

S 41   *The Anointing in Mark 14:3-9 and John 12:1-8*
    Winsome Munro. 127

S 81   *Welfare in the Churches of Asia Minor Under the Early Roman Empire*
    L. William Countryman. 131

vi

S 163   *A Second Look at* The Gospel Before Mark
Pierson Parker .147

S 198   *Virgins, Widows, and Paul in Second*
Century Asia Minor
Dennis MacDonald 169

S 295   *"This Is a Hard Saying; Who Can Be a*
Listener to It?"
The Creation of the Reader in John 6
Gary Phillips. .185

S 296   *It Is Written: A Structuralist Analysis*
of John 6
John Dominic Crossan 197

S 340   *The Agreements That Exist Between*
Luke and John
F. Lamar Cribbs. 215

INTRODUCTORY NOTE

The various papers contained in the two volumes of
Seminar Papers, 1979, will be discussed in the appropriate
program units during the One Hundred Fifteenth Annual Meeting
of the Society of Biblical Literature, 15-18 November, in New
York City. The volumes are produced photographically, from
the copy submitted by the authors of the papers. Both content
and format are therefore the direct responsibility of the
respective authors. Editorial work is limited to assembling
the papers and preparing them for publication. Occasionally a
title is recast to conform to the normal format of the papers,
but there is no further editing.

The volumes are intended to aid the discussion carried
on within the appropriate program units at the annual meeting.
Since the papers are intended to foster and stimulate such discussion, in many cases they represent the first attempt to
formulate the ideas they contain and the theses they propose.
Only rarely do they represent the final product of scholarly
reflection. Rather, they represent for the most part the first
step in the process of scholarly debate and refinement. Publication of the papers in this volume is simply to aid in their
distribution, and represents no claim on the part of the
SOCIETY that they are representative of the mature theological
work of these or other SOCIETY members.

The order in which the papers appear is dictated by their
place within the Annual Program. The identifying number preceding each title refers to the program, and the Book of
Abstracts. The letter *S* indicates they are presentations of
the Society of Biblical Literature.

The editor happily takes this opportunity to thank the
authors and the chairmen and chairwomen of the various Groups
and Seminars, and the Conveners of the various consultations
whose efforts resulted in the papers collected in these two
volumes. Thanks is also due to Sally Hicks, who prepared the
camera-ready copy of the introductory material.

THE <u>KARETH</u> PENALTY IN P: RATIONALE AND CASES

Donald J. Wold

Simpson College

I. THE RATIONALE

The biblical penalty <u>kareth</u>, expressed in its fullest
form by the Priestly Writer's formula "that person shall be
cut off from his people" (ונכרתה הנפש ההוא מעמיה, e.g. Gen
17:14), has been understood in various ways.[1] In general, a
rationale for the imposition of the <u>kareth</u> penalty must be
sought in P's conception of what is pure (טהור) and impure
(טמא) and what is sacred (קדש) and profane (חל).[2] Although
analysis of these concepts in full must await a separate work,
it is important to recognize at this point their relevance to
the <u>kareth</u> curse. Rules delimiting their essence and inter-
relationships within P's cosmology and economy are expressed
with respect to time, space, persons and objects. The categories of holiness and impurity in P's system have, beyond
their religious function and theological significance, the
practical purpose of lending order to P's society.

Anthropologist Mary Douglas has recently emphasized the
importance of pollution beliefs in the structuring of society.
Briefly, her view of holiness and impurity concepts may be
summarized as follows:

> Defilement is never an isolated event. It
> cannot occur except in view of a systematic
> ordering of ideas. . . .The only way in which
> pollution ideas make sense is in reference to
> a total structure of thought whose keystone,
> boundaries, margins, and internal lines are
> held in relation by rituals of separation.[3]

She continues:

> Holiness requires that individuals shall con-
> form to the class to which they belong. And
> holiness requires that different classes of
> things shall not be confused. . . .Holiness
> means keeping distinct the categories of
> creation. It therefore involves correct def-
> inition, discrimination and order.[4]

Finally, Professor Douglas observes:

> . . .when the sense of outrage is adequately
> equipped with practical sanctions in the social
> order, pollution is not likely to arise. Where,
> humanly speaking, the outrage is likely to go

unpunished, pollution beliefs tend to be called
in to supplement the lack of other sanctions.[5]

The principles outlined by Douglas aptly apply to the
Priestly Writer's schematism. In P, the binary oppositions
of impurity and holiness are means to preserve the identity of
the theocratic nation. P's theology links holiness with God;
hence, the violations of his pollution rules by bringing the
impure into contact with the holy are deemed to be offenses
against God. Inasmuch as the kareth crimes then are perpe-
trated against the divine order and therefore cannot be punished by man,[6] the Priestly appeal to the divine curse of
kareth for deliberate cultic violations is axiomatic.[7]

The biblical categories of holiness and impurity are opposite but they are not passive--they are, in fact hostile.
Both holiness and impurity are capable of being transferred
according to the Preistly tradition, though greater space is
allocated in P to regulating the contagion of impurity. This
is due, in part, to the fact that the dynamic power created
by impurity poses a greater threat to society. When the impure comes into contact with the pure, the latter is always
defiled; the impure is never purified.[8] Thus, individuals
and objects may have their positive ritual status altered by
contact (whether direct or indirect) with sources of impurity.

Pollution for P is, as regards both objects and living
persons, temporary and situational; impurity, like holiness,
is an acquired status. Only God is inherently and permanently
holy. The holiness of persons and objects may be placed on
a graduated scale.[9] The negative ritual status of persons
may be acquired voluntarily by flouting certain behavioral
guidelines or involuntarily as a result of natural processes
such as menstruation, birth, death, etc. Personal impurity
is automatically a threat to the equilibrium of the Priestly
society. Thus, specific measures are prescribed by P for the
removal of ritual impurity as a prerequisite for admission to
or reinstatement into a positive ritual status that allows for
continuance in the camp of Israel and execution of the individual's right to participate in Israel's cultic worship.
The Priestly kareth formula ultimately is aimed at making
Israel a pure and holy people, patterned after the holiness
of God himself (Lev. 20:26).

In the exposition which follows, it will be shown that
the Priestly Writer invokes the kareth curse for deliberate
treespasses against the rules of personal conduct which define
and preserve the distinction between the sacred and the impure,
embracing such ordinary activities as eating, working, speaking, and sexual intercourse, as well as matters peculiar to
worship and religious ceremony.[10] Whatever the individual
Israelite's personal appetites or affectations in these areas
might be, they must be subordinated to the divine ordinances
expounded by P. Willful transgressions of the border between
holiness and impurity are thought to defile the residence of
the Deity in the adytum of P's Tabernacle (among other things),

thereby creating the situation for the potential withdrawal
of God's presence and protection from Israel.[11]

II. THE CASES OF <u>KARETH</u> IN THE PRIESTLY SOURCE

A. Violations Against Sacred Time

1) <u>Failure to observe Passover at its proper time</u>
(Num. 9:13). The Israelite or the resident alien (גר) who
has been circumcised and is otherwise ritually pure is ob-
ligated to observe Passover at its appointed time (במועדו)
beginning on the 14th of Nisan. A second date one month
later (14th of Iyar) is designated by P to accommodate those
persons who had legitimately missed the first Passover cele-
bration for reasons of ritual impurity or travel (Num. 9:9f).
Early rabbinic opinion extended P's rule to allow for performance of the second Passover by those who had missed the
first unintentionally or accidentally, but they were liable
to <u>kareth</u> should they miss the second.[12] Observance of Passover is a positive precept; the accompanying motive clause
makes the reason for <u>kareth</u> explicit: ". . .for he did not
present the Lord's offering at its appointed time" (Num.
9:13).

The importance which the Priestly Writer attaches to
observance of Passover at its appointed time finds a striking
analogue in the festivals of the Hittite cult. The Hittite
examples are significant because violations against sacred
time are punishable by the gods and, as with the Priestly
<u>kareth</u>, the penalty befalls not only the sinner but also his
progeny. In the following case, a temple official is threatened with extinction should he not enforce observance of the
sacred festivals at their prescribed times:

> You who are the temple officials, if you do not
> celebrate the festivals at the time proper for
> the festivals and (if) you celebrate the festi-
> val of spring in the autumn, or (if)--when in
> the course of time a festival is about to be
> celebrated--he who is to perform it comes to
> you, the priests, the "anointed," the mothers-
> of-god, to the temple officials and embraces
> your knees (saying): "The harvest is before
> me, or arranging for (my) marriage, or a jour-
> ney, or some other business. Do me a favor
> and let me finish that business first. But when
> that business of mine is finished, I shall per-
> form the festival as prescribed"--do not yield
> to a man's whim, let him not take precedence
> (of the gods). You must not make a deal of
> the god's pleasure. Should with you a man
> take precedence (of the gods) and should you
> make a deal for yourselves, the gods will seek
> to take revenge on you in the future. They
> will hold a grudge against you, yourselves,
> your wives, your children (and) your servants.

4

So act only according to the pleasure of the
gods! And you will eat bread, drink water
and establish a family.[13]

In a similar fashion, those who are responsible to provide sacrifical animals in the Hittite cult must have them
ready as scheduled:

You who are the gods' cowherds (and) the
gods' shepherds, if there is a rite for
any god at the time of bearing young and
you are supposed to have ready for him
either a calf, a lamb, a kid or choice animals, do not delay them! Have them ready
at the right time; do not let the gods wait
for them. Before a man eats of the young
animals, bring it promptly to the gods. Or
if there is a "festival of the cup" for any
god, (even) while they repair the cup, do
not allow it to lapse; celebrate it for him.
If you do not bring the young animals promptly to the gods, but eat first of them your-
selves or send them to your superiors, but
it afterward becomes known, it is considered
a capital sin for you. If it does not become
known--at whatever time you will bring them,
you will bring them before the god with these
words: "If we have given this young animal
to ourselves first, or have given it to our
superiors, or to our wives, our children or
to anyone else, we have offended the gods'
feelings." Then you will drink dry the rhy-
ton of the god of life. If you are found
innocent, (it is due to) your patron god;
but if you are found guilty, you will perish
together with your wives and children.[14]

Further, it is demanded of the Hittite border guards
that they observe sacred time: ". . .They shall worship the
gods on the right dates. If a certain date is set for some
god, they shall worship him on that date."[15] Although no
penalty is specified in this case, it is not improbable that
the usual threat of divinely imposed extinction should be
inferred.

Specific details aside, it is evident from our sources
that the importance given to the principle of sacred time,
the prohibition against desecration of sacred time, the violation of sacred time as an offense against the Deity, and
the divine removal of the sinner's name from the earth are
aspects of cultic belief which ancient Israel and the Hittites
appear to have held in common.

2) Eating leaven on Passover and the Feast of Unleavened Bread (Exod. 12:15,19). Since two originally separate
feasts are combined in the Bible so that the Passover sacr-
fice on the eve of the 14th of Nisan inaugurates the Feast of
Unleavened Bread (חג המצרה),[16] both are sometimes subsumed

under the single rubric "Passover."[17] The eating of leavened
bread on any other festival is not prohibited, but, like all
the other crimes of <u>kareth</u> except for two (the previous case
and the neglect of circumcision), eating leaven during the
week of Passover festivities is a transgression of a negative
command.[18] R. Judah said sour dough (שאר, Exod. 12:15) must
be burned, but whoever eats it is exempt unless it has become
strongly sour; the Sages said he who eats it is liable to
<u>kareth</u> in any case.[19] In the Bible, leaven is not expressly
called impure.[20] It is proscribed to the altar in the offerings for the Lord,[21] but it is permitted to the officiating
priest with the thank offering (זבח תודה, Lev. 7:13). The
order to abstain from leaven during Passover is based on the
importance of hallowing sacred time--to eat leaven on the days
of Passover was to treat them contemptuously, not only in de-
fiance of a negative command, but also in outright rejection
of the <u>Heilsgeschichtliche</u> significance of Passover itself.[22]

Etiologically, Passover commemorates the sparing of the
Israelite firstborn when the Lord struck down all the first-
born of the Egyptians (Exod. 12:27). According to our understanding of <u>kareth</u>, its imposition for desecrating the Passover graphically recalls the measure for measure principle so
frequently expressed in the curses of the ancient Near East:
if God's sparing of Israel's children is not ceremonially remembered, God will bring a curse on the offender's children so
as to leave him without descendants.[23]

The variations in language as regards the third element
in the <u>kareth</u> formula, viz. מישראל (Exod. 12:15) and מעדת
ישראל (Exod. 12:19), are paradigmatic. The second expression
merely emphasizes the sphere of the sinner's existence as the
cultic community of Israel as a whole. After disallowing
<u>kareth</u> for an act committed under duress, Rashi comments on
the variation מישראל as follows:

> I might understand from this that he shall
> be cut off from Israel and that he will be
> able to betake himself to another nation!
> Scripture therefore says (Lev. 22:3) "from
> My presence"--in every place that is My ter-
> ritory (i.e. everywhere).[24]

Elsewhere Rashi correctly understands the <u>kareth</u> penalty to be
not annihilation in general but a premature and childless
death.[25] Neither Rashi nor any other commentator, to the best
of our knowledge, attempts to explain the nature of <u>kareth</u>
when the offender already has children at the time of his infraction. In our view, God will demand the death of the children as well, perhaps simultaneously with the death of the offender,[26] or the children themselves will be without progeny
so that the lineage comes to an end in a later generation. Unfortunately, the Priestly Writer gives us no clear-cut cases at
this point.[27] It is precisely here, however, that we might
suppose the <u>kareth</u> penalty to have been most successful as a
deterrent. For we may naturally expect that the parent, while
being concerned for the preservation of his own name, at the
same time would have a strong emotional attachment to his

children and would scarcely do anything intentionally to harm
them, least of all to expose them to the threat of extinction.[28] If this supposition is correct, one senses here the
intimate relation that P's pollution rules have with the nu-
clear family, the keystone of ancient Israel's social structure.

3) <u>Working on the Sabbath</u> (Exod. 31:14).[29] The Priestly
Writer's rationale for the Sabbath (Exod. 31:17) is based on
the divine prototype of rest on the seventh day of creation
(Gen. 2:1-3).[30] Man's physical labors must cease on the Sabbath so as not to act against the divine model of holiness:
The Sabbath is expressly sacred time (מקרא קדש, Lev. 23:3).
Desecration (חלל)[31] of the Sabbath is punished by death if de-
tected by man (Num. 15:32-36)[32] <u>and</u> by <u>kareth</u>, whether in addition to מות יומת or in the absence of it should man fail to
perform the execution out of negligence or out of ignorance
that a violation had occurred. In his treatment of the Sabbath, M. Tsevat insightfully notices that the sĕmittā text of
Lev. 25:3f. shows correspondences with the Sabbath laws, suggesting that the Sabbath is essentially a day when one desists
from his own pursuits and sets it aside for God: he "re-
nounces his autonomy and affirms God's dominion over him."[33]

Some rabbis granted the priority of circumcision,[34] Passover,[35] and the sacred festivals over the Sabbath should they
coincide.[36] Such displacements of the Sabbath are not desecrations since sacred time is not thereby usurped by man's in-
terests--observance of one holy day is replaced by observance
of another or by the performance of a positive command for
which one could not be penalized. The rabbinic view of <u>kareth</u>
as premature death is expressed by R. Hanina b. Antigonas with
respect to Sabbath desecration as follows:

> An old man who eats forbidden fat or one
> who desecrates the Sabbath dies by <u>kareth</u>.
> And what is there to show that he died by
> <u>kareth</u>? But he who dies after (an illness
> of) three days dies by <u>kareth</u>.[37]

Although the premature death of the offender may accompany or
inaugurate the <u>kareth</u> curse, we maintain that it is not the
exact equivalent of <u>kareth</u>.[38]

The poet at Isaiah 56:5 may have been aware of <u>kareth</u> as
childlessness-extinction as he graphically describes the eu-
nuchs who keep the Lord's sabbaths: "To them I will give in
My house and within My walls a memorial, and a name better
than that of sons and daughters; I will give them an everlast-
ing name which will not be cut off" (אשר לא יכרח). According
to Ezekiel,[39] it is precisely desecration of the Sabbath which
threatened the wilderness generation with destruction (Ezek.
20:13,16,21,24). That generation becomes a paradigm for
Ezekiel's castigation of Judah for committing the defiling
transgressions deserving of <u>kareth</u> in P, expressly for blasphemy (Ezek. 20:27),[40] idolatry (20:28-30), and Molech worship
(20:31). Exile results from these violations in order to
purge the land of its impurities (20:38).[41] Ezekiel does not

mention the <u>kareth</u> formula for these crimes in chapter 20 but we may presume <u>its</u> relevance from Ezek. 14:8, at least as regards idolatry.[42]

4) <u>Working or eating on the Day of Atonement</u> (Lev. 23: 29,30). Like the Sabbath and Passover, the Day of Atonement is a holy day (מקרא קדש, Lev. 23:27).[43] It is a day set aside for penitence and repentance. Only on the Day of Atonement is fasting enjoined upon Israel,[44] perhaps, as P. Gerlitz has proposed, as a symbolic means of purifying the individual.[45] The important rituals of the Day of Atonement, however, are centered in the sanctuary (Lev. 16) and involve the blood of the two purgation-offerings and the scapegoat's dispatch into the wilderness. The effect of the Day of Atonement rituals is threefold: 1) purgation of the sanctuary; 2) propitiation of the Deity; and 3) expiation of the sinner.

Purgation of the sanctuary is primary. J. Milgrom has recently shown that the dynamic, aerial quality of impurity penetrates the sanctuary in three stages according to the nature of its source:[46]

> a) The individual's inadvertent misdemeanor or severe physical impurity pollutes the courtyard altar which is purged by daubing its horns with the <u>hatta't</u> blood (Lev. 4:25,30; 9:9ff.).

> b) The inadvertent misdemeanor of the high priest or the entire community pollutes the shrine which is purged by the high priest by placing the <u>hatta't</u> blood on the inner altar and before the <u>parōket</u>-veil (Lev. 4:5-7,16-18).

> c) The wanton, unrepented sin not only pollutes the outer altar and penetrates into the shrine but it pierces the veil to the holy ark and <u>kap-poret</u>. . . .Since the wanton sinner is barred from bringing his <u>hatta't</u>[50] . . .the pollution wrought by his offense must await the annual purgation of the sanctuary on the Day of Atonement, and consists of two steps: the purging of the Tent and the purging of the outer altar.

On this basis it become clear that the <u>kareth</u> crimes in P are of the most heinous variety inasmuch as the impurity generated by them is thought to lodge in the adytum of the Tabernacle on the earthly throne of the God of Israel. The presence of this obnoxious miasma in His shrine ignites the Deity's anger aginst the deliberate sinner.

Accordingly, it is necessary to maintain that in purging the sanctuary, the slain <u>hatta't</u>'s blood effects the correlative propitiation of God, assuaging His wrath.[48]

Rabbinic exegetes maintained that the scapegoat brings
about the expiation of the people,[49] except, according to
some,[50] for the transgressions of eating sacred foodstuffs in
an unclean condition (Lev. 22:3, see below) and entering the
sanctuary in an unclean state--these, deserving of kareth,
are said to be atoned for by the blood sprinkled within the
shrine.

But regardless of the ritual agents of expiation, how can
the deliberate sinner who is condemned by kareth be absolved?
Not automatically by the Day of Atonement rituals to be sure.
Unlike his ancient Near Eastern contemporaries, as far as we
know, the Priestly Writer makes a merciful concession to the
kareth-cursed in that the deliberate sinner may at any time
repent. It is a basic postulate of the Priestly soteriology
that the only sin which cannot be forgiven is the sin which
is not repented of. This was recognized already by the rabbis,
e.g., by R. Ishmael b. Eleazar ha-Kappar:

> If a man transgressed a prohibition punishable
> by kareth or death at the hands of the court
> and repented, the repentance and the Day of
> Atonement together suspend (the punishment) and
> sufferings in the course of the year will purge
> the sin.[51]

It is a distinctive feature of the biblical writer's theology
that the sword of God's wrath is always wrapped in the mantle
of His mercy. Nevertheless, God's mercy is not to be presumed
upon:

> If one say, "I will sin and repent, I will sin
> and repent," he will not be given (from on high)
> an opportunity to repent. (If one say) "I will
> sin and the Day of Atonement will effect atone-
> ment," the Day of Atonement will not effect
> atonement.[52]

With the provision of the Day of Atonement the Priestly
Writer opens a window on the uniqueness of his monotheistic
religion. By his contrition and repentance and confidence in
the Day of Atonement rituals the deliberate sinner may have
his curse of extinction removed; his deliberate crime is
reduced to an inadvertency by this repentance and confession.[53]
Thereby the purgation-offerings become efficacious for him.
Failure to observe the Day of Atonement is in itself an act of
supercilious conduct, leaving the deliberate sinner exposed to
the imminent imposition of kareth, and, because of the severity
of the defilement generated by him, threatening the entire camp
of Israel with disaster through the removal of God's presence
from His desecrated sanctuary (cf. Ezek. 5:11). This situation
must persist until a succeeding Day of Atonement cleanses the
shrine. According to P, deliberate sin not only jeopardizes
the sinner and his seed but it is a threat to the national
security of Israel.

B. Violations Against Sacred Substance

1) <u>Eating blood</u> (Lev. 7:27; 17:10,14). The Priestly
Writer permits the consumption of meat as a supplement to
man's originally vegetarian diet,[54] but in no event may the
blood of an animal be eaten with the flesh (Gen. 9:4).[55] P's
rationale for the prohibition against eating blood is that
life is seated in the blood (Lev. 17:11)[56]--as blood flows
from the victim so does life.[57] Many peoples forbid the consumption of blood, in Durkheim's view precisely because in
this act contact with the numinous powers which are thought to
reside in the blood is most intimate. For example, to eat
blood is an abomination among certain North American Indians--
game is passed over fire so the blood will be dried up, and
elsewhere the blood is gathered in the skin of the slain animal and interred.[58]

It may be that the Priestly prohibition against consumption of blood was in fact a polemic <u>ex tacito</u> against pagan
notions that animistic or totemistic powers believed to be
resident in blood could be appropriated by its ingestion.
The correlation between consumption of blood and idolatrous
practices was suggested by Maimonides who made no distinction
between eating blood and "eating on the blood" (אכל על הדם,
Lev. 19:26; I Sam. 14:24-35; Ezek. 32:25): "For the eating of
blood leads to a kind of idolatry, to the worship of spirits."[59] J. Grintz, whose article "Do Not Eat on the Blood"
gives the most recent survey of the meanings attributed to
this expression,[60] follows Maimonides, associating the phrase
with the practice of consulting the dead (i.e. in the אוב-
cult): "The people performed this ritual in order to gain
knowledge of the future."[61]

Positively speaking, the blood of sacrificial animals was
forbidden to man because, to use Ezekiel's expression, it was
designated as God's "food" (Ezek. 44:7).[62] Moreover, there was
power in the blood of animals assigned to the altar to make
atonement for sin (Lev. 17:11). J. Milgrom has properly emphasized two instructive points with regard to Lev. 17:11 and its
context (Lev. 17:10-14): 1) P's concern in this pericope is
with the problem of how to eat meat without partaking of the
blood--a problem concerning only the offering of well-being
(שלמים); and 2) "improper disposal of the animal's blood is a
capital violation."[63] The special appointment of the blood to
the altar makes its use for other purposes a sacrilege, hence
the Priestly appeal to <u>kareth</u>. As an apparent extension of
P's concern for the blood of sacrificial animals, perhaps as
an attempt to curb man's appetite for all meat, and on the
principle that blood is somehow equal to life, even the blood
of hunt animals is forbidden as food (Lev. 17:13,14).[64]

The prohibition against eating blood persisted as an
essential doctrine of post-biblical Judaism. <u>Kareth</u> for the
consumption of blood was known to the Qumran sectarians[65]
and to the author of the pseudepigraphic <u>Book of Jubilees</u>.[66]
The haggadic passage at <u>Jubilees</u> 21:18ff. sets forth the nature
of <u>kareth</u> as it was perceived by the first century B.C. writer.
The writer places his language in the mouth of Abraham as the

latter instructs Isaac to beware of committing (among other
grievous sins) the "uncleanness, abomination, and pollution"
of eating blood. The threat of the divine curse is presented
at v. 22b:

> Else he will hide His face from thee,
> And give thee back into the hands of
> thy transgression,
> And root thee out of the land, and
> thy seed likewise from under heaven,
> And thy name and thy seed shall perish
> from the whole earth.[67]

This language is clearly reminiscent of the divine curses of
extinction which we have suggested provide the ancient Near
Eastern prototype for the _kareth_ curse in the Bible.[68]

2) _Eating sacrificial suet_ (Lev. 7:25). The same principle of desecration applies to the eating of sacrificial suet
as to the consumption of blood--the fat is assigned to the
altar as God's "food" (Ezek. 44:7).[69] _Kareth_ is invoked for
eating the fat of all animals consecrated to the altar.[70] It
is commonly held that the fat was in ancient times considered
to be the choicest part of the sacrifice.[71] According to T.H.
Gaster, the blood and the fat were tabooed because in them
were ". . .the primary seats of vitality and energy."[72] One
might speculate that P's restriction of the fatty portions of
the omenta, the kidneys, and the lobe of the liver to the
altar flames was a deliberate attempt to prevent the use of
these parts of the purpose of divination.[73] But such speculation can be defended only from P's silence and his legislation
explicitly regulates only the _eating_ of the tabooed portion.[74]
Students who are familiar with the Akkadian expression _assak-_
kam akālu, "to eat the asakku," used to describe a tresspass
against the sacred property of the Deity or king,[75] may find
in this idiom a parallel motivation for the Priestly prohibition: whatever belongs to the Deity must not be used by man
for any common purpose.

3) _Compounding and/or misusing the oil of installation_
(Exod. 30:33). The oil of installation is inherently holy
(Exod. 30:28) and is used to sanctify (i.e. to elevate to the
proper level of positive ritual status) the sacred objects of
the sanctuary as well as Aaron and his sons. The _kareth_ penalty is imposed for purposely desecrating sancta by the
adhibition of the oil with respect to an unauthorized person
(זר), ostensibly for such profane purposes as bodily care or
as a beauty-aid in the opinion of L. A. Snijders.[76] Scholars
do not agree as to the identity of the זר. Snijders thinks of
the זר merely as a layman.[77] M. Haran maintains that "In P's
usage, זר implies nothing more than a non-priest."[78] J. Milgrom affirms that the זר may be both a non-priest and a non-
Levite.[79] In any instance, that _kareth_ is imposed for
deliberate profanation of the sacred oil cannot be gainsaid--
the categories of the sacred and the profane must not be com-
mingled.

4) <u>Duplicating and/or misusing the sanctuary incense</u> (Exod. 30:38). The incense in question is most holy (קדש קדשים) and, in contrast to the ordinary incense of the courtyard which is of lesser sanctity (only קדש) and is burned in censers, it is burned only on the altar of gold within the sanctuary proper (Exod 30:7-8).[80] It is unique in terms of its place in the complex of rituals within the sanctuary as well as in its composition.[81] Profanation of this sacred incense by duplication or use of it for any purposes other than those prescribed for the sanctuary ritual is a direct affront against God and is therefore punishable by <u>kareth</u>.

5) <u>Eating of the well-being sacrifices on the third day</u> (Lev. 7:18; 19:8). The offerings of well-being (שלמים) are holy (קרש) as a result of their dedication to the altar.[82] The portions of the votive or freewill offerings permitted to the layman are to be eaten on the day of their presentation and on the following day.[83] What remains to the third day (נותר) is to be consumed by fire.[84] The sacrifices will not be credited to the offerer if the flesh is eaten on the third day; they are designated as "refuse" or "defilement" (פגול).[85] According to Lev. 17:18, "whoever eats of it shall bear his sin." Lev. 19:8 adds a motive clause with the <u>kareth</u> penalty: "whoever eats of it shall bear his sin <u>for he has desecrated the sancta of the Lord</u> (כי את קדש ה' חלל); that person shall be cut off from his people." Only with the sacrifices of well-being is the layman allowed a share; he must be pure when eating of them and he must observe the rules of time with respect to them or be threatened with extinction. According to J.C. Moyer, the prayer of Kantuzili suggests that eating the god's food among the Hittites is not only a sacrilege but an act whereby the offender is made impure. The relevant portion of the prayer reads:

> I have never taken an oath to my god and then broken the oath. I have never eaten what is holy (<u>suppi</u>) to my god and hence not fit for me to eat. I have not brought impurity (<u>paprahhun</u>) into my body.[86]

Moyer comments: "Uncleanness resulted through improper appropriation of the god's food or through improper handling under unclean conditions."[87] It is not impossible that the Priestly restriction in our case had a similar motivation, but we may be certain only of the fact that it is the deliberateness of the act in violation of the negative command which brings on the <u>kareth</u> curse, precisely because sacred substance had been profaned, and this on the third day.

The significance of the third day is not explained in the Bible. Perhaps it was chosen merely to guard against eating sacred food which may have begun to putrefy. It may have its prototype in the account of God's epiphany on Mt. Sinai which also concerns the question of purity-impurity contacts (Exod. 19:10-16). Rabbinic exegesis took note of the importance of the time regulation and defined פגול as sacrificial flesh with respect to which the officiating priest had formed the intention of eating at an improper time.

The general principle is given in the Mishna:

> Whoever slaughters, receives, transports, or
> sprinkles (the blood, intending) to eat out-
> side of its (proper) place anything which it is
> his custom to eat, or to (sacrificially) burn
> outside of its proper place anything which it is
> his custom to burn, it is disqualified (פסול)
> but he does not incur <u>kareth</u> thereby; (if his
> intent is to do any of these things) outside of
> its proper time, it is (a case of) defilement
> (פגול) and he incurs <u>kareth</u> thereby. . . .[88]

The higher priority which is given to proper time above
proper place is established explicitly by R. Judah. P. Black-
man translates:

> This is the general principle: if the intention
> about the time (to eat or offer) preceded the
> intention (to eat or offer elsewhere than in)
> the (proper) place, (the offering) becomes
> abomination (פגול) and punishment by <u>excision</u>
> (כרת) is incurred thereby (by those that eat
> thereof); but if the intention about the place
> preceded the intention about the time; (the
> offering) becomes invalid (פסול) but the penalty
> of <u>excision</u> is not suffered (by those who eat
> thereof). But the Sages say, In both cases
> (the offering) becomes invalid, but punishment
> by <u>excision</u> is not incurred (by those that eat
> thereof).[89]

R. Meir exempted from <u>kareth</u> the heathen who transgress
the law of rejection (פגול), remnant (נרתר), or uncleanness
(טמאה) with respect to the restrictions governing the time and
place of their offerings; R. Jose held the heathen culpable.[90]
R. Eliezer understood a negative command to be imposed upon
whatever among holy things had become disqualified.[91] Rabbinic
opinion maintained that "The law of sacrilege applies to פגול
always."[92] If the rabbis correctly stressed the importance of
time with respect to the sacrifices that had become פגול, it
would appear that two principles are violated in our case: the
principle of sacred substance and that of sacred time.

6) <u>Eating the sacred offerings while ritually impure</u> (Lev.
7:20f.; 22:3,9). The Priestly legislation in this case addresses both the priest and the layman.

a) <u>The layman</u> (Lev. 7:20f.). Not only must the layman's
portion of the well-being sacrifices be eaten before the third
day, but it may not be eaten in a state of ritual impurity.
The sources of impurity generalized at Lev. 7:21 are those
contracted naturally by the layman. As an example, the parturient is expressly forbidden to contact the sacred foodstuffs
(Lev. 12:4b בכל קדש לא תגע). This means that she may not prepare or eat them in her home because of her negative ritual
status, nor may she enter the sanctuary until the prescribed
days of her impurity have elapsed.[93] Although <u>kareth</u> is not

expressly stated with respect to the parturient, we may correctly assume that it was to be invoked for her deliberate violation of the purity-impurity rule. Of course, the lay person is not liable to kareth for merely becoming unclean--impurity in the course of life is routine and the exclusion from the cult is not itself kareth as might be supposed by some; rather, kareth is threatened for the intentional disregard for the Priestly distinction between the holy and the profane.

b) The Priest (Lev. 22:3,9). Lev. 22:1-9 forms a literary unit. Aaron and his sons must be circumspect as regards eating the portions of the sacred offerings guaranteed to them as the emoluments of their office lest they desecrate the name of the Lord (Lev. 22:2).[94] Permission to eat the holy foodstuffs of the priests is not granted to the layman,[95] and the priests themselves are restricted as to both the time[96] and the place[97] of their most sacred sacrificial meals. The threat of kareth hangs over the priest who partakes of the sacred offerings knowing that he is ritually impure.

The sources of defilement for the priest are enumerated in our pericope as follows: 1) dermatologic disorders (צרוע, v. 4),[98] 2) non-seminal discharges from the genitals (זב, v. 4),[99] 3) contact with corpse-contamination (טמא בכל נפש, v. 4),[100] 4) emission of semen (שכבת זרע, v. 4),[101] 5) contact with "swarming things" (שרץ, i.e. with their carcasses, cf. Lev. 5:2),[102] 6) contact with any human uncleanness (טמאה אדם, v. 5),[103] 7) consumption of carrion (נבלה וטרפה, i.e. animals which die naturally or are leavings--any animal which is not slain in the proper ritual manner).[104] Lev. 22:9 shows, in our estimation, that death by God (Qal of מות)[105] inaugurates the kareth curse upon the priest who disdains the rules of purity-impurity contact, thereby failing to live up to his own job description (Lev. 10:10). The Priestly Writer gives no examples of the priest's culpability to kareth for tresspass against the holy foodstuffs.[106]

7) Unauthorized contact with sacred property (Num. 4:18). The Kohathite clan, whose task it is to carry the most sacred appurtenances of the sanctuary while the Israelite camp is in transit, may not approach the sacred pieces until they have been properly covered by the priests. Even then the Kohathites must be carefully supervised in their porterage work.[107] Unauthorized eyes must not gaze upon the holy,[108] nor may the Kohathites "touch any holy thing lest they die" (ולא יגעו אל הקדש ומתו, Num. 4:15, cf. v. 19). Indubitably, the duties of the priests in wrapping the sacred furnishings and in overseeing the actual business of transporting them are designed to spare the Kohathites from the divine kareth penalty: "You shall not cause the Kohathite clans (שבט משפחת הקהתי) to be cut off from among the Levites" (Num. 4: 18).

The Midrash Rabbah to Numbers makes a connection between the warning of Num. 4:18 and the rebellion of Korah (Num. 16: 1ff.):

> The Holy One, blessed be He, foresaw that
> Korah, who would spring from the families of
> Kohath, would oppose Moses--as it says: "Now
> Korah, the son of Izhar, the son of Kohath. . .
> took men. . .and they rose up against Moses. . ."
> Therefore it says, "cut ye not off the
> tribe. . . ."[109]

That Korah and company suffer premature death by God is
clear, but that they suffered <u>kareth</u> cannot be shown beyond
reasonable doubt. The Korah narrative is fraught with textual
problems[110] and the <u>kareth</u> formula is not used with respect to
the death of the rebels. It seems that Korah's crime takes
place in the sanctuary precint and probably involves the offering of non-holy incense brought from the outside.[111] At least
it cannot have been a violation of the incense rule for which
<u>kareth</u> is enjoined at Exod. 30:38, for, as we have already
observed, the incense in question there is most holy and must
be consigned only to the sanctuary's gold altar. Nor, tech-
nically speaking, was Korah's crime of the type warned against
at Num. 4:18ff. We do not see in the Korah episode an example
of <u>kareth</u>.[112]

A possible example, viewed from the perspective of the
LXX, is provided by Achan's filching of the <u>ḥerem</u>-objects
(Jos. 7). As our study of the <u>kareth</u> penalty in the LXX
shows,[116] the verb עכר was understood by the Alexandrians to be
used, in our terms, paradigmatically with כרת. At Jos. 6:18
for MT ועכרתם אותו the LXX reads και εκτριψητε ημας. The verb
εκτριβω, "to rub out, wipe out, destroy," is used at Jos. 7:9
as well as in the <u>kareth</u> formula at Num. 15:31 and 19:13. Further evidence that the LXX understood the Achan incident as an
example of <u>kareth</u> is suggested by the rendering of עכר at Jos.
7:25 by εξολεθρενω, the usual LXX word for כרת in the <u>kareth</u>
formula of P. Joshua addresses Achan: Τι ωλεθρευσις ημας,
εξολεθρευσαι σε κυριος which might be translated, "Why would
you have cut us off? May the Lord cut you off. . ." If the
LXX be followed, our view of <u>kareth</u> as a divine curse of extinction is born out for Achan's deliberate violation against
the sacred <u>ḥerem</u> property.

Some hint of this is found in the MT itself. It is noteworthy that at Jos. 7:7 Joshua expresses fear of perishing
(verb אבד) and at 7:9 of having Israel's name cut off (והכריתו
את שמנו מן הארץ). Moreover, Deut. 7:24, using the paradigmatic
semantic field of כרת, provides what we have determined to be
the exact meaning of P's <u>kareth</u> penalty in the expression "you
shall make their name perish from under the heavens" (ואבדת את
שמם מתחת השמים). . ."until you have destroyed them" (עד השמדך
אתם). Significantly, the context (Deut. 7:25-26) anticipates
and legislates against Achan's crime. The very fate which is
axiomatic for persons in <u>ḥerem</u> status befalls Achan, viz. extinction. Both his sons and daughters are executed with him
(Jos. 7:24).[114] His name is removed from Israel.

C. Failure to Perform Purification Rituals

1) <u>Neglect of circumcision</u> (Gen. 17:14). Circumcision is one of the two performative commands the neglect of which incurs the <u>kareth</u> curse. Circumcision is instituted as a sign of the covenant (לאות ברית, Gen. 17:12) by which God had extended to Abraham a threefold promise of a) numerous progeny (17:5f.), b) God's presence in perpetuity (17:7b), and c) the land of Canaan as an inheritance (17:8).

A satisfactory treatment of the symbolically complex circumcision sign would require its own monograph. The secondary literature on the subject boasts a wide variety of beliefs. For example, in a recent article M. Fox has suggested that:

> . . .circumcision is a cognition sign--like the other 'ôtōt in P--whose function is to remind God to keep his promise of posterity . . . .In plain language that means that God will see the Israelite's circumcised penis during or before sexual congress and will remember to keep his covenant by making the union a fruitful one.[115]

That the promise of progeny is the preeminent feature of the circumcision covenant we do not deny, but we object to Fox's interpretation of the sign. All the reasons for this objection, however, must give way to our present purpose in showing the relevance of the <u>kareth</u> penalty to the central provision of the Abrahamic covenant.[116] Our interpretation of <u>kareth</u> as a divine curse of extinction informs the debate on the meaning of the circumcision sign on at least two points.

First, it supports the view that circumcision was understood by the Priestly Writer as a means of ratifying God's suzerainty over Abraham and his seed, giving to them their identify as a peculiar people in relationship to Yahweh.[117] The covenantal blessings will not ensue if the vassal does not comply with the circumcision requirement.[118] Moreover, the sign acts as the symbol of a curse for the covenant violation.[119] In short, now that we understand <u>kareth</u>, there will be no one to carry on the name of him who is not circumcised-- "that person shall be cut off from his people, he has broken My covenant" (Gen. 17:14 ונכרחה הנפש ההוא מעמיה את בריתי הפר). The principle of <u>lex talionis</u> which we have seen to be operative in the ancient Near Eastern divine curses for treaty violation is also operative here. The reason for the covenant sign being effected on the male genitalia is thus obvious.[120] The sign, however, is not, as Fox suggests, a reminder to God to keep His promises; rather, it is an external evidence, a symbolic gesture--a <u>confirmation sign</u>--of the Patriarch's belief that God can and will miraculously give him progeny through the aged Sarah. In sum, the circumcision sign stands opposite the <u>kareth</u> curse as the external symbol of the assurance that God will not permit the extinction of Abraham and his seed.

In the second place, having earlier affirmed that <u>kareth</u> is imposed for deliberate violation of impurity-holiness rules in P's cult, we now submit that circumcision has a practical aim based on the Priestly Writer's pollution concept. Accordingly, the act of circumcision is a purification rite which grants to the initiate positive ritual status.[121] It transfers him initially from the realm of the ritually impure to that of the pure, serving, so to speak, as his passport to participation in Israel's cultic worship.[122] In particular, P requires circumcision for sharing in the Passover (Exod. 12: 47f.) which commemorates God's sparing of the Israelite first-born in Egypt and the subsequent liberation of Israel as a corporate entity with national status. Both circumcision and Passover require bloodshed.[123] Both rituals are associated with the preservation of children and the affording of an inheritance. Circumcision is required before Passover is to be celebrated as Israel enters Canaan to possess her inheritance (Jos. 5:2ff.). P portrays Israel as a holy people among whom God Himself dwells (Num. 5:3), separated from the nations (Lev. 20:26). The contamination of the sanctuary by the un-circumcised (Ezek. 44:7) is not expressly stated by P but it is certainly consonant with his pollution concept. Though the cult does not exist at the time of Abraham, it is inconceivable to the Priestly Writer that Abraham, the fountainhead of Israel, could be ritually impure; hence, in P's etiology Abraham is made to serve as the paradigm for the practice of circumcision.

While it appears to us that the <u>kareth</u> penalty was in-curred in P's legislation for neglecting circumcision <u>per se</u>, there is a tradition in later Judaism which maintained the importance of circumcision on the eighth day, implying that failure to be circumcised on the eighth day made one liable to <u>kareth</u>. For example, the author of the <u>Book of Jubilees</u> felt constrained to add ביום השמיני after ערלתו in his version of Gen. 17:14,[124] giving the following midrash on the meaning of <u>kareth</u>:

> And everyone that is born, the flesh of whose foreskin is not circumcised on the eighth day, belongs not to the children of the covenant which the Lord made with Abraham, but to the children of destruction; nor is there, moreover, any sign on him that he is the Lord's, but (he is destined) to be destroyed and slain from the earth, and to be rooted out of the earth, for he has broken the covenant of the Lord our God.[125]

The same author, with reference to Gen. 34, considers intermarriage with the uncircumcised a defilement worthy of <u>kareth</u>:

> But if they transgress and work uncleanness in in every way, they will be recorded on the heavenly tablets as adversaries, and they will be destroyed out of the book of life, and they will be recorded in the book of those who will

> will be destroyed and with those who will be
> rooted out of the earth.[126]

Aside from the importance which the author of <u>Jubilees</u>
attaches to circumcision on the eighth day, he confirms, in a
general way, what we have been suggesting with respect to the
<u>kareth</u> penalty, viz., that it is total removal from the earth.
The new feature of <u>Jubilees</u> which goes beyond the original biblical meaning of <u>kareth</u> as extinction of the sinner and his
seed is the reference to the "book of life." Further, it is
likely that <u>Jubilees</u> shared with the Qumran sectarians the
belief that <u>kareth</u> would be imposed upon the wicked en masse
in the eschaton.[127]

2) <u>Failure to be cleansed from corpse-contamination</u>
(Num. 19:13,20). The Priestly legislation categorically requires expulsion from the camp for everyone who has become
defiled by contact with a human corpse (Num. 19:11), expressly
so "they will not contaminate the camp of those in whose midst
I dwell" (Num. 5:2-3). Rabbinic opinion considered corpse
uncleanness, a seven-day impurity, as a progenitor of primary
uncleanness (אבי אבות הטומאה) capable of defiling to the fourth
degree of contact.[128] Unlike other impurities, death was
thought to be transferred by mere overshadowing,[129] affecting
both persons and objects (Num. 19). Persons possessing a
special degree of positive ritual status are placed under
greater restriction regarding corpse-defilement in the Bible.
The Nazirite for the duration of his vow is forbidden all
contact with the dead (Num. 6:6ff.) as is the high priest (Lev.
21:11), and the priest may defile himself only for a member of
his immediate family (Lev. 21:1f.).

For the removal of corpse-defilement, the Priestly Writer
prescribed the distinctive ceremony of the red heifer (Num.
19:1ff.).[130] The nature of this ceremony has vexed biblical
scholars for centuries. J. Blau remarks:

> The recurrent references to the Red Heifer
> in the rabbinical literature should be under-
> stood in terms of the endless capacity of the
> human mind to be fascinated with the insoluble
> problem. . . .[131]

J. Neusner dismisses this rite as "hocus-pocus" and "magical."[132] Yet it is possible that even as late as Qumran this
rite may have been practiced.[133] Although its origin and history have been given diverse interpretations, all would agree
that the purpose of the red heifer in Num 19 is clear: it
is taken outside the camp, slain,[134] and burned with the intent that its ashes will be mixed with water and applied to
the corpse-contaminated person in order that he might reenter
the encampment of Israel without severely defiling the sanctuary and thereby falling heir to <u>kareth</u>.[135] It is to be
expected that deaths would have occurred naturally in the camp
of Israel, but the impurity thus generated was unintentional
and would have affected only the outer alter.[136] The <u>kareth</u>

penalty is imposed for the deliberate desecration of the adytum by bringing the severe impurity of death pollution into
the camp.

Even impurity which is contracted outside the camp is
potentially dangerous. Death pollution poses no serious
threat as long as it remains outside, but whoever brazenly
brings it into the midst of Israel is liable to <u>kareth</u>. This
is the most reasonable explanation for why Moses found it
necessary to go outside the camp to meet the returning soldiers and to advise them to follow the purification procedures
for corpse-contamination. They must not cause the residence
of God to be defiled (Num. 31:19).

Amongst some primitive peoples the area outside the vil-
lage is inherently dangerous. For example, a hunter among the
Jen, a tribe of northern Nigeria, may prepare for his hunt by
cleaning the grave of his ancestors and praying to them as
follows: "I am going on the morrow to the bush to hunt, the
bush is not the town; it is the place of death. . . .[137] Y.
Kaufmann has suggested that the area outside the camp in ancient Israel was the source of impurity:

> The Priestly Code preserves traces of the
> notion that impurity is grounded in the
> realm of demons and satyrs. Illicit sacri-
> ficing "in the open fields" is done to satyrs
> (Lev. 17:5-7); lustral birds of the leper and
> the "leprous house" are released there (Lev.
> 14:7,53). The open field. . .is the abode of
> such satyrs as Azazel. . . .Contact with this
> domain is apparently the source of the defile-
> ments listed above.[138]

We demur. P does not consider the entire area outside the
camp of Israel unclean and dangerous since man alone is the
source of the impurity which defiles God's sanctuary, not demons, not magic, not the realm of the impure, etc.[139] In
short, impurity is not geographically or metaphysically generated according to the Priestly Writer.

W. Robertson Smith believed that P's laws of contagion
"have nothing in common with the spirit of Hebrew religion"
and are "remains of a primitive superstition."[140] There is no
better place to look for justification of this statement than
in P's portrayal of death pollution. But, as we have already
stated, P removes death pollution from the realm of the demonic
and the magical. Moreover, he attaches to the deliberate violation of purity rules concerning death the harshest penalty
imaginable to the oriental mind. With the threat of <u>kareth</u>
P defends the jugular of Hebrew religion against the jaws of
paganism--in this case against the likelihood of participation
in a cult of the dead. The Israelite who placed stock in
joining his ancestors at his death and in being joined by his
children would not be likely to risk involvement in a cult of
the dead if there were extended to him the possibility that he
himself might be punished with extirpation and thus be deprived

of whatever benefits he thought such a cult might afford. The
concern for having children to carry on one's name would militate against flirting with the kareth curse.

P's pollution rules regarding contact with the dead, with
graves, bones, etc., are given yet another motivation. Contact with the dead is not only severely restricted by P, but
he gives to his kareth clauses a theological incentive as well.
Fear of the dead, magic, etc., are all subordinated to one
principle: corpse-contamination must not be brought into Israel's camp because it offends the divine presence there--
"the dwelling place of the Lord has been defiled" (Num. 19:13).
Thus P's concept of death pollution is an incentive to enforce
the distinction between the sacred and the profane--to moti-
vate the individual and Israel as a people to emulate the holiness of God. What could be closer to the heart of Hebrew
religion?

As a final note, the kareth penalty for deliberate desecration of the sanctuary by corpse-pollution must be related
to P's laws of homicide. The murderer or the manslayer was
perceived by P as one who had been contaminated by corpse contact. It is unthinkable that such a person could be allowed
to seek asylum at the altar![141] This profane-sacred contact,
according to P's own legislation, would bring about an injus-
tice, invoking the kareth penalty and penalizing the homi-
cide--unintentional as well as deliberate--with a judgment
worse than death, and this without so much as a fair trial.
Based on his view of corpse-pollution, the Priestly Writer
innovatively appoints asylum cities to which the homicide
might flee for refuge until justice could be expedited by his
community.[142]

D. Illicit Worship

1) Slaughtering outside the sacred precinct (Lev. 17:4).
The purpose of the pericope Lev. 17:1-7 is to legitimate
slaughter of sacrificial animals only at the central sanctuary.
As Ramban recognized, the slaughter of an animal outside the
camp is tantamount to murder: "it (blood) shall be imputed to
him as if he had shed blood (of a fellow man).[143] R. Patai,
commenting on the kareth clause of Lev. 17:4, has observed
that ". . .it is quite evident that regarding the sin of
bloodshed and its punishment, no difference was made between
the blood of a man and the blood of an animal."[144]

Yet a distinction exists in P, not as regards the pollut-
ing power of all blood, but in the nature of the punishment
for bloodshed: kareth is never imposed for homicide. P rules
that the intentional murderer, after a trial, is to be executed by the blood avenger (גאל הדם) while the manslayer, after
his innocence has been proved, is given refuge in an asylum
city where he is detained until the death of the high priest
(Num. 35:9-34).[145]

At first blush, it is surprising to find <u>kareth</u> imposed
for theriocide and not for homicide. Why is there a more
severe penalty for the profane slaughter of animals than for
taking a man's life? Not because P takes a low view of man,
to be sure, for according to P's creation story man is made in
the image of God (Gen. 1:26f.). The answer is simple. While
man has a means of redressing the homicide in the blood avenger, thus providing what P deems to be an adequate deterrent
to wholesale homicide, the innocent animal has no such avenger
and is therefore totally vulnerable to be slain according to
man's will. By making the slaughter of sacrificial animals
outside the sacred precinct a sin against God, P makes God the
animal's avenger! Sins against God, we affirm again, may be
punished only by God. One of P's motives in limiting the
slaughter of the domestic animals mentioned in our case might
well be sought in his concern to enforce a vegetarian diet.[146]
In any event, the Priestly Writer, in order to provide a strong
deterrent against theriocide, imposes <u>kareth</u> as the stronger
penalty for the crime which is more easily committed but which
is equally as defiling to the land as the shedding of man's
own blood. If these ratiocinations are correct, it goes without saying that the Priestly appeal to <u>kareth</u> on behalf of
sacrifical animals supports our view that <u>kareth</u> was only a
divine penalty.

2) <u>Sacrificing outside the sacred precinct</u> (Lev. 17:9).
The brief statement at Lev. 17:8-9 follows logically the pericope discussed in the previous section. Here another evidence
for <u>kareth</u> as a divine penalty is afforded. Profane slaughter
naturally leads to the possible offering of sacrificial victims to pagan cult deities--an overt repudiation of God; hence,
as in the previous case, God alone can exact punishment. In
addition to being sins against God, the cultic activities
envisioned by P must certainly have been clandestine and therefore could not have been justly punished by man, even if he had
the right to do so. In this case, as in all cases of <u>kareth</u>,
the executive power to maintain order in P's society was vested
in God, not man.

3) <u>Worshipping Molech</u> (Lev. 20:2-5). The worship of
Molech was probably also related to the cult of the dead.[147]
The syntagmatic relationship between <u>kareth</u> and מות ירמה has
already been discussed in Chapter One; we concluded there that
<u>kareth</u> happens in addition to the capital sentence. Man brings
about the offender's death, but God causes the offender's extinction. Two motive clauses are supplied by P to show that
Molech worship is an offense against God worthy of <u>kareth</u>:
1) the sanctuary is defiled (20:3c מקדשי את טמא למען) and
2) God's holy name is desecrated (20:3d קדשי שם את ולחלל).

The precise nature of Molech worship has been the subject
of an extensive debate. The passing of children through fire
was given a covenantal significance by some early rabbis.[148]
M. Weinfeld has recently assembled convincing evidence to support the view of Josephus that Molech worship involved the
dedication of children as acolytes to pagan cult service.[149]
It seems clear from Ezek. 23:37-39 that children in the cult
ceremony were actually slaughtered and given as food to

idols.[150]   At v. 39 Ezekiel recalls the defiling effect of
this idolatry: "For when they had slaughtered their children
for their idols, they entered My sanctuary on the same day to
profane it--behold, thus they have done within My house."[151]
Moreover, Ezekiel does not appear to be unaware of the meaning
of the kareth penalty as extinction and its measure for measure application to this rebellion: the rebels are given into
the hand of foreigners and are slain along with their sons and
daughters (Ezek. 23:47). Thus they "bear the sin" of their
idolatry (v. 49 וחטאי גלוליכן תשאינה).

For whatever reason children were mistreated and/or
murdered in the Molech cult, we may be sure that the parents
who offered them considered their actions to be personally
advantageous. If the context of Molech worship had anything
to do with a cult of the dead, it is plain to see that the
kareth penalty would be the Priestly Writer's best means to
discourage its practice in Israel. Anyone who believed in the
importance of having children to carry on his name, if not to
assure himself of vitality in the future life, would not
offend God so as to expose himself to the divine curse of
extinction.

4) Consulting the dead (Lev. 20:6). The nature of the
אובות and ידענים has also been widely debated. The lexicon of
Gesenius-Buhl renders אוב as "der Geist eines Verstorbenen, den
der Totenbeschwörer heraufbeschwört." Following Anton Jir-
ku,[152] H. Schmidt rejects this view and suggests that the אוב
was an instrument, perhaps similar to the bull-roarer commonly
found among modern primitives, which, when swung through the
air, was supposed to simulate or symbolize the voices of the
spirits of the deceased.[153] Most recently, E. F. de Ward has
assembled the major opinions on the אוב,[154] including those of
W.R. Smith--"the spirit"; W. F. Albright--"revenant" A. Lods--
"ancestor spirit";[155] C. Rabin--"ventriloquist"; H. P. Smith--
"a fetish"; N. H. Tur-Sinai--a bag made of skin and used by
wizards; C. J. Gadd--a pit from which the spirits could be
called up. De Ward himself believes the ידעני to be the spirit
of the dead who is possessed with esoteric knowledge rather
than the necromancer as the term is more traditionally understood.[156]

We agree with J. Grintz[157] that the view espoused by M.
Vieyra[158] and H. Hoffner[159] has much to commend it. If these
authors are correct, Hebrew אוב, akin to Ugaritic ib/eb from
an original aybi, Hurrian ay(a)bi, Assyrian abu, etc., should
be understood, to use Hoffner's words, as ". . .a ritual hole
in the ground to give infernal deities or spirits of the deceased access to the upper world for a brief period of time."
He further says, ". . .the name which at first designated only
the pit itself came to be applied to the spirits which issued
from it."[160] Now Professor Anne Kilmer has shown that the
basic meaning of the related Akkadian uppu is "concavity, sock-
et," illustrated, for example, in the form of the Mesopotamian
hand drum by that name.[161] We have already pointed out the
likelihood that blood of profanely slain animals was associated with the cult of the dead,[162] probably used as a libation
to be poured into the אוב-hole as a drink offering to the

chthonic deities. Accordingly, kareth is imposed by P to discourage participation in the practice of necromancy.

Two classes of criminals are described in P's legislation with respect to necromancy: 1) the male or female practitioner whose business it is to summon the dead (Lev. 20:27), and 2) the client of these practitioners (Lev. 20:6). In the former case death by stoning is demanded[163] while in the latter it is kareth which is required by P. Superficially, it might appear that kareth would not befall the "pusher"-practitioner but two logical points militate against this: 1) since we have demonstrated that kareth is a more severe punishment than mere death, it is difficult to imagine that the "user" would receive a harsher sentence than the "pusher"; and 2) the nature of the crime is such that the "pusher" is at the same time a "user." This being so, we may correctly suppose that the death penalty should apply at Lev. 20:6 in the event that the offender is caught and that kareth will ensue; if he is not caught he still need fear the imminent kareth penalty. On the other hand, we should also expect kareth to apply to the practitioner at Lev. 20:27 for his/her involvement in necromancy; they too are idolators. God will seek out the sinner and inflict the kareth penalty and death by man will launch this kareth if the sinner is apprehended. In this way all involvement in necromancy incurs the kareth curse as long as the acts in question are deliberate. Of course, as we have observed in our treatment of the Day of Atonement, repentance and the Day of Atonement will acquit even the kareth-cursed. But the death of the sinner without true repentance and the efficacy of the Day of Atonement will not turn aside the divine kareth.

5) Idolatry (Ezek. 14:8). According to Ezekiel, the deliberate practice of idolatry defiles not only the sanctuary and God's holy name but also the people themselves (Ezek. 14:11 לא יטמאו עור בכל פשעיהם). The catch-phrase "you shall know that I am the Lord" (וידעתם כי אני ה') used in our verse appears frequently in Ezekiel as an indicator that God Himself will have performed some act whereby His sovereignty is affirmed.[164] For idolatry this act is the kareth penalty.

It should be understood, however, that the original meaning of kareth, while not rejected outright by the prophet, has undergone a transformation at his hand. Specifically, Ezekiel seems to nationalize it. Only at Ezek. 14:8 is the Priestly formula used, but the Hiph'il of כרת with a divine subject is applied to Judah for the commission of crimes worthy of kareth in P (cf. Ezek. 22:32; 23:49). The means of effecting the kareth curse nationally for Judah is the Exile. However, kareth is not the expulsion from the land per se but is rather the total annihilation of the wicked outside the land so that none return. It is fundamental to Ezekiel's interpretation of the Exile that a faithful remnant will be spared this destruction. Other nations too are victims of the divine kareth in this larger sense, including the Ammonites (25:5,7),[165] Edomites (25:13), Philistines (25:16), and Egyptians (29:8; 30:15). The original meaning of kareth as extinction of the individual sinner and his lineage may of course be encompassed by Ezekiel's large-scale destructions.

E.   Illicit Sexual Relations (Lev. 18:29)

Numerous sexual relations are proscribed by the Priestly
Writer for the defiling effect they are said to have upon the
land.[166] Rabbinic tradition informs us of the importance of
intention in cases of incest: whoever acts deliberately is
liable to kareth but if one partner acted unintentionally he/
she is exempt.[167] P's list at Lev. 18:6ff. is representative,
not exhaustive.[168] Some of the crimes listed are expressly
assigned the death penalty elsewhere by P,[169] presuming that
guilt will have been established by man in these cases.[170]
The following incestuous relatons are specified by P: 1) mother (Lev. 18:7);[171] 2) father's wife (v.8);[172] 3) sister (v.9);
4) granddaughter (v. 10); 5) half-sister (v. 11); 6) paternal
aunt (v. 12); 7) maternal aunt (v.13); 8) uncle's (father's
brother's) wife (v. 14); 9) daughter-in-law (v.15);[173] and
10) sister-in-law (v. 16).[174]

Further unlawful connections include 11) sex with a woman
and her daughter and/or granddaughter (v.17); 12) relations
with a woman and her sister while the former is still living
(v.18); 13) intercourse with a woman in her menses (v.19 and
cf. Lev. 15:24,31,33);[175] 14) adultery (v.20);[176] 15) giving
of one's seed to Molech (v.21);[177] 16) homosexuality (v.22);[178]
and 17) bestiality (v.23).[179]

Numbers 5 (P) provides the most probable example of
kareth in the Bible. The suspected adulteress is made to participate in an ordeal to prove her innocence or guilt. The
special potion she is made to drink is prepared by the priest
from sacral water and earth taken from the Tabernacle floor
(vv. 16f.). The woman must stand before the Lord for the
ordeal. Clearly it is God who causes the curse to befall her
if she is proven guilty: "May the Lord make you a curse and
an imprecation among your people" (vv. 21,27). "But if the
woman has not defiled herself and is pure, she shall be un-
harmed and able to retain seed" (v.28, ונזרעה זרע). In
addition to this childlessness, the kareth penalty may be inferred from the paradigmatic expression נשא עון used at v. 31
"but that woman shall bear her punishment" (והאשה ההרא חשא
את עונה).

Coming as it does from the Priestly Writer's own hand,
this case is of importance for two reasons: 1) it demonstrates
that kareth is a divine curse incurred for the defiling act of
adultery (Lev. 18:20)--man cannot judge fairly here because he
has no way of proving the woman's infidelity. And certainly
she would not be likely to volunteer her guilt in exchange for
the death penalty both for herself and her paramour (Lev. 20:
10). 2) Since the woman is able to retain seed if she is
innocent, we must infer that she is not able to bear children
if she is guilty; her childlessness is one way of effecting the
kareth curse.[180]

F. Blasphemy (Num. 15:30-31)

The verb נדף used at Num. 15:30 has a cognate in Arabic
جدف, "to cut, cut off," in the second form of the verb
"to blaspheme, curse."[181] H. Brichto has affirmed that the
term has reference not to an imprecation per se but to "cutting
taunts."[182] Our verses apply the term מגדף to anyone who acts
defiantly against God so as to break His commands. Hence the
term נדף is a general designation which must include the desecration of God's name through profane use of it (Lev. 24:10ff.)
but which might also be extended to include other crimes. This
was recognized by the early rabbis who maintained that the
blasphemer is one who worships idols.[183]

As J. Milgrom has suggested with reference to the blasphemer at Lev. 24, the reason for the imposition of the death
sentence is based on P's pollution concept: "The blasphemer
has contaminated all within earshot and only his immediate
destruction (preceded by 'hand laying') can remove the impurity."[184] The kareth penalty which is imposed for blasphemy
heightens the seriousness of the crime. Once again the lex
talionis is observable in the execution of kareth: if one
deliberately desecrates God's name, God will remove his name
from among his people--he shall be made extinct. He has com-
mited a sacrilege against God. Blasphemy was considered a
sacrilege among the ancient Greeks,[185] and Hittite sources
confirm the biblical postulate that deliberate trespass against
sancta (מעל), for which blasphemy qualifies (Ezek. 20:27), is
punishable only by God.[186] Even when the stoning of the blasphemer takes place at Lev. 24 it is done at the express command of the Lord (v.23); hence man is only God's agent to
inaugurate the kareth curse.

III. CONCLUSION

In this essay we have discussed all the crimes for which
kareth is incurred according to the Torah. These crimes are
found to be deliberate violations of the Priestly Writer's
holiness/purity-impurity rules, the effect of which is the
desecration of sacred time, sacred substance, sacred place, and
God's holy name as well as the people of Israel themselves.
Nothing has been found in the biblical cases to suggest that
kareth was perceived as anything but a divine curse of extinction visited upon the sinner and his seed. Extrabiblical
sources discussed in this essay not only frequently sustain
the principles of P's pollution concept, but in several cases
the kareth penalty itself is found to have a parallel, in
particular in the praxis of the Hittite cult.

Although the Bible offers no systematic presentation of
examples of kareth, the LXX version of the Achan incident
(Jos. 7) and the case of the suspected adulteress from the
Priestly Writer's own hand (Num. 5) provide measurable support
for our interpretation of kareth.

Positively speaking, the Priestly Writer's appeal to kareth is aimed at discouraging Israelite participation in activities which would compromise Israel's holiness as a people separated unto God (Lev. 20:26).

NOTES

[1]See the author's doctoral dissertation, The Meaning of the Biblical Penalty KARETH, University of California at Berkeley, 1978, passim.

[2]Cf. Lev. 10:10f.; Ezek. 42:20; 44:23. W. Paschen, who accurately stresses the place of kareth in a purity-impurity matrix of ideas, inaccurately equates kareth with the death penalty: "Ferner ist hier die Kultverpflichtung des Kult-fähigen (שחרר) bei Androhung des Todes ausgesprochen (Num. 9:13). Ebenso wird Lev. 15:31 (טמאה) die Beseitigung von Unreinheit unter Todessanktion zur Pflicht gemacht." Cf. his Rein und Unrein = StANT 24 (München: Kösel-Verlag, 1970), p. 43.

[3]Mary Douglas, Purity and Danger (New York: Praeger Publishers, 1970), p. 41.

[4]Douglas, p. 54.

[5]Douglas, p. 132.

[6]Cf. Jacob Milgrom, Cult and Conscience (Leiden: E. J. Brill, 1976), p. 34. For the divine privilege of collective retribution in ancient Israel, cf. also M. Greenberg, "Some Postulates of Biblical Criminal Law," in M. Haran (ed.), Kaufmann Jubilee Volume (Jerusalem, 1960), pp. 5-28. With the kareth curse, divine collective punishment is "vertical" encompassing one's lineage. It may of course be "horizontal" so as to effect total annihilation of a population. Cf. further J. Scharbert, Solidarität in Segen und Fluch, pp. 126-132.

[7]It is noteworthy that during the monarchy in Israel, when the state had power to enforce order, concern for pollution as a source of danger sharply decreased. Witnesses to ritual impurity in the historical and prophetical books of the Old Testament are few, being dominated by the voice of the prophet-priest Ezekiel. Thus, it is precisely at the end of the monarchy, when the ship of state is sinking, that the pollution concerns are underlined.

[8]So also among the Hindus pollution always overcomes purity. For example, "If a ritually pure Brahman touches an outcast, it is the Brahman who becomes temporarily polluted; the outcast does not become purified." Cf. H. N. C. Stevenson, "Status Evaluation in the Hindu Caste System," Journal of the Royal Anthropological Institute 84 (1954), p. 50.

[9]See especially M. Haran, "The Priestly Image of the Tabernacle," HUCA 36 (1965), 191-266.

[10]The individual is perceived as a microcosm of society--order in the individual brings order to the society. The controls placed upon the individual's conduct presume that the body functions on the basis of a principle which might be called "symbolic homeostasis," defending society against dis-solution. For the body as a symbol of society, see provisionally

Mary Douglas, Natural Symbols (New York: Vintage Books,
1973), esp. pp. 93-112.

[11]The Tabernacle design, having its prototype in the
heavens (Exod. 25:9,20; 26:30; 27:8; 39:43), was revealed to
Moses by divine fiat as was customary in the ancient Near
East: cf. the instructions of the gods Ninzigga and Ninsikila
to Gudea to build the temple of Ningursu (ANET, p. 268) and
of Anu and Adad to Tiglath-Pileser I to build their shrine
(ANET, p. 275). According to R. Clifford, "the similarity in
form between the earthly dwelling of the god and its heavenly
prototype brings about the presence of the god," cf. The Cosmic Mountain in Canaan and the Old Testament (Cambridge,
Mass.: Harvard University Press, 1972), p. 123. More likely,
as far as P is concerned, the divine residence was thought to
establish order in what M. Eliade has called "the chaos of the
homogeneity and relativity of profane space," cf. The Sacred
and the Profane (New York: Harcourt, Brace & World, 1959),
p. 22. For the significance of the temple in the ancient Near
East in general, see BAR, I (Garden City: Doubleday, 1961),
pp. 145-200; also Eric Burrows, "Some Cosmological Patterns in
Babylonian Religion," in S. H. Hooke (ed.), The Labyrinth
(New York: Macmillan, 1935), pp. 45-70. For the Priestly
Tabernacle in particular: F. M. Cross, Jr., "The Priestly
Tabernacle," BAR, I, pp. 201-228.

[12]M. Pesachim 9:1.

[13]ANET, pp. 208-209, "Instructions for Temple Officials,"
ii, 59-79. The excuses not tolerated are all of a secular
nature (note the inclusion of a journey as with P's Passover
rule); the layman's purity is not an issue here. It is the
priestly responsibility to police sacred time among the Hittites and it is the priest who is expressly culpable if an
infraction occurs, though we do not know for certain that the
layman is free from punishment.

[14]ANET, p. 210, iv, 34-55.

[15]ANET, pp. 210-211, "From the Instructions for the Commander of the Border Guards," ii, 43-44.

[16]On the history: H. G. May, "The Relation of the
Passover to the Feast of Unleavened Cakes," JBL 55 (1936),
pp. 65-82; and H.-J. Kraus, "Zur Geschichte des Pessah-Maṣṣot-
Festes im AT," ET 18 (1958), pp. 47-67.

[17]Discussed by J. C. Rylaarsdam, "Passover and Feast of
Unleavened Bread," IDB, Vol. III, pp. 663-668, citing the
Mishna (Pesachim, passim.) and Josephus, War II. xiv. 3;
VI. ix. 3; Antiquities XVII. ix. 3; XX. v. 3. Cf. also Deut.
16:2-3; Ezek. 45:21-25.

[18]So M. Pesachim 5:4: "If one slaughter the Passover
sacrifice while in possession of leaven, he transgresses a
negative precept." Kareth is imposed for contempt of the
divine commandment, cf. Num. 15:30f.

28

[19] M. Pesachim 3:5.

[20] However, in later Judaism and in the New Testament leaven became almost synonymous with corruption or evil desires, cf. H. F. Beck, "Leaven," IDB, Vol. III, p. 105. Leaven is used anthropomorphically at I Cor. 5:7 of the man in the Corinthian church who had committed incest with his father's wife, a crime which was to be punished by kareth according to P (cf. infra., Sec. E). Paul applies kareth terminology only to the body (παραδουναι τον τοιουτον τω Σατανα εις ολεθρον της σαρκος) while the sinner's soul is spared judgment from God (I Cor. 5:5).

[21] Exod. 23:18; 34:25; Lev. 2:11; 6:10.

[22] The first and last days of the Passover week are designated as holy (מקרא קדש, Exod. 12:16; Lev. 23:8), as were, according to Sifre R'eih et. al. cited by Ramban, all the half-festive days in between. No work was to be done on the holy days. Ramban (Commentary Torah--Lev. 23:7) says "all servile work" (מלכת עבדה), i.e. excepting preparation of food. So essentially Maimonides, Mishneh Torah, Sepher Zemanim 7:1,2.

[23] For a recent survey of the lex talionis in the curses under discussion see R. O. Brauner, "Some Aspects of Offense and Penalty in the Bible and the Literature of the Ancient Near East," AJS 3 (1974), pp. 9-18.

[24] Rashi, Commentary in Miqra'ot Gedeloth, Exod. 12:15, s.v. מישראל.

[25] Ibid., Gen. 17:14 s.v. הולך ערירי חמו ונכרתה הנפש: רמת קודם. U. Cassuto remarks in his Commentary to Exodus (Jerusalem: Magnes Press, 1967, pp. 141f.) with respect to kareth: "Probably, as rabbinic tradition maintains, it was a punishment imposed by Heaven, that is, the transgressor died before his time, leaving no children. Others consider that the term connotes excommunication or even execution." We reiterate that childlessness is only one way to effect the kareth curse.

[26] Possibly illustrated outside of P by the Achan incident, at least according to the LXX, cf. infra, Sec. B, 7.

[27] Prima facie it might appear that Nadab and Abihu, whose sin of bringing strange fire before the Lord resulted in their immediate death by God (Lev. 10:1ff.), may supply an example of kareth for according to P's genealogy (Num. 3:4) and the Chronicler (I Chr. 24:2) they did not have children (ובנים היו לא ובנים). But the kareth formula is not applied to Nadab and Abihu and their childlessness cannot be related to their crime with any degree of certainty. We do not rest any part of our argument on their case.

[28] The loathsome practice of child-sacrifice notwithstanding. One does not, of course, love children who do not yet exist; love demands a personality for its object. Hence, a parent loves a one-year-old child more than a newborn, a six-

year-old more than the one-year-old, etc., because of the development of the child's personality. So Maimonides, Guide, III, p. 269 in Friedländer's translation.

[29]The early rabbis enumerated thirty-nine principal categories of work prohibited on the Sabbath, c.f. M. Sabbath 7:2.

[30]The Bible records different motivation for Sabbath observance, c.f. Exod. 20:11; Deut 5:13,15.

[31]For מחלליה (Exod 31:14) the LXX has ο βεβηλων αυτο. The noun βεβηλος (verb: βεβελοω, "to desecrate") denotes what is accessible as distinct from αβατον and αδυτον, corresponding to Latin profanus and is the usual rendering for חל (e.g. Lev. 10:10; Ezek. 22:26; 44:23), cf. F. Hauck, TDNT, I, p. 604. Thus, sacred time is "inaccessible" to man for the performance of his usual labors.

[32]Maimonides comments: "What penalty does he deserve for doing work? If he did it voluntarily, willfully (ברצונו בזדון), he deserves kareth; if he acted in the presence of witnesses who forewarned him, he is stoned; if he acted unintentionally, he must bring a standard sin offering (קרבן חטאת קבועה), cf. Mishneh Torah, Hilchoth Shabbath, 1, 1.

[33]M. Tsevat, "The Basic Meaning of the Biblical Sabbath," ZAW 84 (1972), p. 455.

[34]M. Nedarim 3:11; T.B. Shabbath 132a; infra., pp. 102ff.

[35]M. Pesachim 6:1ff.

[36]For discussion cf. Strack-Billerbeck, Kommentar zum Neuen Testament, I (München: C. H. Beck, 1961-1963), pp. 620-622.

[37]M. Semachoth 3:10. Further on kareth as premature death according to the rabbis, cf. Ch. V. infra. pp. 224ff.

[38]Consequently, we disagree with M. Tsevat's analysis of I. Sam. 2:27-36 as the "only true kareth narrative," cf. his "Studies in the Book of Samuel," HUCA 32 (1961), pp. 191-216.

[39]For the transformation which kareth appears to have undergone at the hand of Ezekiel, cf. infra. Sec. D, 5.

[40]Note the use of מעל with גדף here and גויף with כרת at Num. 15:30 suggesting that these terms be added to the semantic field of kareth. Further on blasphemy, cf. infra. Sec. F.

[41]Cf. Lev. 18:29 and Lev. 26:34ff.

[42]Molech worship also qualifies for idolatry as does, according to some, blasphemy. Cf. our discussion infra., at Sec. D, 3,5; and F.

[43]According to rabbinic tradition, the difference between the Day of Atonement and the Sabbath is that the latter is punishable by man (Exod. 31:14), the former only by kareth; cf. M. Megillah 1:5; Sopherim 10,3; Massekoth Ketannoth, 1, p. 256. Maimonides says (Mishneh Torah, Hilcoth Shevithoth 'Asor I:2 = Birnbaum translation, p. 79): "Whenever the penalty for work done willfully on the Sabbath is stoning, the penalty for doing it willfully on Yom Kippur is kareth; whenever the penalty on the Sabbath is a sin-offering, the penalty on Yom Kippur is equally a sin-offering."

[44]So according to tradition, derived from the expression העני את נפשתיכם (Lev. 16:29; 23:29), cf. Maimonides, ibid., I: 4,6.

[45]Peter Gerlitz, "Fasten als Reinigungsritus," ZRGG 20 (1968), pp. 216f. Not the fasting itself expiates--it is merely an external evidence of the sinner's repentance.

[46]Jacob Milgrom, "Israel's Sanctuary: The Priestly 'Picture of Dorian Gray'," RB 83(1976), pp. 393f.

[47]Cf. Num. 15:27ff.; M. Kerithoth 1:2--the purgation-offering is efficacious only for unintentional sins.

[48]We insist on the propitiatory function of the blood against the thesis of C. H. Dodd, "Ἱλασκεσθαι, Its Cognates, Derivatives, and Synonyms in the Septuagint," JTS 32(1931), pp. 352-360. We agree with Leon Morris, The Apostolic Preaching of the Cross (Grand Rapids: W. B. Eerdman, 1965), pp. 144-213; idem., "The Use of Ἱλασκεσθαι, etc., in Biblical Greek," ExpT 62 (1950-51), pp. 227-233; and Roger Nicole, "C.H. Dodd and the Doctrine of Propitiation," WTJ 17 (1955), pp. 117-157.

[49]M. Shevuoth 1:7.

[50]M. Shevuoth 1:6.

[51]'Aboth D'Rabbi Nathan, in A. Cohen (ed.), The Minor Tractates of the Talmud, p. 142. Also cf. Tosephta Yoma IV,6.

[52]M. Yoma 8:9. Cf. Maimonides, Mishneh Torah, Hilchoth Teshubah 2:3 (Birnbaum, p. 37): "Anyone who makes a verbal confession without resolving in his heart to abandon his sin is like one who takes a ritual bath while grasping a defiling reptile. The bath is useless unless he first casts the reptile away."

[53]For commutation of deliberate crimes by confession, cf. J. Milgrom, "The Priestly Doctrine of Repentance," RB 82 (1975), pp. 187-205.

[54]In his creation story the Priestly Writer portrays man in his pristine state as a vegetarian (Gen. 1:29), but this reflects P's ideal and not the historical reality which faced him. The real situation is represented by the post-diluvian Noah to whom the Priestly Writer concedes the right to eat

meat (Gen. 9:3). The dietary regulations to which P appends the kareth curse as an incentive may be deliberately designed to return man to his ideal herbivorous fare. P's ideal demonstrates a humane ethic motivated by a theocratic pollution concept. The Priestly Writer's aim to sublimate man's carnivorous appetite through the rigors of the sacrifical system and purity-impurity rules may find a parallel in Indian history where the Brahmin caste gained control and through purity rules and sacrificial regulations imposed vegetarianism on the society:

> "As in Indian history the Aryan meat-eating priests gradually became Brahmin vegetarians, passing through the stage of eating meat only after sacrifice, so now many tribes eat domestic animals only after sacrifice. Not only among Hinduized tribes, but also among communities little affected by ideas of ahimsa (i.e. non-injury), there may be a certain uneasiness about killing animals. This uneasiness seems to be due less to ethical motives than to the fear of offending the gods." Cf. G. E. Ferro-Luzzi, "Food Avoidances of Indian Tribes," Anthropos 70(1975), p. 395.

Certainly P's concern for profane slaughter is motivated by the fear of offending Israel's God, but the ethical principle also pervades P's dietary regulations.

[55]Cf. Lev. 3:17; 7:26f.; Deut 12:16ff. Talmudic law exempted from kareth one who had eaten less than an olive-sized amount of blood of cattle, beasts, and fowls, cf. M. Kerithoth 5:1.

[56]Blood is tantamount to life also in the Sumerian and Babylonian creation stories; man is made from clay activated by the blood of a slain god. Cf. W. G. Lambert and A. R. Millard, Atra-Ḥasis (Oxford: Clarendon Press, 1970), I: 208ff.: "Let one god be slaughtered so that all the gods may be cleansed in a dipping. From his flesh and blood may Nintu mix clay, that god and man may be thoroughly mixed in the clay. So that we may hear the drum (uppu) for the rest of time let there be a spirit from the god's flesh." Also ANET, p. 68, IV; 33: "Out of his (the god Kingu's) blood they fashioned mankind." Prof. Anne Kilmer has asserted that uppu in this context is not "drum" but refers to the "heartbeats"; cf. her "Notes on Akkadian uppu," Ancient Near Eastern Studies in Memory of J. J. Finkelstein. Memoirs of the Connecticut Academy of Arts and Sciences 19 (New Haven, Conn., 1978--). Further, cf. A. L. Oppenheim, "On the Observation of the Pulse in Mesopotamia," Or 31(1962), pp. 27-33.

[57]So also Deut. 12:23: "the blood is the life" מדה הוא הנפש). D does not present the kareth formula, but it adds a most interesting motive clause to the blood prohibition: "in order that it might be well with you and your children after you" (Deut. 12:25 למען ייטב לך ולבניך אחריך). Does D obliquely refer to the Priestly kareth-curse which befalls the descendants of the sinner as well as the sinner himself?

[58]Emile Durkheim, Incest: The Nature and Origin of the Taboo (New York, Lyle Stuart, 1963), pp. 83-84.

[59]Maimonides, Guide, III, p. 233, Friedländer's translation.

[60]ASTI 8 (1970-1971), pp. 78-105.

[61]Ibid., p. 89, and see our discussion infra., D, 4.

[62]As were the fat and the burnt offerings ('ה אשי, Lev. 21:6).

[63]Jacob Milgrom, "A Prolegomenon to Leviticus 17:11," JBL 90(1971), p. 155. The kareth penalty for theriocide is explained infra., D, 1.

[64]Further on blood, cf. Dennis J. McCarthy, "The Symbolism of Blood and Sacrifice," JBL 88(1969), pp. 166-176; idem., "Blood," IDBS (1976), pp. 114-117; idem., "Further Notes on the Symbolism of Blood and Sacrifice," JBL 92(1973), pp. 205-210.

[65]Cf. CD III, 6,9 discussed infra., Ch. IV, Sec. II, 8.

[66]E.g. Jubilees 6:12f.

[67]Translated by R. H. Charles (ed.) The Apocrypha and Pseudepigrapha of the Old Testament, II (Oxford: Clarendon Press, 1913), p. 44.

[68]According to Abraham Kahana's version of Jubilees in Hebrew (Jerusalem, 1959), the verb "to root out" at 21:22b is כרת and the verb "to perish" is אבד. Further cf. Jub. 15:34 (for neglect of circumcision); 30:10ff. (for sexual relations with father's wife); 20:4-6; 31:20; 36:9; 37:23; and I Enoch 7:5; 98:11. The Ethiopic root, graciously checked for me by Professor Thomas Leahy, is SWR, cf. R. H. Charles, The Ethiopic Version of the Hebrew Book of Jubilees (Oxford: Clarendon Press, 1895).

[69]Also among the Hittites the god's food was holy and could not be consumed by anyone else, cf. KUB XXX 10 i 13-14.

[70]Unlike the blood prohibition which is universal, the prohibition against eating fat is not expressly extended to include that of hunt animals. However, the fat of all carrion (נבלה וטרפה) is strictly forbidden as food but it may be put to any other purpose (Lev. 7:24). Further, cf. M. Kerithoth 3: 1,2; T.B. Kerithoth 3b-4b.

[71]E.g., NJPS at Gen. 4:4.

[72]Theodor H. Gaster, "Sacrifices and Offerings, OT," IDB, Vol. IV, p. 150.

[73] As illustrated in the Babylonian hepatoscopies and extispicies performed by the bāru-priest, cf. I Mendelsohn, "Divination," IDB, I, pp. 856-858 for summary.

[74] A warning against eating fat occurs in Akkadian: lipâ la takkal u dama la teteşşi "eat no fat and you will not excrete blood." Cf. BWL 240:9; CAD, lipû, Vol IX, p. 203.

[75] E.g. at Mari, cf. A. Malamat, "The Ban in Mari and the Bible," Proceedings of the Ninth Meeting of Die Ou-Testamentiese Werkgemeenskap in Suid-Afrika) (= Biblical Essays, 1966), pp. 40-49.

[76] L. A. Snijders, "The meaning of זו in the Old Testament," OTS 10(1954), p. 126.

[77] Ibid., p. 127. In a general way, he correctly understands the kareth penalty to be "annihilation."

[78] Menahem Haran, "The Priestly Image of the Tabernacle," HUCA 36(1965), p. 222.

[79] Jacob Milgrom, Studies, I, p. 5 and n. 6.

[80] M. Haran, "The Complex of Ritual Acts Inside the Sanctuary," SH 8(1961), pp. 276f.

[81] See conclusively, M. Haran, "The Uses of Incense in the Ancient Israelite Ritual," VT 19(1960), pp. 113-129.

[82] Cf. T. B. Kerithoth 2b: "As the peace-offerings are dedications to the altar, and for this reason one is liable on their account to kareth, so also whatever are dedications to the altar, one is liable on that account thereof to kareth; this excludes dedications for the Temple Repair (Fund)."

[83] Thus, during two days and one intervening night, cf. M. Zevachim 5:7.

[84] As Ramban says (Commentary--Leviticus, p. 85), "on the third day in the morning"--the usual time of sacrifice. Cf. also T. B. Zevachim 55a.

[85] The term פגול appears only four times in the Old Testament: Lev. 7:18; 19:7; Ezek. 4:14; Isa. 65:4 (plural). In the latter passage--part of a cultic poem--the eating of פגול is associated with eating swine's flesh and other cultic crimes including the misuse of incense, unlawful sacrifice, etc. פגול at Ezek. 4:14 is clearly a term for ritually unfit food whose consumption is shunned by the prophet.

[86] KUB XXX 10 i 12-14: nu-(...) DINGER-YA natta kuššanka linkun lingain-ašta natta kuššanka šarrahhat šiuni-mi-ma-mu kuit šuppi adana natta ara n-at natta kuššanka edun nuza tuekkan-man natta paprahhun, rendered by James C. Moyer, The Concept of Ritual Purity Among the Hittites (Brandeis Ph.D. Dissertation, 1969; Ann Arbor Microfilm), pp. 30,41,109.

34

Further on the "close connection between the notion of ritual
impurity and the notion of being consecrated to God" cf. the
opinion of R. de Vaux, Ancient Israel (New York: McGraw Hill,
1965), pp. 460ff.

[87]J. C. Moyer, ibid., p. 110.

[88]M. Zevachim 2:3: כל השוחט והמקבל וכמהלך והזורק . . .
לאכל דבר שדרכו לאכל להקטיר דבר שדרכו להקטיר חוץ למקומו פסול
ואין בו כרת חוץ לזמנו פגול וחייבין עליו כרב. . .

[89]M. Zevachim 2:5: זה הכלל, אם מחשבת הזמן קדמה
למחשבת המקום פגול וחייבים עליו כרת; ואם מחשבת המקום קדמה
למחשבת הזמן פסול ואין בו כרת. וחכמים אומרים זה וזה פסול
ואין בו כרת. Further, as regards the sprinkling of the blood
of the purgation-offering, cf. M. Zevachim 4:1: "If the first
act of sprinkling were not carried out at its proper time and
the second not in its proper place, it is rejection and kareth
is incurred thereby" (נתן את הראשונה חוץ לזמנה ואת השניה ...
חוץ למקומה פגול וחייתיו עליו כרת). Cf. T.B. Zevachim 28a. See
also M. Zevachim 6:7.

[90]Cf. M. Zevachim 4:5.

[91]T.B. Me'ilah 17b, in reference to the statement at Exod.
29:34 that "it (i.e. the ordination ram) shall not be eaten
for it is holy." The exceptions for which kareth is not
imposed for transgressing the law of פגול with respect to time
are given at M. Zevachim 4:3.

[92]T.B. Me'ilah 5b. For the exceptions cf. the previous
note.

[93]Similarly, Hindu women in Tamilnad observe birth pollution with regard to the sacred: "Birth pollution is treated
like death pollution in most smṛtis and made to last for 10
days. The magical number 40 also appears with regard to birth,
but Yaj. (III, 19) arrives at it by stages: The mother becomes touchable after 10 days, but it is not fit to take part
in religious rites for another 20 days (i.e. 30 days in all),
if the child is male; and for another 30 days (i.e. 40 days in
all), if the child is female." Cf. Gabriella Eichinger Ferro-
Luzzi, "Women's Pollution Periods in Tamilnad (India),"
Anthropos 69(1974), p. 115. Sacred foods and territory are
proscribed against trespass throughout the ancient Near East as
indicated earlier in the expressions asakkam akālu, anzilla
kabāsu, etc. and see the occurrences of these terms infra. Cf.
further, R. Pettazzoni, "La confession des pêches en Syrie
aux epoches préchrétiennes," Melanges syriens offerts à R.
Dussaud, I (1939), pp. 197-202.

[94]Their portions are described at Exod. 29:26-28,31; Lev.
2:3,10; Ezek. 44:29-31.

[95]Exod. 29:33; only the priest and his dependents who are
part of his household, including the slave he has purchased,
may partake, but explicitly not a stranger (גר) nor a hired
day-laborer (Lev. 22:10-16). At Lev. 22:9 the kareth penalty

is implicit in the expression ולא ישאו עליו חטא as we should
expect for the encroachment of the priest who is unclean. On
the meaning of "encroachment" (cf. v. 3 ויקרב), cf. J. Milgrom,
Studies, I, pp. 16ff. whose suggestion that contact and intention are involved for the usurper follows rabbinic tradition.
Further, cf. Judith 11:13.

[96]E.g. Exod 29:34. Although kareth is not specified by
P at this verse it is only because no priestly violation
regarding the eating of נותר has been mentioned. Kareth may
be deduced according to the rabbinic exegetical principle of
gezerah sh^ewah, i.e. the application to one case of a rule
known from another case when both cases share the use of a
common expression, here ושרפת את הנותר באש לא יאכל כי קדש
הוא, Exod. 29:34 and . . .באש ישרף ואם האכל יאכל., Lev. 7:17b-
18a. If kareth applies to the layman's violation it must also
apply to the priest.

[97]Exod. 39:31f.; Lev. 10:13-20; Ezek. 42:13.

[98]Cf. M. Neḡaim, passim. Among the Babylonians "leprosy"
was inflicted by the moon-god Sin (cf. MDP 2 pl. 23 vi 53):
"May Sin cover his body with leprosy so that adi ūm balṭu bis-
su lizammima kīma umām ṣēri ṣēra lirpud as long as he lives he
shall be deprived of his own house and have to roam outside
the city like a wild animal." Cited by CAD, zummû, Vol. XXI,
p. 156. P also requires expulsion of the leper, cf. Num. 5:2f.

[99]Cf. M. Zavim, passim. The LXX specifies γονορρυης.

[100]According to Ezek. 44:25f. the corpse-contaminated
priest must wait seven days after his cleansing and then bring
a ḥaṭṭa't before entering the sanctuary, but Ezekiel refers to
direct corpse-contact. Our case involves secondary contact
with corpse-uncleanness which requires of the priest only the
ritual bath and one day of waiting before eating his sacred
portions.

[101]The LXX reads κοιτη σπερματος, limiting the emission
to the sexual act (cf. Lev. 15:16-18), but this is, in our
view, too narrow. More than likely all seminal emissions were
considered by P to be defiling just as they were by Israel's
contemporaries in the Near East.
    The Hittite temple servant must not knowingly postpone his
ritual bath after intercourse lest he approach the gods' sacrificial loaves and libation bowl in an unclean condition
(šaknuanza)--this is a capital crime if he is caught, else one
expects for him the divine curse of extinction, cf. KUB XIII
4 iii 78-89, translated in ANET, p. 209, cf. also ii 80ff.
ibid., and see J. C. Moyer, The Concept of Purity Among the
Hittites, p. 44.
    Emission of semen was considered defiling among the Baby-
lonians, cf. the examples of nocturnal emissions and intercourse under balālu, CAD, II, p. 44. A prayer to Marduk
includes the fragment: "the sperm (let. the excretion from his
prepuce) which is abhorrent to all gods, is. . .for mankind. . .": mušu ša libbi urulatišu ikkib ilī kalama ana niši;

cf. CAD, ikkibu, Vol. VII, p. 56. Further citations by R. D.
Biggs, ŠA.ZI.GA, p. 30.
Also among modern pollution conscious peoples bodily
emissions are ritually disqualifying, e.g., among the Coorgs
the festival priests of Ketrappa must not have sexual rela-
tions during the 21 days of the bienniel festival, cf. M. N.
Srinivas, Religion and Society Among the Coorgs of South India
(Oxford: Clarendon Press, 1952), p. 104.

[102]A ḥaṭṭa't is required at Lev. 5:2 for the unintentional
error; in our case the act of the priest must be assumed to
be deliberate. Indeed this is clear from the use of קרב, "to
encroach" at v. 2, cf. supra. n. 98. Further on שרץ uncleanness, cf. M. Tevul Yom 2:1.

[103]The reference is not to the contamination derived from
contact with a human corpse but to all the perimeters of defilement which a man might encounter, cf. Lev. 7:21. So also
B. Levine, In the Presence of the Lord (Leiden: E. J. Brill,
1974), p. 109, n. 132.

[104]The layman is permitted to eat carrion but must be purified by a ritual bath and remain unclean for one day or he
will be liable to kareth (Lev. 17:15f.); the priest may not
partake of carrion at all. Further on נבלה, cf. W. M. W. Roth,
"NBL," VT 10(1960), pp. 394-409 but with caution as to his
conclusion regarding outcasts and sacrilege. Here we must
disagree with his position.
A sept among the Dravidian Kamar is forbidden to eat
animals, birds and fish that die a natural death. G. E. Ferro-
Luzzi, "Food Avoidance of Indian Tribes," Anthropos 70 (1975),
observes: "Association with untimely death explains why the
meat of animals which died while giving birth, died by drowning or killed by wild beasts are shunned. . .Kills of animals,
though occasionally eaten, are considered to be impure general
agreement. Apart from being carrion, they are also leavings.
Leavings are thought to retain the possible dangerous qualities
of the eater and to be defiled by contact with the eater's
saliva" (pp. 391, 398f.).

[105]Cf. J. Milgrom, Studies, I, p. 7, and n. 20.

[106]However, see the example of kareth for priestly violation against sacred offerings which is afforded by Eli's sons
(I Sam. 2:27ff.; 4:11,17).

[107]The possible hendiadys at Num 4:19 is suggested by the
LXX's κατα την αναφοραν αυτου, noticed and approved by J.
Milgrom, Studies, I, pp. 65ff. and Suzanne Daniel, Rescherches
sur le vocabulaire du culte dans le Septant (Paris: C. Klincksieck, 1966), pp. 78ff.

[108]Cf. Exod. 19:21ff. Desecration of sancta by mere sight
is also attested for the Mesopotamians, e.g. in "The Curse of
Agade: The Ekur Avenged," ANET, p. 649: 128ff.: "The
(unauthorized) people (now) say its cella, the house that knew
not light. The Akkadian saw the holy vessels of the gods."
For this desecration, the religious poet explains, divine

appointments ravage Sumer. From Agum-Kakrime we read: "The
initiate may show it (only) to (another) initiate, the unini-
tiated must not see it, it is a sin against DN, etc." mudû
mudâ likallim la mudû la immar (NĪG).GIG ᵈHaniš u ᵈŠullat
ᵈŠamaš u ᵈAdad, cf. CAD, ikkibu, Vol. VII, p. 56, citing 5R
33 viii 30.

Various Akkadian expressions, some which we have already
had occasion to refer to, describe desecrations of sancta,
e.g. asakkam iltanagge (verb leqû, "to take,"): "he continually appropriates what should not be touched" cf. CAD, asakku,
Vol. I, p. 258. Similarly, the verb לקח is used with the חרם-
objects at Jos. 6:18; 7:1. The bĭt asakki is a forbidden
place, perhaps in the adytum of the temple. Death will befall
the individual "who brings (the stela) into a bĭt asakki where
no one can penetrate and sets it up" cf. CAD, erēbu, Vol. IV,
p. 259. Similarly, "into the holy temple, shadowy as a (sacred) grove, nobody may enter" (ibid.: ina bĭti ellu ša kīma
gišti sillašu tarsu ana libbišu mamma la irrubu). anzillu,
according to the editors of the CAD originally an object with
which contact was to be avoided lest one become ritually unclean, is frequently found with kabāsu, "to walk, tread upon,"
as: "Unknowingly I trod upon (what is) forbidden by my goddess": CAD, ikkibu, Vol. VII, p. 55: anzil ištarija ina la
idê ukabbis. The same passage illustrates the use of ikkibu
with akālu, "to eat,": "Unknowingly I have eaten the proscribed food of my god" (ikkib ilija ina la [idê] ākul). anzillu also appears with amāru, "to see,": "I have looked at
and trod upon what is an abomination of my god and my goddess"
CAD, anzillu, Vol. I, p. 153: anzilla ilija u ištarija ša
(. . .) ātammaru ukabbisu.

Mutilated persons, children, women, dogs, pigs, etc. could
not enter the Hittite temples without defiling them, cf. e.g.,
KUB V 7; KUB XIII ii 7ff (ANET, "Instructions," p. 208).

The pig is also tabooed in the Babylonian cult: šaḫû la
simat ekurri. . . .ikkib ilī kalama "The pig is unfit (to enter)
the temple, this is a sin against all gods." Cf. BWL 215 iii
16 (fable) and CAD, ikkibu, Vol. VII, p. 56.

Mutilated persons are among those barred from the congregation of Israel at Deut. 23:2ff.

[109] Midrash Rabbah, Vol. 5, trans. by Judah J. Slotki
(London: Soncino, 1939), p. 148.

[110] See S. R. Driver, Introduction to the Literature of the
Old Testament (New York: Charles Scribner's Sons, 1916), p.
63; F. Cross, "The Priestly Houses of Early Israel," in Canaan-
ite Myth and Hebrew Epic (Cambridge: Harvard University Press,
1973), esp. pp. 205ff., and above all, J. Liver, Korah, Dathan
and Abiram," SH 8(1961), pp. 197-217. The question remains
moot.

[111] M. Haran, "The Uses of Incense," pp. 115f.

[112] Rabbinic opinion has long been divided as to the nature
and extent of Korah's punishment, cf. T.B. Sanhedrin 52a; 108a;
109b; 110a; Tosephta Sanhedrin XIII, 4; Rosh-Hashanah 17a.
Some say he was denied a share in the world to come. Others
dispute the status of his children in the world to come. Still

38

others question the complicity of his family in his crime and
hence the extent of the punishment to them. Discussion and
further citations to the literature may be found in A. Büch-
ler, "Die Todesstrafen der Bibel und der jüdisch-nachbib-
lischen Zeit," MGWJ 50(1906), pp. 554ff.

[113]Cf. my Meaning of the Biblical Penalty KARETH, Ch. III,
Tables 5 and 6.

[114]We are not suggesting that herem-annihilation is the
exact equivalent of kareth, only that in Achan's case the
kareth penalty is effected by the herem execution. Once the
notion that kareth is the equivalent of death is abandoned,
our suggestion becomes more than specious. For example, biblical scholars have struggled with why Achan's children (to
say nothing of his property) are destroyed with him. The
problem has been set forth by J. Milgrom in his Cult and Conscience, p. 34. He cites B. Jackson (Theft in Early Jewish
Law, pp. 61, 164f.) and M. Greenberg ("Some Postulates of
Biblical Criminal Law," pp. 23f.) as supporters of the view
that the principle of contagion lay behind Achan's execution,
hence the destruction of his children and his property. Milgrom demurs, affirming that Achan's sin of sancta tresspass--
a מעל, a sin against God--can only be punished by God who
alone may justifiably punish collectively. He explains
Achan's execution by man as being ordained specially by God,
cf. v. 15a: "whoever is caught with the herem-(objects) shall
be burned with fire--both he and all he has." According to
Lev. 27:29, people in herem status are non-redeemable and must
be put to death (מות יומח). We submit that the human and divine penalties are not mutually exclusive as has heretofore
been supposed; they operate simultaneously. The fact that
Achan's sin is against God and that it was intentional causes
us to expect the divine kareth, but the extinction is effected
by the agency of man. The motive clause כי עבר את-ברית ח' at
Jos. 7:15b recalls P's clause את בריתי הפר used with kareth
(Gen. 17:14; Num. 15:31). The motive clause with the herem
penalty at Deut. 13:18b (which anticipates Achan's case as
well) recalls the circumcision covenant as well as kareth.

[115]Michael V. Fox, "The Sign of the Covenant: Circumcision
in the Light of the Priestly 'ôt Etiologies," RB 81(1974), p.
595.

[116]For an introduction to covenant concepts consult D. R.
Hillers, Covenant: The History of a Biblical Idea (Baltimore:
Johns Hopkins Press, 1970); D. J. McCarthy, Treaty and Cove-
nant: A Study in the Ancient Oriental Documents and in the
Old Testament (Rome: Pontifical Biblical Institute, 1963);
G. E. Mendenhall, "Covenant Forms in Israelite Tradition," BA
17(1954), pp. 50ff.; idem., Law and Covenant in Israel and the
Ancient Near East (Pittsburgh: The Biblical Colloquium, 1955);
J. A. Thompson, "The Near Eastern Suzerain-Vassal Concept in
the Religion of Israel," JRH 3(1964), pp. 1-19; M. Weinfeld,
"Covenant Terminology in the Ancient Near East and Its Influ-
ence on the West," JAOS 93(1973), pp. 190-199; idem., "ברית,"
TDOT, II, pp. 253-279.

[117]E.g., E. Isaac, "Circumcision as a Covenant Rite," Anthropos 59(1964), pp. 444,453; F. J. Helfmeyer, "אות," TDOT, I, p. 182; O. Betz, "Στιγμα," TDNT, VII, p. 662; and M. C. Kline, By Oath Consigned (Grand Rapids: W. B. Eerdman, 1968), p. 87.

[118]They are in this sense conditional. M. Weinfeld believes the Abrahamic covenant to be of the "grant" type rather than the "treaty" type. He says: "While the 'treaty' constitutes an obligation of the vassal to his master, the suzerain, the 'grant' constitutes an obligation of the master to his servant. In the 'grant' the curse is directed towards the one who will violate the rights of the king's vassal, while in the treaty the curse is directed towards the vassal who will violate the rights of the king," cf. his "The Covenant of Grant in the Old Testament and in the Ancient Near East," JAOS 90 (1970), p. 185. In the light of our analysis of kareth (which Weinfeld ignores, incidentally), it is inconceivable that the curse could befall anyone but the vassal, thus, according to Weinfeld's definition, confirming the circumcision covenant as being of the treaty variety. This does not eliminate the promisory nature of the Abrahamic covenant.

[119]On the use of dramatic acts to "sign" legal contracts in the ancient Near East, cf. provisionally Anne D. Kilmer, "Symbolic Gestures in Akkadian Contracts From Alalakh and Ugarit," JAOS 94(1974), pp. 177-183, and the literature cited by her.

[120]For the use of Akkadian ittu, cognate to אות, as "acknowledgement," or "proof" of legal contracts, cf. CAD, Vol. VII, p. 309.

[122]According to Ezek. 44:7, uncircumcised foreigners have been permitted entrance into the sanctuary so as to defile it. P rules that the foreigner (בן נכר) ipso facto cannot share in Passover (Exod. 12:43). The foreigner (lúarab-zenaš) is denied participation in the Hittite cult as well, while the ubāra, like the Hebrew גר, is permitted, cf. J. C. Moyer, The Concept of Purity Among the Hittites, p. 99. Outside of P, circumcision as a mark of in-group identity is recognizable at Gen. 34:16,22, cf. the expression לעם אחד. Nations that are uncircumcised bear the mark of their disgrace to Sheol: Jud. 14:3; 15:18; I Sam. 14:6; 31:4; Ezek. 31:18f.; 32:24,26,29,30,32; I Chr. 10:4. Uncircumcision of the heart is not a Priestly metaphor, cf. Deut. 10:16; 30:6; Jer. 4:4; 9:24f.

[123]Passover and circumcision are intimately related in a midrash by Maimonides: ". . .the blood of the Passover and that of the circumcision flowed together. The prophet Ezekiel (16:6), referring to this event says: 'When I saw thee sprinkled with thine own blood, I said to thee, Live because of thy blood,' i.e. because of the blood of the Passover and that of circumcision" (Guide of the Perplexed, III. p. 232).

[124]Agreeing with the LXX and Samaritan versions, against the MT, Syriac, and Vulgate. R. H. Charles, Apocrypha and Pseudepigrapha of the Old Testament, II, p. 36, gives numerous

references to the debate regarding the necessity to circumcise
on the eighth day, including the presentation of the following
halacha in a second century A.D. work of Justin Martyr: "Did
God wish those to sin who are circumcised or do circumcise on
the Sabbaths? For he commands that on the eighth day--even
though it happen to be a Sabbath--those who are born should
always be circumcised. . . .Could not He have the infants circumcised one day before or one day after the Sabbath, if He
knew that it was a sinful act on the Sabbath?" Further, cf.
T.B. Shabbath 132b, and, in the NT, John 7:22f.

[125] Jubilees 15:26. According to E. Meyer, this passage is
best understood against the background of Hasmonaean politics,
cf. "Περιτεμνω," TDNT, VI, p. 78, n. 38.

[126] Jubilees 30:22. Cf. p. 261, n. 9 for text.

[127] See our discussion in Meaning of the Biblical Penalty
KARETH, ch. IV.

[128] M. Oholoth 1:1-4. Extensively on the rabbinic views cf.
Jacob Neusner, A History of the Mishnaic Law of Purity, Vol.
1-10 (Leiden: E. J. Brill, 1976), s.v. Index.

[129] M. Kelim 1:4.

[130] Cf. M. Parah, passim.

[131] J. Blau, "The Red Heifer: A Biblical Purification Rite
in Rabbinical Literature," Numen 14(1967), p. 78.

[132] J. Neusner, The Idea of Purity in Ancient Judaism
(Leiden: E. J. Brill, 1973), p. 23.

[133] J. Bowman, "Did the Qumran Sect Burn the Red Heifer?"
RQ 1(1957), pp. 73-84.

[134] The reason for the priest's sprinkling of the blood
seven times in the direction of the sanctuary is not stated by
P. It may be merely dedicatory. The procedure is strikingly
similar to that which the priest performs in cleansing the in-
fected house, but whether a symbolic cleansing of the sanctuary
was intended is uncertain.

[135] The expulsion from the camp for death pollution (Num.
5:2f.) is not itself kareth as might be supposed if one thought
kareth to be excommunication or some other form of temporary or
permanent exclusion. G. Forkman's comment at Num. 19:20 that
". . .if anyone omits to cleanse himself, the people (italics
mine) have to cut him off" is totally without support, cf. his
The Limits of The Religious Community (Lund: CWK Gleerup,
1972), p. 18.

[136] It is noteworthy that no ḥaṭṭa't is required of the person cleansed from corpse-contamination as in the case of the
parturient (Lev. 12:6), the leper (Lev. 14:10,19,22,30), and
the woman with a hemorrhage (Lev. 15:30). This may suggest
that death pollution was, comparatively speaking, of a less

severe category. However, only the corpse-contaminated person
must be cleansed in stages--on the third and seventh day (Num.
19:19), thus suggesting a greater degree of impurity for death.
If, as we conjectured at n. 137, the blood of the red heifer
acted symbolically to cleanse the outer altar, this would be
done before the corpse-contaminated person was himself
cleansed, perhaps because the greater impurity caused by death
pollution should not remain on the altar until the eighth day.
If this were so, to require a ḥaṭṭa't as in the other cases of
severe natural impurities would be superfluous. Nevertheless,
hermeneutical difficulties nag this view. For example, one
sprinkling of the blood must do for all future cases of corpse-
contamination as long as the ashes of the cow last. Such pro-
phylactic measures (unless one think of the Passover blood in
this way) are without precedent for Israel's cult. The question remains open and we rest no part of our understanding of
kareth on this discussion.

[137]J. G. Frazer, The Fear of the Dead in Primitive Religion
(1933/1966), p. 80.

[138]Yehezkel Kaufmann, The Religion of Israel (New York:
Schocken Books, 1972), p. 105.

[139]So correctly in our view, J. Milgrom, "Two Kinds of
Ḥaṭṭa't," VT 26 (1976), pp. 334ff. Enemy land is unclean
according to the Hittites just as Hatti land is pure (parkui-)
cf. KUB XV 34 ii 6ff. Demons are not a feared source of
impurity among the Hittites according to J. C. Moyer, The Concept of Purity Among the Hittites, p. 118, n. 321 and p. 142.

[140]W. Robertson Smith, The Religion of the Semites (New
York: Schocken 1889/1972), p. 447. See the cogent objections
to Smith's method and conclusions by Franz Steiner, Taboo
(New York: Philosophical Library, 1956), pp. 59ff.

[141]A practice legitimated at Exod. 21:12-14; cf. I Kings
1:50; 2:28.

[142]For literature on biblical asylum cf. n. 145.

[143]Nachmanides, Commentary to the Torah--Leviticus, p. 234.

[144]R. Patai, "The 'Egla 'Arufa or the Expiation of the Polluted Land," JQR 30 (1939), p. 65. Cf. Deut. 21:1-9

[145]On asylum cf. M. Greenberg, "The Biblical Conception of
Asylum," JBL 78(1959), pp. 125-132; idem., "City of Refuge,"
IDB, I, pp. 638-639; M. David, "Die Bestimmungen Ueber die
Asylstädte in Josue 20," OTS 9(1951), pp. 30-48; M. Lohr, Das
Asylwesen im Alten Testament (Halle, 1930); N. M. Nicolsky,
"Das Asylrecht in Israel," ZAW 48(1930), pp. 146-175; and B.
Dinur, "The Religious Character of the Cities of Refuge and the
Ceremony of Admission into Them," Eretz-Israel 3(1954), pp.
135-146 (Hebrew with English summary).

42

[146]Cf. supra., n. 54. Related to this legislation is the ban on eating blood which follows immediately at Lev. 17:10ff. See further on the consumption of blood: Jubilees 22:27.

[147]Cf. the next section.

[148]Sifre Deut., 171, cf. Deut. 12:31.

[149]Moshe Weinfeld, "The Worship of Molech and of the Queen of Heaven and its Background," UF 4(1972), pp. 141ff.

[150]Cf. also Ezek. 16:20. The association of Molech worship with the Valley of Gehennom (בגיא בן חנם) is well known, cf. 2 Kings 23:10; 2 Chr. 28:3; 33:6 (mentioned with אוב וידעוני); Jer. 7:31 (where the idolatrous practice is said to defile the temple in Jerusalem); 19:6; 32:35.

[151]Molech worship defiles the individual too (Lev. 19:31). Entrance into the temple while ritually unclean was an offense against the deity in Mesopotamia also: "I used to enter the temple without being cultically clean, I repeatedly violated your severe interdiction, I transgressed many times the limits you (imposed) which is displeasing to you" ina la elēlija ēterrub ana ekur(ri) NÍG. GIG-ka danna ēteppus anāku ša mariṣi elika ētettiq ahâtka, KAR 45 r. i,16, cf. CAD, Vol. VII, p. 56.

[152]Die Dämonen und ihre Abwehr im Alten Testament (Leipzig, 1912), pp. 6ff.

[153]Hans Schmidt, "אוב," BZAW 41(1925), p. 260.

[154]E. F. de Ward, "Superstition and Judgment: Archaic Methods of Finding a Verdict," ZAW 89(1977), pp. 9-12.

[155]Lods derives אוב from the same root as אב, "father." Incidentally, J. A. Fitzmeyer, at Job 8:8, reads אתיחם "their ghosts" for MT אבותם "their fathers," quoted by W. F. Albright, Yahweh and the Gods of Canaan, pp. 123ff.

[156]De Ward "Superstition," p. 12.

[157]ASTI 8(1970-71), pp. 89ff.

[158]M. Vieyra, "Les noms du 'mundus' en hittite et en assyrien et la pythonisse d'Endor," RHA 21, fasc. 69(1961), pp. 47-55.

[159]Harry A. Hoffner, Jr., "Second Millennium Antecedents to the Hebrew 'ŌB," JBL 86(1967), pp. 385-401.

[160]Ibid., p. 401.

[161]Anne D. Kilmer, "Notes on Akkadian uppu," Ancient Near Eastern Studies in Memory of J. J. Finkelstein. Memoirs of the Connecticut Academy of Arts and Sciences, 1978 (New Haven). It is possible that musical instruments were used in the necromancy cult, cf. infra., p. 138, n. 29.

[162]Supra., pp. 83f. Further, see Rashi at Lev. 19:26,
s.v. לא תאכלו על הדם and idem., at 19:31, s.v. אל תפנו אל
האבת where he anticipates Rabin's view of the אוב as "ventriloquist." See also T.B. Sanhendrin 55a.

[163]Originally, according to R. Hirzel, "Die Strafe der
Steinigung," Königlich Sächsischen Gesellschaft der Wisen-
chaft 27(1909), pp. 233-266, the essential purpose of stoning
was "nicht die Tötung sondern die Ausstossung aus der Gemeinde"
(p. 244), but this purpose is not reflected in the Bible. In
Judaism, stoning became the most severe human means of execution, especially, as among the Greeks, for crimes against the
Deity or His sanctuary. The Greeks viewed stoning as a communal ritual act of atonement (Sühnnungsakt, pp. 252ff.) by
which the impurity (miasma) generated by the criminal was
removed. The community (e.g. the עם הארץ at Lev. 20:2 or the
עדה at Num. 15:35f.) in Israel also carried out the execution,
probably for similar reasons.

[164]Often with idolatry: Ezek. 6:7,14; 7:4,9; 15:7 (with
the expression ונתתי את פני ב- which is used in positive syntagmatic relation with P's kareth formula two out of its other
three appearances in the Bible, cf. Lev. 17:10; 20:3); 20:30,
42,44.

[165]Note the synonyms of kareth in Ezekiel's language:
והכרתיך מן העמים והאבדתיך מן הארצות אשמידך.

[166]Sexual pollution, for normal as well as aberrant relations, is common the world over, e.g. cf. M. Douglas, Purity
and Danger (1966), esp. pp. 140-158; M. N. Srinivas, Religion
and Society Among the Coorgs of South India (1952), pp. 103ff.;
H. N. C. Stevenson, "Status Evaluation in the Hindu Caste System," JRAI 84(1954), pp. 45-65 and see the reviews of Srinivas
and Stevensen by Dumont et.al. in Pure and Impure, Contributions to Indian Sociology, III, pp. 9-39. On incest cf. Laura
Makarius, "The Magic of Transgression," Anthropos 69(1974), pp.
541ff.; L. N. Rosen, "Contagion and Cataclysm: A Theoretical
Approach to the Study of Ritual Pollution Beliefs," African
Studies 32(1973), pp. 229-246.

[167]Cf. M. Kerithoth 2:6.

[168]Thus sex with one's daughter is not mentioned but must
certainly have been forbidden. Lev. 20:11 adds the stepmother.
Cf. HL 190.

[169]For a comprehensive study of the death penalty which
touches on some of our cases, cf. Edwin M. Good, "Capital
Punishment and its Alternatives in Ancient Near Eastern Law,"
Stanford Law Review 19(1967), pp. 947-977.

[170]Maimonides (Guide of the Perplexed, III pp. 197ff.)
says that death is assigned to those cases "in which the criminal act can easily be done, is of frequent occurrence, is base
and disgraceful, and of a tempting character; otherwise exci-
sion-kareth is the punishment." Thus he appears to view kareth

44

as a punishment less severe than death, just as do the medie-
val halachists in general. We view this situation as a transformation, indeed a reversal, of P's original presentation of
the law. Death by drowning is a widespread penalty for incest
outside the Bible because ". . .the degree of defilement is so
great that even shedding the blood of the guilty is avoided in
order that the earth may not be polluted," cf. E. N. Fallaize,
"Purification (Introductory and Primitive)," ERE 10(1956), p.
460. Fire acts as a purifier in P; hence, burning is prescribed for some incest cases, cf. Lev. 20:14.

[171] Cf. CH 157-158; HL 189, both of which demand the death
penalty. The social significance of incest prohibitions is
widely recognized as lending coherence to society, cf. Lord
Raglan, "Incest and Exogamy," JRAI 69(1931), pp. 167-180. It
is of interest to our interpretation of kareth that incest
among some primitives is regarded as the cause of barrenness,
cf. E. N. Fallaize, ERE 10(1956), p. 460 and cf. Lev. 20:20f.

[172] Cf. Deut. 23:1 (Eng. 22:30).

[173] Cf. CH 155.

[174] HL 189 and 195 include one's own daughter and step-
daughter.

[175] Among the Nuer it is believed that intercourse with a
menstruous woman will result in death or abnormality for the
unborn child, cf. J. W. Burton, "Some Nuer Notions of Purity
and Danger," Anthropos 69(1974), p. 530.

[176] Cf. Deut. 22:22; CH 129,133; MAL 15A; LE 28. All
require death.

[177] Its place among the sexual crimes may suggest that
giving of one's seed to Molech involved sexual abuse, perhaps
a form of temple prostitution.

[178] Cf. HL 189. The destruction of Sodom (Gen. 19:12ff.)
shows diving destruction as a penalty for homosexuality. The
story portrays the extinction of the Sodomites. The Edomites
and Ammonites are pictures as the product of incestuous unions.
Coincidentally, it is interesting that Ezekiel invokes the
kareth curse on both nations (25:5,7 and 25:13).

[179] Exod. 22:18 demands death; HL 187,188,199 require death
for sexual relations with a cow, sheep or pig. HL 200A does
not require death for relations with a horse or mule, though
such relations apparently cause the sinner to become impure and
disqualify him from ever becoming a priest (cf. J. Moyer,
Purity Concept Hittite, pp. 78ff.). E. Good, "Capital Punishment," p. 961, n. 63 misunderstands kareth by suggesting it is
mere "severance for the guilty party from his people." Jub.
22:21 requires extirpation for homosexuality.

[180] Abimelech is portrayed at Gen. 20 as being suspected of
adultery, though he is cleared in the matter. Nevertheless,
the narrator would have us know that God had already set His

curse in motion: "Abraham then prayed to God, and God healed Abimelech, his wife and his slave girls, so they bore children; for the Lord had closed fast every womb of the household of Abimelech because of Sarah, the wife of Abraham" (vv. 17f.). This passage, usually assigned to E (e.g. E. A. Speiser, Genesis), is in perfect harmony with P's legislation of kareth for adultery.

[181]Hans Wehr, Dictionary of Modern Written Arabic, p. 115.

[182]H. Brichto, The Problem of "Curse" in the Hebrew Bible (Philadelphia: Society of Biblical Literature and Exegesis, 1963), p. 147.

[183]T.B. Kerithoth 7b.

[184]J. Milgrom, Studies, p. 57, n. 214.

[185]Louis Moulinier, Le pur et l'impur dans la pensee des Grecs (Paris: Librairie C. Klincksieck, 1952), p. 381.

[186]Jacob Milgrom, "The Concept of Ma'al in the Bible and the Ancient Near East," JAOS 96(1976), pp. 236-247.

WINDOWS AND MIRRORS: LITERARY CRITICISM AND LUKE'S SITZ IM LEBEN*

Robert J. Karris
Catholic Theological Union

In this paper I pursue one question: What contributions does contemporary, non-structuralist literary criticism make to the goal of detecting Luke's Sitz im Leben? I borrow the terms "windows" and "mirrors" for my title from Norman R. Petersen, who rightly insists that we need to look at New Testament texts, literarily, as both windows and mirrors.[1]

In the first part of this paper I employ the device of a Forschungsbericht both to determine what recent literary critical approaches to Luke-Acts say about its Sitz im Leben and to high- light questions of method.[2] My main investigative tool is the rubric of genre. In the second part of the paper I propose addi- tional literary approaches as means of ascertaining the Lukan intention, community, and situation.

I. RECENT LITERARY CRITICAL STUDIES OF LUKE-ACTS

In organizing this section, I use the presupposition that from an analysis of the author's literary genre we can determine his/her intention in writing the work.[3] In analyzing the contri- butions of each author surveyed, I pointedly raise the methodologi- cal question: Does the author carefully and explicitly show how he moves from an analysis of the genre of Luke-Acts to an hypothe- sis about the Lukan Sitz im Leben?

1) Charles H. Talbert

a) In Literary Patterns, Theological Themes and the Genre of Luke-Acts[4] Talbert is a pace-setter, as he generally is in his work on Luke-Acts, in his application of literary criticism to Luke-Acts. His conclusion is:

> The life of the founder is counterbalanced by the re- cord of his followers. The Evangelist's choice of the principle of balance for his basic architectonic scheme, therefore, is integrally intertwined with his adoption of a certain type of ancient biography as the vehicle for his communication. Both Luke's choice of genre type for his message to the church and his development of the type chosen were rooted in the Sitz im Leben of his community. The Lucan community was one that was troubled by a clash of views over the legitimate understanding of Jesus and the true nature of the Christian life (p. 135).

Norman Petersen's review of Talbert's work sets the pro- blematics well.[5] Petersen rightly criticizes Talbert for using the restrictive model of "architecture analysis." Talbert should not have ignored "other and more comprehensive literary models that might have served him better" (p. 456). Such a comprehen- sive model "will enable us to see how the aspects of style, structure, and genre inform the message of the narrative, and having done this provide us with evidence for answering the question of the historical occasion for Luke's writing, and of his theological investment in it" (p. 457).

48

While agreeing to a large extent with Petersen's assessment of Talbert's monograph, I ask whence Talbert has arrived at his view of the Lukan Sitz im Leben. Does his view of the Lukan Sitz im Leben help him arrive at his position of the genre of Luke-Acts, which genre helps him interpret the Lukan Sitz im Leben?

b) Talbert's What Is a Gospel? The Genre of the Canonical Gospels[6] is a learned and insightful study in which he provocatively and persuasively challenges the Bultmannian consensus about the nature of the genre, gospel. For our purposes, though, we must be content with his conclusion about Luke-Acts:

> Luke-Acts is basically a Type D Life of Jesus. It was written so that (a) the life of the founder was followed by (b) a narrative of his successors and selected other disciples so as to indicate where in the Evangelist's present the true tradition was to be found. At the same time, the a component of the Life has been assimilated to Type B biographies so as to prevent misunderstanding of who Jesus really was and to portray an accurate picture of the founder. Luke-Acts is thus a mixed type. It is also composed in terms of the myth of the immortals which gives the two-volume work an outer form and which is a clue to its Sitz im Leben. It is a myth of origins for an early church (p. 134).

I am impressed with the biographical parallels which Talbert has brought to bear on our analyses of Luke-Acts, but I do not immediately see how he has accounted for Luke's multiple use of the Old Testament. Perhaps, Talbert offers a guide to his way of handling this OT material when he writes in another context:

> The major argument, I contended, which Luke used against this overrealized eschatology was the setting up of certain stages that must transpire before the end arrives. Such a scheme of stages was employed by the Evangelist to locate each part of the Jesus tradition in its proper context in salvation history. Luke was written, locating individual Jesus traditions in a controlling context, in order to indicate the legitimate hermeneutical use of the earthly Jesus. In this view, the Third Gospel belonged to a debate over the legitimacy of certain kerygmata. Its method of operation was the inclusion of the various parts of the Jesus tradition in a new whole which controlled the way the parts were read (p. 119).

In conclusion, I ask whether Talbert might have better integrated into a unified genre his insights into Luke-Acts as biography, myth of origins, and salvation history. Is his evidence for the Lukan Sitz im Leben derived directly from his literary analysis of Luke-Acts or postulated from some other source or method?

2) Luke T. Johnson

In The Literary Function of Possessions in Luke-Acts[7] Johnson sets the Lukan passages on possessions within the literary pattern he discerns for the entire two-volume work. He writes:

> Two major questions therefore shaped the course of the study, and from the search for the answer to those questions emerged the two theses advanced by the study. The questions: what is the literary pattern of the story Luke is telling, and how do possessions figure within that literary pattern? The theses: a literary analysis of

Luke-Acts at the level of story reveals a dominant
dramatic pattern which structures the work as a whole;
we have called this pattern the story of the Prophet
and the People. Within the telling of that story, Luke
uses the language of possessions symbolically (p. 220).

Johnson's analysis of the genre of Luke-Acts as that of story
of the Prophet and the People[8] leads to these sentences on
the Lukan Sitz im Leben:

> In his story, Luke does not describe a total or defi-
> nitive rejection by all the Jews, but a division in the
> Jewish people. And in every way, he tries to show that
> the majority of Jews accepted the Word. Why was he con-
> cerned to show this? We can perhaps find a clue in Luke's
> insistence that the 'things brought to fulfillment among
> us' were in fact the fulfillment of God's promises made
> to Abraham in the Old Testament ... These promises con-
> cerned Israel. But for the promises to Abraham to have
> been fulfilled, for God's promise therefore to have proven
> true, there must have been an Israel within which those
> promises were realized in a real way. This is basically
> a question of theodicy. If Israel totally rejected God's
> visitation and was itself totally rejected from salva-
> tion, then God Himself was untrue to His Word. But if
> God was untrue in his promise to Israel, how can the
> Gentiles have asphaleia in their own belief? The Gospel
> now is among the Gentiles. In all likelihood, Luke wrote
> from within a church that was almost totally Gentile and
> wrote for the sake of those Gentiles .... In order for
> the Gentiles now to enjoy the promises that were made in
> the first place to Israel, those promises had to have
> found fulfillment within Israel and been extended in a
> continuous line to the Gentiles (pp. 122-23).

Johnson's monograph is excellent and has shown me how
literary critical analyses can open a scholar's eyes to multiple
and new insights into Luke-Acts. I raise one question: How does
Johnson move from his literary analysis of Luke-Acts as story[9]
to his assessment of Luke's purpose and historical situation?

3) Donald Juel

Juel's analysis[10] of the genre of Luke-Acts provides a
neat contrast with those of Talbert and Johnson in that he
underscores Luke-Acts as history:

> In this sense Luke tells Jesus' story not as a bio-
> grapher but as a historian, interested in relating that
> life and teaching to a larger context. In detail, he
> traces lines from the time of Jesus to the time of the
> church; more broadly, he carefully integrates the combined
> story of Jesus and the Christian movement into the history
> of Israel.... The writer of Luke-Acts, in other words,
> is updating the history of Israel.[11]

> In sum, the story of Jesus and of the Christian move-
> ment is one of controversy, and Luke-Acts does not tell
> it from a neutral point of view. This dispute about who
> are the real Jews lies behind Luke's entire narrative.
> It seeks to convince the reader that the events described
> constitute "fulfillment" (pp. 222-23).[12]

From his literary analysis of Luke-Acts as pertaining to the
genre of history, Juel maintains this about Luke's purpose and
Sitz im Leben:

One of Luke's main purposes is to provide legitimacy
to a religious movement .... despite the strong objections from other Jews - probably the recognized leaders
of the Jewish community. He needs to explain a seeming
paradox: the history of God's people, Israel, will continue to involve more and more Gentiles, while the gulf
separating these 'true' Jews from the rest of the Jewish
community will continue to widen. Those Jews who have
believed in Jesus are the legitimate heirs of the patri-
archs, the true defenders of the Mosaic Law and the Jewish
way of life. If the two-part work was not written specifically for Jewish-Christians, they certainly must have
represented an important element in his constituency
(pp. 234-35).[13]

I find Juel's analysis of the genre and Sitz im Leben of
Luke-Acts supportive of my past and current thinking.[14] But now I
must ask Juel (and myself) how he argued from his literary analysis of Luke-Acts to his position on Luke's Sitz im Leben.[15]

4) Norman R. Petersen

I place Petersen's brief study[16] after those of Johnson
and Juel because Petersen gives a literary analysis of the
"confrontation" aspects of Luke-Acts on which Johnson and Juel
build a considerable amount of their cases for Luke's Sitz im
Leben. Petersen maintains that the Gospel of Luke and Acts are
story:

Each volume's total action thus constitutes a story.
But what are these stories? In each case the story concerns the confrontation between an accredited agent of
God and the people of God in their sanctuaries (synagogues and temple), with the confrontation climaxing in
the legal rejection of the agents by the official representatives of the people of God, which is in turn followed by God's reaffirmation of his agents and by the extension of God's plans beyond his traditional people and
holy places to others (p. 85).

Petersen's goal in his literary analysis is the following:

In what follows I want to show that in both the
sequential and parallel aspects of Luke's composition
the rejection of God's agents by God's people in connection with God's sanctuaries (synagogues and temple) is
the plot device by which the movement of the narrative
as a whole is motivated (p. 83; emphasis his).

I believe that Petersen has substantially achieved his
goal. Working from the position, then, that the rejection of
God's agents by God's people is a plot device, we can ask
whether Johnson and Juel are correct in using what is a literary
plot device as evidence for their evaluations of the Lukan Sitz
im Leben. They seem to have too quickly moved from the text as
mirror to the text as window onto Luke's situation. Incidentally,
Johnson and Juel are not the only ones being interrogated here.
The presuppositions behind my article, "Missionary Communities,"
need closer scrutiny.[17]

5) John Drury

Drury's Tradition and Design in Luke's Gospel: A Study
in Early Christian Historiography[18] is a brilliant book, but one
which is not easy to summarize.[19] Drury's clearest statement
about the link between the genre of Luke-Acts and its purpose is:

Luke is Jewish in the story-telling tradition of the
books of Genesis, Judges, Samuel and Kings and the tales
in the Apocrypha, a tradition still alive in Josephus'
grand historical midrash, The Jewish Antiquities, and in
Joseph and Asenath. The young community's search for its
past is resolved by being thoroughly at home in it - a
home which, according to Luke, it has never left. The
elder brother was the apostate (pp. 8-9).

But if Luke's purpose in his two-volume work is to give
his community roots, how does Drury account for Luke's preten-
sions of being an historian as evidenced in Luke 1:1-4? In a
discussion of Luke 1-2 Drury writes this about Luke and history-
writing:

The structure shows a clever and much used device of
Luke's. Great and momentous matters emerge gradually,
catching the reader's attention by prophetic hints before
they happen. He is aware of the divisions between times,
the distinction between one era, its predecessor and its
successor. In this conscious and sophisticated sense of
the past, rather than in a modern attention to hard facts,
lies his claim to be called an historian, skilled in the
ancient Jewish discipline of weaving skeins of prophecy
and fulfillment from one event to another... They (Luke's
first two chapters) have strong resemblances to the story
books of the Jewish dispersion, Tobit, Esther and Judith,
which carry into the rest of the gospel and Acts. Theology comes in the form of a tale in which the poor and
meek are exalted, the great and proud brought low
(p. 64).[20]

In summary, Drury has made astute observations about Luke's
art of writing history. He seems to be saying that Luke creates
in midrash-fashion much of what is contained in his work.
Luke-Acts is a theological story, whose story elements Luke has
linked together by means of the Deuteronomic historian's art of
promise and fulfillment. I ask Drury whether he arrives at
the Lukan Sitz im Leben from his analysis of the genre of Luke-
Acts as theological story. It is not obvious to me that Drury
explains how and why Luke gives his community roots by telling
them a theological story which is Luke-Acts.

6) A. J. Mattill, Jr.

In his article, "The Jesus-Paul Parallels and the Purpose
of Luke-Acts: H. H. Evans Reconsidered,"[21] Mattill amasses a
wealth of evidence for a literary critical approach to Luke-Acts.
I will summarize his argument from his conclusions:

By thus personifying his theological program in the
life and work of Jesus and Paul, Luke has succeeded in
drawing an unmistakable Jesus-Paul parallelism which
functions as an irresistible apology for Paul (p. 37).

If Luke presents these parallels so thoroughly and yet
so unobtrusively, we might suspect that he has given us a
verse which adequately and yet unobtrusively points to
these parallels, even as names of persons in Acts may
indicate Luke's sources of information. We suggest that
this verse is Lk. vi 40 ... 'The disciple is not above
his teacher: but every one when he is perfected shall be
as his teacher' (pp. 40-41).

For whatever reason, Luke placed this key verse in a
position where it unobtrusively points to the Jesus-Paul
parallelism which concerns so much of his two volumes and

which forms Luke's supreme apology for Paul; Luke-Acts
shows how Paul is perfected by his experiences, especially suffering, to be like his Model and Master, and
thus himself be a model for his churches (p. 46).

Mattill's article opens up many interpretive vistas. Its
major weakness lies in his attempt to too quickly move from the
"mirror" of the Jesus-Paul parallelism to the "window" onto
Luke's Sitz im Leben. One can ask him to give more detailed
justification, from an analysis of the overall genre of Luke-
Acts, for his contention that Luke is writing an apology for
Paul.

7) Geoffrey F. Nuttall

In his booklet of sixteen pages, <u>The Moment of Recognition:</u>
<u>Luke as Story-Teller</u>,[22] Nuttall makes some refreshing and highly
provocative observations. He analyzes Luke' stories, e.g.,
Luke 24:13-35, on the level of imagination and investigates
Luke's art of "'changing the very being of man through the
education of his imagination'" (p. 6). He suggests that Luke is
a poetic historian in this sense: "'The poet's purpose, when he
makes use of history is to discover ... the metaphoric, the representative, the perennial significance of what happened'"
(p. 14). Also in this sense, "'At their best they (inspired
words) communicate something so powerful that it makes us live
more abundantly'" (p. 14).

If Nuttall's evaluation of the genre of Luke-Acts as
poetic history is accurate - and there seems much to commend it -
then it seems that we learn little, if anything, about Luke's
Sitz im Leben from an analysis of Luke-Acts. Luke's goal is
the communication of the perennial significance of what he
recounts, not its evidential value for what happened in the
first century of the Common Era.[23]

8) Conclusions and Prognostications

What sense do I make of the conflicting views of the genre
of Luke-Acts and thus the conflicting views of Luke's Sitz im
Leben which my Forschungsbericht has uncovered? It seems that
the Forschungsbericht has established the validity of Hirsch's
contention that by selecting a genre in which to write, an author
wills the meaning implied in that genre and also reveals his
intention for writing. But how does one determine what genre
the author has selected? Is the determination of a work's genre
a sophisticated guessing game,[24] in which some guesses are more
"institutionally acceptable"[25] than others? Are we fated to
explore, in turn, each of the approaches singled out above by
running it through a number of readings of or courses on Luke-
Acts to see what sense it makes of the whole? Will pressures to
find scholarly comfort in numbers and to unify disparate items
prompt us to select the common elements from the various approaches and fashion them into a common consensus on the genre
of Luke-Acts and Luke's Sitz im Leben?

I propose another way. It seems to me that one of the
chief problems so far encountered in the young life of a literary
critical approach to Luke-Acts is that we scholars have been
playing the game of all-or-nothing. Luke-Acts is either biography or history or story, but not all three together. In this
regard I find the remarks of Frank Kermode, a leading literary
critic, both liberating and visionary for our discipline:

A genre is not what used to be known as a <u>kind</u>, with
rules prescribed by institutional authority; it is a

context of expectation, an 'internalized probability system' ... New genres are formed from realignments of existing genres. To prove that a gospel is evidently not a chria or an aretalogy or a beracah or an apocalypse is by no means to demonstrate that these genres did not contribute to the set of expectations within which Mark wrote and his audience read or listened. Historically, like any new form of literature, the gospel is a genus mixtum ... If genre is a consensus, a set of foreunderstandings exterior to a text which enable us to follow that text, whether it is a sentence, a book, or a life, its existence explains why readers who share those foreunderstandings rather exactly with the author of the text can read him more easily; but it also explains why we must read him differently.[26]

If we view Luke-Acts as a genus mixtum, then we New Testament literary critics have our work cut out for us. How do we weigh the contributions the various genera make to the genus mixtum we call Luke-Acts? How do we employ the method hinted at by Petersen whereby we note "the cooperation of the poetic and generic principles of arrangement in the shaping of one and the same text"?[27]

My working hypothesis of the genus mixtum of Luke-Acts[28] will be: Luke-Acts is an historical novel. That is, Luke bases his work on the events of Jesus and the primitive church, but embellishes these events by such means as narrating them according to the scheme of promise and fulfillment in order to give a vision of who God is and to share insight into the mystery of human life. At this point I do not explore all the implications of this hypothetical literary genre for a delineation of the Lukan Sitz im Leben.

II. AVENUES WHICH FUTURE LITERARY CRITICAL STUDIES OF LUKE-ACTS
    MIGHT FOLLOW

1) The Implied Author and The Implied Reader

In this section I summarize the thrust of two literary approaches and give an example of the possible insights they might generate for appreciating Luke-Acts.

In his The Rhetoric of Fiction[29] Wayne C. Booth pursues[30] "the author's means of controlling his reader." In putting their own comments into the work, "authors are in effect exercising careful control over the reader's degree of involvement in or distance from the events of the story, by insuring that the reader views the materials with the degree of detachment or sympathy felt by the implied author."[31] In this context, think of passages like Luke 1:1-4, 7:29-30, 15:1-2 and the speeches of Acts where "the implied author" tells us how he views the work he writes.

In his The Implied Reader: Patterns of Communication in Prose Fiction from Bunyan to Beckett,[32] Wolfgang Iser opens up many a perspective for re-reading Luke-Acts. I quote from one of his many valuable insights:

As we read, there occurs an artificial division of our personality, because we take as a theme for ourselves something that we are not. Consequently when reading we operate on different levels. For although we may be thinking the thoughts of someone else, what we are will not disappear completely - it will merely

remain a more or less powerful virtual force. Thus,
in reading there are these two levels - the alien 'me'
and the real, virtual 'me' - which are never completely
cut off from each other. Indeed, we can only make someone else's thoughts into an absorbing theme for ourselves, provided the virtual background of our own
personality can adapt to it (p. 293).

Take the well-worn example of Luke 1:1-4, in which Luke
tells his readers how he wants us to read his two-volume work
and how we are to fictionalize ourselves as its readers.[33]
In working through these four verses, we are becoming the implied reader. We are in search of things fulfilled among us;
we want to know the "truth" (RSV) concerning the things of which
we have been informed. And Luke, the implied author, is working
on us almost unconsciously through our reading of these four
verses he has created. He invites us to view him as someone who
has done his homework well and who is trustworthy and who will
give us reliable "information."[34]

By a study of the phenomena of "the implied author" and
"the implied reader" we may be able to more closely define the
genre of Luke-Acts and its Sitz im Leben.[35]

2) Vision of Life

We have all had the experience of reading a book which has
changed us, a book with whose message we have struggled, a
book with which we have disagreed vehemently. I categorize this
phenomenon under the rubric "vision of life." Giles Gunn
expresses clearly what I imply by "vision of life":

My own view (of literature) is to be distinguished from
all three of these, at least to the degree that each assumes, as criticism so consistently has from the end of
the eighteenth century to the present, that the meaning
of any given literary text is to be found either behind
it, in the Sitz im Leben of its first readers, or be-
neath it, in the deep-flowing currents of sentiment and
belief that link the individual talent to the traditions
of collective experience that surround him, or within it,
in the internal configuration of its various parts.
While aspects of any work's meaning are to be located in
each of these realms, I still agree with theorists
otherwise as different as Dorothy Van Ghent and Paul
Ricoeur, that the fullest portion of every work's meaning lies rather, to continue the awkward figure, out in
front of it, in the hypothetical world - or, better,
hypothetical way of looking at the world and orienting
oneself within it - which the work is designed both to
project and, through some alchemy of its own devising,
to assess.[36]

In Gunn's view we interpret a work like Luke-Acts "by
assessing the experiential paradigm that makes sense out of the
individual work's logic and outcome against those more familiar or traditional paradigms from our larger cultural life and
experience by which we otherwise do, or should, make sense to
ourselves" (p. 123). Perhaps, as we scholars begin to wrestle
with Luke-Acts' "hypothetical way of looking at the world and
orienting oneself within it," we will get to know more about the
author's intention and Sitz im Leben.

3) Inconsistency, Thou Art A Jewel[37]

Luke's inconsistencies on such topics as rich and poor, eschatology, and the stance of the _laos_ towards Jesus and the apostolic messengers, have often been noted. The question is: How does one interpret these inconsistencies? Some scholars tend to see them as a sign of Lukan muddleheadedness, that he was not in control of his material. In this connection, it is sobering to recall that early critics explained the frustrating inconsistencies which peopled Emily Brontë's Wuthering Heights in these ways: she was from the "boondocks" of Yorkshire, she was uneducated, she was a woman!

Other scholars have interpreted Lukan inconsistencies more positively. G. W. H. Lampe observed:

> The author does not follow any one line of interpreta-
> tion to the exclusion of all others; on the contrary, he
> prefers to make a synthesis. Nor does he press any one
> idea to its ultimate conclusion or content himself with
> drawing out the significance of a single scriptural image.
> He prefers to hold a large number of threads in his hand
> at once, introducing first one and then another into a
> somewhat untidy and ill-defined pattern, without allowing
> any one of them so to predominate over the rest as to
> give unity and coherence to the whole.[38]

In trying to rid Luke-Acts of its inconsistencies, might the scholarly community have fallen victim to the presupposition of organic unity? What if a work of literature like Luke-Acts and other classics are governed by the principle of hetero- geneity, that is, no one interpretation exhausts their meaning. Luke-Acts might be further governed by the principle of hetero- geneity in that many of its symbols conflict with one another, e.g., in the Travel Narrative of Luke 9:51-19:44, and do not form an obvious unity.

It seems to me that the interpreter's task is to rejoice in the literary riches of the Lukan inconsistencies and try to ascertain the meaning Luke placed in their very contrast and contradiction.[39] I cannot guarantee at this time that by taking the Lukan inconsistencies seriously the scholarly community will arrive at a clearer idea of the Lukan Sitz im Leben. At the very least we scholars will have a positive view of Luke's inconsist- encies and be able to evaluate the weaknesses of those positions of Lukan Sitz im Leben which try to refashion the mosaic of Luke-Acts with stones of one color.

CONCLUSION

Even though the application of literary criticism to Luke-Acts is a young discipline, it has yielded much and promises an even greater harvest of insights. Remembering to evaluate Luke-Acts as both window and mirror, we scholars should con- tinue to explore the many ways in which literary criticism can open our eyes to appreciate Luke's literary genius, vision, and situation more clearly and nearly.

56

NOTES

I gratefully acknowledge the rich help I have received in the preparation of this paper from conversations with Prof. Dolores Frese of the University of Notre Dame and Prof. David M. Rhoads of Carthage College. In a brief compass this paper covers the territory of a book I am authoring for Paulist Press.

[1]On the use of the imagery of windows and mirrors, see Petersen, Literary Criticism for New Testament Critics (Philadelphia: Fortress, 1978) 24: "Texts as windows, texts as mirrors, or texts as both. Murray Krieger, a literary critic, uses these metaphors to characterize the main stages in the modern history of literary-critical thinking. Nineteenth- and early twentieth-century critics thought about texts as though they were windows to meaning that lay beyond them, but against this the Anglo-American New Criticism and similar movements in other countries in the early decades of this century rebelled by construing texts as mirrors within which meaning was locked up. Krieger, however, is one among many critics who today deny the sharp alternatives posed by the two metaphors and insist that we must see 'the mirrors as windows too,' for literature both traps us in the looking glass and takes us through it."

[2]For a recent Forschungsbericht on the results of the application of the historical critical method to Luke-Acts, see my article, "Missionary Communities: A New Paradigm for the Study of Luke-Acts," CBQ 41 (1979) 80-97.

[3]See E. D. Hirsch, Jr., Validity in Interpretation (New Haven: Yale University Press, 1967) 86,101,121,124.

[4]SBLMS 20; Missoula: Scholars, 1974.

[5]JBL 96 (1977) 455-58.

[6]Philadelphia: Fortress, 1977.

[7]SBLDS 39; Missoula: Scholars, 1977.

[8]See section four below and Petersen's analysis of the people's acceptance/rejection of the Prophet. Petersen uses the model of "confrontation."

[9]For further comments on Johnson's masterful work, see my article, "Missionary Communities," 87-90 and my forthcoming review in CBQ.

[10]Donald Juel with J. S. Ackerman and T. S. Warshaw, An Introduction to New Testament Literature (Nashville: Abingdon, 1978) 202-40.

[11]Pp. 219-20.

[12]See note 8.

[13]Also see his formulation on p. 237: Luke-Acts is "an apologetic for a movement whose legitimacy was in question."

[14]See my Invitation to Luke: A Commentary on the Gospel of Luke with Complete Text from The Jerusalem Bible (Garden City: Doubleday Image, 1977); Invitation to Acts: A Commentary on the Acts of the Apostles with Complete Text from The Jerusalem Bible (Garden City: Doubleday Image, 1978); "Missionary Communities"; What Are They Saying About Luke and Acts? A Theology of The Faithful God (New York: Paulist, 1979).

[15] On p. 238 Juel hints at a rationale when he writes that his suggested Sitz im Leben is hypothetical, "but it does provide a plausible relationship among major themes, literary devices, purpose, and the period in which Luke-Acts was composed."

[16] Literary Criticism 81-92.

[17] I wonder whether Petersen himself does not rush to the "window" aspect of Mark too readily. It is not clear to me how it follows that since Mark's narrative is non-fictional, "its narrative world corresponds to the narrator's and addressees' real world" (Literary Criticism 79).

[18] London: Darton, Longman and Todd, 1976/Atlanta: John Knox, 1977.

[19] In the summary I omit any argument with Drury's position that Luke used Matthew as a source. It does not seem to me that Drury's case stands or falls with that theory.

[20] See p. 31 where Drury hints at biography as part of the genre of Luke-Acts. See also p. 44 where in the context of stressing the necessity of studying midrash, Drury says this about the gospels: "But to be thoroughly historical we still need to study the gospels in their matrix of contemporary theological story-writing." It seems that Drury comes closest of any of the authors studied to calling Luke-Acts a genus mixtum. See section eight below.

[21] NovT 17 (1975) 15-46.

[22] London: The Athlone Press, 1978.

[23] I have omitted discussing various other opinions, chiefly those held by authors who view Luke-Acts as "factual history" and by the school of Hans Conzelmann, because of space limitations. See my "Missionary Communities" for some discussion of these opinions.

[24] On the "art" of guessing what the genre of a work is, see Hirsch, Validity in Interpretation 88-89,203.

[25] In his The Genesis of Secrecy: On the Interpretation of Narrative (Cambridge: Harvard University Press, 1979) 12,37, 68,71 and passim Frank Kermode alludes to the phenomenon and influence of "institutional acceptability." An interpretation of the genre of Luke-Acts would have to be stamped "acceptable" by the institution of the biblical guild.

[26] Genesis 162-63 n. 20.

[27] Literary Criticism 44.

[28] My notion of "working hypothesis" in regard to the genre of Luke-Acts is equivalent to what Hirsch calls "heuristic genre." See Validity in Interpretation 88.

[29] Chicago: University of Chicago Press, 1961.

[30] See the first page of the unpaginated Preface of Rhetoric.

[31] Rhetoric 200.

[32] Baltimore: Johns Hopkins University Press, 1974.

[33]See Walter J. Ong, "The Writer's Audience Is Always a Fiction," Interfaces of the Word: Studies in the Evolution of Consciousness and Culture (Ithaca: Cornell University Press, 1977) 53-81.

[34]On the translation of asphaleia (Luke 1:4) as "truth," see Northrop Frye, The Secular Scripture: A Study of the Structure of Romance (Cambridge: Harvard University Press, 1976) 16-23, who reminds us that truth and falsehood are not literary categories. What Frye says on p. 16 about the "truth" of myth is suggestive for Luke-Acts: "Myths are usually assumed to be true, stories about what really happened ... The anxiety of society, when it urges the authority of myth and the necessity of believing it, seems to be less to proclaim its truth than to prevent anyone from questioning it. It aims at consent, including the consent of silence, rather than conviction." Frye's point is well illustrated by a recent Amtrak incident. Tommy, the older brother, is teasing his sister Marie. In exasperation Marie appeals to her mother: "Mommy, Tommy says that the story of Jesus is just a story. Tell him that it's true." Mommy reassured Marie that the story of Jesus was true.

[35]This approach to literature seems especially useful for an appreciation of Luke's motif of poor and rich, and seems to be behind some of the recent and exciting work of Stanley Hauerwas in the field of ethics. See his Truthfulness and Tragedy: Further Investigations into Christian Ethics (Notre Dame: University of Notre Dame Press, 1977) chapters 1 and 4; "Jesus: the story of the Kingdom," Theology Digest 26 (1978) 303-24.

[36]The Interpretation of Otherness: Literature, Religion, and the American Imagination (New York: Oxford, 1979) 120. See also David Tracy, "Metaphor and Religion: The Test Case of Christian Texts," Critical Inquiry 5 (1978) 97.

[37]For the insights in this section I am much indebted to the oral communication, "Wuthering Heights: The Motive of Narration," given by J. Hillis Miller at the University of Chicago Divinity School, May 3, 1979.

[38]"The Lucan Portrait of Christ," NTS 2 (1955/56) 160.

[39]Perhaps investigations into the style of thinking which issues in coincidentia oppositorum and in mandalas would benefit our scholarly investigations of Luke's inconsistencies. On the fruitfulness of the latter approach, see P. Joseph Cahill, "The Johannine Logos as Center," CBQ 38 (1976) 54-72. Also, might there be something we can learn about Lukan inconsistencies from those who have studied the nature of myth? On p. 19 of a fine article, "The Symbolism of Transcendence in Jewish Apocalyptic," BR 19 (1974), John J. Collins, building upon insights of Paul Ricoeur, observes: "The juxtaposition of conflicting viewpoints is typical of myth." He also notes: "Like literature it (myth) is probing to formulate the meaning of life and can never be tied to one formulation" (20). See also Claude Levi-Strauss, Structural Anthropology (Garden City: Doubleday Anchor, 1963) 202-28 (chapter eleven) on the nature of contradiction in mythology.

LUKE, JOSEPHUS AND ROME:
A COMPARATIVE APPROACH TO THE LUKAN
SITZ IM LEBEN

Benjamin J. Hubbard
St. Jerome's College

This paper seeks to shed light upon the Sitz im Leben of the Lukan community by comparing Luke's stance towards the Roman state and the Jewish people with that of Josephus in The Jewish War. After a brief discussion of the appropriateness of the comparison, we shall examine Josephus' situation when he wrote War and the corresponding point of view which he adopted. Comparisons will then be made with Luke.

I. An Appropriate Comparison?

It might well be asked whether anything is to be gained from a comparison of two figures as different as were Flavius Josephus and the author of Luke-Acts. Those differences can be summarized under three headings.

1. Background. Josephus was a Judean Jew of priestly lineage on his father's side and Hasmonean royal descent on his mother's (Life 1:1-2; War 1:3). The person whom we call, for convenience' sake, "Luke" was an anonymous gentile Christian living somewhere outside the Palestinian region.   1

2. Standpoint. Josephus was a participant in the Jewish-Roman war of A.D. 66-74 seeking to justify his complex role as a Jewish general turned Roman intermediary. Luke, though no neutral chronicler of Christian origins, was not attempting a personal justification of his role and never refers to himself except briefly in connection with his patron, Theophilus (Lk 1:1-4, Acts 1:1).

3. Subject Matter. In seven volumes Josephus narrates a war to which Luke merely alludes in the two predictions of Jerusalem's and the temple's destruction respectively (19:43 f., 21:6) and in the mention of the city being surrounded by armies and trodden down by the Gentiles (21:20-24). Luke's subject matter, on the other hand, is the birth of Christianity which is never mentioned by Josephus in War.   2

Despite these significant differences, similarities do exist.

1. Method. Both writers are influenced by the literary conventions of ancient Greek historiography and write in Greek (though Josephus' first edition of War was in Aramaic; War 1:3). Also, neither can be considered an unbiased historian. Both are writing from a definite vantage point which considers the other side dead wrong.   3

2. Time. The two works are nearly contemporaneous. Luke's two volumes were probably composed, with some interval between them, in the 80's. Josephus' Greek version of War is dated between 75 and 79.   4

3. <u>Stance towards the Romans and the Jews</u>. Though for differing reasons, both writers view the Romans favorably and the Jews, or some segment of the Jewish people, unfavorably. As will be shown, this stance is theologically justified by both authors.

II. Josephus' Situation

Josephus wrote <u>War</u> for several reasons, all of which influenced his point of view. (1) He wished to justify theologically his controversial role as Jewish general turned Roman agent. (2) He wished to magnify his patrons, the emperor Vespasian (A.D. 69-79) and his son, and successor as emperor, Titus (79-81) who had successfully waged the war. (3) He wished to defend Judaism by blaming the war not on the people as a whole but on the revolutionaries who instigated it, victimized the general populace and pressed the conflict to the bitter end. 5 He believed that the survival of God's chosen people throughout the Roman Empire depended upon their willingness to accept Rome's power and authority. They should, in other words, follow his example. He puts it as follows at one point:

> If I have dwelt at some length on this topic,
> my intention was not so much to extol the Romans
> as to console those whom they have vanquished
> and to deter others who may be tempted to revolt
> (<u>War</u> 3:108). 6

In his preface to the entire work, Josephus provides an excellent summary of his viewpoint.

> I have no intention of rivalling those who extol
> the Roman power by exaggerating the deeds of my
> compatriots. I shall faithfully recount the
> actions of both combatants; but in my reflections
> on the events I cannot conceal my private sentiments,
> nor refuse to give my personal sympathies scope to
> bewail my country's misfortunes. For, that it owed
> its ruin to civil strife, and that it was the Jewish
> tyrants who drew down upon the holy temple the un-
> willing hands of the Romans and the conflagration,
> is attested by Titus Caesar himself, who sacked the
> city; throughout the war he commiserated the populace
> who were at the mercy of the revolutionaries, and
> often of his own accord deferred the capture of the
> city and by protracting the siege gave the culprits
> time for repentance (1:9-10).

With this axiomatic quotation as a springboard, we are now in a position to examine the principal theological themes in <u>War</u>. I shall attempt to state Josephus' point of view in a single sentence: Divine providence favored Rome, as various prophecies and portents attest, whereas the revolutionaries totally disregarded their own religious and ethical standards and thus got what they deserved.

1. Divine Providence on Roman Side

Josephus constantly notes the fact that God is with the Romans. In his speech to dissuade the Jews from war, King Agrippa II declares that only divine assistance could save them, but it is on the side of Rome. Otherwise, so vast an empire could never have been built (2:390). Nero is said to have been

divinely influenced in appointing Vespasian as commander in Syria
(3:6). With his continued success in the war, Vespasian was led
to think that providence had assisted him to grasp the empire
(4:622, cf. 5:1). In Josephus' first speech to the revolutionaries before the walls of Jerusalem he points out that God, who
had brought the rod of empire to various nations, now "rested
over Italy" (5:367) and had actually "fled" from the "holy
places" of Judaism (5:412). In an address to his troops during
the siege of Jerusalem, Titus states that God is cooperating with
the Romans and is angry with the Jews (6:38).

2. Attested by Prophecies and Portents

While Josephus was trying to decide if he should surrender to Vespasian, he suddenly remembered a series of dreams
"in which God had foretold the impending fate of the Jews and
the destinies of the Roman sovereigns" (3:351). He then tells
his readers that he was a skilled interpreter of dreams and, by
virtue of his priestly heritage, was also aware of "the prophecies in the sacred books" (3:352; cf. 4:385-88). What prophecies he meant we are not told, but he then interpreted them
and his dreams to mean that he should surrender "not as a traitor
but as thy [God's] minister" (3:354). 7 He later speaks of an
oracle "found in their sacred scriptures" - again, we are not
told where - stating that at that time one from Judea would
become ruler of the world. The Jews took this to mean one from
their own race but in reality it referred to Vespasian who was
proclaimed emperor on Jewish soil (6:312-13). Josephus also
lists a series of portents which the revolutionaires did not
believe and thus disregarded "the plain warnings of God" (6:288).
These included a star resembling a sword which stood for a year
over Jerusalem; a cow which gave birth to a lamb during Passover
in the court of the temple; the spontaneous midnight opening at
the same feast of the massive bronze gate of the inner court;
the apparition seen throughout the whole country a short time
later of chariots and armed battalions hurtling through the
clouds and encompassing the cities; etc. (6:288-309).

3. Total Disregard by the Revolutionaries of Their Religious and Ethical Standards

Not only does Josephus excoriate the revolutionaries
for coercing the general population into waging the war, he condemns their behaviour as utterly barbarous and contrary to Jewish
standards. For example, those Jews who tried to escape from
Jerusalem in the face of the Roman advance and could not buy
their way out were slaughtered and left unburied. The penalty
for not burying a relative was death (4:381-83). In matters of
religious law, the conduct of the revolutionaries was just as
bad. They took upon themselves the election of the high priesthood and cast lots for a high priest. The lot fell to Phannai,
son of Samuel, who was not descended from high priests and "was
such a clown that he scarcely knew what the high priesthood
meant" (4:155). They also committed a sacrilege by invading the
temple sanctuary with polluted feet (4:150).

4. Revolutionaries Justly Punished

In another of his appeals to the revolutionaries,
Josephus sums up the three previous points as well as the present
one.

> Who knows not the records of the ancient
> prophets and that oracle which threatens
> this poor city and is even now coming true?
> For they foretold that it would then be
> taken whensoever one should begin to slaughter
> his own countrymen. And is not the city, aye
> and the whole temple, filled with your corpses?
> God it is then, God Himself, who with the Romans
> is bringing the fire to purge His temple and ex-
> terminating a city so laden with pollutions
> (6:108-110, cf. 6:249-51).

Earlier in the narrative Josephus had reported that after a
Roman garrison had surrendered and then been deceitfully massacred on the Sabbath, the inhabitants of Caesarea massacred
her Jewish residents at the same hour "as if by the hand of
providence" (2:449-57). Twenty thousand were slaughtered in
the space of an hour (2:457).

There thus emerges in Josephus a view of history which
considers the Judean Jews to have acted so contrary to their own
Law that God must use the Romans to "purge" Jerusalem and its
temple of "pollutions". Fate has gone over to the Roman side.[8]

It is a well-accepted fact of scholarship that the
Jewish revolutionaries were not as devoid of virtue as Josephus
pictures them. As Thackeray puts it,

> The narrative of the war is one-sided, and,
> to balance it and to see the other side of the
> picture, we would gladly recover the lost work
> of Justus of Tiberias, or, better still, have
> the story presented by Johanan ben Zakkai or
> by another of those who witnessed the siege
> from within. The villain, John of Gischala,
> cannot have been quite so black as he is here
> painted; and the "robbers" or Zealots would
> have another tale to tell of their patriotism.[9]

In a similar vein Rhoads talks of a "reverse polemic" employed
by Josephus against the revolutionaries. It consisted of his
turning back upon them their own reasons for opposing Rome.[10]
For example, in replying to John of Gischala's words that he
could never fear being captured since Jerusalem was God's,
Josephus shouts back to him and his associates these words:

> Most impious wretch, should anyone deprive
> you of your daily food, you would consider
> him an enemy; and do you hope to have God,
> whom you have bereft of His everlasting
> worship, for your Ally in this war? And do
> you impute your sins to the Romans, who, to
> this day, are concerned for our laws and are
> trying to force you to restore to God those
> sacrifices which you have interrupted? Who
> would not bewail and lament for the city at
> this amazing inversion, when aliens and
> enemies rectify your impiety, while you, a
> Jew, nurtured in her laws, treat them more
> harshly even than your foes? (6:100-102)

From the words "and do you impute your sins to the Romans...,"
it appears that the revolutionaries themselves had charged the
Romans with disregarding Jewish laws and customs and defiling
the holy city and temple. Josephus is attempting to turn the
charge back upon them so as to further discredit their cause.
He himself states that one of the revolutionaries' aims was to
keep their "religious rules from contaminations" (2:391) and to
preserve the traditions of their forefathers (2:393). Yet he
turns around and accuses them, as we have seen, of doing just
the opposite (e.g., 4:348, 385).

In summary, Josephus' _Sitz im Leben_ could be described
as follows. He was an adopted Flavian, dependent in all respects on the good will of imperial Rome (_Life_ 422 f.). He was
a former Jewish revolutionary leader who had to explain to Jew
and gentile alike at Rome why his life was spared and why he
was so favored by Caesar. He himself notes that, "my pri-
vileged position excited envy and thereby exposed me to danger"
(_Life_ 424). He describes how a Jew named Jonathan, leader of
an abortive revolt in Cyrene, falsely asserted that Josephus
had supplied him with arms and money (_Life_ 424 f.). He also
notes that Titus "never credited the accusations to which I
was constantly subjected" (_Life_ 428) and that Domitian, Titus'
successor, punished his "Jewish accusers" (_Life_ 429). Still,
he was a Jew proud of his roots and his traditions but dis-
mayed by the suicidal course which he felt the Jewish revolutionaries had taken during the war. He hoped to awaken diaspora
Jews (and perhaps those left in Judea, Samaria and Galilee) to
the folly of further resistance against Rome.

III. Luke's Stance Towards the Synagogue and the Government

The Gospel of Luke shares with the other three a
largely negative view of official Judaism. In some instances,
moreover, he sharpens this view. For example, after Jesus'
encomium to John the Baptist, Luke parenthetically and redactionally observes that

> when they heard this all the people and the
> tax collectors justified God, having been
> baptized with the baptism of John; but the
> Pharisees and the lawyers rejected the purpose
> of God for themselves, not having been baptized
> by him (7:29 f.; cf. Matt 21:32). 11

In a similar fashion, all four gospels tend to
mitigate Pilate's (and, thereby, Rome's) responsibility for
Jesus' death and heighten that of the Jewish leaders. However,
Pilate's innocence is emphasized in Luke more than in the others.
Whereas Mark and Matthew each refer to one protestation by Pilate
of Jesus' innocence (Matt 27:23 f., Mk 15:14), Luke has Pilate
expressly state his innocence three times (23:4, 13-6, 22; cf.
Jn 18:38; 19:4,6). Pilate is described at one point in the
Lukan trial scene as addressing the chief priests, rulers and
people "desiring to release Jesus" (23:20, no par.). Finally,
Luke has sharpened the awareness that it was "their will" (the
chief priests' and the multitude's) that Jesus be handed over to
the executioners (23:24 f.; cf. Mk 15:15). Lloyd Gaston has
accurately observed:

> Jesus' real trial is before the Jewish people
> as part of Luke's apologetic against the Jews

of his own day. It was not with respect to the
trumped up political charge (22:67 f.; 23:2,5) but
with respect to the religious charge of Luke's time
(claiming to be the Son of God, 22:70 f.), that
Pilate declares Jesus to be innocent. [12]

It would seem, furthermore, that in having Pilate declare, so
unequivocally, Jesus' innocence Luke is strengthening his pro-
Roman apologetic. This is further corroborated by the fact that
Luke alone of the Synoptics mentions the actual political charge
against Jesus: "We found this man perverting our nation, and
forbidding us to give tribute to Caesar, and saying that he himself is Christ a king" (23:2, cf. 23:5 and Jn 19:12). Pilate
then expressly acquits Jesus of the charge.

The negative attitude towards Jewish leaders in Luke's
Gospel continues in the early chapters of Acts. We learn, e.g.,
that the high priest and the Sadducean party were "filled with
jealousy" at the apostles' missionary success and had them arrested (5:17 f.).

In a parallel way, Paul's accusers during his series
of trials in Acts 22-26 are "the chief priests and the elders"
or words to that effect (22:30; 23:2, 6, 9, 14; 24:1; 25:2, 15;
26:10, 12; 28:17). As with Jesus and Pilate, Roman officials
declare Paul not guilty of the charges brought against him by
their Jewish counterparts. Claudius Lysias (23:29) and Festus
(25:25, 26:31) both declare that he has done "nothing deserving
death or imprisonment."

Furthermore, Paul's entire career as recounted in Acts
is punctuated with favorable responses by officials of the Roman
government: Sergius Paulus, the proconsul in Salamis (13:7-12);
the jailer in Philippi (16:27-34) and the magistrates there
(16:35-39); the authorities in Thessalonika (17:5-9); Gallio,
the proconsul of Achaia (18:12-17); the Asiarchs (19:31) and
town clerk in Ephesus (19:35-41); Claudius Lysias, the tribune
at Jerusalem (21:31-40, 22:24-30); the governors at Caesarea,
Felix (24:22 f.) and Festus (25:1-6, 12); Julius, the centurion
on the ship (27:3, 43); and Publius, a high official on Malta
(28:7-10). [13]

Gaston views this entire pro-Roman stance as a Lukan
device to portray the governmental officials as "character
witnesses testifying to Paul's innocence of the charges made
against him at his real trial - before the Jewish people." [14]
He explains that Luke's predominantly gentile Christian community
was being challenged by members of the local synagogue. They'
were questioning these Christians' self-understanding and were
calling Paul an apostate from the faith of Israel. [15] Gaston
denies, however, that a political apologetic is operative in
Luke's pro-Roman stance. You cannot, he seems to be saying,
have it both ways. Yet the actual historical conditions - as
far as these can be reconstructed - do make possible a coordi-
nated anti-Jewish, pro-Roman point of view. By Luke's time the
Jewish mission was virtually a thing of the past, and Church and.
Synagogue were locked in an ideological struggle. By Luke's
time as well there had been sporadic Roman persecutions of
Christians, including the martyrdoms both of Peter and of Paul
(cf. Clem 5:1-7). [16] A pro-Roman political apologetic could
be Luke's way of telling potential converts from the Greco-
Roman world that they need not fear the government if they become Christians. [17] Luke, of course, could not report the one

event which would have really proved the good will of the state towards Christianity: Paul's release from his imprisonment at Rome. Yet nowhere has he prepared his readers for a happy ending to his legal proceedings. Instead, he has stressed Paul's innocence - he <u>deserved</u> neither death nor imprisonment. Moreover, in his farewell speech at Miletus to the Ephesian elders, Paul tells them that they will never again see his face (20: 25, 38). The Neronic persecution in which Paul was martyred did not bind the Roman state twenty years later in Luke's time. 18 Thus the parade of benevolent Roman officials serves to accentuate the positive in Church-state relations in the 80's. The Jews, on the other hand, are the culprits who continually forced the hand of the Romans and made them suspicious of Christianity.

There are three speeches by Paul in Acts which indicate clearly Luke's attitude towards Jews and gentiles: 13:44-52, 18:5 f. and 28:23-28. A similar pattern appears in each: (1) Jewish rejection of Paul's preaching, (2) Paul's condemnation of their attitude (3) his statement that he will turn to the gentiles (i.e., converts and potential converts from the Greco-Roman world) who will listen (4) the use of scripture to support his position (missing in 18:5 f. but perhaps supplied by the terse, Genesis-like theophany to Paul in 18:9 f. which assures him that his work among the gentiles is divinely inspired). 19

IV. Parallels Between Josephus and Luke

The use of scriptural support, just discussed, is important for my argument because it parallels in some respects Josephus' appeal to scriptural prophecies as justification for his own actions and as confirmation of the differing destinies of the Romans and the Jews (see #II, 2 above).

One speech in Acts, that of Gamaliel to the council of Jewish leaders (5:33-9), parallels Josephus' view that divine providence has gone over to the Roman side (see #I, 1 above). He cautions them that if the Christian movement is of human origin it will fail. If divine, however, it will be indestructible.

The Josephan view that the Jewish revolutionaries have disregarded their own ethical standards (see #I, 3 above) is frequently paralleled in the speeches in Acts:

this Jesus...you crucified and killed by the hands of lawless men (2:23).

But you denied the Holy and Righteous One, and asked for a murderer...and killed the Author of life (3:14 f.).

The God of our fathers raised Jesus whom you killed (5:30).

You always resist the Holy Spirit...the Righteous One, whom you have now betrayed and murdered...(7:51 f.).

Though they could charge him with nothing deserving death, yet they asked Pilate to have him killed (13:28).

With respect to Josephus' view that the revolutionaries got what they deserved (#I, 4 above), the parallels are
evident in the uniquely Lukan prediction of Jerusalem's destruction (Lk 19:41-4). The city's "enemies" will surround and
destroy it (cp. Lk 23:28-31). It is also clear in the Lukan
redaction of the Markan apocalypse where Jesus states: "But
when you see Jerusalem surrounded by armies, then know that
its desolation has come near" (21:20). H. Conzelmann defends
the non-apocalyptic character of this saying by noting that
Jesus had already severed the connection between Jerusalem
and the End:

> ...he proceeded to tell a parable, because
> he was near to Jerusalem, and because they
> supposed that the kingdom of God was to
> appear immediately (19:11). 20

Thus, the comparisons between Luke and Josephus indicate that each pronounced similar judgments upon the two
outside groups with whom they had to contend. For Luke these
were the government and the synagogue, for Josephus the government and certain Jews who were suspicious of his motives. Of
course, Luke writes out of a communal Sitz im Leben and Josephus
a more personal and isolated one. Still, their historical viewpoints operate in some remarkably parallel ways.

This comparative exercise has been intended to
facilitate a refocusing upon the Lukan community to draw some
overall conclusions. To this we now turn.

V. The Lukan Sitz im Leben

Luke's community had to contend with ideological opposition from Judaism. Serious questions were being raised
about Jesus' status as well as Paul's relativizing of Torah
(his apostacy from the faith of Israel). How, furthermore,
could Christianity claim to be rooted in Judaism when its
membership was predominantly gentile? To such questions, Luke
tries to provide his community - especially its missionaries -
with answers. Jesus' suffering, death and resurrection were
divinely ordained. Paul remained a loyal Pharisee and always
began his missionary work in a given area by appealing to its
Jewish community. The Church was largely gentile because the
Jewish people had deliberately rejected its hour of salvation.

Luke's community also had to contend with the power
of the state. Persecution had been a reality under Nero, and
the threat of a new outbreak was always a possibility. It was
important, therefore, that as positive a stance as possible be
taken towards Rome. This would assist "Lukan" missionaries in
trying to attract to Christianity gentiles of the Greco-Roman
world. It might also assist the Christians in Luke's community
in adopting a balanced outlook towards the state, neither timid
nor belligerent. 21

Both Luke's description of Christian beginnings and
Josephus' account of the war were narrated from very specific
vantage points. It is hoped that this comparative study has
helped clarify those vantage points.

NOTES

1. W. Kümmel, Introduction to the New Testament[14] (ET: Nashville: Abingdon Press, 1966), pp. 104-6.

2. There are, of course, a few brief references to Christianity in Antiquities: 18:63 f. (Jesus), 18:116-19 (John the Baptist), 20:200 (James, brother of Jesus).

3. Cf. D. Rhoads, Israel in Revolution: 6-74 C.E. (A Political History Based on the Writings of Josephus.) (Philadelphia: Fortress Press, 1976), pp. 11-14, 17.

4. H. Thackeray, Josephus, The Man and the Historian (New York: Jewish Institute of Religion Press, 1929), pp. 34 f. On the question of whether Luke knew any of Josephus' writings, I follow the now generally accepted negative view. Cf. W. Gasque, A History of the Criticism of the Acts of the Apostles (Grand Rapids: Wm. Eerdmans, 1975), p. 104, n. 22.

5. Josephus singles out one group of Jews as exemplary citizens, the Essenes, to whom he devotes a lengthy and praiseworthy description (War 2:119-61).

6. See also 2:388 f. and 5:19. Josephus would have viewed the unsuccessful Bar-Kokhba revolt (A.D. 132-35) as a confirmation of his warnings. All translations are from Thackeray, R. Marcus, A. Wikgren and L. Feldman, eds. and trans., Josephus, 9 Vols. (Cambridge: Harvard University Press, 1926-65). All subsequent references to Josephus are from War unless otherwise indicated.

7. Josephus' claim in this passage that his own prophetic gifts were based on a combination of exegetical skill and divine inspiration is similar to what he says of the Essenes:

> There are some among them who profess to fortell the future, being versed from their early years in holy books, various forms of purification and apophthegms of prophets; and seldom, if ever, do they err in their predictions (2:159; cf. 1:78, 2:113 and Antiquities 15:373 ff.)

He may, in fact, have learned about prophetic interpretation of the Bible during his stay with the Essenes (Life 9-11). Cf. J. Blenkinsopp, "Prophecy and Priesthood in Josephus" JJS 25 (1974), 247, 258 f.

8. Cf. H. Lindner, Die Geschichtsauffassung des Flavius Josephus im Bellum Judaicum (Leiden: Brill, 1972), pp. 42-48.

9. Josephus, p. 49.

10. Israel in Revolution, p. 166.

11. For other uniquely Lukan examples, see 13:14-17, 16:14 f. and 18:9-14.

12. "Anti-Judaism and the Passion Narrative in Luke and Acts". Paper read at the Annual Meeting of the Canadian Society of Biblical Studies, Saskatoon, Saskatchewan; May, 1979, p. 18.

68

13. It is also no accident that Luke stresses the conversion
    by Peter of Cornelius, centurion of the Italian Cohort
    at Caesarea and a man of great virtue even before his
    conversion (10:1 ff.)

14. "Anti-Judaism", p. 8.

15. Ibid., p. 9.

16. B. Reicke, The New Testament Era. ET: Philadelphia:
    Fortress Press, 1968, pp. 245-51.

17. R. Karris, "Missionary Communities: A New Paradigm for
    the Study of Luke-Acts", CBQ 41 (1979), 86, n. 18.

18. E. Haenchen, The Acts of the Apostles[14] (A Commentary).
    ET: Philadelphia: Westminster Press, 1971, pp. 731 f.

19. Cf. 15:15 and Lk. 24:46 f. The theme of scriptural ful-
    fillment is prevalent in Luke-Acts. See, especially,
    the recurring statements in the mission speeches to the
    Jews that Jesus' suffering and death were foretold by the
    prophets: Acts 2:23, 29-31; 3:19; 4:11; 10:43; 13:27.
    See also Stephen's words (7:51-3) to the effect that the
    Jewish people "always resist the Holy Spirit" and per-
    secuted the prophets in the past just as they have be-
    trayed and murdered the "Righteous One" in the present.

20. The Theology of St. Luke. ET: New York: Harper and
    Row, 1960, p. 134.

21. Cf. G. Schneider, "Der Zweck des lukanischen Doppel-
    werks", BZ 21 (1977), 60 f.

THE PROBLEM OF FOOD IN ACTS:
A STUDY OF LITERARY PATTERNS WITH PARTICULAR REFERENCE
TO ACTS 6: 1-7

Joseph B. Tyson

Southern Methodist University

This paper will deal with Luke's approach to the problematic character of food, but that treatment will be preceded by
a discussion of literary patterns in the Book of Acts. I wish
to raise certain literary critical questions about Acts (and
Luke) without presupposing a solution to the source problem.
This means, in general, that this paper will look more like a
composition critical analysis, though concentrating on a rather
small section of the book, than a redaction critical analysis.
What I hope to show is that there is a significant literary
pattern in Acts which reveals something about the author's
point of view and that one aspect of it has something to do
with food. At the end I will make a very tentative suggestion
that the author works within a community in which food still
has something of a problematic character.

I. Literary Patterns

The questions I wish to raise are, at least initially,
literary, as distinguished from historical. They are such as
to direct our attention to the text itself and not to questions
about the historical nature of the narratives, characters, and
references in the text. In order to resolve these questions,
it is necessary to employ a method that will allow us to examine the text as we have it (assuming that we have a reasonably
accurate reconstruction of the text of Acts) and to trace the
hand of the author by working through those literary patterns
and features that appear in his work.

A recent book by Charles H. Talbert, Literary Patterns,
Theological Themes and the Genre of Luke-Acts,[1] may serve as a
starting point for this discussion. Talbert has attempted to
use "architecture analysis" in order to understand the Lukan
literary style and then to question the implications of Luke's
literary patterns for his Christology and finally to draw some
conclusions about the genre to which Luke-Acts belongs.

Talbert's study has the merit of being comprehensive so far
as the Lukan corpus is concerned. Although he concentrates
only on one literary feature, it is one that would reflect the
author's conception of his work and would expose something about
his way of perceiving things. It also has the advantage of
being firmly grounded in the criticism of classical literature.
His analysis shows that Luke-Acts is structured by means of
parallels in which similar themes, topics, images, characters,
or even statements appear. This parallel structure is examined
first in the two major parts, the Gospel and the Acts, and
Talbert lists 32 parallel narratives in the two parts. In addition, he finds that there is parallelism within the Gospel and
within Acts and within smaller sections of each.

Three observations about Talbert's study are germane.
First, he does not make an effort to include every narrative

70

or saying as part of the architecture of Luke-Acts. Second, in
some cases a rather short section in one place is considered to
be parallel to a large block of material in another place. For
example, Luke 10:1-12 is parallel to Acts 13-20; and Acts 12 is
parallel to Acts 21-28. There are, of course, similar features
within each of the sections, but the parallelism of the two in
their entirety is not obvious. Third, and perhaps of greatest
significance, the points of comparison are highly varied. In
the 32 parallels cited between the Gospel and the Acts, the following features serve as points of comparison: similar literary
forms (prologues); similar activities (praying, healing, traveling, raising the dead); the same name (Theophilus); similar
characters (a lame man, a centurion, widows); the same group
(Pharisees); the same geographical reference (Jerusalem); numbers (four trials, three declarations of innocence; seven references to Jerusalem); similar statements; similar themes.

These observations do not cancel the real value of Talbert's study. Although some of his parallels may be questioned,
he has shown that there is a series of parallel structures in
Luke-Acts and that these structures form the basic architecture
of these books.[2]

It is likely that an author would make use of more than
one literary pattern. Two or more patterns might be employed
simultaneously over the entire work or separately in smaller
sections of a book. Some patterns may be thought appropriate
for certain themes, and others for others. So it seems reasonable to grant that Talbert has rightly pointed to one pattern
in Luke-Acts, that of parallelism. His discovery should not
require us to cease looking for others.

One such pattern that seems to operate in Acts is used in
narratives which describe potentially threatening situations.
In general, these stories begin with an introduction which describes the church prior to the threat. The threat is then
described, sometimes in a brief note but often in a lengthy
narrative. Then follows a resolution of the threat, i.e. a
decision is made or something occurs which directly nullifies
the threat. The conclusion to the story then describes the
situation after the threat has been resolved, and frequently it
is written in terms similar to those used in the introduction.

It is plausible to read the entire Book of Acts in this
way. After the introductory preface (1:1-5) and a narrative
which partially duplicates the end of the Gospel (1:6-11; cf.
Luke 24:52-53), the Book of Acts begins by placing the apostles
in Jerusalem. They are all together in an upstairs room, living in harmony and praying. In fact it is precisely Acts 1:12-
14 that picks up the ending of Luke. The description of Jesus'
ascension and its aftermath in Acts is simply a fuller narration of the brief note in Luke 24:50-53, and the situation of
the apostles at the end of Luke is almost exactly the same as
in Acts 1:12-14. They have returned to Jerusalem, and they are
in devotion to God. Acts then picks up where Luke leaves off,
with a description of the pious harmony enjoyed by the apostles.
At the end of Acts we find Paul in Rome, for a period of two
full years, during which he preaches and teaches freely (28:30-
31). The book ends as it began, with a picture of well-being
and harmony, although the reference to the limited time period
may hint that further threats will occur. Between these points
the harmony of early Christianity is threatened over and over
again. There is a shortage among the twelve (1:15-20); Ananias

and Sapphira lie about their property (5:1-2); the apostles are
arrested (5:17-18; 21b-33); there is grumbling between Hellenists and Hebrews (6:1b); Stephen is killed, and a persecution
breaks out (6:9-8:3); Simon Magus poses a threat (8:9-12;18-19);
Saul threatens the church (9:1-2); Peter is criticized for eating with Gentiles (11:1-3); Herod kills James and imprisons
Peter (12:1-5). Paul meets with a long series of dangers. So,
Acts moves from a description of peace to a series of threats
to a restoration of the peace.

The pattern is, however, more complex than this. Not only
is there a kind of overarching pattern for the book as a whole,
but each of the threatening situations is met by a resolution
which restores the peace of the church. The analyses that follow will show how the pattern is utilized, and in some cases
varied, in the narratives about the threats in chapters 1-12.
For purposes of brevity, we shall designate the component parts
of the pattern as peace/threat/resolution/restoration.

1. The shortage among the twelve (1:12-2:1).

Peace: The eleven have returned to Jerusalem and are living
together, along with women, Jesus' mother, and his brothers.
They engage unanimously in prayer (proskarterountes homothumadon
tē proseuchē)---1:12-14.

Threat: Peter says that Judas' defection was necessary
(dei) and in accordance with the scriptures. But the number of
the apostles must be twelve---1:15-20.[3]

Resolution: Matthias is selected as Judas' replacement---
1:21-26.

Restoration: The introductory verse to the Pentecost narrative suggests a situation in which harmony has been restored---
they were all together in the same place (ēsan pantes homou epi
to auto)---2:1.

2. Ananias and Sapphira (4:32-5:11).

Peace: All the believers are of one heart and soul; no one
regards anything as his own, and all things are held in common.
The apostles witness to the resurrection; no one is in need,
and distribution is made according to need. The action of
Barnabas is cited as an illustration---4:32-37. This is a
rather full description, which serves both as a general summary and as an introduction to the story of Ananias and Sapphira.[4]

Threat: Ananias and Sapphira retain some of the profit
from a sale of property---5:1-2.

Resolution: Peter condemns the two, and they both die,
i.e., they are excluded from the community---5:3-10.

Restoration: Fear comes upon the whole church---5:11.

3. The arrest of the apostles (5:12-42).

Peace: The apostles are performing signs and wonders; all
are of one mind (homothumadon hapantes); the apostles are honored by the people; the size of the believing group is being
enlarged (prostithēmi); and Peter heals large numbers of people,

even by his shadow---5:12-16. This too is a fairly long section which serves both as a general summary and as an introduction to the story of the arrest of the apostles.

Threat: The high priest and the Sadducees put the apostles in prison---5:17-18.

Resolution: The apostles are released by an angel---5:19-20.

Restoration: The apostles teach in the temple---5:21a.

Now we have a variation of the pattern, for a second threat occurs.

Threat: The high priest convenes the Sanhedrin; the escape of the apostles is discovered, and they are rearrested. Peter and the apostles make a defense, but the members of the council decide to kill them---5:21b-33.

Resolution: Gamaliel persuades the members of the Sanhedrin to dismiss the apostles---5:34-40.

Restoration: The apostles leave with joy, and they resume teaching and preaching---5:41-42.

4. Grumbling between Hellenists and Hebrews (6:1-7).[5]

Peace: The disciples are increasing in number (plēthunō)---6:1a.

Threat: The Hellenists complain because their widows are being overlooked in the daily service---6:1b.

Resolution: The seven are appointed for service of tables ---6:2-6.

Restoration: The believing community continues to grow (plēthunō)---6:7.

5. Stephen and the persecution (6:8-8:8).

Peace: Stephen performs signs and wonders---6:8.

Threat: Stephen disputes with some synagogue members and is charged with blasphemy. He is brought before the Sanhedrin, speaks in his own defense and is killed. A persecution breaks out against the rank and file in Jerusalem, and Saul drags off many to prison---6:9-8:3. From a literary point of view, the long speech in 7:2-53 should probably be regarded as intruding into the usual pattern.

Resolution: The persecution results in a scattering, through which the gospel is presented to Samaria, notably through Philip---8:4-5. In 11:19, there is another note about the result of the persecution: it makes possible the evangelization of Jews in Phoenicia, Cyprus, and Antioch.

Restoration: Philip preaches in Samaria, performs signs, and heals. Crowds unanimously (homothumadon) respond, and there is great joy---8:6-8. These verses also serve to introduce the next narrative about Philip and Simon Magus.

6. Simon Magus A (8:6-13).

Peace: Philip preaches in Samaria, performs signs, and heals. Crowds unanimously respond, and there is great joy---8:6-8.

Threat: Simon is a competitor of Philip---8:9-12.

Resolution: Simon believes and is baptized---8:13a.

Restoration: Simon and Philip remain together, and Simon is amazed at the signs and wonders---8:13b.

7. Simon Magus B (8:14-25)

Peace: Peter and John come to Samaria, and the holy spirit comes upon the believers there---8:14-17.

Threat: Simon offers to buy the secret to the power of the spirit---8:18-19.

Resolution: Peter condemns Simon, who asks for his prayers ---8:20-24. Luke may intend to signify in v. 24 that Simon has repented.

Restoration: They (i.e. Peter and John) return to Jerusalem; they testify and preach---8:25.

8. Saul (9:1-31)

The material on Saul in this chapter generally follows the same literary pattern that we have seen elsewhere, but there are alterations. We have here a series of five threats and resolutions before there is a description of a restoration.

Peace: Not described.

1st Threat: Saul breathes threats and murder against believers, and he secures permission from the high priest to search for Christians in Damascus---9:1-2.

1st Resolution: Saul is converted and baptized; he preaches in the synagogues---9:3-20.

2nd Threat: He is met with distrust---9:21.

2nd Resolution: Saul grows stronger, confuses and teaches the Jews in Damascus---9:22.

3rd Threat: The Jews plot to kill Saul---9:23-24.

3rd Resolution: He escapes in a basket---9:25.

4th Threat: He is met with distrust in Jerusalem---9:26.

4th Resolution: Barnabas speaks on his behalf, and he preaches in Jerusalem---9:27-29b.

5th Threat: The Hellenists try to kill him---9:29c.

5th Resolution: He is dispatched to Caesarea and Tarsus---9:30.

Restoration: The church in Judaea, Galilee, and Samaria is at peace and is being built up. Believers walk in the fear of the Lord, and the community increases (plēthunō) with the help of the holy spirit---9:31.

9. Peter (11:1-18).

A body of Petrine material begins at 9:32, the chief portion of which is the vision and the acceptance of Cornelius and other Gentiles. In 11:1-18 we have something like another version of the Cornelius material, and its form is a fragment of the peace/threat/resolution/restoration pattern.

Peace: Not described.

Threat: Peter is criticized for eating with Gentiles---11:1-3.

Resolution: Peter tells of his vision and his experience with Cornelius, and there is agreement that God has given repentance to Gentiles---11:4-18.

Restoration: Not described.

10. Herod (12:1-24).

Peace: Not described.

Threat: Herod kills James and imprisons Peter---12:1-5.

Resolution: Peter makes a miraculous escape, and Herod dies a horrible death---12:6-23.

Restoration: The word of God grows and multiplies (ēuxanen kai eplēthuneto)---12:24.

Fragments of the pattern may also be found in chapters 13-28, but space does not permit an analysis of those sections. There seems to be sufficient evidence to establish the fact that a literary pattern is at work in many of Luke's narratives. Literary patterns may be artistic means for conveying to the reader an impression. In the case of this movement from peace through threat and resolution to restoration, the reader should finally get a definite impression of what is positive and what is negative, and we may presume that such is in the mind of the author. In any event, the description of the peaceful situations and the restorations must be put on the positive side, and the threats on the negative. In a sense, the positive represents a kind of ideal situation, and it is instructive to pull together those features that appear to be included in that ideal situation.

But before we do so, it will be necessary to look at another passage in which the peace of the church is described, namely 2:41-47. These verses function as a conclusion to the Pentecost narrative and the speech of Peter. If that had been regarded as a threatening situation, these verses would have described the restoration. As they stand, however, they function as a general summary which describes the peace of the church. There is growth, religious devotion, and the breaking of bread. There is fear; the apostles perform signs and wonders; believers are together (epi to auto); they hold all things in common; they all

(homothumadon) remain (proskarterountes) in the temple; they
break bread and eat.[6]

Now we may pull together those passages which function to
describe peace and restoration. They are: 1:12-14; 2:1; 2:41-
47; 4:32-37; 5:11; 5:12-16; 5:21a; 5:41-42; 6:1a; 6:7; 6:8;
8:6-8; 8:13b; 8:14-17; 8:25; 9:21a; 12:24.[7] There is a good deal
of common language in these passages, and some of the expressions are virtually stereotypical. So it is possible to list
the major features which are included in these sections on the
assumption that they form a description of the ideal church.
The following features are the chief ones:

(1) Unanimity, usually expressed by homothumadon. The ideas of
living together and being together (epi to auto) also express
unanimity---1:12-14; 2:1; 2:41-47; 4:32-37; 5:12-16; 8:6-8;
8:13b.

(2) Growth of the community. The feature of popular esteem also suggests the idea of growth---2:41-47; 5:12-16; 6:1a; 6:7;
9:31; 12:24.

(3) Religious devotion, prayer, joy, fear, or fear of the Lord
---1:12-14; 2:41-47; 5:11; 5:41-42; 8:6-8; 9:31.

(4) Signs, wonders, healings; the spirit---2:41-47; 5:12-16;
6:8; 8:6-8; 8:14-17; 9:31.

(5) Testifying, preaching, and teaching---2:41-47; 4:32-37;
5:21a; 5:41-42; 8:6-8; 8:25.

(6) Common property---2:41-47; 4:32-37.

(7) Eating---2:41-47.

The general procedure in Luke seems to be to include for
each of the features some illustrative story showing how in that
respect the church was threatened and how the threat was met.
There seem to be no direct threats to the continuation of religious devotion, but the growth of the community is threatened
by persecution and by Saul. Unanimity is threatened by the
grumbling of Hellenists against Hebrews and by the criticism
against Peter. The performance of signs, wonders, and healings
is threatened by Simon Magus, as is the understanding of the
holy spirit. Preaching and teaching are directly threatened
by the killing of Stephen, the arrest of the apostles, the
killing of James, and the arrest of Peter. Saul's threats may
also be regarded as threats against preaching. The threat
against common property is, of course, described in the story
of Ananias and Sapphira. The threat against the common meal
comes up explicitly in the criticism against Peter and, as we
shall see, in the grumbling of the Hellenists. Clearly there
is an inter-relationship among these features and the narratives. A threat against common property and the common meal is
a threat against unanimity. A threat against preaching and
signs is a threat against growth.

II. The Threat and the Resolution in Acts 6:1-7.

Against the background of the literary pattern that is described above, it is possible to investigate the nature of the
threat and the resolution of the threat in Acts 6:1-7. We have

already seen that the passage is structured along the lines of
the literary pattern we have found and that it describes a
threat to the church. Yet the specific nature of the threat,
and hence its resolution, have not become clear.

The narrative is formed along the lines of the literary
pattern we have observed. There is an initial description of
the peaceful situation, followed by a threat and by the resolution of the threat. In the concluding verse we have a description of the restoration of peace. The narrative itself is in
the form of an inclusio, in which the multiplication of the disciples forms a frame for the action. A brief outline will show
how the narrative is structured:

A. The disciples are multiplying (plēthunō, v. 1a).

B. Hellenists grumble against Hebrews, because their widows are
being overlooked in the daily service (v. 1b).

C. The twelve call the community together (v. 2a).

D. The twelve propose a plan (v. 2b-4).

E. The community accepts the plan (v. 5a).

F. The plan is implemented, and the seven are ordained (v. 5b-
6).

G. The disciples continue to multiply (plēthunō, v. 7).

The inclusio should remind the reader of the peaceful situation of the church, and it emphasizes the feature of growth.
When all is going well, the community increases; and when the
threat is resolved, the community resumes its natural growth.
In this case the natural growth of the community is threatened
by a grumbling of one group against another. Factionalism and
discontent appear to be the threatening factors, so the unanimity of the community is also threatened. The basis for the
discontent appears to be discrimination: the widows of the
Hellenists were being overlooked in the daily service. The
plan which the twelve propose is to appoint a group of seven
qualified men who will wait on tables. This is done, and the
growth of the community resumes.

The fact that this narrative has long been regarded as
troublesome means that the problems in it are familiar. To be
sure, some of the problems are those that accompany a historical approach to the narrative, but there are also problems for
literary criticism. The literary approach, however, requires
a certain way of casting the questions. It requires us to look
for the literary meaning of the passage within its context and
to examine its possible function in Luke's writings. The questions that will now be faced relate to the precise nature of the
threat and the resolution.

In order to analyze Luke's understanding of the threat and
the resolution, it is necessary to raise four major questions:
(1) What does Luke mean by the daily service? (2) What does he
mean by Hebrews and Hellenists? (3) What does he mean by the
"overlooking of widows"? (4) How is the reader to understand
the resolution?

1. What does Luke mean by the daily service?

Arndt and Gingrich give various meanings to diakonia: service; service necessary to the preparation of a meal; the office of prophet, apostle, deacon; aid, support; distribution. The cognate verb, diakoneō, means to wait on someone at table; to serve; to help, to support, etc.[8]

Luke uses both diakoneō and diakonia several times, and a study of them shows that he utilizes the following connotations:

a. Hospitality, entertaining of guests, preparing and providing meals. In Luke 4:39, Simon's mother-in-law served the people in their house after Jesus had cured her of a high fever. Such activity would probably be regarded as hospitality and may have included the serving of food. In Luke 10:40, Martha is said to be burdened with service. The service must be that which is incidental to the entertainment of guests, for Martha is the one who welcomed Jesus to the home in v. 38. The contrast between the two women is between Martha, who is engaged in domestic service, and Mary, who is attentive to Jesus' word. In Luke 12:37, the master is pictured as putting on a belt, having the slaves sit down, and serving them. In Luke 17:8, a slave is told to put on a belt, prepare and serve a meal for the master. This verse is a close parallel to 12:37, but the roles are reversed. In both cases, the activity of putting on a belt is associated with preparing and serving a meal. In Luke 22:26-27, there is a triple contrast: greatest/youngest; leader/servant (diakonōn); the one who sits at table (ho anakeimos)/the one who serves (ho diakonōn). Clearly the connotation of ho diakonōn in v. 27 is of one waiting on tables. The contrast, leader/servant, should probably be the same. But in 22:27, Jesus claims to be the one serving (ho diakonōn); so we have here another role reversal which reminds us of 12:37.

b. Support by available means. In 8:3, some female followers of Jesus served with their means. The participle, huparchontōn, designates things that are present and available to someone, so we should not confine its meaning here to money or property. The verse probably means that the women did whatever they could to help the community.

c. Emergency aid. In Acts 11:29, there is a decision to send eis diakonian to the brothers living in Judaea. It is sent via Barnabas and Saul, who complete the service (diakonia) in 12:25, i.e., they complete their assignments, since they have taken the emergency relief to Judaea.[9] Note that what precipitated the diakonia was Agabus' prediction of a famine in 11:28.

d. Testimony, apostleship. In Acts 1:17, Peter says that Judas had been counted among the twelve and had "received the share of this service."[10] Diakonia must refer to whatever it is that Luke understands to be the duty of the twelve. In 1:25, the community prays that Judas' replacement will "take the place of this service and apostleship." In 20:24, Paul refers to his service, which is described as testifying "about the good news of the grace of God." Probably 21:19 should be read in this way also, where Paul meets with James and other Jerusalem Christians and speaks about his service among the Gentiles.

e. General aid. In Acts 19:22, Timothy and Erastus are described as the ones serving (diakonountōn) Paul. Other references in Acts to Timothy's activity (16:3; 17:14-15; 18:5; 20:4; Erastus is not mentioned again) indicate that Luke thought of his service as general aid and mostly as accompaniment.

Although we might expect to find any of these connotations in Acts 6:1, the narrative of 6:1-7 itself will help us to define the meaning more precisely. In 6:2, we have: "So the twelve convened the community of disciples, and they said, 'It is not acceptable (areston) for us to leave behind the word and to serve tables (diakonein trapezais). A trapeza is a table, usually a dining table.[11] According to Arndt and Gingrich, it may stand figuratively for a meal or for food.[12] In 6:4, the twelve say, "We, however, will continue in prayer and in service to the word (tē diakonia tou logou)." This must be a kind of service like that in Acts 1:17,25; 20:24; and 21:19, i.e., diakonia here has the connotation of testimony and apostleship. The contrast in 6:2,4, is between two kinds of diakonia: the service of the apostle; and the preparation of meals, which is a task assigned to the seven. In the light of the entire narrative of 6:1-7, therefore, the primary connotation of diakonia in 6:1 must be a meal.

An alternative interpretation is to take diakonia in 6:1 in the sense of financial relief or welfare, as in 11:29. On that verse, Foakes-Jackson and Lake comment: "The general term διακονία was perhaps beginning to have a special usage as an undertaking for financial relief."[13] They call attention to Romans 15:31 and II Corinthians 8:4, where Paul uses the word with this connotation, and they so interpret diakonia in Acts 6:1. If, however, the phrase diakonein trapezais, which describes the task assigned to the seven, connotes the serving of meals, it is difficult to avoid the conclusion that the daily diakonia of 6:1 was an actual meal.[14]

Thus far it appears that Acts 6:1-7 describes a threat to the peace of the church. The threat is caused by a tendency to overlook some widows at the daily common meal.

2.   What does Luke mean by Hebrews and Hellenists?

The major problem has always been the identification of the Hellenists. Everett Ferguson[15] has provided a handy classification and appraisal of the various options, and he lists these alternatives as follows: (1) Hellenists were Greek-speaking Jews. This is said to be the prevailing view, and Ferguson lists F. F. Bruce, Ernst Haenchen, Hans Conzelmann, F. C. Grant, Johannes Munck, and Paul Gaechter among its supporters.[16] (2) "Modifications of the linguistic interpretation."[17] Ferguson refers to J. A. T. Robinson, who "introduces a geographical qualification, interpreting the Hellenists as 'Greek-speaking Jews of the Diaspora living in Palestine.'"[18] Actually, Haenchen also agrees with Robinson, and should be included here.[19] (3) Racial. This is the identification of the Hellenists as Greeks, and Henry Cadbury is its chief proponent. (4) Sectarian. Oscar Cullmann makes them similar to Essenes. Marcel Simon identifies them as "a religious party in Judaism opposed to the temple and its sacrificial cultus."[20] But in another study, Simon says that to Luke Hellenists meant Greek-speaking Jews.[21] (5) Cultural, i.e., "those who follow the Greek manner of life."[22] Ferguson agrees that several scholars have included the cultural meaning as secondary to the linguistic, but he believes it needs to be understood as the primary meaning. He is convinced that such an understanding satisfies all three appearances of the term in Acts (6:1; 9:29; 11:20). To Ferguson, the Hellenists were Jews who felt that they were retaining basic Jewish religion but accommodating to the larger culture. He suggests that the observance of dietary regulations might have been a point of controversy: "The dietary laws of Judaism have historically been among the first to go as Jews have made cultural accommodations."[23]

Ferguson's five options can better be reduced to two, one of which has several variants. Either Luke understood the Hellenists as Jews or as Gentiles. If they were Jews, they may have spoken Greek, or belonged to a heterodox movement, or have come from the Diaspora, or have compromised religious practices by cultural accommodation, or any combination of these possibilities. Over against these views, Cadbury's understanding of the Hellenists as Greeks appears to be a significant and distinctive alternative.[24]

Cadbury recognizes that, etymologically, _Hellenistēs_ should designate "anyone who practises Greek ways---whether a Greek himself or a foreigner."[25] He emphasizes the points that such aping of Greek ways is not limited to foreigners and that there is no "special reference to language."[26] He also claims that _Hebraioi_ does not refer to language, but to people, i.e. Jews. Cadbury then focuses on the three uses of the term Hellenists in Acts---6:1; 9:29; 11:20. In 9:29, Saul debates with the Hellenists, who try to kill him. The brothers in Jerusalem, however, rescue him. In 11:19-20, those persons who had been scattered as a result of the persecution that started with Stephen began to preach, but only to Jews. Some others, however, from Cyprus and Cyrene, preached to Hellenists, at Antioch.[27] The contrasts in the three verses are:

> Hebrews and Hellenists, 6:1.
> Brothers and Hellenists, 9:29.
> Jews and Hellenists, 11:19-20.

In 6:1, both groups are Christians; in 9:29, the Hellenists are apparently not Christians; in 11:19-20, both are potential Christians. Cadbury shows that Hellenists in 11:20 cannot be Jews, or else the contrast is meaningless. On 9:29, he says: "The context has nothing in it to indicate who are meant. But there is no reason why the author may not be supposed to have introduced here a prompt fulfillment of the prediction made at Paul's conversion that he would be a missionary to Gentiles."[28] So Cadbury is able to conclude that Hellenists in all three verses of Acts probably means Greeks.

One of the major obstacles to Cadbury's view is the apparent problem caused by the introduction of Gentile Christians at such an early point as Acts 6. It seems to conflict with the structure of Acts, in which Gentiles only come into the Christian movement with the conversion of Cornelius in chapter 10. Cadbury believes, however, that Acts does not present a picture of a straight-line movement from a Jewish to a Gentile setting. He says there are "successive and, one might almost say, repeated beginnings of Gentile Christianity."[29] He is able to point to five such beginnings, each one narrated in apparent ignorance of the former ones. The five are:

Pentecost, chapter 2.[30]
Philip's conversion of the Ethiopian eunuch, 8:26-40
Cornelius, 10:1-11:18
Preaching by men from Cyprus and Cyrene---11:19-20
The missionary journey of Paul and Barnabas,
        chapters 13-14.

The situation in chapter 2 is not clear, since Peter's speech at
Pentecost is addressed to the men of Israel (2:22). But it does
seem more natural to understand the Ethiopian eunuch as a Gentile rather than a Jew, although he is reading from Isaiah. One
may also wonder if Luke thought of Simon Magus as a Gentile. In
any event, Cadbury concludes that "there is therefore no difficulty in supposing that Acts vi.1 may have introduced a story
(perhaps from a new source, as is often supposed) in which Gentiles and Jews already formed the two national divisions of the
Jerusalem church."[31]

    Cadbury's argument seems persuasive, and there seems to be
no substantial literary argument against understanding the terms
as he does.[32] We may conclude, therefore, that Luke intends the
reader to understand that the threat in Acts 6:1 is one involv-
ing some controversy between Jewish and Gentile Christians about
the daily meal.

3. What does Luke mean by the overlooking of widows?

    If the controversy is as described above, then it seems as
if Luke is alluding to a situation in which the Gentile widows
were being overlooked at the daily meal. Although the grumbling
is against the Hebrews, the text does not explicitly say that
the Hebrews are the ones overlooking the widows. The verb,
paretheōrounto[33] is an imperfect passive, which indicates a hab-
itual neglect rather than a single incident; but the agent of
the neglect is not specified. The grumbling against the Hebrews may, however, indicate that they were perceived to be responsible for the meal.[34] In any event, the plain meaning of the
complaint is that the Gentile widows were not allowed to participate in the daily meal.

    In Luke-Acts, as in other early Christian literature, wid-
ows appear to form a special and respected group. Luke always
portrays them in a positive light, and he presents them as persons who have special needs. Widowhood appears to add a special
ingredient of piety---to Anna the prophetess in Luke 2:36-38.
It is an additional burden of grief for the mother at Nain,
whose son has died (Luke 7:11-17). A widow is a person who is
in extreme need (Luke 18:1-8); she is vulnerable to scribes, who
may take her home away from her (Luke 20:47). She is poor but
mindful of the need to make a contribution, no matter how small
(Luke 21:1-4).[35] For Luke-Acts, widowhood means grief, poverty,
vulnerability, and piety. The exclusion of widows from the
daily meal would therefore appear as an act of extreme cruelty
and impiety, but also as a condition which underlined the urgent
need for a solution. The reader should recognize immediately
that here is an intolerable situation, one which can have only
one solution: the widows must not be excluded.

    If we now put together what we have found about the nature
of the threat in 6:1, we find that Luke has presented a mean-
ingful account. The problem was that Gentile widows were habit-
ually being excluded from the daily meal. Luke does know that

the problem of a common meal was a serious one in early Christianity, for he comes back to it in the material in chapters 10-11, where Peter is criticized for eating with Gentiles. If he means to signify Jews and Greeks by his terms Hebrews and Hellenists, then surely the reader is correct to think of the Jewish dietary regulations and of the problems these might cause for a common daily meal, although it is not clear if Luke would intend this in a statement about widows.

We may conclude that the threat, as Luke presents it in 6:1, involves the observance of a common meal and of the propriety of Gentile widows participating in it.

4. How is the reader to understand the resolution?

It has frequently been observed that the solution is not appropriate to the threat. For this reason, some commentators reject the suggestion that a common meal was in any way part of the threat. Many commentators have also questioned the effectiveness of a solution in which the representatives of one side only, the Hellenists, are put in charge of the solution.[36] This turns out to be an unnecessary question, however. The seven are not called Hellenists, and their names do not require us to assume that they were.[37] Other objectors point to the rather menial character of an assignment for such highly qualified persons. Why do we need spiritual men to wait on tables, a task which the twelve specifically disavow?

If, however, we approach the narrative from the other end, as we have, it is necessary to see the solution in a different way. It now becomes clear that the problem of the daily service is a problem which requires serious attention. If the question has to do with dietary regulations, the appointment of the seven should be seen, not simply as the appointment of a group to distribute food, but of a council of wise and spiritual persons who are commissioned to solve this problem. Although it may seem natural to understand table service as inferior to service to the word, the main idea of the narrative is that these represent alternative modes of service.[38] The seven are described as persons who are approved by the disciples, full of spirit and wisdom, full of faith and spirit, and appointed by the twelve. Clearly the seven are not prohibited from preaching, as the subsequent narratives about Stephen and Philip show. We are not to think of the seven as performing a menial task. They are commissioned to solve the problem of the common meal and the exclusion of the Greek widows from it, one of the serious problems that threatened the peace of the church. Unfortunately, Luke does not tell us what the solution was, although he clearly implies that a solution was reached. The speech of Stephen, which follows, may be understood as a hint that liberal tendencies prevailed. The material about the criticism of Peter in 11:1-18 also shows that Luke feels that Christians should eat together. Perhaps he also means that the dietary restrictions in 15:20, 29; 21:25, are to be understood as the real solution to the problem. In any case, Luke means for the reader to understand that the food problem is a serious one and that the solution to it required the best efforts of the early Christians.

III. Acts 6:1-7 and the Lukan Community

We have seen that one of the literary patterns in the Book of Acts is one that treats various threats to the peace of the

church. This pattern works in a fairly regular fashion in those
narratives in which Luke describes the threats to the church.
An analysis of this pattern has enabled us to identify those
features that Luke conceives of as being important to the peace
of the church, and they serve to describe the ideal ecclesiastical situation. Among those features is the observance of a
common meal. There are threats to the common meal as there are
to the other ideal features. Luke's narrative in 6:1-7 shows
how the threat works and how it should be solved. He must feel
that, although it might be threatened, it is of sufficient importance that the leaders must assure its survival. That survival, by implication, means a new understanding of the Jewish
dietary regulations.

Since the topic this year for the Luke-Acts seminar is one
which asks about Luke's community, it now becomes necessary to
say something about that topic. There are, however, serious
hazards involved in painting a picture about an author's community which is drawn from the literary patterns he uses. In the
past several decades literary critics have been involved in a
vigorous discussion about the relationship of author and text,
and the arguments which sever the two, while they may not be
altogether persuasive, are weighty. The so-called new criticism
has seriously challenged the view that we can understand a book
by studying the biography of the author and can discover what an
author is like by reading his book. The point is not that the
new critics are right, but that, in New Testament studies, their
viewpoint has not yet been given full consideration, and their
challenge has not been met. Until it is, it seems the better
part of discretion to avoid any but the most tentative claims
about the author's community.[39]

The best that we may do at present is to suggest, tentatively, the kind of community in which Luke's treatment of the
food problem might have been appropriate. His description of
the early days of the church may have served as a kind of ideal
for his own church. If we could plot a "trajectory" of various
Christian communities, designed to show something about their
attitudes toward the common meal, we should probably find the
Pauline churches at one end and the community of Justin at the
other. Clearly, Paul is in immediate struggle with the question
of Jews and Gentiles eating together, and he feels that the act
of eating together is non-negotiable.[40] Justin is aware of no
such problem, and he can say that dietary regulations pertain
only to Jews and were given to them to help them remember
God.[41] Luke is between the two of them, but closer to Paul.
He agrees with Paul that the act of eating together is non-
negotiable, but he presents a modification of the Jewish dietary
regulations as, at least, acceptable. The kind of community in
which this attitude appears to be appropriate is one in which
the common meal is still controversial. Such a community may
have included some Jews who felt reluctant to eat with Gentiles.

Notes

1. SBL Monograph Series, 20.(Missoula: Scholars Press, 1974).
   The study by H. J. Cadbury, The Style and Literary Method of
   Luke (Cambridge: Harvard University Press, 1920), is still
   indispensable for the literary critical study of Luke-Acts.
   Talbert's analysis concentrates on the large patterns in
   Luke-Acts, while Cadbury discusses such things as vocabulary

and syntax. Cf. also Cadbury, The Making of Luke-Acts, 2nd edition (London: S. P. C. K., 1958).

2. Two other recent literary critical studies of Luke-Acts are: Luke T. Johnson, The Literary Function of Possessions in Luke-Acts, SBL Dissertation Series, 39 (Missoula: Scholars Press, 1977); and Earl Richard, Acts 6:1-8:4: The Author's Method of Composition, SBL Dissertation Series, 41 (Missoula: Scholars Press, 1978).

3. Johnson says that the integrity of the twelve is important for Luke because that group represents believing Israel. "The betrayal of Judas was not simply the failing of an individual; it splintered the numerical and therefore symbolic integrity of that group which constituted the beginning and essential authority of the believing Israel . . . As the others of the Twelve died there would be no need to replace them, for once the Twelve had been definitively constituted and the Spirit bestowed, the faithful Israel would have come into existence, and have fulfilled its role in God's plan." Op. cit., p. 176. Cf. Jacob Jervell, Luke and the People of God (Minneapolis: Augsburg, 1972), pp. 75-112.

4. Johnson, op. cit., pp. 200-203, calls attention to the symbolic significance of laying one's possessions at the feet of the apostles (vs. 34b-35). He writes: "When the believers lay their possessions at the Apostles' feet, therefore, they were symbolically laying themselves there, in a gesture of submission to the authority of the Twelve." (p. 202)

5. This narrative will be examined in greater detail below.

6. The act of breaking bread is mentioned twice in this passage, and the most probable denotation is that of a common meal. The passage speaks of living together, holding common property, and worshiping in the temple as acts of the community. If the breaking of bread is not to be understood as a common meal, the reference to it here would have no significance. In Acts 20:7, 11; 27:35, the act of breaking bread is understood to be a common meal. The scene of the meal in 2:46 is set kat' oikon, in apparent contrast to en tō hierō. Cf. F. J. Foakes-Jackson and Kirsopp Lake, The Acts of the Apostles, paperback edition (Grand Rapids: Baker Book House, 1979) IV, 29, for a discussion of the various possible translations of the phrase, kat' oikon.

7. Several of these passages are treated as general summaries by H. J. Cadbury, in Foakes-Jackson and Lake, op. cit., V, 392-402.

8. W. F. Arndt and F. W. Gingrich, A Greek-English Lexicon of the New Testament and Other Early Christian Literature (Chicago: University of Chicago Press, 1957), in loc.

9. Although eis Ierousalēm has better textual support than any of the other readings, it does not fit in with the geographical scheme in this section of Acts. Saul and Barnabas must be thought of as having returned from Jerusalem.

10. Cf. Luke 22:3, where Judas is said to be ek tou arithmou tōn dōdeka.

11. Arndt and Gingrich, op. cit., in loc., say that it also designates a table used by bankers and may stand figuratively for a bank.

12. Ibid.

13. Foakes-Jackson and Lake, op. cit., IV, 131.

14. Marcel Simon, St. Stephen and the Hellenists in the Primitive Church (London: Longmans, Green and Co., 1958), p. 51, takes the word trapeza in the sense of a banker's table and says that serving tables means "to deal with material problems and to take up the commissariat of the community."

15. "The Hellenists in the Book of Acts," Restoration Quarterly 12 (1969), 159-180.

16. Martin Hengel, "Zwischen Jesus und Paulus," ZTK 72 (1975), 151-206, should also be included here. C. F. D. Moule, "Once More, Who Were the Hellenists?" Expository Times 70 (1958), 100, says that the Hellenists were "Jews (whether by birth or as proselytes) who spoke only Greek and no Semitic language."

17. Ferguson, op. cit., p. 159.

18. Ibid.

19. Cf. Ernst Haenchen, The Acts of the Apostles (Philadelphia: Westminster, 1971), p. 267.

20. Ferguson, op. cit., p. 160.

21. Simon, op. cit., p. 18.

22. Ferguson, op. cit., p. 160.

23. Ibid., p. 180.

24. Cf. H. J. Cadbury, "The Hellenists," in Foakes-Jackson and Lake, op. cit., V, 59-74.

25. Ibid., p. 60.

26. Ibid.

27. Cadbury considers the alternate reading, Hellēnas, in 11:20, to be inferior; ibid., pp. 70-71.

28. Ibid., p. 70.

29. Ibid., p. 66.

30. Cadbury argues that, on textual grounds, Ioudaioi should be omitted from 2:5, so that the verse refers to "devout men of every nation under heaven." Ibid., p. 68.

31. Ibid., p. 69.

32. But consider the position of Martin Hengel, op. cit., who interprets the Hellenists as Jewish inhabitants of Jerusalem who spoke Greek. Cf. also Stephen G. Wilson, The Gentiles and the Gentile Mission in Luke-Acts, SNTS Monograph Series, 23 (Cambridge: Cambridge University Press, 1973), pp. 129-138. Wilson says that Luke saw the Hellenists as Jews, because he has Stephen speak as a Jew. But the text does not say that Stephen is a Hellenist.

33. This verb appears only here in the NT.

34. D* makes the Hebrews directly responsible.

35. Cf. also Luke 4:25, 26; Acts 9:39, 41.

36. For a brief history of the criticism of this narrative, cf. Haenchen, op. cit., pp. 264-269.

37. Although all seven carry Greek names, this fact does not constitute conclusive evidence. Cadbury, op. cit., p. 62, says: "They could have been borne, on the one hand by Palestinian Jews, who must often have been partly bilingual, or on the other hand by non-Jews." Hengel, op. cit., pp.175-6, is convinced that the seven were Hellenists, and he remarks about the total absence from the list of any typically Jewish name. He writes: "Ein Vergleich mit den jüdischen Namen in Papyri und Inschriften und bei Josephus zeigt nur bei Philippus eine gewisse Häufigkeit." (p. 175)

38. Cf. the motif of role reversal in Luke 12:37; 17:8; 22:27.

39. Cf. René Wellek and Austin Warren, Theory of Literature (New York: Harcourt, Brace, and Co., 1949); René Wellek, Concepts of Criticism (New Haven: Yale University Press, 1963); John M. Ellis, The Theory of Literary Criticism (Berkeley: University of California Press, 1974). For a position opposed to the new criticism, cf. E. D. Hirsch, Jr., Validity in Interpretation (New Haven: Yale University Press, 1967).

40. Cf. especially Galatians 2:11-21.

41. Dialogue with Trypho, 20. Justin claims, however, that Christians observe a common meal once a week, using bread, wine, and water. Cf. Apology, 65-66.

On Finding the Lukan Community
A Cautious Cautionary Essay

Luke T. Johnson
Yale Divinity School

We have all heard the old fable of the blindfolded sages and the elephant, and have learned its moral: the limited perception of a part can only with hazard be trusted to explain the whole. The sage who, upon feeling the elephant's trunk, concluded he was handling a snake was not wrong in his perception, only in his conclusion. There are more possibilities to wriggly things than snakes. But having learned that moral from the tale, we may find ourselves tempted in the opposite direction, so that whenever we touch something slick and vaguely prehensile, we conclude there is an elephant attached. Wrong again, and for the same reason.

I am reminded of this tale when I consider the signs of a stirring interest among Lukan scholars in finding the Lukan community.[1] Why should there be this interest? How has it arisen? Is it the text of Luke-Acts itself which impels the search, or is it a set of presuppositions regarding the reading of New Testament documents generally, presuppositions which may not apply in this case?

Since it is no longer the fashion to regard Luke as the companion of Paul, or as writing to specifically Pauline communities,[2] the basis for a description of the Lukan community would seem to be limited to the text of Luke-Acts. Any optimism accompanying the search is provided by certain presuppositions concerning the relationship between the author, his work, and his readers: a) the author was writing for a specific group of people with definable and distinct characteristics;[3] b) the author's text reveals, at least by inference, hard information about this group; so that c) on the basis of that information the Lukan audience can be described with some accuracy. A further presupposition would seem to be that this description of the community's life situation will provide sharper insight into those very themes which have provided the basis of the description. In short, we can move from the text to its life-setting, and from the life-setting to the meaning of the text.

As you recognize, these presuppositions are those of the exegetical approach which has come to be called the "mirror method".[4] I suggest that the hope of discovering a Lukan community derives less from the shape of the Lukan documents than from the presumed validity of this method for the study of any New Testament document. Since it has been successful elsewhere, it should work here, as well.

In this short essay, I will try to draw some lessons from what I perceive to be the limits of the mirror method in general, and apply them by way of caution to the reading of Luke-Acts. Skepticism, after all, has its functions. If a legitimate doubt can be raised about the validity or fruitfulness of this way of reading Luke-Acts, perhaps the way to a more appropriate approach can be cleared.

The Limits of the Mirror Method: Lessons from Paul

In the case of the Corinthian letters, which are

occasional in nature, which are addressed to a concrete and
identifiable group, and which describe specific problems within
that group, the mirror method has had some success. It has not
been an unqualified success, since there are as many opinions
about the precise dimensions of the Corinthian social setting,
attitudes and problems as there are investigators.[5] But at least
the method makes sense here, indeed is almost necessary.[6] And
there are some controls. We know the author, and what he has
written elsewhere. He explicitly refers to the attitudes of the
members of the community, and even alludes to aspects of their
social standing.[7] He appears to cite the slogans of his inter-
locutors, and takes up their positions in his argument.[8] There
is, furthermore, some exegetical reward. By piecing together
the diverse bits of information (and fitting them to what we
know of Corinth from elsewhere, including Acts), we can con-
struct a more or less coherent picture of a community and its
problems. This portrait, in turn, helps us recognize the significance of parts of Paul's argument we might otherwise have
overlooked.

The method's success in the Corinthian correspondence has
not been matched in the other Pauline letters. In Galatians and
Colossians (granting the authenticity of the latter), we are
able to make some guesses about the identity or practices of the
respective "opponents",[9] but are not able to say much about the
"Galatian Community" or the "Colossian Community" apart from the
fairly obvious facts that both were young Gentile churches. The
letters simply do not yield that sort of information, in spite
of the clear "occasionality" of both writings.[10] In these cases
we do not have the support of evidence from Acts or other
ancient sources (at least not directly). Even though both letters were written in response to a crisis, we can only with
great difficulty reconstruct the "heresy", much less describe
the make-up of the community as a social organism.[11]

The Letter to the Romans should stand as an example of the
mirror method's limits. Romans 14 (and 16) appear to give us information for the reconstruction of the Roman church's situation, and some scholars have tried to read Romans through the
lens of that reconstruction.[12] The legitimacy of this has been
questioned before.[13] To what extent does Paul in Rom 14, by a
kind of literary inertia, carry over into Romans the concerns
of I Cor 8-10?[14] The thematic and theological connection between Rom 1-11 and 14 should not be doubted. But that the "life-
setting" of Rom 14 explains or adequately accounts for the theological exposition of 1-11 is not likely. Romans reminds us
that life-setting, occasion, purpose and meaning should not
hastily be identified. Why? Precisely because of the literary
shape of the writing. Rom 1-11 gives no indication of having
been stimulated by local difficulties, but gives every sign of
being a carefully constructed scholastic diatribe of more universal significance.[15]

Recognition of the literary structure of Romans leads to
the analysis of passages within that structure. Few would want
to argue, I think, that the vice-list of Rom 1:30-31 reveals
the characteristic failings of the Roman community. We know that
Paul is using a literary convention, and recognize as well that
this topos has a place within a broader literary set-piece (the
polemic against idolatry), which, in turn, prepares for the argument of chapter four. Neither would many of us want to conclude from Paul's positive remarks about the state in Rom 13:1ff
that the Roman church was caught up in revolutionary fever.

Again, we see that Paul is employing stereotyped ethical teaching whose variation is due less to the situation of his readers than his own perceptions.

There is a lesson to be learned from Romans. Where references to local situations are few and ambiguous, and where there is clear evidence of literary technique, it is hazardous to move from the presence of a theme or topos to the situation of the readers. The more a Pauline letter moves toward being an "epistle", the more generalized the applicability of his teaching becomes. And the more clearly a theme or topos serves a literary function within a broader argument, the less likely its presence is to be accounted for by the particular circumstances of the readers.

Within the Pauline corpus itself, therefore, the mirror method has only limited applicability. The reconstruction of a Pauline community must take into account the literary structure of the individual letters, together with the degree of occasionality and specificity these suggest. The study of Paul's letters reminds us that even in documents of a genuinely occasional nature, not every element in the writing is determined by the place, the people, or the occasion. Some things are there because of the demands of genre, the impetus of tradition, the logic of argumentation, the inertia of scriptural citations, and the idiosyncratic perceptions of the author. Responsible exegesis takes these factors into account before using passages as a mirror to community problems.[16] Where they are not taken into account, the reading of documents can become fantastical.

The Mirror Reading of the Gospels: Lessons Yet to be Learned

The categories and perceptions of form-criticism are still alive in redaction-criticism of the Gospels.[17] If form-criticism tended to draw the tightest sort of connection between individual units of tradition and the life-setting of communities, redaction-criticism generally assumes a similar symbiotic connection between the evangelists and individual communities. The recent efflorescence of heresy-hunting going by the neutral rubric of "traditions in conflict" has simply given a distinctive coloration to this perception.[18]

Redaction of traditional material, we are to understand, points to the pastoral and theological concerns of the evangelist. Fair enough. But another, less legitimate assumption is too frequently made: that these concerns are invariably determined by some crisis among the evangelist's readers, his community. Still further down the logical road is the assumption that these crises involved eschatological or Christological heresies. Once these assumptions are in place -- and they are assumptions, whose roots cannot be traced here[19]--then it appears possible to move from the themes of the text to the social setting and theological stances of the text's readers. Where there is a plus in the text we are to infer a minus in the community, or in part of the community, and so forth.

The purpose of the evangelist's redaction, then, is to shape the story about Jesus in such fashion as to correct or counter such misunderstandings or opposing theologies.[20] It has been pointed out before that the resulting polemic is extraordinarily subtle,[21] and that we should have no notion of the

opposition at all were it not for the positive presentation of
their supposed positions within the Gospels themselves.[22]But
these criticisms have not had much impact, and the assumptions I
have stated appear to be gaining ever more dominance in redactional studies, even though their validity has not been tested by
anything more rigorous than popularity.The danger posed by this
methodological hegemony is real. By limiting the possible relations between author and text, text and audience, the mirror
method not only gives off implausible historical refractions, but
can lead to the distortion of those texts which form the only
starting place and inevitable homing of our shared investigation.

The method has had some success in the study of John's
Gospel. But there, we have the evidence given by the three letters, which points to a divided community. And in the letters,
the terminology of the Gospel is placed in the context of an
ecclesiological and theological dispute.[23] The Gospel also has
observable redactional seams which open to reveal, within the
narrative, the community concerns. The corpus as a whole, therefore, and the literary structure of the document, give some
justification for reading elements of the Gospel as reflections
of internecine quarrels within Johannine Christianity. Whether or
not an obsessive preoccupation with these factors has led to an
enrichment of our understanding of John's Gospel as a whole, I
leave to you.

But it is essential to stress that in the Synoptics, we have
no such supporting evidence for intra-communitarian disputes, and
no controls to the fantasies of heresy-hunting. Consider, if
you will, the logical steps necessary to justify the leap from
the "Scribes" of Mark's narrative to the Jacobean party of the
Jerusalem church.[24] Or those required to identify the "Pharisees"
of Luke's narrative as "antinomians" within the Lukan church.[25]
Reading everything in the Gospel narratives as immediately addressed to a contemporary crisis reduces them to the level of
cryptograms, and the evangelists to the level of tractarians.

An objection may be raised here. Isn't it axiomatic for New
Testament scholarship that a document's meaning is determined by
its purpose, and for that purpose to be real it must be seen
within a concrete life-setting?[26] Doesn't every writing (ancient
or modern) emerge from and address itself to a specific situation? Without being grounded in a "life-setting", don't the
documents of the New Testament become floating fragments, mot-
ivationless and purposeless productions of whose meaning we cannot be certain?

The objection touches on the heart of the matter. It raises
the difficult issue of how texts are to be read. I have no intention of getting into those murky waters. But even when we
grant the legitimacy of the classical historical-critical method
as such, which method uses the documents of the New Testament as
sources for the depiction of primitive Christianity, logic must
be observed. Certainly if, from other sources, a concrete life-
setting for a document is available, we would do wrong to neglect
it. But even in such a case, we could not facilely equate life-
setting, occasion, motivation, purpose and meaning. These aspects
of authorship are interrelated, to be sure; but they are not
identical, nor do they flow automatically from one to the other.
The possibilities are multiple.[27] With regard to the Gospels,
then, to agree that they emerge from a life-setting does not
allow us to conclude that the life-setting is determinative of
the document's meaning, either as a whole or in its parts. If

this is so, neither can we move directly from the concerns of
the text to its life-setting, or the attitudes of its readers.
Without the clear and unequivocal indication by the author in
his text, we cannot establish the connection between the presence of a particular motif and the stance of the readers. At
the most, we can learn something about the author's perception
of his readers' situation.

The Search for the Lukan Community

If the quest for the Pauline community is difficult, and
that for the communities behind the Synoptics suspect, how realistic are our expectations of finding the profile of a community
in a document like Luke-Acts, whose author we do not know, which
is addressed to an individual, not a church, and in which, of
all the documents of the New Testament, there are the clearest
marks of literary intention and artifice? If we take the Gospel prologue seriously as an indication of publication,[28] we
have a writing which proclaims its presentation to a larger
world than that defined by a particular community's concerns.
If we choose not to take this aspect of the prologue seriously,
how far are we able to go beyond the certainty that the audience
read Greek, very probably was already Christian, and possibly
knew something about the scriptures? What sort of connection
are we assuming between the author of Luke-Acts and a specific,
sociologically definable grouping? With what justification do
we see his text as mirroring that group's situation? It comes
down again to attaching the presence of a theme to the needs
of a hypothetical community.

For the sake of argument, let us suppose there was such a
community, and the author had as one of his purposes the instruction of this community in the demands of discipleship. It
need not be shown again that prayer was an important aspect of
discipleship for Luke.[29] But from what Luke says about prayer,
what can we learn about his readers' appreciation of it? Are
we to suppose that Luke stresses praying because his community
does not pray (or that some in the community are not praying)?
Or, are we to conclude that people are praying wrongly, and he
wishes to correct an incipient doxological heresy by providing
proper models of prayer? How specific should we get? By using
a special title in two of his prayers,[30] is Luke intending to
counter a theological tendency manifested by the use of other
divine titles in prayer?[31] But there are still other possibilities. There may be no problem with prayer at all. Perhaps
Luke emphasizes prayer as a way of congratulating his community
on its practice, or as a way of showing that its practice was
rooted in the example of Jesus and the first disciples.[32]

I may be accused of engaging in parody. But the importance
of teasing out the logical possibilities in a neutral case is
to stress the essential point. Even if, by redactional analysis,
we are able to arrive at one or the other of these possibilities, we are still only in contact with Luke's perception of
the community's needs, not the situation of the community as
such.[33] Certainly, if it were not for the popularity of the
assumptions governing so much redaction-criticism, a fair reading of the text would lead us to conclude that the motif of
prayer is important in Luke-Acts because of a) the strength of
the tradition concerning Jesus' own prayer, b) the tradition of
prayer among Christians , and c) Luke's appreciation of its

importance. In any case, the interpreter's first task is to take into account everything Luke has to say about prayer, not only by way of command, but also by way of modelling in the narrative, before suggesting that some tendency is being countered.[34]

The same logical possibilities are present for other themes in Luke-Acts, such as missionary images, almsgiving, and hospitality. Even if we grant that Luke's purpose was specifically to instruct a particular community concerning these ideals, we cannot automatically conclude that the practices or ideals being inculcated were either lacking or misunderstood within that community.[35]

But what is there about the text of Luke-Acts which leads us to think that such a particular, problem-centered instruction was the purpose for writing in the first place?[36] To say that the evangelists were teachers of the Church is one thing. To say that everything included in the Gospels was aimed at the problems of any particular community is something else altogether, and goes beyond the evidence. Quite apart from the influence of the tradition, and Luke's interest in writing a historical account,[37] there is every reason to believe that the composition of Luke's work was motivated above all by the demands of his overall literary and theological aims.[38]

The lesson learned from Romans should be applied to Luke-Acts. The more generalized and pervasive a motif, the less likely it is to be attached to a specific community stimulus, and this is particularly the case when it can be shown that a passage or motif serves a literary function. This is the biggest hurdle placed between the text of Luke-Acts and the discovery of a community. In Luke-Acts we should recognize that: a) the literary structure as a whole has meaning; that is, there is some correspondence between the author's intentions and the literary vehicle employed; b) individual elements within this structure have as their primary meaning a literary function (so that to treat them in isolation from this setting can distort the meaning of the text as surely as lifting Rom 1:30-31 out of context); and c) composition can be motivated as much by aesthetic or theological aims as by instructional or polemical ones.[39]

Given a fairly intricate and intelligible literary structure which, taken as a whole, conveys a coherent message, our first assumption with regard to individual parts within that structure should not be that they point to a specific community problem, but that they are in service to the larger literary goal of the author.[40] To put it simply, exegesis cannot forget the importance of literary context for the determination of meaning.[41]

By stressing the primacy of literary function, however, I am by no means sounding the call for a new methodology, or for the importation of alien literary critical methods to save the day. I simply want to remind myself and you of the elementary rules of our discipline, one of which demands the careful analysis both of structure and of content. Some studies which call themselves literary tend to move exclusively at the level of structure; some redactional studies exclusively at the level of content.[42] Both extremes point to a deficient appreciation of narrative as the vehicle of theological expression.[43]

Now, what is the literary context of Luke-Acts? Obviously, the two volumes taken together. Everyone agrees with this in principle, but the exegetical implications are not always appreciated. There are at least two important consequences of taking Luke-Acts as a literary unit. First, the redaction of Luke's Gospel vis-a-vis Mark or Matthew is not the sole or even the most important indicator of Luke's intentions. In Acts, Luke provides the first and authoritative interpretation of his Gospel story.[44] Whatever the legitimacy of moving from the narratives of Mark or Matthew to their respective communities, the same cannot be done in the case of Luke without considering all of his story. Not only does the further development of some motifs in Acts illuminate aspects of the third Gospel which are not obvious from synoptic comparison,[45] but the cessation or change of themes in Acts should caution against taking a synoptic comparison as definitive.[46] Second, the temptation to read the Gospels as cryptograms directed to the contemporaries of the evangelist is countered in Luke by the plain fact that the story of the first disciples continues in Acts, not only with elements of coninuity, but also of discontinuity. In Luke's writing, the past is really past. The story of Jesus and his first followers is significant for Luke's readers, but not as a direct mirror of their situation.[47]

What are some of the features of Luke-Acts as a literary work which should be attended to? First, that Luke-Acts taken as a whole, is a story.[48] It has a beginning and an end, and whatever the elements of circularity, the story is linear; things change and develop. The exegetical importance of this simple observation cannot be overemphasized. If this is a story, the reader must attend to the place in the story a passage occurs. Does a pericope or thematic statement serve a function which is appropriate here and only here in the story? Second, the story of Luke-Acts is carried by the main characters, who are uniformly presented by literary stereotyping, which is itself of first importance for grasping their significance. Third, the story line has a consistent pattern of acceptance and rejection; ignoring the placement of passages within this pattern can lead to misreading. Fourth, not only is Luke a theologian of the promise-fulfillment school; he makes fulfillment of prophecy a literary mechanism. The context of a pericope in Luke-Acts is established not only by what happens immediately before and after, but as well by the way a whole series of passages flow from and illuminate thematic (prophetic) statements within the narrative.

In another place, I tried to deal with the language about possessions within Luke-Acts, by placing it within the literary structure as I construe it. Whether or not my thesis regarding the symbolic function of possessions language within the story of the Prophet and the People is correct in every detail (and it would be surprising if it were), I maintain this kind of analysis is necessary before speaking of the economic state of Luke's community, or its use of possessions. It is necessary to notice, for example, where Luke talks about possessions, and in what connection.[49] Not all talk about possessions is really about possessions.[50] Still less is everything said about possessions intended to stand as a mandate to the Church.[51] Finally, there is no indication that the ideals concerning the use of possessions form some sort of subtle polemic against members of Luke's community.

The task of discovering the literary function of the diverse elements in Luke-Acts does not by itself preclude the possibility of ultimately finding out something about Luke's readers. But it obviously makes the enterprise more arduous. On the other hand, any search for the life-setting of this document which does not adequately take into account the context and function of passages and themes is likely to be arbitrary and superficial.[52]

The understanding of Luke's purpose which seems to do most justice to the literary form of his work as well as his expressed intention, is that he intended to write the continuation of the biblical story.[53] Certainly, the story he tells revolves around the acceptance and rejection of God's prophetic Christ by Israel, and the inclusion of the Gentiles among the "people for His name."[54] Although the characterization of Luke-Acts as a hellenistic biography is a step in the right direction, it should be noted that this is a story in which the fate of the people is as significant as the fate of the heroes.[55] Luke's readers probably were Gentile (or at least predominantly so). But it is not likely that some heretical tendency among these Gentile believers stimulated the writing of this work. The story is so vast and inclusive, the elements it contains so diverse, it seems more likely that it emerged from the author's contemplation of the theological mystery of God's faithfulness to His people. The problem, if you will, is one of theodicy. Within this understanding, Luke-Acts can be seen to function as a kind of aetiological myth for the Gentile Christian Church, in which Luke conveys to his readers how the People of God has come to be what it now is.

NOTES

[1] S. Brown, "The Role of the Prologues in Determining the Purpose of Luke-Acts," Perspectives on Luke-Acts ed. C.H. Talbert (Danville: Association of Baptist Professors of Religion, 1978) 108; (hereafter this volume cited as Perspectives). R.J. Karris, "Rich and Poor: The Lukan Sitz-im-Leben," Perspectives 112-125, and "Missionary Communities: A New Paradigm for the Study of Luke-Acts," CBQ 41 (1979) 80-97; C.H. Talbert, Literary Patterns, Theological Themes, and the Genre of Luke-Acts (Missoula: Scholars Press, 1974) 134-136; R. McDonnell, "Luke's Sitz-im-Leben: An Early Christian School," (Unpublished Paper for the CBA Luke-Acts Task Force, 1978).

[2] Cf. W.G. Kuemmel, Introduction to the New Testament rev.ed., tran. H. Kee (Nashville: Abingdon, 1975) 147-148. The recent attempt by J. Quinn to connect the Pastorals to Luke-Acts is imaginative and deserves attention. cf. "The Last Volume of Luke: The Relation of Luke-Acts to the Pastoral Epistles," Perspectives 62-75.

[3] The problem of terminology corresponds to the problem of definition. What sort of grouping is denoted by "community"? Among the possibilities: a) members of a household or household based Church; b) members of an intentional grouping such as a school; c) Christians of a particular city; d) Christians of a district or Province; e) the readers, generally. The wider the net is thrown, the more combinations of sociological factors are possible.

4 Whether there is a literary origin to this term I do not know. It has been part of the shorthand of the discipline since I began scripture studies.

5 By way of sample, A. Schlatter, Paulus der Bote Jesu 4th ed. (Stuttgart: Calwer Verlag, 1969) 11-46; W. Schmithals, Gnosticism in Corinth tran. J. Steely (Nashville: Abingdon, 1971) 117ff.; J. Munck, "The Church without Factions," Paul and the Salvation of Mankind tran. F. Clarke (Atlanta: John Knox, 1959) 135-167; H. Conzelmann, I Corinthians tran. J. Leitch (Philadelphia: Fortress, 1975) 14-16; N.A. Dahl, "Paul and the Church at Corinth according to I Corinthians 1:10-4:21," Studies in Paul (Minneapolis: Augsburg, 1977) 40-61;R.A. Horsley, "'How can some of you say that there is no resurrection of the dead,' Spiritual Elitism in Corinth," NovTest 20 (1978) 203-240. On the excesses of the mirror reading of II Corinthians, cf. C.J.A. Hickling, "Is the Second Epistle to the Corinthians a Source for Early Church History?" ZNW 66 (1975) 284-287.

6 "Die Rekonstruktion derselben ist eine wesentliche Aufgabe der Auslegung der beiden Korintherbriefe," H. Conzelmann, Der Erste Brief an die Korinther (Goettingen: Vandenhoeck & Ruprecht, 1969) 28.

7 Cf. G. Theissen, "Soziale Schichtung in der Korinthischen Gemeinde: ein Beitrag zur Soziologie des hellenistischen Urchristentums," ZNW 65 (1974) 232-272; A. Ehrhardt, "Social Problems of the Early Church," The Framework of the New Testament Stories (Cambridge: Harvard U. Press, 1964) 275-312; A.J. Malherbe, Social Aspects of Early Christianity (Baton Rouge: LSU Press, 1977) 71-91.

8 J.C. Hurd, The Origin of I Corinthians (London: SPCK, 1965) 114-209.

9 For Galatians, cf. J. Tyson, "Paul's Opponents in Galatia," NovTest 10 (1968) 241-254; R. Jewett, "The Agitators and the Galatian Congregation," NTS 17 (1970) 198-212; A.E. Harvey, "The Opposition of Paul," Studia Evangelica IV ed. F.L. Cross (Berlin: Akademie-Verlag, 1968) 319-332; R.McL. Wilson, "Gnostics--in Galatia?" ibid, 358-367. For Colossians, cf. F.O. Francis and W.A. Meeks, Conflict in Colossae (Missoula: Scholars Press, 1975).

10 H.D. Betz has illuminating remarks on the coherent literary structure of Galatians in the light of hellenistic rhetoric, despite its "occasional" nature, in "The Literary Composition and Function of Paul's Letter to the Galatians," NTS 21 (1975) 353-379.

11 Cf. The epilogue of Conflict at Colossae, 209-218.

12 H.W. Bartsch, "Die historische Situation des Roemerbriefes," Studia Evangelica IV, 281-291; E. Trocmé, "L'Epitre aux Romaines et le Méthode Missionaire de l'Apôtre Paul," NTS 7 (1960) 148-153; P. Minear, The Obedience of Faith (Naperville: A. Allenson, 1971) 1-35; K.P. Donfried, "False Presuppositions in the Study of Romans," CBQ 36 (1974) 332-355.

13 R.J. Karris, "Rom 14:1-15:13 and the Occasion of Romans," CBQ 35 (1973) 155-178, and "The Occasion of Romans: A Response to Professor Donfried," CBQ 36 (1974) 356-358; from the point of view of rhetorical analysis, W. Wuellner, "Paul's Rhetoric of Argumentation in Romans," CBQ 38 (1976) 330-351.

14 Karris, "Rom 14:1-15:13," 162ff; G. Bornkamm, Paul, tran. D. Stalker (New York: Harper and Row, 1971) 93-94; W.A. Meeks, The Writings of St. Paul (New York: W.W. Norton, 1972) 67-68.

15 On this now, cf. S.K. Stowers, A Critical Reassessment of Paul and the Diatribe: The Dialogical Element in Paul's Letter to the Romans (Unpublished Yale Dissertation, 1979) 233-249, 263-268, 270-275. On the basis of a thorough examination of the form and function of diatribal elements, Stowers argues convincingly that Romans should be read as "the self introduction of Paul as a teacher and preacher of the Gospel", and that the specific problems of the Roman community are not to be read out of the document.

16 Cf. the cautious remarks concerning the Thessalonian community in Malherbe's Social Aspects, 25-27.

17 Cf. J. Rohde, Rediscovering the Teaching of the Evangelists (Philadelphia: Westminster, 1968) 1-46; S. Simonsen, "Zur Frage der grundlegenden Problematik in form- und redaktionsgeschichtliche Evangeliensforschung," StudTheol 27 (1972) 1-23; R.H. Stein, "The Proper Methodology for Ascertaining a Markan Redaction History," NovTest 13 (1971) 181-198; P. Stuhlmacher, "Thesen zur Methodologie gegenwaertiger Exegese," ZNW 63 (1972) 18-26.

18 C.J.A. Hickling, "A Problem of Method in Gospel Research," RelStud 10 (1974) 339-346 (in review of Weeden).

19 However remote (but real) the influence of F.C. Baur, the debt these assumptions owe to W. Bauer's Orthodoxy and Heresy in Earliest Christianity ed. R. Kraft and G. Krodel (Philadelphia: Fortress, 1971) is clear, and is explicitly acknowledged in H. Koester's "GNOMAI DIAPHOROI, The Origin and Nature of Diversification in the History of Early Christianity," Trajectories Through Early Christianity (Philadelphia: Fortress, 1971) 114,n.1, and in E. Kaesemann's The Testament of Jesus tran. G. Krodel (Philadelphia: Fortress, 1968) 75, n.1.

20 "To some extent all of our canonical gospels are shaped so as to dispel a false image of the Savior and to provide a true one to follow," C.H. Talbert, What is a Gospel? (Philadelphia: Fortress, 1977) 98; cf. also his Literary Patterns, 114-119, and Luke and the Gnostics (Nashville: Abingdon, 1966) 15. The approach is rampant in the study of Mark. cf. T. Weeden, Mark--Traditions in Conflict (Philadelphia: Fortress, 1971); N. Perrin, What is Redaction Criticism? (Philadelphia: Fortress, 1969) 56; W. Kelber, The Kingdom in Mark (Philadelphia: Fortress, 1974) 144-147; E. Trocmé, The Formation of the Gospel according to Mark (Philadelphia: Westminster, 1975) 107ff.

21 Cf. W.A. Meeks, "Hypomnēmata from an Untamed Skeptic: A Response to George Kennedy," The Relationships among the Gospels: An Interdisciplinary Dialogue ed. W.O. Walker (Trinity U. Press, 1978) 162-163; Hickling, "A Problem of Method," 343.

[22] Despite the genuine contribution made by Talbert's What is a Gospel?, the case for the polemic function of "Type B" biographies has not convincingly been made. Talbert notes (94-95), "Other lives aim to dispel a false image of the teacher and to provide a true model to follow...in these lives material that had been used to discredit a teacher was often times taken up and neutralized by its inclusion in a new whole." But the slanders against Apollonius and Epicurus (to which Talbert alludes) are explicitly stated as such; they are not "neutralized" without being identified (cf. Philostratus' Life of Apollonius of Tyana I,2; I,13; IV,18; IV,26; IV, 43-44; V,33, 37,39; VII,4,17; and Diogenes Laertius, Lives of Eminent Philosophers X, 4-8. Furthermore, it is one thing to rebut slanders from without; it is another to polemicize against heterodox tendencies within a school by means of such materials. The latter is what Talbert is suggesting, but I do not find evidence for this function in the hellenistic biographies.

[23] Among others, cf. W.A. Meeks, "The Man from Heaven in Johannine Sectarianism," JBL 91 (1972) 44-72; J.C. Martyn, History and Theology in the Fourth Gospel rev.ed. (Nashville: Abingdon, 1979); R.E. Brown, "'Other Sheep not of this Fold': The Johannine Perspective on Christian Diversity in the Late First Century," JBL 97 (1978) 5-22, and The Community of the Beloved Disciple (New York: Paulist Press, 1979). For another, non-theological reading of the situation in III John, cf. A.J. Malherbe, "The Inhospitality of Diotrephes," God's Christ and His People ed. J. Jervell and W.A. Meeks (Oslo: Universitetsforlaget, 1977) 222-232.

[24] E. Trocmé, The Formation of the Gospel according to Mark, 120-137.

[25] R.J. Karris, "The Lukan Sitz-im-Leben: Methodology and Prospects," 1976 SBL Seminar Papers ed. G. MacRae (Missoula: Scholars Press, 1976) 226.

[26] R.J. Karris, "Missionary Communities," 96.

[27] Clearly, there are diverse possibilities at each level, even when there is a specific life-setting and occasion. Take, for example, the inaugural speech of A. Bartlett Giamatti to the Yale community in 1978. Knowing the setting and the situation does not tell us what his motivations were for giving the speech, or the purposes he wished to achieve. Even though his talk dealt at length with the "state of the university", moreover, the meaning of the speech derived less from some objective base of data on this, than from his own vision of the nature and task of a university in any time and place.

[28] H.J. Cadbury, The Making of Luke-Acts (New York: Macmillan Co., 1927) 194-204, and "Commentary on the Preface of Luke," The Beginnings of Christianity (London: Macmillan and Co., 1922) II, 490; H. Von Campenhausen, The Formation of the Christian Bible (London: Adam and Charles Black, 1972) 123-124; N.A. Dahl, "The Purpose of Luke-Acts," Jesus in the Memory of the Early Church (Minneapolis: Augsburg, 1976) 87.

[29] Cf. A. Trites, "The Prayer Motif in Luke-Acts," Perspectives 168-186.

[30] despotēs in Lk 2:29 and Acts 4:24.

[31] The vagaries of Christological critique by title can be illustrated for Lk 24:21 by J. Wanke, Die Emmauserzaehlung (Leipzig: St. Benno Verlag, 1973) 61 and 64; and for Lk 7:13 by H. Shuermann, Das Lukasevangelium (Freiburg: Herder, 1969) 403.

[32] Trites, 179.

[33] This is true as well, of course, for the Pauline letters; cf. Hickling, "II Corinthians" 285.

[34] As Trites does, 179-184.

[35] The same caution should obtain with regard to materials as pervasive as those dealing with persecution. Karris, "Missionary Communities," 84, says that Luke's readers were undergoing "persecution, harassment and distress," and seeks to find what might have come from Jews and what from Gentiles. He concludes that Luke "has given diverse answers to his persecuted Christian reader," (87). The problem here is that the motif of tribulations is at once so widespread in the New Testament writings, so stereotyped, and so attached to apocalyptic expressions, that it is very difficult to derive specific information about the kind of sufferings a particular community might be undergoing.

[36] Cf. the typically sane remarks of Dahl in "The Purpose of Luke-Acts," 93.

[37] Cf. W.C. van Unnik, "Once More St. Luke's Prologue," Essays on the Gospel of Luke and Acts (Neotestamentica 7; The New Testament Society of South Africa, 1973), 19.

[38] The assessment of P.Schubert, "The Structure and Significance of Luke 24," Neutestamentliche Studien fuer Rudolf Bultmann (Berlin: A. Toepelmann, 1954), 185, stands firm: "Luke is a littérateur of considerable skill and technique. His literary methods serve his theology as his theology serves them."

[39] The literary function of Lukan materials has been well recognized by Talbert, Literary Function 120, 136, and What is a Gospel, 11. I have two criticisms of his application. In my judgment, he tends to identify the unique in Luke's redaction with the important (cf. Literary Patterns 112-118); and he moves too quickly from the purported architectronic (literary) function to the theological (polemic) function, via the suggested function of certain biographies, ibid., 135.

[40] It is striking, for example, that Luke's parable of the pounds (Lk 19:11-27) is usually interpreted as a response to eschatological or messianic expectations, and rarely if ever seen as interpreting the narrative of Jesus' entry into Jerusalem. Cf. L.T. Johnson, The Literary Function of Possessions in Luke-Acts (Missoula: Scholars Press, 1977) 168-170.

[41] Cf. Talbert, What is a Gospel?, 11.

[42] For the first, cf.,e.g., R. Morgenthaler, Die lukanische Geschichtsschreibung als Zeugnis 2 Vols (Zuerich: Zwingli-Verlag, 1949) and M.D. Goulder, Type and History in Acts (London: SPCK, 1964); for the second, cf.,e.g.,

E. Franklin, Christ the Lord (Philadelphia: Westminster, 1975), and I.H. Marshall, Luke: Historian and Theologian (Exeter: Paternoster, 1970).

[43] Cf. H. Frei, The Eclipse of Biblical Narrative (New Haven: Yale U. Press, 1974).

[44] Here, I strongly disagree with the methodological preference of Talbert, Literary Patterns 121, n.10, concerning the determination of Lukan Christology, and agree with G.W.H. Lampe, "The Lucan Portrait of Christ," NTS 2 (1956) 160-175.Cf. Literary Function of Possessions,70-78.

[45] E.g.,the allusion to Deut 18:5f. in Luke 9:35 is made certain by the strength of the Mosaic imagery in Acts 3 and 7. cf. F. Gils, Jésus Prophète d'après les Evangiles Synoptiques (Louvain: Publications Universitaires, 1957) 36.

[46] E.g.,the perplexing Lukan view of the Pharisees. The recent article by J.H. Ziesler, "Luke and the Pharisees," NTS 25 (1979) 146-157, is helpful, but tends to soften the negative picture of the Pharisees in the Gospel, in favor of Acts' more positive shading.

[47] Although certainly not agreeing with Conzelmann's artificial epochal breakdown, nor with his view that the writing was stimulated by the issue of the delay of the parousia, I do agree with him that Luke "recognizes the uniqueness of the events of that time, and his picture of the early church is not meant to harmonize with the present, but stands in contrast. The characteristic summary statements about the life of the early community do not reflect present conditions, neither do they represent an ideal for the present," Theology of St. Luke tran. G. Buswell (London: Farber and Farber, 1960) 14-15. On the other hand, Talbert's suggestion that Acts 20:29-30 points to a conviction of the author that his generation "participates in post-apostolic decadence," goes too far, especially when used as a lens for detecting a Christological heresy combatted by the evangelist. Cf. Literary Patterns, 102, 119.

[48] For this and the following points, cf. Literary Function of Possessions in Luke-Acts, 9-126.

[49] Typically, Karris, "The Lukan Sitz-im-Leben," 116, ignores the differences between Acts 2:41-47 and 4:32-37. There are significant differences in the two accounts, which raise exegetical questions concerning the function of each passage in its context. Cf. Literary Function of Possessions, 9-12.

[50] The thematic statements concerning the rich and poor in Lk 4:18; 6:20,24; 7:22, 14:7-24 and their parabolic expression in 16:19-31 do not really have to do with the use of possessions, but serve a twofold literary and theological function: a) signalling the mission of the prophetic Messiah, and b) expressing the acceptance of the outcast and the rejection of the powerful. cf. J. Dupont, Les Béatitudes III, Les Evangelistes (Paris: J. Gabalda, 1973) 47-64, and Literary Function, 132-144. It should also be noted that passages which do not at first sight appear to be about the use of possessions nevertheless are important for Luke's understanding of

the power of possessions, e.g. Lk 15:11-32; 11:21-22; 9:10-
17; 12:41-48; 19:11-27; 17:22-33.

51 The inconsistency of Luke's teaching about possessions, when taken at the level of mandate, has led to such
attempts at reconciliation as H. Flender's St. Luke, Theologian
of Redemptive History tran.R. and I. Fuller (London: SPCK,
1970) 75-78, S. Brown's Apostasy and Perseverence in the Theology of Luke (Rome: Pontifical Biblical Institute, 1969) 100-
105, and H.-J. Degenhardt's Lukas Evangelist der Armen (Stuttgart: Katholisches Bibelwerk, 1965) 41,185. Failure to take
seriously the inconsistency mars Karris's "Lukan Sitz-im-
Leben". Let us, ex hypothesi, grant that Luke wanted to
present the ideal way for community leaders to handle possessions. We not only have the instructions of 9:3-4 and
10:4-7 revoked by 22:35-36; we also see members of the 12
standing at the head of the community of goods in Acts 4:32ff,
and handing over this duty to hellenistic missionaries in
6:1ff; then we see that Paul worked for a living (18:3, 20:34),
travelled with money (21:24, 24:36, 28:30), and recommended to
the   Ephesian Elders that they too work for the support
of others as he had done (20:35). Does Luke want the preach-
ers of Good News (the element which unites all these figures)
to be destitute itinerants, self-sufficient laborers,
supporters of others, or administrators of the community's
wealth? The lack of clear mandate makes us question whether
Luke is interested in the mandate, and forces us to consider
his language about possessions at another level.

52 Precisely the sort of genre studies of Talbert, and
the insights offered by works like E. Pluemacher's Lukas als
hellenistischer Schriftsteller (Goettingen: Vandenhoeck &
Ruprecht, 1972) are valuable is helping define the intellectual
milieu of Luke's writing. It is possible, furthermore, to
make at least plausible suggestions concerning the social
milieu from these analyses of literary level. Cf. Malherbe,
Social Aspects, 29-59. But this is not the same as doing a
mirror reading. Nor does it locate a "community" as such.

53 N.A. Dahl, "The Story of Abraham in Luke-Acts," Studies in Luke-Acts ed. L. Keck and J. Martyn (Nashville: Abingdon,
1966) 152-153, and "The Purpose of Luke-Acts," 88.

54 N.A. Dahl, "'A People for His Name' (Acts 15:14),"
NTS 4 (1957) 324-326; cf. also Literary Function of Possessions, 123, n.2.

55 This aspect of Luke's story has not adequately been
considered by Talbert. If Luke's writing can be considered
as a hellenistic biography, it can also be considered as the
work of a "minor hellenistic historian" (Dahl, "Purpose",88),
who tells not only of the founder and his successors, but also
of the formation of God's People.

THE FEEDING OF THE FIVE THOUSAND:
                A MARKAN COMPOSITION

                    Robert M. Fowler
              Yankton College, Yankton, SD

    When discussing the presence in both Mark and John of a
feeding story followed by a sea story (Mark 6:30-52; John 6:1-
21), the issue most often raised is the origin of the connection
between the two stories. Should we attribute the connection of
feeding story + sea story to a pre-gospel tradition that was
available to both Mark and John, or should we instead hold one
of the evangelists responsible for this connection? Of course,
once one begins to consider the possibility of a traditional
connection between two miracle stories, one finds oneself
moving into the more general discussion of the possibility of
pre-gospel miracle cycles or catenae. In my dissertation
("The Feeding Stories in the Gospel of Mark," University of
Chicago, 1978) I examined the question of pre-Markan miracle
cycles and more specifically the connection between the feeding
story + sea story in Mark. For my initial contribution to the
Mark-John discussion, I would like to share the results of this
work on the gospel of Mark. Interested readers are invited to
consult my dissertation for a fuller discussion of the points
raised below.

    After a careful examination of the literature one must
conclude that the attempts to recover pre-Markan miracle cycles
containing one or both of the feeding stories in Mark have not
succeeded. Many attempts to recover one or more pre-Markan
miracle cycles lying behind the present text of the gospel do
not employ a clearly stated methodology; they appear to be
based solely on an intuition that clusters of miracle stories
must have existed prior to the writing of the gospels. Other
attempts do employ a clearly stated methodology, but the
methodology is not employed consistently and rigorously. For
example, some scholars have noted the presence of particular
motifs in a number of miracle stories in Mark (Jesus portrayed
as a θεῖος ἀνήρ, the use of a boat, the motif of Jesus touch-
ing and being touched, etc.), and they have argued that a pre-
Markan miracle cycle may have been centered around or united by
one of these motifs. Invariably, however, there will be some
material left out of the reconstituted miracle cycle that also
contains the motif, but no good reason is ever given why some
material containing the motif is left out of the cycle, while
other material containing the motif is confidently placed within the cycle. The criterion that functions as the chief tool
in this case, i.e., the recurrence of a motif in several
stories, is not sufficiently exact for the task of isolating
pre-Markan cycles. Still other attempts to recover pre-Markan
cycles focus on the connections or seams between stories. Too
often one encounters the argument that if a connection between
two stories is smooth, unobtrusive, and graceful, then it must
be traditional. Unfortunately this is fallacious reasoning;
there is no reason why an evangelist must have been clumsy nor
any reason why his sources must have been artfully constructed.
Indeed, when one actually examines the vocabulary and syntax
of the connections between the miracle stories in Mark 4-8, one

                         101

often finds them to be full of Markan language and Markan
themes. They seem to be Markan in origin and not traditional.
Lastly, one should observe that even though many attempts to
recover pre-Markan miracle cycles are inspired by the doublet
problem in Mark 4-8 (i.e., "Why are there two feeding stories
in Mark?"), the doublet problem has never been adequately
explained by appeals to pre-Markan tradition. One need only
look at the ingenious suggestion by P. Achtemeier that the two,
parallel feeding stories are parallel climaxes of parallel
miracle catenae. This does not solve the doublet problem; it
only modifies the question into a new, even more intense,
formulation: "Why are there two, parallel miracle catenae?"
Again, as I assess the literature, I can only conclude that
the quest for pre-Markan miracle cycles has so far failed.

To this point I have been speaking rather generally of
pre-Markan miracle cycles. What can we say about the more
specific linkage between the feeding story + sea story in Mark?
It is important to observe that Mark 6:30-56 is a continuous
narrative in which the boat is present from beginning to end to
move the characters of the story from one location to another.
Such use of a boat to shift the scenery from one episode to the
next is a recurring Markan technique. The feeding story + sea
story in Mark is neatly bracketed by the second of three major
boat trips in Mark--Mark's use of the boat motif here makes
Mark 6:30-56 a carefully framed literary whole. (The three
boat trips in Mark, each of which consists of two parts, are
as follows: I. A. 4:1-2,35-36; 5:1-2; B. 5:18,21; 5:21; II. A.
6:32-33; 6:34-35; B. 6:45-47; 6:53-55; III. A. 8:9-10; 8:9-10;
B. 8:13-14; 8:22.) John also employs a boat in his version of
the feeding story + sea story, but this is the only place in
his gospel where the boat appears (outside of John 21), so its
sudden, unforeseen introduction into the story is somewhat
awkward, especially in the peculiar passage in John 6:22-24.
So the use of the boat in Mark 6:30-56 is both graceful and
typically Markan, while the use of the boat in John 6:1-24 is
somewhat less than graceful and not at all typical of John.

On the basis of this evidence alone, I would be inclined
to argue that Mark is the architect of the feeding story + sea
story connection. Even more importantly, however, a redaction-
critical examination of the two feeding stories in Mark reveals
that the Feeding of the Four Thousand (Mark 8:1-10) is largely
a traditional story inherited by Mark, but the Feeding of the
Five Thousand (Mark 6:30-44) is entirely a Markan composition
based on the model provided by the traditional story in Mark 8.
Except for a few redactional verses, Mark 8:1-10 is full of
non-Markan vocabulary and syntax. In particular, the striking
number of hapax legomena in this passage has often been noted;
the following are probably from Mark's source: προσμένω,
νῆστις, ἐκλύομαι, ἥκω, ἐρημία, περίσσευμα, μέρος (?),
Δαλμανουθά (?). Other non-Markan usages in Mark 8:1-10 include:
the use of ἀποκρίνομαι without λέγω, the use of χορτάζω instead
of ἐσθίω, and the use of ἐρωτάω instead of ἐπερωτάω. These
instances of non-Markan language are especially prominent in
Mark 8:3-6,8-9, indicating that Mark has preserved the wording
of his source with little modification. At the same time,
Markan redaction may be found in Mark 8:1-2,7,10 where the
following Markan characteristics predominate: the Markan

insertion technique, genitive absolute, πάλιν, the ὄχλος πολύς, ἔχω, προσκαλέομαι, the historical present, λέγω in introductory phrases, ἐπί and the accusative with σπλαγχνίζομαι, ἤδη, the boat motif, εὐθύς, fondness for diminutives, and εἶπεν followed by an infinitive with the sense of "to command." So Mark 8:3-6,8-9 is pre-Markan tradition with Markan redaction occurring in Mark 8:1-2,7,10. The vocabulary and syntax of Mark 6:30-44, on the other hand, is thoroughly Markan from beginning to end--this story is clearly a Markan composition. The familiar characteristics of the Markan literary style in 6:30-44 are as follows: συνάγω, naming Jesus in introductory phrases, πρὸς τὸν Ἰησοῦν/πρὸς αὐτόν, ἀπαγγέλλω, ὅσος with ποιέω, πᾶς/ὅλος, the historical present, λέγω in introductory phrases, δεῦτε, κατ' ἰδίαν, ἔρημος τόπος, parenthetical statement introduced with γάρ, ἔρχομαι and its compounds, ὑπάγω, the Markan insertion technique, ἐσθίω, impersonal plural, the boat motif, ἔχω, the teaching motif, ἄρχομαι auxiliary, adverbial πολλά, genitive absolute, ὅτι recitative, adversative δέ, κύκλῳ, ἀποκρίνομαι with a form of λέγω, εἶπεν with the sense of "to command," fondness for numbers, γινώσκω, ἐπιτάσσω, distributive doubling, series of three, ἀναβλέπω, and πλήρωμα. As a result of the discovery that the Feeding of the Five Thousand is a Markan composition, I am inclined to believe that Matthew, Luke, and John each borrowed the story from Mark's gospel. In the case of John, in particular, John alone preserves the mention of 200 denarii in Mark's story, thereby betraying dependence on the original Markan version of the story.

With regard to the significance of the feeding story + sea story, in Mark's gospel the focus is on the confrontation between Jesus and his disciples. Mark is intent on portraying the disciples negatively: "their hearts were hardened," he says (Mark 6:52). John, however, redeems the disciples; their peevish, callous nature in Mark's gospel is softened considerably by John. For example, spending 200 denarii on the crowd is no longer a matter of serious economic concern, as it is in Mark, but is now only a casually mentioned hypothetical situation. Also, John deflects attention away from the disciples to crowds who publicly witness and acclaim the feeding miracle and who also exercise their powers of observation and logic to infer that a sea miracle has occurred as well. Thus John is able to make a public event out of a private experience of the disciples in the middle of the lake.

If Mark is the author of the Feeding of the Five Thousand, then he is of course the first to link that story to the following sea story. But what of the doublet problem in Mark? What light can be shed on this perennial scholarly concern? I would like to suggest that the feeding story and the sea story are each one-half of a doublet in Mark, but when I use the word doublet I am not referring to variant versions of a single traditional story. Rather, in Mark 4-8 it is appropriate to use the term doublet to refer to two stories shaped and then put to use by the evangelist as a 'matched pair': a pair of stories that somehow must be regarded together as one reads the gospel. In Mark 4-8 there are three doublets in this sense of the word: the two sea stories (4:35-41; 6:45-52), the two feeding stories (6:30-44; 8:1-10), and the two healing stories

(7:31-37; 8:22-26). Each of these six individual stories is
somehow incomplete without its companion story. Furthermore,
each of these six stories is a dual miracle: 4:35-41 and 6:45-
52 both demonstrate Jesus' mastery over wind and sea; 6:30-44
and 8:1-10 both have to do with meals of bread and fish; 7:31-
37 describes the healing of a man who was deaf and dumb while
the companion story describes the healing of a blind man in
two distinct stages. "Duality" itself is a recurring Markan
characteristic (so F. Neirynck). More importantly, however,
there is major significance to the "duality" of these particular
cases, viz., in contradistinction to the men in Mark 7:31-37
and 8:22-26 who were given hearing, proper speech, and sight
by Jesus' double-touch, the 'double-touch' of two sea episodes
and two feeding episodes is not enough to give Jesus' own
disciples 'hearing,' 'proper speech,' and 'sight' (see Mark
8:14-21!).

In summary, Mark 6:30-44 is filled from beginning to end
with the characteristics of the Markan literary style--one can
only conclude that it is a Markan composition. Consequently,
the connection between feeding story + sea story is Markan as
well. The feeding story + sea story is bracketed by the
typically Markan use of the boat motif, the feeding story and
the sea story are each one-half of a 'matched pair' in Mark 4-8,
and both stories are dual miracles. As a result, Mark 6:30-56
functions as an integral part of Mark 4-8, and there is no
legitimate reason to manipulate or rearrange these chapters
into supposed pre-Markan miracle cycles. These chapters have
been carefully constructed by an author; they are not a jumble
of tradition. Since Mark is the author of the Feeding of the
Five Thousand and is the first to connect feeding story + sea
story, other occurrences of this narrative in other gospels
imply knowledge, direct or indirect, of Mark's gospel.

Mahlon H. Smith III, Rutgers College

0.0. The Marcan and Johannine accounts of the feeding of the
5000 and subsequent sea-crossing have enough structural and
verbal similarities to claim a single tradition behind both.
Those scholars who hold to the historical priority of Mark view
John's version of these incidents as a creative reconstruction
of the synoptic material (e.g., B.H. Streeter, Four Gospels,
pp. 395-426). C.H. Dodd, however, pointed to details in John
that reflect a pre-Marcan source (Historical Tradition, pp. 196-
217) and R. Bultmann (John, tr. p. 210) conceded as much.
Detailed comparison of the Johannine stories with parallel
synoptic passages reveals *John* to be a conservative reporter
and *Mark* the more original redactor.

1.0. The differences in dramatic detail between Johannine and
Marcan feeding accounts are redactionally significant. Mark's
editing is often evident in his version, whereas John as often
presents wording that clearly antedates his Gospel.

1.1. Mk. 6.37f claims *Jesus* responded to the *disciples'* concern
for food (6.35f) with instructions to use *their own* resources.
But Jn. 6.8f has *a disciple* react to *Jesus'* question (6.5) by
volunteering *someone else's* provisions. Mark's account reflects
his preoccupation with the disciples' lack of confidence and
understanding (cf. 8.4,14ff). But John's details -- apart from
the naming of Philip and Andrew, whom he mentioned earlier
(1.40ff) -- are unrelated to themes found elsewhere in his work.
The very fact that the fourth evangelist interjects a caution
not to interpret Jesus' question as a sign of ignorance (6.6)
shows that this detail is not a reworking of the Marcan material.

1.2. The structure and phrasing of Mark's feeding of the 4000
(8.1-9) echoes his own account of the feeding of the 5000. Yet
in three words Mark's second story is closer to John's single
account than to his own version of the same incident. Mk. 8.4
and Jn. 6.5 pose the question πόθεν can bread be found, while
Mk. 6.35ff makes the problem one of *who* is to fetch food. And
John's words for blessing (εὐχαριστήσας) and seating (ἀναπεσεῖν)
occur in Mk. 8.6 in place of the εὐλογησεν and ἀνακλιθῆναι of
Mk. 6.39,41. Otherwise the dramatic action of the two Marcan
stories is identical, while John differs from both. Since
Jn. 6.11 omits the *breaking* of bread it is not simply a conflation of the consecrations in Mark's accounts. Moreover, John
has Jesus give the loaves directly to the crowd, whereas Mark
presents the disciples as intermediaries (6.41, 8.6). Whatever
influence liturgical tradition may have had on Jn. 6, the wording of v.11 remains unrelated to other motifs in the Gospel.
For John interprets Jesus' role in the feeding not by stressing
his *agency* but by identifying him as the *matter* given by God
(6.32ff) and consumed by others (6.51ff). Mark's version, however, points up his claim (8.14-22) that the feedings carried
implications for the conduct of the apostolic mission. And the
terms Mark used for the consecration in 6.41 are those he later
attributed to Jesus at the last supper (14.22). But if the
liturgical action in Mark's version of the feeding of the 5000
reflects his editing, then its pre-Marcan wording may have been
closer to John's, which explains the Johannine words in Mk. 8.6.

1.3. Although Mark sets his feeding stories in the wilderness (6.31f,35; 8.4), he does not press parallels to Israel's Exodus tradition. Instead he prefers to stress an ambiguous pastoral motif. Mk. 6.34 may have been inspired by the choice of *Joshua* to lead the people lest they be "like sheep without a shepherd" (Num. 27.17). Yet the shepherd who *feeds* Israel was a standard symbol for the Davidic Messiah (Ezek. 34.23). But by stressing Jesus' compassion (6.34, 8.2) and order to *recline* on *green* grass (6.39), Mark associates Jesus with traditional descriptions of God himself (Ps. 23.1ff, 78.19,52; Ezek. 34.11ff). John's omission of these terms from his feeding story makes it unlikely that he was even remotely dependent upon Mark. For he would hardly have suppressed a motif that he developed elsewhere (cf. 10.11ff, 21.15ff). The fact that both Matthew and Luke also fail to echo Mk. 6.34 and do not mention the color of the grass indicates the the second Gospel does not always present the feeding of the 5000 as it was best known in the early Church.

1.4. Though John links the feeding of the 5000 to Passover (6.4) and manna (6.31ff) he does not set the incident in the ἔρημος. In fact, Exodus motifs are limited to peripheral details in both Johannine and Marcan feeding accounts. A better model for the structural elements of the story is 2 K. 4.42ff. For Jesus, like Elisha, was given literal bread, not a metaphorical substitute as Moses was (Ex. 16.4,15). Jesus and Elisha were each offered fewer loaves than were thought needed to feed the number present, while the manna was superabundant (16.8f). Jesus and Elisha gave skeptical associates instructions to distribute what was available, whereas Moses countered the people's own protest with orders to go out and gather for themselves (16.2f,16). But most importantly, the stories about Jesus and Elisha stress that some bread was left over. Exodus tradition, however, insisted that no surplus manna be gathered except when needed for the Sabbath (16.19ff). Since these parallels and discrepancies are integral to the outline of the story common to Mark and John, they are hardly the invention of either. Although John claims that the crowd recognized the incident as a sign that Jesus was a *prophet*, the context makes it clear that he took this to mean the figure modeled on Moses (Deut. 18.15ff). And Mark insists that to claim Jesus to be a prophet of any kind is inadequate (8.27-30). Yet the fact that both admit that this was Jesus' *popular* reputation makes it likely that the elements of the feeding story that identify Jesus with Elijah's successor reflect the purpose for which it was originally composed. If so, then two other details in John probably present the original better than Mark: the specification of the bread as *barley loaves* (6.9,13) and the identification of someone *outside* the prophet's circle as their source (6.9). For both increase the parallels with the Elisha saga.

2.0. At several points Matthew and Luke present material that resembles the feeding story in John rather than those in Mark. It is easier to account for these echoes with the theory that the later synoptics knew *both* Marcan *and* Johannine versions than to suppose that John drew details from all the synoptics only to retell the incident contradicting their combined witness regarding the plot.

2.1. Jn. 6.1-4 has only two words (ἀπῆλθεν and πολύς) found in Mark's introduction to the feeding of the 5000 (6.30-33) and has no verbal contact with Mark's preface to the feeding of the 4000 (8.1). Yet there is a striking similarity between these Johannine verses and Mtt. 15.29f (Dodd, p. 208f). Both authors say Jesus went εἰς τὸ ὄρος and ἐκάθητο ἐκεῖ *after leaving* the sea of Galilee. Mk. 7.31ff, however, has Jesus return *from* Phoenicia *to* the sea without reference to a mountaintop seat. And while Mark mentions a single healing in this context, Matthew like John talks of many. Since Matthew's account of the feeding of the 4000 is practically identical with Mark's it is striking that he should depart so much in the passage immediately preceding. Since there is no real connection between the healings and feeding in either Mark or Matthew, it is not likely that John borrowed the phrasing of Mtt. 15.29f to emend the synoptic setting for the feeding of the 5000. But it is quite possible that familiarity with a non-Marcan feeding story that began like Jn. 6.1-4 led Matthew to emend Mk. 7.31ff.

2.2. Mtt. 14.13 and Lk. 9.11 agree with Jn. 6.2 that the ὄχλος (pl. in synoptics) *followed* Jesus prior to the feeding of the 5000. Mk. 6.33 says instead that πολλοί knew his destination and *ran ahead*. This triple witness against Mark makes it difficult to hold his account to be the prime source of the others. Moreover, Mtt. 14.17 and Jn. 6.9 claim the disciples told Jesus they "have here" (ὧδε + form of ἔχω) πέντε ἄρτους καὶ δύο fish, hardly a coincidental elaboration of Mark's brief formula. Yet it is clear that John did not use Matthew as his prime source, since the latter omits the recommendation to *buy* bread for 200 denarii, common to John and Mark. Nor did John conflate the synoptic accounts, since his phrasing is independent of the elements they have in common. But Matthew's departures from Mark can be accounted for by presupposing Johannine influence.

2.3. Both Matthew and Mark present two feeding stories related to material in surrounding passages. Each frames the section with verses which raise the question of Jesus' identity (Mk.6.2f, Mtt. 13.54f) and others which give the answer (Mk. 8.27ff, Mtt. 16.13ff). But rather than link one to the other, the feeding accounts in the first two Gospels provide a mystifying interlude. Luke, however, recounts only the feeding of the 5000 (like John) and omits all contiguous material in the other synoptics except Herod's question (Lk.9.7ff, Mk. 6.14ff) and Peter's confession (Lk. 9.18ff, Mk. 8.27ff). Both passages concern Jesus' popular reputation as a prophet. But as neither Matthew nor Mark relate this motif to any feeding story, the inspiration for Luke's redaction must have come from another source. Since the Johannine account presents the feeding as a *sign* of Jesus' prophetic status, Luke likely knew this version.

2.4. Both Matthew and Mark end their feeding stories by noting the size of the crowd. Yet each has Jesus focus the disciples' attention on the amount of bread left over (Mk. 8.18ff, Mtt. 16.9ff). In Lk. 9.14 as in Jn. 6.10 the number of people is mentioned *prior* to the feeding as a point of contrast with the slight resources Jesus started with. Luke's transposition of this single detail in an account that is otherwise a paraphrase of his synoptic sources is striking evidence that the original denouement of the feeding was where John has it: the gathering of the 12 baskets.

3.0. Although the story of the sea-crossing probably originated independently, it clearly circulated as the sequel to the feeding of the 5000 prior to the composition of both Mark and John. While it makes for awkward transitions in both Gospels, John represents the elements that originally linked it to the feeding more faithfully than Mark.

3.1. Unlike the feeding of the 5000, the account of Jesus' appearance ἐπὶ τῆς θαλάσσης has few parallels to prophetic or Torah tradition. Israel's sea-crossing was regularly told in conjunction with the feeding in the wilderness, but as prelude rather than aftermath and with the *people* as well as Moses walking on *dry ground* (Ex. 14.16,22,29). And the latter condition is constant wherever Israel's sea-crossing is echoed in later tradition (Josh. 3.17, 2 K. 2.14, Ps. 106.9). Yet the fact that both Mark and John tell of the sea-crossing as the conclusion to the feeding of the 5000 even though it makes them delay their discussion of the motifs implicit in that event is sure evidence that for early Christians there was logical necessity not only to the conjunction but to the sequence of these two stories. Jn. 6.21 does provide a fit conclusion to Exodus motifs in the feeding by claiming that Jesus' presence brought the disciples ἐπὶ τῆς γῆς εἰς ἥν ὑπῆγον. Mark uses the first three of these words *at the beginning* of his story (6.47) to describe Jesus' solitary condition in contrast to the storm-tossed disciples. And, perhaps through clumsy editing, he has the incident take the disciples to a destination other than they intended (6.45,53). Instead of setting the disciples in the promised land, Mark has Jesus' presence still the storm but leave the boat at sea (6.51). The Marcan emphasis on the wind ceasing echoes the conclusion of the second Gospel's earlier account of a tumultuous passage (4.39). But the Marcan version obscures any thematic relationship between the feeding and the sea-crossing.

3.2. The focal point of both Marcan and Johannine versions of the sea-crossing is on Jesus' words: Fear not! ἐγώ εἰμι (Mk.6.50, Jn. 6.20). The clear purpose of this introductory formula is the identification of Jesus in terms traditionally associated with the *LORD and Deliverer* of Israel. While no historical paradigm for the evangelists' account is found in the OT, the situation presented by both Mark and John is strikingly close to that described in Ps. 107.23-30. But the Psalmist claims the LORD *both* stilled the storm *and* brought the sea-farers to their intended port. Thus it is possible that John and Mark independently preserve portions of the original sea-crossing narrative while omitting others. John emphasized the Exodus motifs that he was concerned with in this context, whereas Mark fastened on Jesus' power over cosmic forces. Yet Mark claims that the significance of the event was missed because the disciples failed to understand the feeding (6.52), which he himself associated with the wilderness tradition. Therefore, John's version of these two stories better presents their pre-recorded form than does Mark.

PETER'S DENIAL REEXAMINED:
          JOHN'S KNOWLEDGE OF MARK'S GOSPEL

Kim E. Dewey
Hamline University

    In an earlier article /1/, I argued that the denial story,
as found in Mk 14.53-54, 66-72, is a combination of both Markan
and non-Markan elements, such that the evangelist has taken a
simple one-denial story and amplified it into a story of three
denials. This same basic conclusion has been reached independently by several others recently. /2/ In my estimation, Mark
had a tradition containing the following points: Jesus is led
to the High Priest (14.53a), Peter follows into the courtyard
of the High Priest, sits with the guards and warms himself by
the fire (14.54); one of the maids of the High Priest confronts
Peter: "You were with Jesus," Peter denies: "I neither know nor
understand what you are saying," and then exits into the fore-
court (14.66b-68), where he remembers Jesus' prediction of denial and then weeps (14.72b,d and par.). The remainder of the
story in Mark is a product of that author's own hand.

    If this analysis is correct, the existence of a story of
three denials is attributable to Mark, and the fact that all of
the other gospels, including John, contain stories with three
denials is traceable ultimately to the influence of Mark, regardless of what differences between the four versions of the
story might exist. Indeed, there is some evidence to suggest
that the gospel of John reveals a knowledge of the Markan denial
story./3/

    To demonstrate a relationship between John and Mark a care-
ful methodology is required. In assessing the connection between John and Mark in the denial story, the following guidelines were used:
    1) Verbal agreements may indicate John's knowledge
        of Mark.
    2) Agreements in structure (e.g., sequence of events,
        details, setting, patterns) may indicate John's
        knowledge of Mark.
    3) We are on firmer ground when we can point to ver-
        bal and structural agreements between John and
        Mark which are absent from Matthew and Luke, thus
        eliminating the possibility of their intermediate
        influence.
    4) If it can be shown that those elements which John
        shares with Mark derive not from pre-Markan tra-
        dition but from Markan redaction or composition,
        the case for John's knowledge of Mark strengthens.
        However, in Markan studies, the burden of proof
        has gradually shifted to those claiming the exis-
        tence of pre-Markan tradition.
    5) It is important to acknowledge the creativity of
        each of the evangelists. Differences between
        gospels are not necessarily an argument for some
        independent source nor do they negate absolutely
        one gospel's knowledge of the other.

In light of these criteria, my analysis of the Markan denial story revealed a set of points which may indicate that John knows Mark's denial story.

1. <u>Both Mark and John intercalate a hearing story within the denial story.</u> Intercalation is recognized Markan technique./4/ Mark split the denial story and inserted within it the story of Jesus' hearing before the High Priest. The repetition of information from 14.54 in 14.66-67a reinforces the observation that this framing has taken place; the setting, broken by the insertion of the hearing story, is reestablished. I am aware of Fortna's /5/ criticism that because both hearing and denial are set in the High Priest's courtyard, "it <u>seems</u> predictable that as soon as traditions were gathered into larger continuous narratives, and possibly earlier, these two would have been joined together because of their common locale." However, Fortna misses the point. What betrays the hand of Mark is not the juxtaposition of stories with a common locale, but precisely the <u>act of intercalating</u> the two stories. Note that while Matthew (26.57-75) follows Mark's pattern, Luke (22.54-71) dismantles it, presenting first the complete denial story and then the hearing. The fact that John follows the pattern (18.15-27) suggests a knowledge of Mark (or perhaps Matthew). The sharing of this structural element remains true even though John inserts the hearing at a slightly different point in the denial story.

2. <u>Both Mark and John frame the hearing story with references to Peter's warming himself (Mk 14.54,67/Jn 18.18,25).</u> This is a second structural element which builds upon the intercalation. Fortna /6/ states that this parallel between John and Mark "<u>seem(s)</u> as likely to be accidental as due to any dependence." On the contrary, there would seem to be little liklihood that the double reference to Peter's warming himself which frames the hearing story in each gospel would be accidental. Such a parallel seems very deliberate. The recognition that both Luke and Matthew eliminate completely the references points up how deliberate the retention of those references must be in John. Particularly telling in demonstrating John's knowledge of Mark is Jn 18.18 which uniquely among the gospels reports that the servants and guards were warming themselves and then in somewhat redundant fashion goes on to state that Peter was warming himself. Why? The redundancy occurs precisely where John moves to follow the pattern of framing the hearing with references to Peter's warming himself.

3. <u>Both Mark and John use the term thermainomenos.</u> This verbal agreement gives additional weight to the deliberateness of the structural agreement discussed above. The persuasiveness of this observation is greater in light of the fact that neither Matthew nor Luke ever use this term, nor do Mark and John use it outside of these verses. I have argued that Mark's use of this term reflects both tradition (14.54) and redaction (14.67). Therefore, John's use of the term indicates a knowledge of Markan redaction.

4. <u>Both Mark and John have one stage in the story where Peter's denial has no direct discourse.</u> Mark's second denial (14.70) and John's third denial (18.27) both simply state that he denied. While this element may not seem to have the significance of the others, it is nevertheless a structural element

that the two gospels have in common and an element that is due
to Markan redaction. Moreover, as with the other points above,
both Matthew and Luke diverge by reporting direct discourse in
all three denials. Again, Fortna's comment that this "seem(s)
as likely to be accidental as due to any dependence," seems an
inadequate treatment of this item. What is curious is that
only Mark and John share this point.

These four points, /7/ along with some minor verbal agreements, /8/ provide some evidence for a knowledge of Mark on the
part of John. The point in isolating these particular items is
not to establish that John is a carbon copy of Mark, but to
show that in the midst of similarities and differences between
these two versions of the denial story there are clues of an
influence of Mark upon John. How this influence is finally
conceived is open to a number of options, from a direct dependence of John upon Mark to the existence of a post-Markan oral
tradition influenced by the Markan text, and so on. Obviously,
the discussion above does not attempt to deal with Markan redactional elements that John does not have, nor with outright
differences, but a sensitivity toward authorial creativity
ought to be taken into account in assessing these differences.

The fact that there is a "complex mixture of parallels and
differences between John and Mark in the denials"/9/ points
also perhaps to Johannine redactional activity incorrectly perceived in John's denial story and perhaps an overly eager
desire to assign material to a source. It is not clear that it
is necessary to argue for "parallel but distinct traditions" to
account for the similarities and differences between the two
denial stories.

What is clear is that any resolution of the question of
the relationship between John and Mark will only be forthcoming
when the methodologies of both source and redaction critics can
be assessed, but even more so the presuppositions which guide
them.

112

/1/ "Peter's Curse and Cursed Peter," in The Passion in
Mark, ed. Werner Kelber (Philadelphia: Fortress Press,
1976) 96-114.

/2/ Wolfgang Schenk, Der Passionsbericht nach Markus
(Gütersloh: Gerd Mohn, 1974) 215-223; Detlev Dormeyer,
Die Passion Jesu als Verhaltensmodell, NTAbh,n.f. 11
(Münster: Aschendorff, 1974) 150-157.

/3/ Robert T. Fortna, "Jesus and Peter at the High Priest's
House: A Test Case for the Question of the Relation
Between Mark's and John's Gospels," NTS 24 (1978) 378:
Fortna states, "The threefold scheme seems to me more
probably the product of developing tradition, or of
pre-Markan redaction." He offers nothing, however, to
refute my arguments that in fact Mark has created the
threefold denial story. (First italics mine)

/4/ See the references for this in Dewey, p. 97 n.2

/5/ Fortna, p. 373. Italics mine.

/6/ Fortna, p. 378. Italics mine.

/7/ I do not discuss two other elements produced by Markan
redaction, the cockcrow and the triple denial (see n.3),
because they are shared by all four gospels and thus do
not present a clear case of John's knowledge of Mark.
Fortna's (p.378) belief that cockcrow was an original
part of the denial story does not necessarily follow
from his observation that cockcrow is a basic element
in the denial saying. I am also not persuaded by his
(p.373) argument that Mk 14.26-31 is "clearly pre-Markan" or that it seems dependent on the prior (and therefore traditional) connection of stories of the disciples'
flight, the arrest and the denial. Is Fortna observing
the chronological relationship between these units or
rather the literary relationship between them in the
narrative? Mk 14.26-31 is not evidence for a pre-Markan
connection of flight,arrest and denial, but for the
Markan connection of them.   One methodological point
that deserves discussion is the apparent assumption
that a rough or clumsy text indicates redaction or the
combining of sources, while a smooth text does not (see
Fortna 379 n.2 for example). And a second point: how is
the author viewed (mechanic or artist) and how is the
text perceived (mechanism or literary creation); is it
correct to speak of a "wooden repetition" (Fortna,379;
my italics) for example? Methodological implications
flow from our choice of assumptions.

/8/ E.g., Mk 14.66-67: "one of the maids of the High Priest
says (legei) to him (Peter)," and Jn 18.17,26; Mk 14.54:
eis tēn aulēn tou archiereōs, and Jn 18.15 (cf.Lk 22.54,
55 and Mt 26.58); use of hypēretēs in Jn 18.18, Mk
14.54, Mt 26.58, but missing in Luke.

/9/ Fortna, p.382

S 38 THE CLEANSING OF THE TEMPLE AND THE ANOINTING AT BETHANY:
THE ORDER OF EVENTS IN MARK 11/JOHN 11-12

Edward F. Glusman, Jr.

Hammond, LA

When Raymond Brown divided his Anchor Bible commentary on
the Gospel according to John into two volumes, he chose to
treat Jn. 1-12 as the Book of Signs and Jn. 13-21 as the Book
of Glory. This division recognizes a structural feature
shared by the Fourth Gospel with the Second, viz., that the
latter part of both is esoteric, dealing with the community of
disciples and the passion, in contrast to the earlier public
ministry. The shift from ministry to passion as Jesus moves
from Galilee to Jerusalem is consistent with the kerygmatic
formulations preserved in Acts and Paul, and it is significant
that John, which does not preserve the Galilee to Jerusalem
movement at this point, nevertheless shares with Mark this
change in point of view. At this same general stage in their
gospels, Mark and John share one specific episode and perhaps
two others. The triumphal entry occurs at precisely the same
point in the chronology of both gospels. But it is preceded
in John by the anointing at Bethany, which Mark places later
in Jesus' last week, and it is followed in Mark by the cleansing of the temple, which John, of course, places at the beginning of the ministry. With these events and their order we
propose to deal.

These three episodes present a multitude of difficulties
to the attempt to elucidate the literary relationship between
Mark and John. The triumphal entry is the only one which appears at the same point in both gospels, yet it provides the
smallest number of parallels. Clearly the evangelists deal
with the same events, but the context and details vary widely.
Indeed, other than in the quotations from the Old Testament,
there is really little agreement between John and any of the
synoptics. The situation is much the same in the temple-
cleansing, where the list of verbal agreements is almost invisible, and consists mostly of words or phrases without which
the story could not be told. Differences are numerous.

The anointing at Bethany, on the other hand, provides
some striking verbal agreements between Mark and John, agreements which are really unique among all the parallel material.
These have caused C. K. Barrett and others to conclude that
John is here drawing on Mark as a source. The difficulty with
this position is that in the description of the woman's action
John reproduces the language and action of Luke at least as
closely as that of Mark. Yet Luke's story is that of a woman
with a notorious past, whose sins are now forgiven. Is it
likely that John would compose with Mark and Luke before him,
lifting phrases now from one now from the other? And can John
have transferred the action of Luke's sinner to a character of
whom such a past is never suggested elsewhere, all in the context of a Markan story with an entirely different point?

Brown, following P. Benoit, has suggested that there
were two anointing stories in pre-gospel tradition, one by a
penitent in Galilee with tears on the feet, one by Mary of
Bethany with perfume on the head. The two became easily confused in the oral stage of the tradition. Anointing the feet
is really unparalleled, and Luke's account has mixed details
of the two incidents. John's narrative, then, is a thorough
blend, a version of the second incident overlayed with details
from the same traditional strand as the Lukan form. Brown observes that the omission of tears in John forces the transfer
of the action of wiping to the perfume, an unlikely detail,
and that the letting down of hair to accomplish this is inap-
propriate for the virtuous Mary of Bethany. Cross-contamina-
tion at the oral stage is suggested.[1] This confusion, however,
permits us to focus more or less clearly on what the account
John knew was like. It may have resembled Mark in suggesting
a burial rite, but it cannot have been Mark's account itself.
In the Johannine source, the feet were anointed and dried with
the hair.

The complexity of the verbal parallels and their interpretation makes it quite difficult to support on the basis of
their evidence any particular hypothesis about the Mark-John
relationship. But the considerable differences in the order
of events between the two gospels suggests that the investigation of sequence may provide additional data, and it is to
this study we now turn.

As we have already seen, the story of Jesus' anointing
had a long complex literary history before its inclusion in
the Fourth Gospel, apparently circulating independently in
several quite different versions. This makes it difficult indeed to recover its original place in a traditional sequence
of events, if it ever appeared there at all. There is reason
to doubt that either Mark or John found the story in its present location. As Fortna observes, the Markan location is con-
trived, interrupting what precedes and follows it, and involv-
ing a sudden shift of locale to Bethany. In fact, Mark records a number of trips to Bethany in this period, prior to
the entry (11:1; cf. Jn. 12:12, where the entry is also from
Bethany) and after it (11:11), probably after the cleansing
(11:19), and before the last supper, when the anointing occurs
(14:3).[2] John's account, on the other hand, shows signs of
having circulated more freely in the tradition than Mark's,
and, while this does not necessarily mean the Johannine order
is unreliable, it is prima facie evidence that the story was
not fixed in the Johannine tradition. Theologically, the
story fits equally well in either location: in Mark, it provides a prelude to the breaking of Jesus' body at the last
supper; in John, as Barrett remarks, "It is as anointed king
that Jesus rides into Jerusalem, and as anointed king that he
dies...."[3] The literary evidence is inconclusive, and it may
be that we cannot be sure of the incident's precise location.
But the Lukan version of the story (7:36-50) establishes that
it is not necessarily tied to passion week, and the fact that
both Mark and John employ it in this context suggests at least
that it was so associated in their tradition, if not in a common traditional outline of events.

The chronology of the temple-cleansing remains a problem. Those who support the Johannine dating point out the synoptics, with only one journey to Jerusalem, have nowhere else to place the story, while the mention of the Baptist in Mark 11:30parr. and the difficulty of the witnesses at the trial in recalling Jesus' words both suggest a location for Jesus' statements in the early portions of his ministry. Others, arguing for the synoptic dating, point out that such an act would have forced the hand of the authorities, who in the synoptics put Jesus quickly to death. In John, however, he continues to function for at least two more years. Further, to be in a position to act in the temple precincts, Jesus had to have a substantial following and status, which is far more consistent with the synoptic timing.

The problem is similar in some respects to that of the anointing. On literary grounds the account does not seem firmly fixed in either its Markan or Johannine setting. As we observed in connection with the anointing, the Markan framework in ch. 11 appears forced, if not actually artificial, and there is no real connection between the triumphal entry and the cleansing of the temple, separated as they are by a night in Bethany and the cursing of the fig tree. But it should be noted that if the cursing of the fig tree and its sequel (11:12-14, 20-25) were removed from Mark, a coherent narrative would remain,[4] so it is difficult to be sure whether Mark's tradition connected the two events. The story is even more intrusive in its Johannine context, with the abrupt change of locale in 2:13 required to begin it and the Johannine summary of 2:23-25 following. But even in John the Passover connection of the synoptic accounts is preserved.

Once again, it may be that certainty is beyond us. A possible reconstruction of all the material we have been discussing, however, is suggested by certain features of Jn. 11-12. Brown notes the many Johannine characteristics that abound in this section: The presence of Thomas, Philip, and Andrew; an "I am" saying in 11:25; Johannine misunderstanding in 11:11-14; "lifted up" in 12:32; etc. The phrase "the Jews," which appears here at 11:19, 31, 33, 36, 45 and 12:9, 11, is not used polemically as earlier in the Gospel, but refers to the people of Judea and Jerusalem. Further, the present location of the Lazarus miracle makes the sequence of events difficult, requiring that Jesus move from the Transjordan (10:40) to Bethany, thence to Ephraim (11:54), again to Bethany (12:1), and, after a single day in Jerusalem, into hiding (12:36b). Brown concludes that ch. 11-12 were not an original part of the plan of the Fourth Gospel, but were added to a gospel that moved directly from 10:42 to 13:1.[5] But Brown's observations in fact apply not to ch. 11-12 as a whole, but only to the Lazarus material in these chapters (11:1-44; 12:1c, 2b, 9-11) and to the story of the Greeks who wanted to see Jesus and its accompanying discourse (12:20-50). In the traditional material--the anointing and the triumphal entry--we see none of the Johannine characteristics noted by Brown. Since all of the problems in sequence arise from the Lazarus material, it appears that John has added the accounts of Lazarus and the Greeks to an already existing sequence.

116

If so, it may well be, as Fortna proposes, that the
Lazarus miracle has displaced the cleansing of the temple in
the Johannine narrative, with the former now serving to prepare for the passion narrative:

> Mark's rearrangement then would be the result of
> his natural wish to make the entry the culmination
> of Jesus' journey from Galilee up to Jerusalem;
> the two episodes which...originally preceded it
> (temple cleansing and anointing) are postponed,
> the one coming soon after the entry, the other in-
> serted into the account of the passion proper.[6]

In John's tradition as well, the cleansing of the temple would
have come at the present location of the Lazarus pericope,
serving, with the anointing and the entry which followed it,
as a prelude to the passion.

What are the implications of this reconstruction for the
Mark-John relationship? To begin with, the order of events in
John's Gospel makes it quite problematical to defend his dependence on Mark. If John removed Mark's anointing from passion week, it can only have been for the purpose of making of
Mark's burial rite a royal chrismation, yet there is no trace
of this theology in the Johannine pericope. And why, if such
were his intent, would he import narrative details from Luke
(or a Luke-like account)? It appears far more likely that
John placed the anointing where he found it in his tradition,
immediately preceding the triumphal entry. If this sequence
began with the temple-cleansing, now displaced by the Lazarus
material, a traditional chronology is suggested which also
makes sense in Mark.

Such a reconstruction must of necessity remain hypothetical, especially in light of the probability that both the
cleansing of the temple and the anointing circulated more or
less independently. It does appear, however, to fit the evidence, and to explain why the events seem more or less intrusive in their present contexts, yet are associated by both
gospels with each other. Should John be aware of a pre-Markan
sequence of events, of course, the possibility of Johannine
dependence on Mark is excluded at this point.

NOTES

1: Raymond E. Brown, The Gospel according to John, The
Anchor Bible (Garden City, N. Y.: Doubleday & Company, Inc.,
1966-70), 29:450-52.

2: Robert T. Fortna, The Gospel of Signs, SNTS
Monograph Series, 11 (Cambridge: Cambridge University Press,
1970), p. 152.

3: C. K. Barrett, The Gospel according to St. John
(London: S.P.C.K., 1967), p. 341.

4:   Cf. Ivor Buse, "The Cleansing of the Temple in the Synoptics and in John," ET 70(1958-59):22-24 and Joachim Jeremias, The Eucharistic Words of Jesus, trans. Arnold Ehrhardt (New York: The Macmillan Company, 1955), pp. 62-63.

5:   Brown, Gospel, 29:427-28. Brown also observes that the synoptics know nothing of the Lazarus miracle, which could scarcely be the case if the incident actually occurred in its Johannine location.

6:   Fortna, Gospel of Signs, p. 147, n. 1.

EVIDENCE FROM JN. 12 THAT THE AUTHOR OF JOHN KNEW THE GOSPEL OF MARK

Lloyd R. Kittlaus
Dolton, Illinois

The reader of Jn. 12 who is familiar with the gospel of Mark will notice, as he reads, that this chapter in John contains parallels to materials which are to be found in various parts of our second gospel.

The following chart attempts specifically and succinctly to identify the parallel elements and to indicate their most important similarities and differences.

JOHN	MARK
11:55-57 <u>narrator's summary</u> Passover near chief priests & Pharisees seek information leading to Jesus' arrest they want an informant on his whereabouts (v. 57)	**14:1-2** <u>narrator's summary</u> two days before Passover chief priests & scribes seek to arrest Jesus secretly (see Judas' offer of betrayal in vv. 10-11)
12:1-8 <u>anointing story</u> six days before Passover Bethany, where Lazarus was house of Lazarus, Martha, & Mary (?) Lazarus is present and witnesses the anointing Mary is the anointer; with a λίτραν μύρου νάρδου πιστικῆς πολυτίμου she anoints Jesus' feet (v. 3) Judas Iscariot, the betrayer questions her use of the ointment: Διὰ τί τοῦτο τὸ μύρον οὐκ ἐπράθη τριακοσίων δηναρίων καὶ ἐδόθη πτωχοῖς; (vv. 4-5) the narrator explains: Judas is a thief who regularly steals from the money-box Jesus: Ἄφες αὐτήν, ἵνα εἰς τὴν ἡμέραν τοῦ ἐνταφιασμοῦ μου τηρήσῃ αὐτό· τοὺς πτωχοὺς γὰρ πάντοτε ἔχετε μεθ' ἑαυτῶν, ἐμὲ δὲ οὐ πάντοτε ἔχετε. (vv. 7-8)	**14:3-9** <u>anointing story</u> Bethany house of Simon the leper a woman is the anointer; with an ἀλάβαστρον μύρου νάρδου πιστικῆς πολυτελοῦς she anoints Jesus' head (v. 3) some unnamed persons raise the same question: Εἰς τί ἡ ἀπώλεια αὕτη τοῦ μύρου γέγονεν; ἠδύνατο γὰρ τοῦτο τὸ μύρον πραθῆναι ἐπάνω δηναρίων τριακοσίων καὶ δοθῆναι τοῖς πτωχοῖς· . . . (vv. 4-5) (see the reference to Judas in vv. 10-11) Jesus: Ἄφετε αὐτήν· . . . (v. 6) . . . προέλαβεν μυρίσαι τὸ σῶμά μου εἰς τὸν ἐνταφιασμόν. (v. 8) πάντοτε γὰρ τοὺς πτωχοὺς ἔχετε μεθ' ἑαυτῶν, . . . ἐμὲ δὲ οὐ πάντοτε ἔχετε. (v. 7)
12:9-11 <u>narrator's summary</u> crowds came to see Lazarus, as well as Jesus; therefore, the chief priests plan to kill Lazarus too	**14:10-11** <u>narrator's summary</u> Judas Iscariot went to the chief priests to betray Jesus; they promised him money

120

12:12-19 entry into Jerusalem
ʽΩσαννά· εὐλογημένος ὁ ἐρχόμενος
ἐν ὀνόματι κυρίου, . . . (v.
13)
Jesus found an ὀνάριον
(εὑρίσκειν, v. 14)
one crowd had been with Jesus
when he raised Lazarus; the
other went to meet him on
account of this sign (vv.
17-19)

11:1-11 entry into Jerusalem
two disciples are sent to
find a πῶλος, and they do
(εὑρίσκειν, vv. 2, 4)
ʽΩσαννά· εὐλογημένος ὁ ἐρχόμενος
ἐν ὀνόματι κυρίου· . . . (v. 9)

12:20-36a the coming of
Jesus' hour
Ἐλήλυθεν ἡ ὥρα ἵνα δοξασθῇ ὁ υἱὸς
τοῦ ἀνθρώπου. (v. 23)
metaphorical reference to
the necessity of Jesus'
death
discipleship sayings: ὁ φιλῶν
τὴν ψυχὴν αὐτοῦ ἀπολλύει αὐτήν,
καὶ ὁ μισῶν τὴν ψυχὴν αὐτοῦ ἐν
τῷ κόσμῳ τούτῳ εἰς ζωὴν αἰώνιον
φυλάξει αὐτήν. (v. 25)
ἐὰν ἐμοί τις διακονῇ, ἐμοὶ
ἀκολουθείτω, . . . (v. 26)

cf. 14:41: . . . ἦλθεν ἡ ὥρα, ἰδοὺ
παραδίδοται ὁ υἱὸς τοῦ ἀνθρώπου . .
(cf. 8:31)

cf. 8:35: ὃς γὰρ ἐὰν θέλῃ τὴν
ψυχὴν αὐτοῦ σῶσαι ἀπολέσει αὐτήν·
ὃς δ' ἂν ἀπολέσει τὴν ψυχὴν αὐτοῦ
ἕνεκεν ἐμοῦ καὶ τοῦ εὐαγγελίου
σώσει αὐτήν.
cf. 8:34: Εἴ τις θέλει ὀπίσω μου
ἀκολουθεῖν, ἀπαρνησάσθω ἑαυτὸν
καὶ ἀράτω τὸν σταυρὸν αὐτοῦ καὶ
ἀκολουθείτω μοι. (cf. also 15:
41)

Νῦν ἡ ψυχή μου τετάρακται.

καὶ τί εἴπω; Πάτερ, σῶσόν με
ἐκ τῆς ὥρας ταύτης; ἀλλὰ διὰ
τοῦτο ἦλθον εἰς τὴν ὥραν ταύτην.
(v. 27)
crowd: . . . καὶ πῶς λέγεις σὺ
ὅτι δεῖ ὑψωθῆναι τὸν υἱὸν τοῦ
ἀνθρώπου; . . . (v. 34--the
question recalls Jesus'
statement in 3:14)

cf. 14:34: Περίλυπός ἐστιν ἡ ψυχή
μου ἕως θανάτου· . . .
cf. 14:36: Αββα ὁ πατήρ, πάντα
δυνατά σοι· παρένεγκε τὸ ποτήριον
τοῦτο ἀπ' ἐμοῦ· ἀλλ' οὐ τί ἐγὼ
θέλω ἀλλὰ τί σύ.
cf. 8:31: . . . δεῖ τὸν υἱὸν
τοῦ ἀνθρώπου πολλὰ παθεῖν καὶ
ἀποδοκιμασθῆναι . . . .

12:36b-50 conclusion of Jesus'
public ministry & evaluation
of the response to him
Jesus hid himself (v. 36b)

free quotation of Isa. 6:9-
10 (v. 40)
the narrator's conclusion:
the public has rejected
Jesus (vv. 37, 48)
Jesus: ὁ ἀθετῶν ἐμὲ καὶ μὴ
λαμβάνων τὰ ῥήματά μου ἔχει τὸν
κρίνοντα αὐτόν· ὁ λόγος ὃν
ἐλάλησα ἐκεῖνος κρινεῖ αὐτὸν ἐν
τῇ ἐσχάτῃ ἡμέρα· . . . (v.
48)

cf. 4:11-12: Jesus' teaching in
parables hides the kingdom of
God
cf. 4:12: adaptation of Isa.
6:9-10
cf. 4:11-12: the Markan Jesus'
forecast: outsiders will not
understand the kingdom
cf. 8:38: ὃς γὰρ ἐὰν ἐπαισχυνθῇ με
καὶ τοὺς ἐμοὺς λόγους ἐν τῇ γενεᾷ
ταύτῃ τῇ μοιχαλίδι καὶ ἁμαρτωλῷ,
καὶ ὁ υἱὸς τοῦ ἀνθρώπου ἐπαισχυν-
θήσεται αὐτὸν ὅταν ἔλθῃ ἐν τῇ δόξῃ
τοῦ πατρὸς αὐτοῦ μετὰ τῶν ἀγγέλων
τῶν ἁγίων.

For the reasons to be set forth below, the most probable explanation of the parallels just identified is that the author of John knew the gospel of Mark.

The evidence which points the most clearly toward this conclusion is the extended parallel with which the chart opens, the one which includes not only the anointing stories, but also their respective frames. In the first place, the close correspondence of the second halves of the anointing stories shows that they are the same story. From the point of the disapproving question asked of the anointer through Jesus' rebuke of her questioner(s), the Johannine and the Markan stories exhibit much the same thoughts, expressed in much the same language. This considerable correspondence also rules out an exclusive relation between the Johannine and the Lukan anointings, for the latter story (7:36-50) takes a very different turn right after the act of anointing and from v. 39 onward, no longer corresponds to the story found both in Mark and in John. By contrast, the Matthean story (26:6-13) does exhibit the correspondence with the Johannine, for it closely follows the story in Mark. Nevertheless, that the relationship is between the Johannine and the Markan stories is indicated by two close verbal parallels which only these two share, viz., (1) their similar descriptions of the ointment and (2) their common assessments of its value at or near three hundred denarii.

The decisive factor, however, is the inclusion of the respective frames in this parallel. Their inclusion has three main implications. First, it further rules out an exclusive relation between the Johannine and the Lukan stories, for the latter is set relatively early in Luke's gospel and is not framed by references to the plot against Jesus. Secondly, the inclusion of the frames renders unlikely another alternative suggestion, viz., that the extensive parallelism in our anointing stories is to be attributed to the two authors' having possessed the same oral version of the story. The reason is that at the oral stage, it probably would not have been thus framed. Thirdly, and most importantly, the frames' inclusion suggests that it was John who knew Mark, for the addition of Lazarus to the plot against Jesus (as well as to the introduction to the anointing story) can be seen to be John's way of integrating the whole unit into his narrative, since in the preceding chapter he has made Jesus' raising of Lazarus to be the precipitating cause of the plot (11:53).

Realizing that the imposition of our logic upon an author always is problematic, we, nevertheless, shall hazard, in the space remaining, some guesses at the reasons for which John has selected, arranged, and altered certain elements from the gospel of Mark. These conjectures will show that the other data presented in the chart are amenable to the conclusion which has been advanced.

The placement of the anointing story and its frame after the raising of Lazarus and before Jesus' entry into Jerusalem (the latter is a reversal of the Markan order) probably was motivated both thematically and geographically. This unit's twofold theme of plot and passion, on the one hand, echoes the end of the Lazarus story and, on the other hand, prepares for

Jesus' entrance into that city in which the passion will take place. Likewise, the unit's location in Bethany (Mk. 14:3) both enables the insertion of the integrating references to Lazarus and prepares for the scene of the procession toward the capital. John's having brought in Judas as the objector to the anointing helps to explain his eventual act of betrayal and also prepares for 13:29.

John appears to have had little interest in the entry story itself, for he greatly has abbreviated it, in favor of his own commentary. In fact, he never reports the end of the procession, perhaps because Mark has made the temple the terminus, in preparation for the cleansing. John's referring, instead, to the Lazarus sign both integrates the entry story and prepares for the coming of the Greeks and of Jesus' hour. Jesus' having mounted a young ass _after_ the crowd's cry (again a reversal of the Markan order) may represent another correction of a suggestion that his kingship is this worldly (see 6:15, and perhaps too, the anointing of his feet in 12:3).

For the announcement of Jesus' hour, John has used the language found in Mark and then has continued Jesus' speech with a pattern familiar from the Markan passion prediction units, viz., a saying about the necessity of Jesus' death, followed by some teachings on discipleship. In v. 25, the two prepositional phrases are characteristically Johannine. Moreover, the variants, φιλεῖν, μισεῖν, and φυλάσσειν, all occur elsewhere in John--the first two, in this gospel more often than in any of the others. The antithesis, φιλεῖν/μισεῖν, will recur in 15:18-19. As in Mark, the coming of Jesus' hour causes his soul to be troubled (v. 27). If the next element in this verse has been intended as a question (see the note to the Greek text), it surely seems to presuppose the Markan Gethsemane scene, in which Jesus indeed did pray for divine help (14:36). The Johannine Jesus, however, will not even appear to make such a request, for he already has decided freely to lay down his life (10:17-18). V. 34 recalls not only 3:14, but also the formulation of the passion prediction in Mk. 8:31.

John's having used Isa. 6:9-10 to explain, not the misunderstanding of the kingdom of God (as in Mk. 4:11-12), but rather the rejection of Jesus (vv. 36b, 40), follows his characteristic pattern of reinterpreting the synoptic tradition by shifting emphasis from the kingdom to the person of Jesus.

(Other studies have convinced the present writer that both Mark and John were authors who exercised considerable creative freedom in their use of traditional materials. Therefore, the alternative suggestion that both authors used a common written source has not been pursued for two reasons. First, the parallels noted above can be explained adequately without recourse to such an hypothesis. Secondly, since Mark and John were authors, we do not have, as yet at least, a reliable method for reconstructing precisely the traditions which they used.)

TWO CHANGING PATTERNS: CONFLICTS AND THE NECESSITY OF DEATH
JOHN 2 and 12 and MARKAN PARALLELS

Anitra Bingham Kolenkow
University of California Berkeley

One step toward answering the "Mark-John relationship" question is to delineate the aims of the individual authors -- and especially what a gospel writer may be moving from or toward. If one has two writers working with similar material in different ways, one may ask how their aims differ -- is one moving away from another or are they both moving from a position which is the position of neither. John 2:13-22 and 12: 23-30 and their parallels in Mark seem to reflect similar material, yet they occur in different parts of their gospel's structures and also differ in wording. Thus they provide a suitable focus of study.

The gospels of Mark and John each have a temple story with a structure of driving out, speech to opponents and opponents' request for validation. However, the gospels as wholes present alternative "beginning of strife" and "death cause" structures (miracle or temple scene). Mark makes Jesus' actions in the temple the precipitating cause of the final attempt to destroy Jesus (11:18) Mark makes the controversy section of 2:1-3:6 (beginning and ending with miracle controversies) the first confrontation of Jesus with his opponents in the gospel -- ending indeed with a decision to destroy Jesus . The gospel of John, in contrast, puts the temple story at the beginning of the gospel, making it into a context for showing that Jesus forecast his own death and resurrection. The fulfillments of these forecasts in the gospel show Jesus uniting the ultimate prophetic power of forecasting one's own death (cf. A. B. Kolenkow, "Forecasts of One's Own Death in the Greco-Roman World and the New Testament," ANRW II, 28) and the ultimate miracle power of raising himself (as Mark, vs. Matthew and Paul). John uses the Lazarus miracle as a precipitating basis of final prosecution -- a story reflecting a typical early Christian motif of Christian leaders persecuted because they did miracles (cf. Acts 4:16 and John 11:47b , parallel sayings of opponents who wonder what to do with one who does signs and A. B. Kolenkow, "The Signs Controversy and the Ties of Acts and John against Luke," SBL 1977). John as Mark keeps the motif of healing on the sabbath as a reason for the early persecution of Jesus (John 5:18) in basically similar controversy stories (Bacon et al.). Thus Mark has the temple story at the end of his gospel and John has it at the beginning. Mark begins the confrontations in his gospel with a miracle story; John has miracle-caused confrontations both towards the beginning and at the end of his gospel structure.

If one argued that both gospels had a common source, how would one argue for the structure of this source. It would be probable that this source had a miracle controversy early in its structure since both works contain one early in their structures. As has long been argued, the temple story would

124

normally occur at the end of the gospel. John sets the temple story at the beginning of his gospel. This effective time back dating allows him to heighten the power of Jesus' forecast of his own death -- since the ordinary righteous man received forecasts of his own death only a few days before death. John as Mark has the Jewish request for legitimation (sign) occur as the result of Jesus' temple activities (a prophecy in itself). John makes the "sign" the forecast of a three day rebuilding of a destroyed temple, which John interprets as Jesus' body. (John's evident interest in forecasts of death, cf. the "lifting up" motif and 8:28, 12:33, 13:19, also might be added evidence that John does not know Mark or John would have used the more specific Markan forecasts.) The occurrence of signs or healing after the temple story in both John and Matthew also suggest an "end of gospel" location. Then if one may argue that John is maintaining the correct story line of his source by saying that a resurrection was the present sign for Jesus' temple-action prophecy, one may ask if John and Mark's source is a gospel about a prophet who forecast the fall of the temple. The prophet's power and endtime authority are proved by signs of healing (especially resurrection) which lead to prosecution both on a legal basis (cf. Deut 13) and because leaders feared popular belief resulting from signs. Critics of the gospel of John have maintained that the raising of Lazarus is the greatest sign of the signs source. It (with resultant prophet's death and city fall) would be a likely candidate both for proof-sign of Jesus temple actions and for crossover between temple forecast, sign and death. (Cf. II Kings 5:7-8, bSan 98a, bBM 59b, CDb 2:13-15)

Unlike John, Mark seems to find difficulty with the term "sign," with tying miracles to passion and even with speaking about Jesus' forecast of the fall of the temple. Mark makes Jesus' sayings about the temple into a fabrication of false witnesses. He guards and reilluminates the understanding of the forecast by having Peter question about the sign of the fall of the wonderful buildings. Mark's Jesus gives an apocalyptic-historical "when" answer ; Mark 13:14 and all the preceding events are the sign. Mark will not even speak of miracles after the beginning of the passion story -- thus effectively denying ties between miracle and passion (and being a good reason he would not use a story like that of Lazarus). In the temple story, Mark uses the term "exousia" where John uses semeion. Mark also uses "exousia" in 1:27 where it has always seemed peculiar in its context of talking about teaching but would be a natural description of an exorcism which was a sign for Jesus' typical teaching about the Kingdom of God (1:15). Mark also adds 11:16 to his temple story so that (unlike Matthew and John) he does not have Jesus directly address the pigeon sellers. Thus one may argue that both Mark and John are moving away from the structure of a common source. What is most remarkable about the later history of such a source is that John, Mark and "Q" each move separately to describe Jesus' forecasts of his own death (John 2:21, Mark 8:31 et al. and the sign of Luke 11:29-30, 32, Matt 12:38-41). There is a motion beyond fulfillment of scripture or apologetic (Mark 4:12, John 12:38-40). The prophet's own powers are at stake in this era. How may the church best argue that Jesus knew of his own death, thus his other forecasts were true.

A second set of passages using similar materials is John 12:23-28 and its parallels in Mark 8:34-9:1 and 14:32-42. It may be argued that Mark not only moves away from an emphasis on miracles causing suffering, but that he also moves from an argument that a follower of Jesus should seek suffering (cf. A. B. Kolenkow, "Beyond Miracles, Suffering and Eschatology," SBL 1973 Seminar Papers II, 160-62) -- cf. esp. 4:17 where persecution (like Satan) is one of the causes of seed not growing (scorched), 10:45 and the movement from suffering to service, the Gethsemane story of Jesus not seeking suffering and his advice to Peter not to seek "peirasmos," and Mark 13:14 which suggests that the time of martyrdom is past (now is the time to flee and some will be saved, 13:20). If one argues such a case, the major problem is Mark 8:34-38. Since similar materials occur in John, study of John's use of the materials may highlight what Mark does.

John 12:23-28 is part of the large section, 11-12, on death for the glory of God. In 12:23-28, John gives a context of glory and suffering to the questions which are covered in Mark 8:34-38 and the Gethsemane story. John uses what seems to be a typical early martyrdom statement about the seed having to die (John 12:21, cf. I Cor 15:36 and contrast Mark's seed parable!). John then moves into servant language -- disciples as serving Jesus and therefore following him (cf. 13:16) and being honored by the father. 12:27 might be considered an answer to Mark's picture of the Gethsemane Jesus (with John emphasizing that Jesus was merely asking a hypothetical question). However, John uses quite different language (although knowing "cup" language, cf 18:11, "Shall I not drink the cup which the father has given me) and this question is followed by Jesus' "glory implying suffering" statement and a "bath kol" which Jesus says is for the group's sake -- and the effective end of this glory-suffering section.

Mark 8:34-9:1 occurs in the context of Jesus' forecast of death for the Son of Man. 8:34 uses a "Q" passage which in Luke talks about what disciples should give up -- father and mother as well as life, cf. Mark 10:29-30). What Mark then does is argue for life. His argument starts with the motif of loosing life (as John) "for my sake and the gospel's." He then adds a group of sayings often used concerning lack of care about wealth (II Clement 6:1-2, Justin Martyr Apol 1:15:11-12) and a revelation of shame (not "Q"'s denial) and promise of the end before some here die. Both this passage and the Gethsemane passage would seem to start out with a Jesus who did not avoid death and then a possible modification of the effect of a demand to take up the cross:
         as one may pray to avoid "peirasmos" in Gethsemane,
         so one may know the possibility that one may not
                  taste death before the Kingdom of God comes..
Surveying the arguments of the two gospels, the passages show John indeed emphasizing a glory and suffering motif which Mark denies in 10:37-40. Mark retains the apocalyptic promise that some may live (9:1, 13:30). The above comparison gives few answers to the "source-dependence" problem, but raises some important questions. Is Mark's gospel the apocalyptic answer to an over stress on suffering and martyrdom. Is John typical of the early church or returning to its view in "peirasmos."

THE ANOINTING IN MARK 14:3-9 AND JOHN 12:1-8

Winsome Munro
Siena College, Loudonville, New York

1. Thesis

Though there is much to be said for the view that John
12:1-8 is directly derived from Mark 14:3-9, there are signs
that John's source was not exactly the same as the Markan
version. The position of the story is, moreover, more likely
to have been originally as in John than Mark. Thus a different version of Mark, or another source, is indicated.

2. Presuppositions and Criteria

The presuppositions accepted here are the same as those
of Arthur H. Maynard: "that unless there is a compelling
argument against the use of known documents, it is better to
posit known documents as sources rather than hypothetical
documents or oral traditions"; that Mark is prior to John;
and that John is very free in his use of sources.[1] A further
assumption is that Johannine adaptations are not random, but
issue from his particular tendencies and purposes.

On these bases the following criteria will be applied:
a) that use of Mark by John is to be assumed as a working
hypothesis if there is general agreement in sense and some
identical wording; b) in this case all divergences should be
explainable in terms of Johannine tendencies and purposes,
or use of other sources; c) where any difference cannot be
explained in this way, it is possible that it reflects a
difference from Mark in the Johannine source, particularly
if it is irrelevant to, or in tension with Johannine tendencies; d) if the difference accords with discernable Markan
redactional tendencies, the case for use of canonical Mark
breaks down, and the argument for use of another version
becomes compelling.

3. Agreements between Mark 14:3-9 and John 12:1-8

The story is basically the same in each: while Jesus is
at table in Bethany a woman takes costly ointment and anoints
him, which evokes the protest that it could have been sold
for 300 denarii (or more in Mark), and given to the poor,
whereupon Jesus says, "Let her alone," and refers the matter
to his death and burial.

Next, there are close verbal parallels, amounting to
about a third of Mark 14:3-9, as shown below:

Mark 14	John 12
v 3 murou nardou pistikēs (polutelous)	v 3 murou nardou pistikēs (polutimou)

Mark 14	John 12
v 4 (ēdunato gar) touto to muron prathēnai (epanō) denarion triakosion kai dothēnai (tois) ptōchois	v 5 (Dia ti) touto to muron (ouk) eprathē triakosiōn denariōn kai edothē ptōchois
v 6 ho (de) Iēsous eipen, Aphete autēn	v 7 eipen (oun) ho Iēsous, Aphes autēn
v 7 pantote gar tous ptōchous echete meth' heautōn ... eme de ou pantote echete	v 8 tous ptōchous gar pantote echete meth' heauton, eme de ou pantote echete
v 8 (proelaben murisai to sōma) mou eis ton entaphiasmon	v 7 (hina) eis (tēn hēmeran) tou entaphiasmou mou (tērēsēi auto)

John 12:8 could be due to textual assimilation, for it is absent in D and some other manuscripts, but scribal omission of words found earlier in the story in Matthew and Mark is as feasible. Most significant is the phrase in Mark 14:3 and John 12:3, for both nardos and pistikos occur nowhere else in the New Testament.

These agreements are sufficient to satisfy the first criterion. It is assumed, then, that John has used Mark unless the contrary can be demonstrated.

4. Differences between Mark 14:3-9 and John 12:1-8

These are identified as follows:

Mark 14	John 12
a. Two days before Passover (v 1)	Six days before Passover (v 1)
b. at home of Simon the leper (v 3)	at home of Lazarus, Martha, and Mary (vv 1-3)
c. nameless woman anoints Jesus (v 3)	Mary anoints Jesus (v 3)
d. she breaks alabaster jar, pours ointment (v 3)	she takes pound of ointment (v 3)
e. over Jesus' head (v 3)	(anoints) Jesus' feet (v 3)
f. --	wipes them with hair (v 3)
g. --	whole house filled with fragrance (v 3)
h. some reproach her for waste of what could have been sold for poor (v 5)	Judas, disciple, betrayer, reproaches her, not because he cares about poor, but because he steals from money box (vv 4-5)
i. Jesus asks why they trouble her (v 6)	--
j. commends her for beautiful deed (v 6)	--
k. whenever you will you can do good to poor (v 7)	--
l. she has done what she could (v 8)	--

Mark 14	John 12
m. anointed body beforehand for burial (v 8)	she may keep ointment for day of Jesus' burial (v 7)
n. wherever gospel is preached in whole world this will be told in memory of her (v 9)	--

Item h is explainable as due to the Johannine tendency to stress the diabolical character of Judas (13:2,26; 18:2), and as preparation for the betrayal, perhaps reflecting Mark 14:10-11. Item n may well be embodied in item g (John 12:3), with "house" symbolizing "world," which accords with Johannine use of symbolism.[2] Items i, k, and l could be due to abbreviation.

Items b, e, and f can be ascribed to Johannine conflation with Lukan material, so that the scene is as in Luke 10:38-42, with Martha serving and Mary at Jesus' feet, and the action as in the feetwashing and drying in Luke 7:36-50, with the omission of penitential tears. Why, however, should the anointer have been identified with Mary, sister of Martha, unless she was in fact known as Mary, as John 11:2 indicates?[3] The problem is not why John names her, but why Mark does not, especially in view of her fame. It accords with the Markan tendency to omit names of almost all characters outside the inner circle, and to render the continuous following of female disciples invisible until immediately after Jesus' death, when we hear of two Marys and Salome (Mark 15:40-41). If John found her unnamed in Mark, however, he could have supplied her name from the widespread oral tradition referred to in Mark 14:9, pointing to use of some earlier source material omitted in Mark. Similarly, it is difficult to see why Lazarus is identified as the brother of Mary and Martha unless earlier tradition known to John connected him with one or both of them. Again, the problem is Markan omission.

Next, there is no apparent reason why John should have eliminated the breaking of the alabaster jar and pouring in favor of she "took a pound of costly ointment... and anointed..." (12:30), nor why he should have changed the pre-anointing for burial to permission to keep the ointment for the day of burial. The pre-anointing is irrelevant to him. He knows nothing of it, for he has solved the problem of proper burial by having Nicodemus arrive on the scene loaded with spices (John 19:39-40). On the other hand, Mark accentuates the connection of the incident with Jesus' death and burial by placing it as close as possible to Jesus' death, so that it has the appearance of an insertion in Mark 14, and having the two Marys and Salome bring spices to the tomb (16:1). The latter actually betrays knowledge of the keeping of the ointment for the burial. Thus item d is to be explained as due to Markan adaptation to the notion of burial anointing of the whole body, with its meritorious nature emphasized in j and l. There is then compelling reason for thinking that John 12:3,7 preserve pre-Markan elements from an earlier version.

John 12:7 gains in credibility if the pericope is placed in the context of Mark 10:17-11:10 with the additions from the secret gospel of Mark cited in the claimed Clementine letter discovered by Morton Smith at Mar Saba.[4] Assuming its genuineness, Clement knew of a version of Mark containing an equivalent to the Lazarus story, which in turn has the sister of the dead man acknowledging Jesus as son of David. Assuming that this woman is the anointer, then she like her brother is rich, and subject with him to the call to "sell what you have and give to the poor" (Mark 10:21). This would account for the protest in Mark 14:5 and John 12:5, and for the permission to keep the ointment for the burial.

This motif would have been important in the stage of the community reflected in Acts 2:44-45, 4:32-35, 5:1-11, but more significant initially would have been the implication of messianic anointing of Jesus' head.[5] Confirming this as the original point of the story is its position before the triumphal entry in John,[5] which is all the more convincing because John has obscured it. Thus his "six days before the Passover" and order are vindicated as preserving pre-Markan elements.

5. Conclusion

It is concluded then that there are compelling reasons for thinking that John drew on a pre-Marcan version of the anointing very close to Mark 14:3-9 but not identical, in a gospel differing in order from Mark.

NOTES

[1] "Common Elements in the Outlines of Mark and John," Seminar Papers SBL 1978 2 251-60, 251.

[2] R.E. Brown, The Gospel according to John (i - xii) (New York: Doubleday, 1966), 451.

[3] Op. cit., 453.

[4] Clement of Alexandria and a Secret Gospel of Mark (Cambridge: Harvard, 1973).

[5] C.K. Barrett, The Gospel according to St. John (London: SPCK, 1967), 341-42, among others.

[6] I.e. the anointing story, perhaps plus the reference to Judas' betrayal as in Mark 14:10, 11, before the triumphal entry, six days before the Passover.

WELFARE IN THE CHURCHES OF ASIA MINOR
UNDER THE EARLY ROMAN EMPIRE

L. Wm. Countryman
Brite Divinity School

Part I - The Christian Practice of Almsgiving

The study of the Christianity of the Early Empire is always bedeviled
by the scattered nature of the few historical sources we have, so it
is difficult to devise a complete, confident interpretation of any
aspect of the community life of Christians. One must often combine
sources from different times and places on the grounds that the common
origins of the Christian churches and the frequent contacts among them
will have served to create and to maintain a certain consistency of
practice from place to place. One may also argue that the self-conscious conservatism of Early Catholicism would have retarded change
over time. These presuppositions, however, must be tested while they
are used. We must always stay alert to define the boundaries of our
study realistically and to revise them if there is reason.

In this essay, the boundaries of time are set as those of the Early
Roman Empire. This could take us as late as the final collapse of that
social order in about the 250s; but in fact, the information that is
useful to us here takes us no later than the late second century. Our
geographical boundaries will embrace several Roman provinces: Asia,
Bithynia, and Galatia. These contained a great variety of social set-
tings, ranging from the highly urbanized life of Ionia to the tribal
organization of the ethnic Galatians. This variety may lead us to ask
whether, indeed, these three provinces can be treated at all as a unit.
Yet, to some extent, they shared the same social and economic development in the first two centuries A.D. The emperor Augustus had brought
peace to the region and promoted the return of prosperity by his re-
organization of the government and by gifts to the municipalities. The
prosperity thus inaugurated continued to characterize the region down to
the reign of Marcus Aurelius, when there are signs of an economic setback
which grew steadily worse over the following century. The period up to
the reign of Marcus Aurelius was also a time of increasing urbanization
of the area, so that those parts which were more rural in the time of
Augustus came more and more to approximate the state of the cities on the
Aegean coast.[1]

If this common social and economic experience serves to give some unity
to the area, its effect will have been more decisive for the Christian
communities than for the area as a whole, since Christianity penetrated
the area as an urban phenomenon. We have no evidence for the spread of
the Christian religion outside the cities until early in the second century,
when Pliny the Younger tells us that the superstition was just beginning
to infect the country areas of Bithynia. Thus, Christianity was moving
with the tendency toward greater urbanization and its center of gravity
remained largely in the cities. We may think of our field of study, then,
as one characterized by social and economic continuity: we are dealing
with a small religious subsociety spreading mainly within an urban envi-
ronment of steadily increasing prosperity.[2]

Having drawn the boundaries of our study, I should next like to consider
briefly the kinds of evidence we have available for filling in the picture.

Christianity appears to have entered Asia Minor in more than one movement, so that we have several types of material to deal with. To begin with, there was the Pauline mission in Asia and southern Galatia and the tradition which developed from it. All the Pauline and deutero-Pauline letters are relevant for our task, since even those directed to churches outside Asia Minor reveal something of the nature of this brand of the religion. Again, there is the Johannine type of Christianity, which was certainly represented in the province of Asia. It is possible that not all our Johannine writings were composed there, but we may use them as representative of this tradition of Asian Christianity. Finally, there developed on Asian soil a variety of early forms which owe something to both Paul and John: the catholicism of Polycarp, reinforced and modified by that influential transient, Ignatius of Antioch; the semi-Gnostic Paulinism of Marcion, developed more completely on Italian soil; and the charismatic Christianity of Montanus and his followers.

THE PAULINE TRADITION

One has the impression, both from Acts of the Apostles and from Paul's own writings, that Paul's mission was the first to plant Christianity both in inland Asia Minor and on the shores of the Aegean. We shall begin, then, by examining the way in which his writings treat the question of charity or almsgiving. At this point I use these terms rather than "welfare," for it is not clear that the primary purpose of this activity was the welfare of the poor. What is welfare from the recipient's point of view is charity or almsgiving from that of the giver. Paul, in fact, devotes much more attention to the reasons for giving than to ultimate disposition of the gifts.

The principal reason for giving alms is that it is an expression of love (philadelphia), the kind of love which must automatically be present among Christians (Rom. 12:10 & 13). Indeed, if alms are given without love (agape), they cease to be of any value, so far as Paul is concerned (I Cor. 13:3). The loving sacrifice of the giver imitates that of Christ, who became poor for the sake of humanity (II Cor. 8:9). At the same time, Paul was also capable of arguing that almsgiving was a way of ensuring prosperity for the giver: God gives prosperity to make charity possible, and then he rewards the gift with more prosperity (II Cor. 8:10-15; 9:6-10). Alms may be exchanged for spiritual as well as material goods, for Paul asked the Corinthians (II Cor. 9:11-15) to give to the church at Jerusalem in return for their having shared the Gospel with the Corinthians.[3] In these ways, Paul treated almsgiving as a religious act, proceeding from the initial charity of God toward humanity in Jesus and from the loving interrelationship of all Christians to each other in the church.

Paul could also explain almsgiving as a gift of the Spirit (Rom. 12:8). If we compare this gift with other charismata, we shall understand it to mean that certain people within the church were endowed with both the means and the will to perform a certain task. The easiest way to understand this gift, I should think, would be to suppose that it was the preserve of rich Christians, whose contributions to church life were thus endowed with a religious value comparable to that of teaching or prophesying or speaking in tongues. At the same time, the charism of giving was not limited to the rich. Paul himself spoke admiringly of the Macedonians for having contributed beyond their means and despite "extreme poverty" to the Jerusalem church (II Cor. 8:1-3). Paul or an early follower of his encouraged Christians of moderate means to work with their hands so that they would have something to give the needy (Eph.4:28). Still, Paul's expression in Romans 12:8 suggests that this was primarily the function of the rich, for parallel with almsgiving he lists the charism of him who gives aid (proistamenos), where the Greek expression suggests a patron-client relationship.

The distribution of alms, in the Pauline tradition, is harder to trace than their origin. Paul told the Galatian churches that they should give alms broadly; but he encouraged them to give particular attention to their fellow-Christians (Gal. 6:9-10). There is no clear indication in Paul's letters, however, that he was familiar with a continuing program of welfare for the poor within the congregation. The most we have is a hint in the Thessalonian correspondence, where it appears that some brethren were abusing the church's charity by living in idleness (II Thess. 3:6-13). Paul (or a disciple of Paul's) criticized the idlers sharply and then recommended to the congregation as a whole that they not be "weary in welldoing." Perhaps a few people had been living entirely from the church's alms, and some givers were prepared to halt almsgiving altogether as a result of the abuses.

Paul has more to say of gifts between churches. Perhaps, as an apostle, he was more likely to take cognizance of those gifts which transcended the bounds of individual congregations. The most noted instance of this kind of charity is the collection which Paul made for the Christians at Jerusalem. He seems to have devoted much time and attention to this project over a long period toward the end of his Aegean missionary work. Money was collected, it seems, from the provinces of Galatia, Asia, Macedonia, and Achaia; and Paul set out with delegates from the contributing churches to conduct the gift to Judea.[4] It is still a matter of controversy whether Paul's motive was to alleviate real poverty at Jerusalem or to pay a kind of tribute to the Jerusalem authorities in the hope of maintaining unity with them. We cannot deal with the question here. It is enough to recognize that Paul certainly regarded the gift as a way of reaffirming the bonds between Christians, as he says clearly enough in II Corinthians 9.

It is also worth noting that when Paul encouraged the Romans to "contribute to the needs of the saints," he associated this with a command to "practice hospitality" (Rom. 12:13). This, too, suggests that charity given between churches had a special importance for him. This was practiced partly through hospitality, the reception of Christian travelers, and partly by sending aid to churches in trouble because of persecution or other local disaster.[5] This was the combination of activities Paul urged on the Roman church. With the church at Philippi, this charitable activity took the form of donations made to further the work of the apostle himself (Phil. 4:15-16). Such gifts, however, raised problems, since it was impossible to make the individual recipient accountable for their use. This introduces yet another aspect of the Pauline attitude toward alms and welfare.

Paul was conscious that ministry could become a means of enrichment for those on whom it fell. He felt that even the lesser office of Teacher was entitled to compensation (Gal. 6:6), and he argued that the apostle had a right to full support, both for himself and for his family (I Cor. 9:3-6). Yet, Paul refused to claim such a right for himself; indeed, he condescended to work with his hands rather than do so.[6] Thus, Paul sensed a certain danger in the notion of the apostle as recipient or custodian of the gifts of the faithful. There was even a danger in his handling these

gifts when they were destined for others, so that Paul was careful to
ensure that the collection for Jerusalem should be attended on its way by
the representatives of the churches, not by himself and his companions
alone.[7]

The idea that religious or philosophical missionaries might impose on the
innocent and generous was not a Christian discovery, but it must have made
a deep impression on Christians. The danger of peculation by religious
authorities is a theme that crops up repeatedly in early Christian writings,
most notably in the Didache, where there are regulations designed to limit
it.[8] There is a continuing concern about it in the deutero-Pauline Pastoral Epistles, where one finds complaints about false teachers who are
out to soak the Christian people (I Tim. 6:3-5; Tit. 1:10-11). Indeed, it
is in these epistles that we learn that the love of money is the root of
all evils (I Tim. 6:10). Can it be any accident that we also find, in the
list of qualifications for the local ministry, that bishops and deacons
are not to be greedy (I Tim. 3:2, 8; Tit. 1:7-8)? In the same breath, it
is said of bishops that they must be hospitable men. The implication is
that they will be personally responsible for the administration of the
church's alms and hospitality and they must be as immune as possible to
the temptation of enriching themselves from the common chest.

The Pastorals, with their concern for local church organization, also make
an effort to place limits on the church's charity. I Timothy prescribes
that the church shall support certain aged widows; but the epistle also
restricts this status to those over sixty and married only once. What is
more significant, no widow with a living Christian relative may be enrolled,
for such women are the charge of their own families (5:3-10). The Pastorals thus provide evidence not only of a desire to prevent clerical
peculation, but also of a need to limit the internal obligations of the
congregation. It is not clear whether this represents a change from the
time of Paul--a change in which the burden of internal charity had grown
heavier--or whether this is simply an aspect of the institutionalizing
tendency which marks these documents in any case.

In summary, we can say this of the Pauline tradition which contributed so
much to the foundation of Christianity in Asia Minor. Paul and his followers generally had more to say about the reasons for giving alms than
about their practical applications. Gifts that reached outside the congregation's own boundaries play an important part in Paul's own undoubted
writings, while the deutero-Pauline materials speak more of welfare within
the local congregation. The whole tradition bears witness to a fear within the churches that the handling of money could easily taint the religious leadership of the community. There can be no question, however, but
that almsgiving was stressed within the Pauline tradition and that it
possessed a religious value for these Christians. Paul himself tried to
deal with the problem of peculation by personal restraint and by the use
of congregational delegates to oversee delivery of gifts outside the
congregation. The author of the Pastorals tried to deal with the same
problem by setting high standards for ordination. There is also evident
in the Pastorals a desire to prune the welfare rolls and leave the church
treasury responsible only for the absolute minimum of poor clients.

A comparable picture emerges from another document which is associated
with the Christianity of Asia Minor and also, in some way, with Pauline
Christianity--namely, I Peter. Love of the brotherhood is highly

esteemed (2:17). "Rendering service," perhaps an expression of almsgiving, is reckoned a divine gift (4:11). Elders are told that they must
not look for gain (5:2). It is impossible to state definitively whether
this letter belongs to the Pauline tradition or only to a type of Christianity which had some contact with Pauline ideas. In any case, it was
addressed to churches in the northern part of Asia Minor, outside the
Pauline sphere and so provides valuable evidence that similar ideas were
circulated there.

THE JOHANNINE TRADITION

In the writings associated with the Johannine tradition, there is less
attention devoted to the question of almsgiving. A reasonably clear picture emerges, however, which is basically similar to that we have discovered for the Pauline communities. Almsgiving was a basic practice of
Johannine Christianity--so much so that the Gospel of John traces it back
to the original company of Jesus and his disciples. Valuable gifts to the
community were sold to provide funds for alms. Judas was the keeper of
the purse; and here, again, the responsible official was tempted to embezzle (Jn. 12:4-8). On the other hand, the Johannine communities had no
notion of being able to abolish poverty, nor any feeling that the relief
of the poor was the primary object of Christianity (Jn. 12:8).

If almsgiving becomes a duty of the first rank, it is when the needy person is also a "brother," a member of the Johannine sect. To love one
another is the commandment stressed repeatedly in I John. The love for
one's fellow Christians is, for "John" as for Paul, an imitation of God's
love for humanity (I Jn. 4:8-12). "But if any one has the world's goods
and sees his brother in need, yet closes his heart against him, how does
God's love abide in him?" (I Jn. 3:17). Love must necessarily take the
form of action, not of mere words. Perhaps it was a lack of almsgiving
that led the author of the Revelation to rebuke the church at Laodicea for
glorying in its wealth. The risen Christ advises the Laodiceans to buy
of him "gold refined in the fire" (Rev. 3:18), which reminds one of the
evangelical admonition to lay up treasures in heaven.[9] On the other hand,
he compliments the Christians at Thyatira for their "works and love and
faith and service (διακονία) and patience" (Rev. 2:18).

Hospitality served as a bond among the Johannine churches as among the
Pauline ones; and a breach of it was tantamount to a declaration of schism
(III John).[10] It is not clear from the earlier Johannine writings whether
there might also be an exchange of alms among separate churches, comparable
to Paul's collection for Jerusalem; but in the later Acts of John, we find
the claim that John left large sums of money (gathered elsewhere?) in
Laodicea for distribution (58). This document also confirms the importance
of almsgiving for Johannine Christianity by declaring that the person who
gives no alms will find no pity in hell (35). Receipt of alms was associated to some degree with membership in the sect, for a notoriously
wicked Christian, in being excommunicated, would be cut off from every
form of social intercourse with the church (84). Yet, John and his new
converts at Ephesus are described as willing to care for all old women at
Ephesus, regardless of their faith (30).

In summary, the Johannine tradition was similar to the Pauline in this
matter. Almsgiving was a major expression of Christian faith, being
understood as an imitation of God's own goodness and love. It was a

communal activity, with the community's officers charged with the oversight of alms. The officers who had charge of alms and also of hospitality might be tempted to embezzle or misuse the funds at their disposal. The recipients of the alms were the poor, especially widows; in the Johannine churches, the principal interest was in the Christian poor, although this may not have excluded other needy people.

EARLY CATHOLICISM

Polycarp of Smyrna was a disciple of John, according to tradition; yet, his letter to the church at Philippi is steeped in the language of Paul. No doubt he represented the fusion of these two originally distinct traditions in Asia Minor. In the matter of almsgiving, Polycarp preserved the common motifs of both. To love the brotherhood (10.1), to receive traveling Christians hospitably (1.1; martyrs, in this case)—these were basic Christian practices. Polycarp even quoted with approval the verse from Tobit: "almsgiving sets free from death" (10.2; Tobit 4:10). Most significantly, Polycarp reiterated several times the idea that ministers must be people who are not lovers of money (4.3; 5.1; 6.1; widows are treated in this respect as ministers). The specific reason for Polycarp's concern seems to have been the case of the Philippian presbyter Valens and his wife, whose fall was occasioned by avarice (11). This suggests that alms were still passing, to a great extent, through the hands of church officials.

The same situation is presupposed in the letters of Ignatius of Antioch, most of which are addressed to churches of Asia Minor by an author who had direct acquaintance with some of them. Ignatius repeatedly stresses both the importance of _agape_ and the necessity of complete organizational unity in the congregation under the bishop. In the one letter which he wrote to a bishop (Polycarp) rather than to the congregation, the link between these two concerns becomes clear. The bishop, for Ignatius, was the congregation's chief agent for charity. Ignatius charged Polycarp to let nothing be done without his approval, and to take personal charge of the welfare of the widows. He was also to guard the church treasury from a claim which Ignatius considered unwarranted—the desire of slaves to be emancipated.[11]

Neither Polycarp nor Ignatius argued for the giving of alms; they took it as a given that this was a basic Christian expression of religion. Ignatius encouraged his hearers to expect a reward for their works (Poly. 6.2) and argued that God shares in the good works of Christians (or rather that Christian good works are a sharing in God's works) (7.3). Polycarp, as we have seen, suggested that almsgiving could promote salvation. Neither author, however, offered a more theological reason for almsgiving; the Pauline and Johannine conception of alms as imitation of God's goodness had receded into the background.

Another Catholic document from about this era, the Epistle of the Apostles, is similar in hinting at eternal punishment as the consequence of failure to give alms (24, Coptic version only). No other rationale is offered. Even those Christians who are not rich are bidden to give to the poor, just as in Paul; but in this case they are promised an earthly reward as well as a heavenly one—the coveted title of "benefactors" (46, Coptic; Ethiopic reads "doers").[12] Other catholic writings from Asia Minor do not handle the topic of charity at all, which suggests that the system for gathering and distributing alms was working reasonably well and called for little public debate.

In summary, second-century Catholicism seems to add little to the picture we have gleaned from the Pauline and Johannine traditions. The
basic theological rationales for almsgiving have faded into the background in favor of an occasional personal appeal which connected almsgiving with the individual's hope for salvation. Alms are still being
channeled through the community's officers, with the attendant danger
of peculation. There is enough demand for assistance within the congregation that the Christians must put certain limitations on the purposes for which alms may be used.

ALMS OUTSIDE THE CATHOLIC TRADITION

Almsgiving also seems to have been valued in those forms of Asian Christianity which lay outside the emergent Catholic tradition. On the
periphery of the Catholic churches, there existed a tendency toward
Encratism, which seems not to have broken with Catholicism in its earlier
stages. From such a milieu comes the Acts of Paul, which treats almsgiving as a normal aspect of Christian life. Thus, Tryphaena is said to
have sent a generous gift to Paul's convert, Thecla, some of it for the
poor; Thecla even used some of the money as a kind of bribe to reconcile
her mother to her conversion (Paul and Thecla 41). It is interesting,
here, that the celibate woman serves as the distributor of alms instead
of any regularly ordained minister; this is a contrast to the church order
of the Pastorals. In another episode, a man named Hermocrates is represented as selling a piece of property and distributing the proceeds to
the widows. His immediate object is to gain his son's healing, and it
may be that the alms are a kind of payment for the widow's prayers (P.
Heid., p. 33). Again, no regular clergyman is involved in the procedure.

The Gnosticism of Asia Minor is not well documented--at least as regards
almsgiving. One Marcionite leader, Apelles, is recorded to have suggested
that good works were necessary for salvation (thus Rhodo, in Eusebius, H.
E. 5.13.5). And this seems consistent with Marcion's theology of the good
and loving father of Jesus. But I am unable to be more specific.

Finally, the most important Christian group of Asia Minor outside of
emergent Catholicism was surely the Montanists. Again, our evidence is
meager, but it is clear that the Montanist prophets collected alms not only
from the rich, but from all their followers; (Apollonius, in Eusebius, H.
E. 5.18, even says that they took money from orphans and widows). There
was one signal difference, however, between Montanists and Catholics:
among Catholics, the ordained clergy controlled the church treasury and
the distribution of alms; among Montanists, the prophets did so. Thus,
Apollonius of Ephesus observed indignantly that Montanus actually paid his
clergy salaries--a sign of their subjection to him, and also an example
of gluttony, since the salary, unlike the church treasury, was reckoned to
belong to the cleric (Eusebius, H.E., same reference).

In sum, if the non-Catholic groups differed from the Catholic churches, it
seems to have been in the matter of who controlled the alms and their distribution. Among Catholics, it was the ordained clergy; but other groups,
who valued celibacy or inspiration above "decency and order," invested
control in virgins or prophets.

138

SUMMARY OF THE EVIDENCE

We have, then, the following picture of almsgiving in the Christian
churches of Asia Minor in the period of the Early Empire: alms were
given to the community itself and dispersed through whatever leaders were
most highly regarded by the particular group. There was always a danger
of these leaders' misappropriating funds thus entrusted to them. There
were, moreover, enough legitimate demands on the church treasury that
some efforts were made, in the late first and the second centuries, to
limit the types of cases where aid would be given. Still, the Christian
poor benefited considerably from the system, and the non-Christian poor
probably benefited, too, in an incidental way. Almsgiving was regarded
as a basic expression of Christianity, although the specific rationales
offered for it varied from one period and author to another.

This summary is, of course, a synthetic one, which cannot be demonsrated
wholly from any one author or document. Yet, there is so little development evident within the traditions that such an approach is justified. The
main difficulty here is that we are forced to read the non-Catholic
evidence in terms of the better-known Catholic practice because we lack
any other guide to its meaning.

PART II - CHRISTIAN WELFARE IN THE LARGER SOCIAL CONTEXT

GRECO-ROMAN PHILANTHROPY

The Christian community did not invent the idea of social benevolence. The
concept of almsgiving was rooted in Judaism, which already had a developed
notion of the responsibility of society for the poor as early as the time
when the Torah was formulated. The almsgiving of Palestine has two
aspects: to a certain extent, it was legally incumbent, in the form of
the poor-tithe; for the pious, however, there was an additional voluntary
dimension of almsgiving. The giver of alms directed his efforts to the
relief of the needy, whoever they might be; and there was some feeling
that alms were best given anonymously. God would reward the giver; any
reward in this world, therefore, would be superfluous. These same notions
are to be found in the Gospels, suggesting that early Christianity carried
its Palestinian heritage with it in this respect when it began to move out
into the larger Greco-Roman world.[13]

In studying the Christianity of Asia, however, another social milieu becomes more important for us--that of the Hellenistic city. Christianity
first appeared in Asia on the fringes of Jewish communities in these
cities. The Jewish life of these communities is not well documented; but
it seems likely that it was strongly Hellenized. In any case, the Christian churches soon became Gentile as well as Jewish. Thus, the principal
context for the development of Christian benevolence and welfare consisted
of Greco-Roman concepts of philanthropy. It is this tradition that requires our attention here.

The nature of Greco-Roman philanthropy must be understood in terms of the
social structure of that culture, which was more formal and explicit than
our own, yet did not cut people of different social strata off from each
other so completely as ours. In technical terms, it was a system not of

classes, but of estates or orders. Various orders of society were defined by law: senators, equestrians, members of city councils, and so forth; to each, the law assigned privileges and prerequisites appropriate to it. To be identified as a member of the upper social strata of the Roman Empire, it was not enough to be rich (though that was necessary) or to be well-educated or of a good family (though these things were helpful). One must be formally translated into, for example, the senatorial order.[14]

Despite the apparent gulfs, however, which separated one order of society from another, there was a great deal of interdependence among the orders. The Roman aristocrat was in daily touch with people of a variety of social stations. His private secretary, who might also be his most intimate confidant, was a slave. Before dawn each day, the aristocrat was sought at home by petitioners who wanted his help in legal matters, by clients who sought his advice or needed his financial assistance, by friends who wanted to renew his acquaintance. When he went to the Forum, he was accompanied by a crowd of clients, free men and freedmen, whose presence was valuable to him, since it gave visible evidence of his importance in the city. During the day he was attended by a variety of literati, junior officers and aristocratic ne'er-do-wells, subtly soliciting invitations to dinner. In the evening, he dined not with his family nor, generally, with his social equals, but with people whom we call, from the Greek term denoting their place at table, "parasite."

Greco-Roman society was largely organized around the households of the great, not only at Rome, but in the provincial cities as well. The vertical relationships between people of different ranks were at least as significant as the horizontal relationships between members of the same order; the whole texture of daily life depended heavily on them. Thus, the relationship between rich and poor assumed an immediacy in the Greco-Roman world which it lacks in ours, for it was almost always a face-to-face relationship, with major consequences for the poor person and serious, if less obvious, ones for the rich.

This exchange between rich and poor was a fundamental feature of Greco-Roman society from very early times. Already in the Homeric era, heroes were accompanied to war by their clients. Sophocles caught the sense of interdependence between the two orders of society in his Ajax, where he has the chorus declare:

> . . . humble men without their princes
> Are a frail prop for a fortress. They
> Should be dependent on the great
> And the great be upheld by the lesser ones.

These words were equally applicable in the Athens of Sophocles' own day, where most political leaders were rich men who could count on the backing of large numbers of clients. The Roman Republic was like Athens in this respect, in that clients were an indispensable part of the budding politician's armory; every rich family had to support them, encourage them, and ensure their loyalty. On the other hand, a poor man with no patron was in a precarious position, with little defense against any kind of attack, legal or illegal. The link between patron and client was thus mutually advantageous.[15]

We are concerned here, however, with the period of the Early Roman Empire; and there the picture becomes more difficult to decipher, for the system

of patron and client had entered into its decline. It has been said,
aptly, that with Augustus every social class of the empire became the
client of the Emperor.[16] As the state became the supreme patron, other,
lesser types of patronage began to wither away. We should not, however,
think of some sweeping and dramatic change which at once altered the face
of society. It took many generations before the populace came to feel
that the role of the emperor made certain older social arrangements obso-
lete. Augustus himself was cautious about usurping older customs except
where he might seize a source of power vital to his own function in the
state. He left the cursus honorum untouched at Rome, preserved the Senate
in most of its traditional functions, encouraged local responsibility in
government throughout the Empire, and formed no great, centralized bureau-
cracy. It was Claudius who gave institutional form to the inevitable
claims of centralization through his organization of the government bureaus;
and only in Domitian do we find an emperor making theoretical claims to a
universal dominion which matched the actual powers he and his predecessors
held.

The change that was taking place on the local level was captured by the
poet Juvenal in his "First Satire," where he complains that in the Rome of
his day poor clients were neglected or even rejected, while the rich culti-
vated each other's friendship instead. The patron-client relationship
still existed, but it was beginning to decline in favor of a new emphasis
on "friendship," a relationship between equals. Juvenal's observations are
corroborated by a sober contemporary, the younger Pliny, who criticized
those people who gave their gifts in a calculating way to people from whom
they expected much in return. He implied that the custom was typical of
his day.[17]

Even the person who gave more liberally, according to Pliny, would still
not broadcast his money to the needy in general. Pliny, like other ancient
writers on philanthropy, held that the principal grounds for determining
who should benefit by the liberality of the rich were those of relationship: one gives to one's native place, one's neighbors, one's relatives,
one's friends. Only secondarily, in the case of friends, does need become
a consideration; for Pliny did hold that one should give only to friends
who really needed the gift. "Need," however, should not be thought of as
implying any desperate financial condition. Pliny, as a senator of some
wealth, was prepared to help a friend whose fortune did not quite qualify
him to rise in society. So long as the recipient was not in a position to
repay the giver, the criterion of need was met. But so long as repayment
had not been made, the recipient remained in the giver's debt and so continued to be, in however loose a sense, the giver's client.[18]

Even if exchanges among the rich were a prominent feature of the liberality
of the Early Empire, such men as Pliny are evidence that the patron-client
relationship still existed and that it played an important part in the day-
to-day functioning of society. The patron supplied the poor with goods
vital to their existence: money, food---and also influence. Since the rich
generally belonged to the upper strata of society, they could wield influence with government on behalf of the poor; and since Roman law gave explicit preference to the "better" classes of society, a poor man might well
need the assistance of his "betters" in the prosecution of a suit or to
defend himself in court.[19]

Another kind of gift was that of capital, which was naturally rarer and which we frequently find commemorated in literature or inscription. Thus, Pliny refers to a gift of HS300,000 which he gave to enable a friend to meet the minimum census for an equestrian and a member of the Roman decuriae. This was only the largest of many such personal gifts. The emperors, from time to time, assisted impoverished senators in the same way. Often, the rich gave such gifts of capital not to individual clients, but to groups of people who functioned in a similar role: especially to clubs and to cities.[20]

The role of the rich patron of a club is well known to us from the large number of inscriptions that were erected thanking the rich for their gifts and rewarding them with honorific titles. Sometimes, rich patrons seem to have founded a club themselves as a beneficence to members of their households. At other times, a patron would provide an existing club with new amenities: sometimes he furnished it with a meeting-place, which might also be a small temple honoring the club's guardian divinities; often, he endowed one or more of its feasts, providing also for gifts of money to be distributed to the officers and members on the occasion. Such endowments were given for and restricted to fixed purposes. While the club life of the poor might have been possible in some cases without such benefactions, it would certainly have been less luxurious and entertaining.[21]

In the financing of cities, too, the rich played an important role. Recent analyses suggest that the average city of Greco-Roman antiquity raised only a small part of necessary revenues through taxation, enough to finance only the barest minimum of government. Everything else was provided by the rich. This might come as the result of special levies: the liturgies of fifth-century Athens would be a typical example, in which various wealthy citizens were assigned vital tasks such as shipbuilding. In other instances, the gifts were exacted as the price of public office-- what the Romans called a summa honoraria. On still other occasions, the gifts were purely voluntary, so far as we can now tell. Most often, the rich donor gave to his own city; but sometimes people with an empire-wide reputation to make (for example, Herod the Great or Herodes Atticus) would scatter their benefactions further afield. Gifts to cities might include endowments to pay the expenses of certain public offices, buildings such as temples, porticoes and baths, or alimentary trusts and other provisions for the education of the young. In short, the life of the ancient city was almost inconceivable without the gifts of the rich, whether purely voluntary or dictated in part by the community itself.[22]

These gifts were not simply expressions of the goodness of heart and public spirit of the Greco-Roman rich. The donors fully expected something in return. Despite appearances, the poor had a great deal to give the rich-- the gift of public reputation and honor, which only the "people" could bestow. In the relatively small communities of the ancient Mediterranean world, public reputation was traditionally the principal social goal for the upper strata of society. The competition for such honors among the rich of the Early Empire was still intense, albeit less bloody than the civil strife under the Republic. If there were rich men, who were content to keep to themselves and lead purely private lives, there were more who were eager to see their names recorded in inscriptions as benefactor of this or that city or club.[23]

The idea of liberality was reinforced in a variety of ways. Public recognition was an essential ingredient in social success for the upper strata of the Greco-Roman world Children learned by observation from an early age that the liberal were popular and successful. Classical literature enshrined the virtue of hospitality. The very word philanthropia, originally a reference to the generosity of the gods toward humanity, suggested a divine model for human benefactors.[24] From the negative side, there was a lively fear of the evil eye aroused by envy. Both social function and religious ideas thus converged to make liberality a basic cultural value.

The social function of liberality, however, also determined that limits must be placed on it. As I have already mentioned, need was not in itself the primary criterion for determining the recipients of benevolence. The donor might take need into account, but only within the circle of those who already deserved his consideration because of their relationship to him: family, friends, native place. In such cases, need might well dictate the kind of aid to be offered. The "needy" as such, however, were not regarded as normal objects of benevolence simply by reason of their need.

This feature of Greco-Roman philanthropy arises from its character as exchange. The rich did not normally give to strangers or to people who were marginal to the social order, because they would not have had social goods to offer in return. We must remember that only a minority of residents of any ancient city usually belonged to the citizen-body and so could vote in the assembly. Non-citizens might belong to clubs, which could bestow public recognition. But a person who was simply needy, without other qualifications, was not a suitable partner in the exchange.

Beggars, no doubt, were attended to somehow, for Cynic philosophers were able to make their way about the Empire in that guise. But the gift given to a beggar was small and casual--given partly to escape his curses and the annoyance of having him tag after one. No one took responsibility for beggars; indeed, one avoided them if possible. For the rich person to concentrate his attention on the needy as such, on people totally removed from the normal workings of society, on wanderers or the destitute, would be to undermine the fabric of society. Thus, the anonymous Good Samaritan would not have been accepted readily as a model of benevolence in Greco-Roman society; society could not afford to treat benevolence so casually.[25]

In summary, exchanges between rich and poor were part of the essential texture of the Greco-Roman society in which the churches of Asia Minor found themselves involved. The attitudes toward benevolence were therefore quite different from Jewish ideas of almsgiving. In Palestinian Judaism, the giver was encouraged to make need the primary criterion for bestowing his gift and to remain anonymous while he did so. In the larger Greco-Roman world, neither of these tendencies was fully practicable.

DISTINCTIVE DEVELOPMENTS OF CHRISTIAN CHARITY

In some ways, the Christians of Asia Minor remained within the pattern of Greco-Roman philanthropy. The Christian rich appear in early Christian literature generally as givers of alms and capital gifts to the churches. Most forms of early Christianity stressed giving as a major virtue. Believers of all social strata were encouraged to give what they could; but the principal burden necessarily rested on the richer members of the congregation, who could most easily spare something from their incomes. Already, before their conversion, they were used to having such demands made

on them. In this respect, the new religious community of Christians was
not very different from the existing voluntary religious associations, the
clubs.

In addition to their economic functions, the Christian rich must have
played yet another role, though it is inevitably one for which we have
little evidence. They must have acted as the guardians of the Christian
community in its dealings with the government and the courts. The only
possible explanation for the relative ease with which the churches avoided
persecution under the Early Empire is that they could bring influence to
bear on their behalf. We have a few hints of such situations: Paul was
rescued from serious trouble in Ephesus by the friendly intervention of
some Asiarchs (while they were probably not Christians themselves, some
one must have won their favor for Paul); Ignatius of Antioch was afraid
that the Christians at Rome would pull strings to get him released and
he did not doubt that they could do so.[26] The rich, with their network of
friendships and relationships, must have been the principal defense of
Christianity against the overwhelming might of the government. Thus, the
rich believers contributed to the church in much the same way that a rich
patron contributed to a pagan club or to an individual client.

In two important ways, however, the Christian rich differed from their
pagan peers: first, they did not have direct control over the distribution
of their gifts; second, they were not repaid with comparable public honors.
The two differences are intimately linked. We have already observed the
important role of the clergy in handling the church's treasury--and the
attendant danger of peculation. It was not the individual Christian donor
who acted as patron of the Christian poor; instead, the donor gave to the
church whose clergy then performed the role of patrons of the poor. In
this way, the direct relationship between giver and receiver, which was so
important to Greco-Roman society, was dissolved and recreated in a new
form. It is not surprising, in light of this, that our early Christian
authors do not suggest that the church bestowed any particular honors on
the rich, comparable to those granted by pagan clubs. The authority of
the clergy intervened between the rich and their expected reward.

No doubt the church did have a certain number of direct patron-client relationships in the beginning. How else could the house-church have operated?[27] But such arrangements never became normative, since the Catholic
clergy evolved as a kind of third term in the process, identified with
neither rich nor poor and serving as middlemen in the distribution of alms.
This does not mean that the church altogether rejected the Greco-Roman mode
of philanthropy. Rather, the church accepted and adapted it. The Christian rich, as we have said, were expected to give gifts like those of their
pagan counterparts. The Christian poor could depend on those gifts, within limits. The difference is that whereas the rich and poor would thus
have established a relationship with each other in standard Greco-Roman
practice, both groups established relationships with the church through
the clergy in the Christian version of the process.

How the clergy acquired such importance is too large a question for this
paper.[28] It is connected, no doubt, with the sacred conception of the
clergy in Early Catholicism as representing not merely the human organization of the church but God himself, whether through spiritual endowment,
apostolic calling, apostolic succession, or some other means. As the
holders of sacral wealth (salvation), the clergy were fully the equals of
the Christian rich. An exchange might still take place between the rich

and the clergy, but it was not a patron-client sort of exchange; it comes closer to the model of exchanges between equals--what the ancients called "friendship."[29] The rich gave their gifts of money, property and influence; the clergy reciprocated with guarantees of salvation through membership in the church. Since the earthly wealth, too, was now in clerical hands, the Christian poor related to them.

The ministers could behave toward the poor as patrons toward clients. From Paul to Ignatius, they laid down rules limiting the disbursement of church funds, requiring the poor to work, telling slaves to be content with their lot, distinguishing between widows who deserved church support and those who were ineligible. In return, one must assume that the clients were under obligation to cooperate with their patrons, maintaining an attitude of respectful subordination toward them and of unflinching loyalty to the community that assisted them. One does not, to be sure, find any clear reference to this in the Christian literature that pertains to Asia Minor; but there is no reason to expect it. Rarely does any ancient writer expatiate on the duties of the client, for they were known to all and it was easy for the patron to punish infractions of the code by withdrawing support.

The clergy also served as the mediators of gifts which passed between different Christian churches; and it was they who offered (or denied) hospitality to Christian travelers. Such practices served elsewhere as a basis for the growth of metropolitical authority within Early Catholicism; but I see no evidence of such a process taking place in Asia Minor. Perhaps this was a result of the geography of the area, where many cities of approximately equal size and wealth were grouped close together along the seaboard and there was less opportunity for one church to assume exclusive leadership. The early stages of development in the authority of Carthage over neighboring churches are similar to the relationship of patron and clients; the looser pattern of authority in Asia appears to be rather a relationship among "friends."[30]

In summary, the Christian communities of Asia Minor operated as efficient means for the redistributing of goods from rich to poor. The adaptations which the Christians made in the usual Greco-Roman client-patron relationship "rationalized" this process in that it abstracted it from considerations of prior personal relationships. They also had the effect of strengthening the role of the community's officers, since the larger part of Christian alms passed through their hands. These were significant adjustments in the existing system and it may be that they will go some way toward explaining the expansion of Christianity under the Early Empire, despite its barbarian origins, its rejection of much of the Greco-Roman heritage, and its illegality.

[1]T. R. S. Broughton, "Roman Asia Minor," in An Economic Survey of Ancient Rome, ed. Tenney Frank (New York: Octagon Books, 1975; reprinted from the edition of 1938), vol. 4, pp. 627-48, 696-797.

[2]Pliny, Ep. 10.96.9. The Montanists may have been an exception to the general rule that Christians were mainly urban people, for their holiest sites were located Phrygian villages.

[3]Cf. Paul's suggestion that Philemon might repay a spiritual debt with a material favor (Phlm. 18-20).

[4]See I Cor. 16:1-4 (Galatia and Achaea); II Cor. 8-9 and Rom. 15: 25-27 (Macedonia and Achaea); Acts 20:4 (representatives of Asia in Paul's entourage).

[5]One might compare the gifts given by the Emperor to Asian cities destroyed by earthquake; Broughton, p. 712.

[6]For Paul's social class and his labor as "condescension," see Ronald F. Hock, "Paul's Tentmaking and the Problem of His Social Class," JBL 97(1978):555-64.

[7]I Cor. 16:3-4.

[8]For base motives among non-Christian missionaries, see Apollonius of Tyana, Ep. 3. Didache 11-13. According to Lucian of Samosata, Peregrinus hoodwinked the Christians so successfully that delegations visited him in prison from as far away as Asia (Peregrinus 13).

[9]The reference, however, might equally well have to do with martyrdom, as the "white garments" suggest.

[10]Cf. Abraham J. Malherbe, "The Inhospitality of Diotrephes," in God's Christ and His People: Studies in Honor of Nils Alstrup Dahl, ed. Jacob Jervell and Wayne A. Meeks (Oslo: Universitetsforlaget, 1977), pp. 222-32.

[11]Ignatius, Polycarp 4.1-2.

[12]I have depended, for this and other New Testament Apocrypha, on the translations in Edgar Hennecke, New Testament Apocrypha, ed. Wilhelm Schneemelcher, Eng. trans. ed. by R. McL. Wilson, 2 vols. (Philadelphia: Westminster, 1963-65).

[13]For a collection of illustrative texts, see C. G. Montefiore and H. Loewe, A Rabbinic Anthology (New York: Schocken Books, 1974), pp. 412-39. For Christian borrowing of Jewish principles, see, for example, Mt. 19:21 (". . .give to the poor and you will have treasure in heaven . . .") and 6:3 (". . .do not left your left hand know what your right hand is doing. . .").

[14]My understanding of the Greco-Roman social structure follows, in the main, the work of M. I. Finley, The Ancient Economy (Berkeley: University of California Press, 1973); see especially, pp. 45-51.

[15]Sophocles, Ajax, trans. John Moore, in The Complete Greek Tragedies, ed. David Grene and Richmond Lattimore (New York: Modern Library, 1957), vol. 4, 11. 158-61.

[16]Jean Gage, Les classes sociales dans l'empire romain, 2d ed. (Paris: Payot, 1971), pp. 34-35, 71-77.

[17]I have translated the work by Juvenal in my article, "D. Iunius Iuvenalis: The First Satire, Translation and Afterword," The Classical World 71(1978):373-79.

[18]Pliny, Ep. 9.30. Hendrik Bolkestein, Wohltatigkeit und Armenpflege im vorchristlichen Altertum: Ein Beitrag zum Problem "Moral und Gesell-schaft" (Utrecht: A. Oosthoek, 1939), pp. 95-100, 114-15, 297-99, 337-39.

[19]Peter Garnsey, Social Status and Legal Privilege in the Roman Empire (Oxford: Clarendon Press, 1970), pp. 232-33, 274; John Crook, Law and Life of Rome (Ithaca, N.Y.: Cornell University Press, 1967), p. 97.

[20]Pliny, Ep. 1.19; 4:29. Richard Duncan-Jones, The Economy of the Roman Empire: Quantitative Studies (New York: Cambridge University Press, 1974), pp. 28-32.

[21]Franz Poland, Geschichte des griechischen Vereinswesens (Leipzig: B. G. Teubner, 1909), pp. 271-73, 468, 478-83.

[22]Finley, pp. 150-76. A. R. Hands, Charities and Social Aid in Greece and Rome (Ithaca, N.Y.: Cornell University Press, 1968), p. 39.

[23]Juvenal complained about those of the rich who lived purely private lives, Sat. 1.135-46.

[24]Hands, pp. 35-36.

[25]Bolkestein, pp. vii-viii; cf. pages cited above, note 18.

[26]Acts 19:30-31; Ignatius, Rom. 1-2,7.

[27]Floyd V. Filson, "The Significance of the Early House Churches," JBL 58(1939):105-12. The relationship between the Elder and Diotrephes in III John may be evidence for some struggle between the church's sacral authorities (the Elder, in this case) and its financial sup-porters (Diotrephes, who appears in control of hospitality to trave-lers, though he is not the presiding officer of the community, but only "wants to be first"); cf. Malherbe.

[28]For a partial solution, see my article, "The Intellectual Role of the Early Catholic Episcopate," Church History, forthcoming.

[29]Hands, pp. 32-35.

[30]On the relationship between gifts and the authority of the church of Rome, see Walter Bauer, Orthodoxy and Heresy in Earliest Christianity, Eng. trans. ed. by Robert Kraft and Gerhard Krodel (Philadelphia: For-tress, 1971), pp. 121-24. For Carthage,note Cyprian, Epp. 41, 62.

A SECOND LOOK AT THE GOSPEL BEFORE MARK

Pierson Parker
Claremont, California

I. Introduction

First, and all too briefly, let me express warm thanks
to the chairman and members of the Group on the Relationships
of the Gospels, for taking time to discuss, and permitting me
to discuss, my old book.[1] Especial thanks go to members of
the panel, who have devoted their time out of their very busy
days. Some have been so kind as to say that the book has had
less attention than it merited or, even, that it was ahead of
its time. Be such ideas as they may, the present assignment is
to indicate where my own thinking about the Synoptic Problem
has changed in the past quarter-century and, every bit as important, where it has not.

The book's central thesis still seems, to me, inescapa-
ble. Our Matthew did not derive from our Mark. Instead, both
canonical Gospels were taken from a common Grundschrift which
had first appeared, probably, in Aramaic, and which for convenience I labeled "K" (koinos).

Several corollaries, also, I continue to believe true.
(a) "K" fits, as canonical Matthew does not, what early fathers
said about Matthew. (b) The "K" hypothesis also corresponds to
what some fathers said about the Second Evangelist's procedures. So I concluded (c) that "K" must be a Proto-Matthew;
if, however, you prefer to call it a Proto- or Ur-Marcus, that
is what I at first thought it was. (d) The tone of "K" was
profoundly, perhaps polemically Palestinian and Judeo-
Christian. Our Second Evangelist shortened and altered all
that, to conform the Gospel to Gentile Christian needs. (e)
Canonical Matthew, produced after the Judaizing controversy had
subsided, could afford to keep "K's" Judeo-Christian materials,
but it merged these with other materials of different slant.
Many of the latter reflect a period like the one that produced
the book of Revelation. (f) Other added matter, which Matthew
shares with Luke and which we label "Q," is quieter and more
relaxed. Finally, (g) I still believe, positively, in Proto-
Luke.

These theses and corollaries were based, in 1953, on four
types of evidence: the vocabularies and styles of the various
Gospels, their structural characteristics, their reflection of
the Christian history of their times, and the patristic evidence. Since 1953 further evidence has accumulated. But before
reviewing some of this, let me summarize items I should certainly change, were the book ever to go through a second
writing.

II. Some Departures from 1953

1. As recognized in 1953, the so-called "M" or peculiar
Matthean material is of two sharply different sorts. (a) In
the main, "M" is material from the Grundschrift which canonical Mark left out but canonical Matthew preserved. (b) But
there is material, much less extensive, that the final Matthean redactor added to meet the needs of his own time.

(a) The following are surely marks, in "M," of the
original Jewish-Christian Gospel: persistent assumption, the
stronger for not being stated, that the reader dwells in Palestine; that Jerusalem and the Temple are standing; that the reader worships in the Temple, knows about the high priest, and
his court, and the treasury with its rules; that he confronts
Pharisaism as a live issue; has witnessed the public displays
of some Pharisees at prayer; is likely to be impressed by a Roman soldier; knows the geography of Syria, and the differences
among Palestinian dialects. The reader is commanded to obey
the Mosaic Law, and also obey the Pharisees. He is warned not
to swear by the Holy City or holy places. The author hesitates
to use the word "God," preferring a circumlocution. Like the
Jewish Christian missioners of Acts, he appeals to testimonia.
He repeatedly deplores the Jewish charge that Jesus "practised
magic and deceived and led astray Israel."[2] Often he seems to
oppose any mission to the uncircumcised. His apocalyptic describes so poorly what actually happened that it cannot be from
vaticinia ex eventu, and must antedate the Jewish War. Further, all these "M" materials are permeated by a language and
style that also pervade Matthew's "Markan" material and, yes,
the Second Gospel itself. If such language cannot be the final
arbiter, still it is of enormous help in identifying doubtful
passages.

(b) The hand of the final redactor is probably to be
seen in such "M" features as a positive interest in the Church,
and in the Kingdom as the entire body of Jesus' followers.
That Kingdom was for all mankind. Jesus' followers, it is assumed, are entrapped in a seemingly endless period of agony and
broadside opposition. Their Lord is a long time coming. His
devotees are in danger of growing weary, and slipping away.
They are summoned to be patient, longsuffering, steadfast.
This final redactor had a penchant for mixing passages together, sometimes to the point of incomprehensibility. (See,
e.g., the so-called Parable of the Wedding Feast, 22:1-14.)
Though the totality of his additions is not large, yet they
exhibit their own linguistic quirks, such as hetaire, brugmós
ton odónton, praûs.

Other possible marks of a late redactor might be the
division of Jesus' ministry into five sections; the doctrine of
a transcendental Christ; and a preoccupation with miracle that
reminds one of later Christian romances. These, however, are
not dependable criteria. A five-fold division would have been
congenial to early Jewish Christians. The transcendent Christ
was taught at least as early as Paul and the "Q" material. And
not only had Palestinian Jews a bent toward miracle; Matthew's
most bizarre tale, about a coin in a fish's mouth, is in a con-

text that only an ante-bellum Palestinian Jew could have appreciated.

2. The case for a Proto-Luke seems to me to be stronger than ever. In a series of articles I have pointed out how, when Mark and Acts deal with the same subject-matter, they contradict each other at nearly every turn. Yet Luke's own Gospel continually parallels Mark and, where Acts and Mark differ, constantly compromises or otherwise mediates between the two.[3] So I have come to agree with D. S. C. Williams that the "former treatise," mentioned at Acts 1:1, was an earlier edition of Luke's Gospel, composed before he came across his "Markan" material.[4]

3. On the other hand, I am less sure than I was, that "Q" was ever a separate document. All of us must hesitate to multiply hypothetical documents for which there is no independent evidence. (I was glad that the "K" solution posited only 3 such primary sources, where Streeter had 4!) Also, "Q" is so deucedly amorphous, and so lacking in any apparent purpose! It is not surprising that, in recent years, so many have questioned whether "Q" ever existed by itself.

Yet it simply will not do, just to say, "Raus mit!" "Q" has too many unique features, that cry out for explanation. (a) There is its vocabulary, so distinct from the rest of Matthew. (b) When "Q" material is erased from Matthew, the remainder of that Gospel reads smoothly (albeit with a changed import); whereas, when "Markan" material is erased, the remainder is in shreds. Surely that implies that "Q" at one time stood apart from this Gospel. (c) "Q" has a pro-Gentile slant. It is more easy-going than Mark's, no doubt, but it is nonetheless real: The Chosen People are not "worthy" (Matt 22:8), a favorite "Q" word. John the Baptist disparages descent from Abraham (3:9). The Torah was in force until the Baptist came (10:13). Jesus offers to enter a Gentile house (8:7) and at Luke 7:6 actually sets out to do so. The "sign of Jonah" authorizes a mission to Gentiles (Matt 12:39,41f.). "Leaven" is given a good sense (13:33). Also "Q" may have used one or two distinctively Gentile expressions, kodrantes = Latin quadrans (5:20), a coin that seems not to have circulated in Palestine; and "prayer and fasting" (17:21), a technical term from Gentile magic; but these are not in Luke, and the second is textually doubtful, so they may not be properly "Q." As to the other items, however, if "Q" never stood alone, whence came all these distinctive features?

4. I am somewhat less confident than formerly of the definitive value of statistics. True, it was the vocabulary of "M" that first set me on this track; and, when combined with other evidence, vocabulary counts do most certainly contribute. But what seem to me to be excesses in the work of, say, A. Q. Morton, make me feel that the other evidence, for the prior unity of "Markan" and much "M" material, ought to take precedence. Were I to rewrite the book, I should probably put the statistical argument last, not first.

Having said that, however, I call attention to two articles, one by A. M. Honoré, "A Statistical Study of the Synoptic Problem," the other by Charles E. Carlston and Dennis Norlin, "Once More--Statistics and Q."[5] None of those gentlemen could be accused of espousing the "K" hypothesis; yet their general drift is quite in line with what I have maintained. Honoré argues (a) that Mark usually appears more primitive than Matthew, but (b) the next best answer would be to accept the primitivity of Matthew. Those two points almost paraphrase my own observations that (a) canonical Mark is usually but (b) canonical Matthew often the more primitive. Carlston and Norlin show (c) that Matthew and Luke are closer in their "Q" than in their "Markan" portions--but that was inevitable if these Evangelists used the same "Q" and different "Marks"! (d) Honoré adds that his own statistics point to the possibility of a Proto-Matthew.

5. Further, while I am not--not yet--converted to Griesbach, I am increasingly unsettled by his hypothesis, and by its reflections in the work of Farmer, Buchanan, Longstaff, and Stoldt.

For one thing, there are places where Mark does indeed look like a conflation, therefore a derivative, of Matthew + Luke; for instance:

> Luke 22:53. I was daily with-you in the temple.
> Matt 26:55. I sat daily in the temple teaching.
> Mark 14:49. I was daily with-you in the temple
> teaching.

Here Matthew's picture of a sitting teacher is thoroughly Jewish.

> Luke 18:35. ....as he drew-nigh-unto Jericho....
> Matt 20:29. ....as they went-out-from Jericho....
> Mark 10:46. they come-to Jericho, and as he
> went-out-from Jericho....

This one can be otherwise explained, for Mark's clumsy gap is filled in Clement of Alexandria's Secret Markan Gospel, a document Morton Smith regards as original.[6] But again:

> Luke 21:37. every-night he went out
> Matt 21:17. he went forth out-of-the-city to
> Bethany
> Mark 11:11, he went out unto Bethany....
> 19. and every-evening he went forth
> out-of-the-city

There are many such passages. A few more will be noticed presently. They leave me uneasy.

Toward the end of this essay I shall suggest, very tentatively, a possible way to dispose of the anomalous "Q," and at the same time bring Griesbach and the "K" hypothesis and some others a little closer together.

III. The Second Gospel is Secondary

A more far-reaching departure from 1953 is in picturing
the way in which the Second Gospel came into being. I am more
than ever impressed with the secondary character of this Gospel. Negatively, it cannot be Petrine, and cannot be the work
of John Mark of Jerusalem. These two points were argued at
the 1977 annual meeting of this Society, in a presentation
that need not be repeated here'--though, inevitably, some
points must be recalled. Let me now argue, more positively,
that the Second Evangelist was himself a late-comer and a Gentile.

Some of the following items are discussed in the 1953
book, so are but briefly summarized here. Many, however, have
not hitherto been put in print, or not by me:

1. The Second Gospel is late. Whatever its calendar
date, its viewpoint is often strangely subsequent to those of
Matthew, Luke and, even, John. For instance, the Second is the
only Gospel which, like the Apostles' and Nicene Creeds, never
alludes even remotely to Mary's husband. And it is the only NT
book that calls Jesus "Son of Mary" (6:3). Also seemingly
late, and certainly distinctive, this is the only Gospel that
uses an unqualified to euangelion to designate the Christian
enterprise (1:15; 8:35; 10:29; 13:10; 14:9). Again, only at
Mark 1:8 does the Baptist say "I baptized," past tense; that
looks like an inadvertent throwback from a later standpoint.

In numerous other places, the Second Gospel looks defin-
itely less original than the First. At Matt 3:13, Jesus came
to the Jordan expressly "in order to be baptized" (tou baptis-
thenai) by John--an idea quite alien to the rest of the NT. In
Matthew, moreover, Jesus' teaching is at times almost word-for-
word like the Baptist's: compare Matt 3:2 with 4:17; 3:7f.
with 12:37f., 23:33; 3:10 with 7:19; 3:12 with 13:30. No
Christian would have welcomed these subordinations of Jesus to
John, still less have invented them. Almost certainly, therefore, they came to Matthew out of the earliest tradition.

Again, Matt 15:4, "God said, Honor thy father &c," ad-
heres to earliest Jewish and Jewish-Christian concepts of Scriptural inspiration; at Mark 7:10 it becomes "Moses said....,"
which would be clearer to Gentiles and accord better with their
attitudes toward the Torah. At Mark 11:25, the saying on for-
giveness is put so completely out of context as to make little
sense; its proper context is in Matt 6:14f., besides which,
Mark's "stand praying" seems to echo Matt 6:5. The 1953 book
gives other examples of this sort of thing.

2. Errors in the Second Gospel. The mistakes in Mark are
so various and so numerous that it seems futile to try to explain them away (though many have made the attempt). This Evangelist just cannot have been familiar with Palestine, its people
or its religion.

(a) Mistakes about Judaism. Mark 5:22, "one (heis)
of the rulers of the synagogue." Diaspora synagogues may some-

152

times have had more than one ruler, as at Pisidian Antioch
(Acts 13:15), but Palestinian synagogues normally had only one.

At Mark 7:11, the explanation of <u>qorban</u> is very inadequate.

Mark 14:12, "On the <u>first</u> day of unleavened bread
<u>when they sacrificed the Passover</u>," confuses Nisan 15 with Ni-
san 14. Some will say that this is another conflation, of Matt
26:17, "the <u>first</u> day of unleavened bread" vs. Luke 22:7, "the
day of <u>unleavened</u> bread <u>on which the Passover must be sacri-
ficed</u>." In any case, only the Second Evangelist seems not to
have known the difference.

Mark 14:13 (also Luke 22:10) says the disciples were
to be met by a man carrying a pitcher of water. Since adult
male Jews never did that, it would have aroused jeers, and excited the very attention that Jesus sought to avoid. (Perhaps
the guide had a priestly seal ring with the picture of a water
jar; but neither Mark nor Luke says that.)

Only Mark supposes that, for Jesus' hearing, "the
entire Sanhedrin" met <u>twice</u> (14:55; 15:1). That is most improbable. Some will again be disposed to find conflation here, of
Matt 26:58 and Luke 22:66.

Mark 15:42, "When <u>evening was already come</u>, because
it was Friday (<u>Paraskeue</u>) that is, the day before the Sabbath
....." If this be taken literally, either <u>that</u> Friday began with
<u>that</u> sunset, and Jesus had died on Thursday; or else the Evan-
gelist forgot that the Jewish day began at evening.

Mark 15:46 says that presently, that same evening,
Joseph of Arimathea "<u>bought</u> a linen cloth." Again, either it
was now Friday, and Jesus had died on Thursday; or else somebody
has quietly got around the Jewish Sabbath laws.

No Jew, nor any one familiar with Judaism, would have
produced the caricature at Mark 7:3,4. The caricature is made
worse by the gratuitous remark at v. 13, "and many such like
things you do."

(b) <u>Mistakes about Scripture</u> are less significant,
since the ancients had no easy way to look up texts, and must
depend on memory. Those in Mark are interesting chiefly as
part of a broader pattern:

Mark 1:2 ascribes Mal 3:1 to Isaiah.

Mark 1:11 misquotes Isa 42:1. So does Luke 3:22, but
not Matt 3:17.

Mark 2:26, "Abiathar" should be "Ahimelech."

Mark 10:19 misquotes the Decalogue, and inserts one,
in some MSS two extra commandments, "Do not defraud" (mē apo-
stereses), "Do not practise prostitution" (mē porneuses). Luke
18:20 is like Mark, but without these additions. Matt 19:18f.

quotes correctly and then, like many rabbis, adds Lev 19:18.

Had Jesus quoted Psalm 22:1 in Aramaic ("Eloi"), as Mark 15:34 says, bystanders could hardly have supposed he was calling for Elijah. Jesus must have used Hebrew Eli, as at Matt 27:46. (Did the Aramaic Grundschrift first give Eli, then Eloi as its translation, and did this confuse the Second Evangelist or else a prior Greek translator? One can only guess. All one knows is that the Matthean account makes better sense than the Markan.)

(c) Mistakes about geography. Except at Mark 2:4, where a Palestinian roof-top is more accurately described than at Luke 5:19, the Second Evangelist appears woefully ignorant of Jesus' land.

Only Mark 6:21 says that Antipas' birthday party was for "the chief men of Galilee." Yet (6:27) Antipas had the Baptist beheaded and his head brought in to the party. Therefore the festivities were still in progress, and therefore they must have been at Machaerus--a good 100 miles from Antipas' Galilean seat. Did "the chief men of Galilee" walk all that way to a birthday party? Or did the Second Evangelist simply have no idea how far it was from Tiberias to John's prison?

At Mark 6:45, Jesus and his disciples cross to Bethsaida after the feeding of the five thousand. Yet (6:55) that crossing brings them to Gennesaret! Luke 9:11 puts the feeding itself near Bethsaida, and the same is implied at John 6:1,5,16 and also, probably, Matt 14:13,34.

Mark 7:31 says that Jesus and his companions journeyed "out from the borders of Tyre....through Sidon, to the Sea of Galilee, through the midst of the borders of Decapolis." How many have been the headaches of commentators, trying to make sense out of that!

There apparently was no such place as "Dalmanutha" (Mark 8:10). "Magadan" at Matt 15:39 is likewise a problem; but it, at least, could be an alternative form of "Magdala." It is sometimes suggested that the Second Evangelist here just misread his source; but that itself would not speak well for his knowledge.

Mark 8:27 speaks of "villages of Caesarea Philippi."

Those are too many geographical absurdities. Our author cannot have been told much about Palestine, still less ever have seen the country.

(d) Mistakes about current history. Mark 6:14-27 repeatedly calls Herod Antipas a "king." Except in the confused text of Matt 14:9, no other NT writer commits that error. The correct title "tetrarch" appears at Matt 14:1; Luke 3:19; 9:7; Acts 13:1; but never in the Second Gospel.

Mark 6:17 says that Antipas married his brother Philip's wife. Actually she was wife of a different brother.[8] The name "Philip" is absent from Luke 3:19 and is textually doubtful

154

at Matt 14:3.

It is most unlikely that the Jerusalem populace and their chief priests acclaimed Jesus as the King of the Jews. Only Mark (15:11f.) supposes that they did.

(e) Other mistakes? In virtually all the foregoing, the Second Gospel stands alone. The errors are so eccentric that one is bound to wonder about other Markan statements, when these find no support elsewhere. Whence came the following bits of information?

--that Andrew dwelt at Capernaum, nay, in the very same house as his brother's wife's mother (Mark 1:29).

--that Levi was the son (or brother?) of Alpheus (2:14). And does that make Levi a son, or brother, or nephew, or uncle of James (3:18)?

--that Herod Antipas feared John the Baptist (6:14). Perhaps he did, but both Matt 14:5 and Josephus[9] say he really feared the reaction of the populace.

--that Jesus and the "apostles" took a vacation (6:31). However, that is not in itself inconceivable.

--that it was the high priest's maid who accused Peter.

3. Doubtful Statements about Jesus. In the light of what has been said, some Markan statements about Jesus himself fall open to question. In all the following, the Second Gospel stands alone. In a number of them, there are additional reasons for doubt:

(a) Geography of Jesus' activities. Only Mark (1:9) puts Jesus in Nazareth immediately before his baptism. It achieves this simply by omitting the article. With the article (as at Matt 21:11; John 1:45; Acts 10:38), Iesous ho apo Nazareth would have been only a title, with no indication as to where, in Galilee, Jesus had just been.

Only Mark (2:1ff.) sets the healing of the paralytic in Capernaum. Matt 9:1 seems to put it in Jesus' "own city," whatever that means. Luke is vaguer still, and could be thinking of a desert area (5:16) or Gennesaret (5:1) or some city (5:12) somewhere in Galilee or Judea (5:17).

Only in Mark, Jesus occupies at least six different houses, in Capernaum (2:1; 9:33), on a mountain (3:13 + 19), somewhere in Galilee (7:17), in "the borders" of Tyre and Sidon (7:24), at the foot of the mount of transfiguration (9:28), in Perea (10:10). Moreover, each of these has room also for Jesus' disciples plus other folk! How did Jesus come by all this real estate? We are not told.

(b) Jesus' chronology. Only Mark (3:6) has Pharisees and Herodians conspiring together in Galilee and right after Jesus got there. Elsewhere the conspiracy is set much later and in the southland (Matt 22:15f. = Mark 12:13; Acts 4:27; cf. Luke 13:31).

Only Mark has scribes come from Jerusalem as early as 3:22, and only here (3:23) is Jesus' discourse directed to that group.

Only Mark has no Judean ministry before 10:46. Matt 23:37, a "Q" passage, speaks of such a ministry, while Luke, Acts and John mention it constantly. Perhaps the Second Evangelist's silence here is due to bias in the source he used, and which he did not know enough to correct.

Only Mark (11:15-19) puts the Temple cleansing on the second day of Jesus' last visit to Jerusalem. Matt 21:21ff. and Luke 19:45ff. put it on the first day, and John 2:13ff. of course has it much earlier still.

Only Mark (11:11,15) has two visits to the Temple on those first two days.

Only Mark (11:20ff.) has the aftermath of the fig-tree incident on the third day.

Only Mark (14:17) explicitly identifies the Last Supper with the Passover meal the disciples had prepared. Luke 22:14 may equate them, but is unclear. Matt 26:20 does not say that it was that meal. John 13:1f. says flatly that the Supper was before Passover. This looks like a culminating item in Mark's highly individual calendar of the Passion story.

(c) Jesus' own stance. Only Mark (3:14f.) tells what Jesus' motives were in calling the Twelve, viz., that they should be with him, and go forth to preach, and exorcise demons. These are what any Christian writer could guess, so that they do not demonstrate any personal knowledge.

Only Mark (6:3) says that Jesus was himself a tektōn. Is that history? Or does it reflect the Evangelist's unwillingness to notice Joseph?

At the Temple cleansing, only Mark (11:16) says that Jesus "would not let any one carry a vessel through the temple." Is Jesus here denigrating Temple worship? Or, contrariwise, does he so revere the Temple that he will not let it be made a thoroughfare? In any case, where were the Temple police?

(d) Jesus' desire for secrecy. Granted that Jesus was unwilling to channelize his ministry along lines either of a mere healer or of a political leader, even so, his demands in Mark are carried to irrational lengths. At Mark 5:43, he wants it kept secret that Jaīrus' little girl has been brought back from death! At 7:36, an erstwhile deaf-mute now hears and speaks, and Jesus again demands that he not let any one know about it!

At Mark 7:24, Jesus wants his Tyre and Sidon where-abouts kept secret. No other Gospel reports a desire for se-crecy that early.

We seem to be dealing, here, not with sober repor-tage, but with a literary idiosyncrasy of the Second Evangel-ist. Perhaps it stemmed from his idea of a Messianitätsge-heimnis.[10] In any case, it is not history.

(e) Jesus' teaching. In the Parable of the Wicked Husbandmen, Mark 12:8 says that the husbandmen first killed the son, then cast him out. At Matt 21:39 and Luke 20:15, they first cast him out, then killed him. If, as later Christians thought, the "son" stands for Jesus, the Matthew-Luke order is lectio difficilior, hence likely to be original. It is a for-tiori original if, as I incline to think, the "son" originally meant John the Baptist: that was the order in his tragedy.

John 2:19 reports that Jesus said, "Destroy this temple and in three days I will raise it up." The saying is echoed at Acts 6:14, and is not denied at Matt 26:21. Only Mark (14:57f.) brands the report as false.

4. The Second Evangelist was a Gentile. Of his pro-Gentile sympathies numerous examples are given in the 1953 book. For the most part those passages will be recalled, here, by a mere "See" or "See also." But there are other items, and they lead beyond the findings of a quarter-century ago.

(a) Jesus' mission to Gentiles. At Mark 3:8, Jesus has followers from Idumea. No other Gospel says that.

At Mark 5:18-20, a Gentile, an erstwhile demoniac, goes at Jesus' bidding on an extended mission to the Decapolis. The mission is more restricted in Luke 8:37b-39, and is not men-tioned in Matthew.

At Mark 7:31 + 8:1, Jesus himself conducts a mission to the Decapolis. (See also 8:3.) Matt 15:29 does not say this; at most, Matt 15:39 may mean that the feeding of the four thousand had occurred somewhere on the eastern shore.

Elsewhere in the Second Gospel, Jesus expresses in-tense concern for a world-wide mission. Mark 8:19-21 lays heavy emphasis on the significance, in the two feedings, of 12 baskets on Jewish territory and 7 on Gentile. The treatment is far less explicit at Matt 16:9.

At Mark 13:27, the elect are to be gathered "from the uttermost part of the earth," a phrase absent from Matthew and Luke.

At Mark 14:9, "the gospel shall be preached through-out the whole world." Matt 26:13 is more limited: "this gospel of the woman's deed? shall be preached in the whole world."

See also Mark 11:17 vs. Matt 21:13 and Luke 19:46; also the remarkable differences between First and Second Gospel accounts of the woman near Tyre and Sidon (Matt 15:21-28; Mark 7:24-30).

(b) The larger group. Even amongst Jews, Jesus' mission in Mark constantly reaches a wider circle than in the other Gospels. In the north, only Mark says, "His name had become known" (6:19). In the south, only Mark says, "Ho polús óchlos heard him gladly" (12:37).

At Matt 19:23, Jesus "said to his disciples....," but at Mark 10:23, he "looked round about and said to his disciples...."

Compare also:

Mark 3:34; 4:10; 8:34; 9:35; 10:44; 11:23;
Matt 12:36; 13:10; 16:24; 23:11; 20:27; 17:30 and 21:21.

This difference, between the two Gospels, is much too widespread to be accidental.

(c) Absence of Jewish details. In its parallels to Matthew, the Second Gospel consistently fails to include items where the primary thrust is Jewish. Mark 1:14f. lacks (I should have preferred to say omits) an elaborately Jewish description of Capernaum (Matt 4:13). So does Luke 4:31, which explains instead that Capernaum was "a city of Galilee."

Mark 7:37 lacks the phrase, "they glorified the God of Israel" (Matt 15:31).

The healing of two blind men (Matt 9:27-31) seems to be an addition by the final Matthean redactor, duplicating Matt 20:29ff. = Mark 10:46ff. However, Mark at this point (5:43f.) also lacks the healing of a dumb man (Matt 9:32-34), where the stress is on the Pharisees' reaction and on the faith of Israel. The command to secrecy (Matt 9:30) gets transferred in Mark, as we saw, to a context where it makes no sense.

In the Apocalyptic Discourse, Mark 13:13 is not like Matt 24:9-13, but like Matthew's mission charge (Matt 10:22). In particular Mark lacks, of Matt 24:9ff.,

v. 9, "you will be hated by all Gentiles for my name's sake,"

v. 10, "many will be caused to stumble (skandalisthésontai),"

v. 11, "false prophets will arise and lead many astray,"

v. 12, "because of violation of the Law (anomía), the love of many will grow cold."

Mark 13:17-19 fails to urge Jesus' followers to pray that they not have to fly on the Sabbath (Matt 24:20).

Jewish Christians, in propagandizing fellow Jews,

made heavy use of testimonia. Such apologetic would carry far
less weight with Gentiles. (That is doubtless why the first
half of Acts has 14 appeals to testimonia, the second half only
3, of which 2 are addressed to Jews.) The Second Gospel lacks
nearly every testimonium of Matthew (Matt 4:15f.; 8:17;
12:18-21; 13:14f.,35; 17:5; 21:4,5,15,16); and it has none to
take their place. In fact, Mark's only testimonia are four
that it shares with Matthew and Luke, viz., two about John the
Baptist (Mark 1:2 = Matt 11:10; Luke 7:27; and Mark 1:3 = Matt
3:3; Luke 3:4), and two spoken by Jesus himself (Mark 12:10 =
Matt 21:42; Luke 20:17; and Mark 12:36 = Matt 22:44; Luke
20:42f.).

See also Mark 6:7-13, which lacks Matt 10:5; and
Mark 9:33ff., which lacks Matt 17:24-27. These two Matthean
passages would have been both unclear and, probably, offensive
to early Gentile Christians.

(d) Mosaic Law abrogated. Matt 12:5-7 appeals to
the Torah, and also to Hosea. Mark 2:27 makes no such appeal,
but simply sets aside or, at least, modifies the Sabbath requirement.

In a comment by the Evangelist, Mark 7:19 asserts
that Jesus declared all foods clean. (Recall that at Acts
10:11-14 and 11:5-8, Peter has never heard of this.)

Mark 9:4 names Elijah before Moses. To subordinate
the Law-giver in that way would have struck Jews as bizarre.
Matt 17:3 and Luke 9:30 name Moses first.

See also Mark 12:31,33,34, where the Torah is subordinated to love, and to the Kingdom; contrast Matt 22:40.

It is interesting that Luke lacks every Markan passage where a Mosaic ordinance is abrogated or toned down.

(e) Jewish features explained. The Second Evangelist does not explain matters of Gentile knowledge, such as who
Pilate was. He does explain Jewish customs and traditions, as
though these were unfamiliar to his readers. Sometimes his explanations are not quite accurate.

After quoting Jesus' simile, Mark 2:19 explains that
"as long as they have the bridegroom with them, they cannot
fast."

Mark 2:25 explains that David took the showbread
"when he had need."

Not only is Mark 7:2ff. a caricature. No Jew would
have needed any explanation here, however accurate.

Matt 22:31 reads, "spoken to you by God." Mark
12:32 has "in the book of Moses, in the account of the bush,
how God spoke to him." However, Luke 20:37 reads, "Moses
showed, in the account of the bush, when he called on the Lord
....," so that, to some, Mark here will look like a conflation.

Only Mark (12:42) explains that a lépton, a coin used in Palestine, was worth half a quadrans.

(f) Adapts gospel to Gentile interests. Sometimes, instead of explaining, the Second Evangelist just uses phrasing that was more readily understood by non-Jews. Where Matthew's "Heaven" means God, Mark always reads "God," as does Luke. Where Matt 12:50 has "my father in heaven," again Mark 3:35 (and Luke 8:20) reads simply "God." Matt 24:15 reads, "standing in the Holy Place," but Mark 13:14 has, "standing where he ought not."

This may be why Mark 15:25 sets the crucifixion at "the third hour." By Jewish ways of counting time that would mean 9 a.m., which is much too early; but by Roman it meant noon, and that agrees with John 19:14, and also, apparently, with Matt 27:45; Luke 23:44. Besides, the whole of Mark 15:25 is an awkward interruption.

Other Gentile adaptations involve not just forms of expression, but a whole range of ideas. The concept automatos (Mark 4:28) is most un-Jewish, whereas it appears repeatedly in Greek literature. (Its only other NT occurrence is at Acts 12:10.)[11]

Matt 8:30 says that the herd of swine was "a long way off" from Jesus and the group. But Mark 5:11 (also Luke 8:32) says the swine were right there. Only Mark adds that there were about two thousand of them.

Only Mark (10:38f.) has Jesus ask the sons of Zebedee, "Are you able to be baptized with the baptism I am baptized with?" Baptizesthai was a common Greek metaphor for overwhelming calamity. It was not Semitic. (Cf. Luke 12:50.)

Only at Mark 10:12 does Jesus forbid women to divorce their husbands and remarry. But Jewish law already forbade that! The teaching would have seemed outlandish to a Jew of Palestine,[12] but was an appropriate expansion for those of pagan background.

(g) Aramaic is, to the Second Evangelist, a foreign and exotic tongue. He includes it at 7:34 (Ephphatha) and 8:41 (Talitha cumi) as if these were incantations for healing, which he then explains. At 3:17 and 10:46 he similarly explains the meanings of Aramaic surnames. We have seen how, at Jesus' cry from the cross (15:34), the Evangelist appears confused about both Aramaic and Hebrew.

(h) Derogatory of apostles. The Second Evangelist displays almost unremitting impatience with the Jerusalem apostles--which is understandable if they opposed admission of the uncircumcised to the Church. As pointed out in 1953, this Gospel pictures the Twelve as uncomprehending (6:52; 9:32; Luke 9:45 agrees with the latter, but explains that a divine decree kept them in the dark). They were extremely discourteous to Jesus (Mark 4:38; 5:31; 6:37; 9:34). Jesus himself upbraided them severely (4:13; 8:17f.; 9:19).

Further, these disciples had no idea what "rising from the dead" meant (9:10)--even though their forebears had been discussing that topic for two centuries!

At Mark 10:24 the disciples are amazed at Jesus' words about riches, and Jesus enlarges on the subject. Neither Matthew nor, surprisingly, Luke have this.

Again at Mark 10:32 the disciples are "amazed.... afraid."

At Mark 10:35-45, the disciples James and John try to undercut their fellows, whereas at Matt 20:20-28 it is their mother who tries that. I have already noted reasons for thinking Mark secondary here. Further, Matthew would hardly have let a woman play so significant a role unless she really did so. Also, in both Gospels, the other ten get angry not "at" the two brothers (pros or epí) but "about" them (perí); that fits the Matthean context, but is out of place in Mark. (Incidentally, Matt 20:20 + 29 places the mother in Jericho. Does that say anything about Zebedee's habitat?)

Mark 14:20 underscores the fact that one of the Twelve betrayed Jesus. The sentence itself comes in awkwardly (unless there were others at the table).

At Mark 14:40, the disciples "did not know how to answer him."

Mark 9:14-29 fails to include Jesus' word to his disciples, "Nothing shall be impossible to you" (Matt 17:20).

Also peculiar to this Gospel are the derogation of Jesus' "friends" (3:21) and "his own kin" (6:4), but it is hard to say whether these belong with the foregoing.

(1) Attitude toward Peter. The Second Gospel names Peter less often than the others do, though perhaps not in disproportion to its length. Also, however:

It never acknowledges Peter's authority. Contrast Matt 16:17-20; Luke 22:28-32; John 21:15-17.

It never calls him "Simon Peter." Contrast Matt 16:16; Luke 5:8; and 16 times in John.

It says nothing about his walking on water. Contrast Matt 14:28-31.

Where, at Matt 15:15, Peter asks Jesus to explain a parable, at Mark 7:17 it is only "his disciples" who ask.

Regarding Peter's perfidy, both Matthew and Mark say he had promised to be loyal, but only Mark (14:31) says Peter declared his faithfulness "exceeding vehemently." At the Sanhedrin hearing, only Mark (14:54) has the bitter note about Peter "sitting and warming himself" at the officers' fire. (John 18:18,25 is much milder.) Note, further, that only Matthew

(26:70-74) puts Peter's denials in proper Jewish form, (a) a simple denial, (b) denial with an oath, (c) denial with a curse.

Recall, then, that the Second Gospel contains very little that reads like personal reminiscence, and nothing at all that need have come from Peter. Peter ignored, Peter denigrated--are these the ways that John Mark would write of his friend?

To sum up, the Second Gospel favors Gentiles. It proclaims a marked universalism. It ignores matters of interest to Jews. It plays down their Torah. It runs down the Jerusalem Christian leaders. It reinterprets the Christian message along Gentile lines. And it displays vast ignorance of Judaism, of Palestinian geography and history, and of the Hebrew Scriptures. Often it seems misinformed about Jesus himself. Not only can these things not have come from Peter or John Mark. They cannot have come from any first century Jew or Jewish Christian. The author must have been a Gentile convert. If his name was Marcus, it was some other Marcus.

On the positive side, this Gentile Evangelist has left us some of the subtlest and deepest theology in the NT. But its very subtlety and depth make "Markan" thought a vast and separate field of study.[13] In the present essay, I have ventured to adduce only a few of the most striking theological considerations.

IV. Some Items of Literary Criticism

Regarding several items of literary criticism, there are points to add to the 1953 discussion.

1. Prolixity. As between two stories of the same event, the more prolix or verbose is commonly taken--other things being equal--to be the more primitive. That is because the tendency of a later writer is usually to condense. Now while the Second Gospel is usually more prolix than the First, in 1953 I noted 23 places where Matthew is the more wordy. Recently I marked 31 other instances. (It would be tedious to list them here, but I shall be happy to supply the list to any one who writes for it.) Often, furthermore, through extended passages the two books alternate in their verbosity, Matthew being more wordy for a sentence or two, then Mark, then Matthew, and so on; see Matt 24:1-25:46 and Mark 13:1-17; Matt 26:1-16 and Mark 14:1-11; Matt 26:36-46 and Mark 14:32-43; Matt 26:57-75 and Mark 14:53-72.

Interestingly, of the 54 instances where Mark is the more succinct, 36, or exactly two-thirds, fall after the point (Matt 19:1; Mark 10:1) where Jesus finally departs from Galilee.

2. Direct Discourse. It is frequently the case that direct discourse is a sign of primitivity, indirect the mark of a later writer. Here again, in parallel passages Mark sometimes has direct discourse where Matthew has indirect. In all the

following, however, Matthew quotes directly, Mark indirectly.
For the starred items, we have seen other reasons to think
Matthew the more original:

Matt 12:10; 13:10; *15:15; *15:22; 17:9; *22:42b; 26:15;
Mark   3:2;   4:10;   7:17;   7:26; 9:9; 12:35b; 14:10;

Matt *26:42; 26:66b; 26:72;
Mark 14:39; 14:64b; 14:70.

    3. Gaps in the Second Gospel, Acknowledged. In 1953 I
noted some 13 places where the Second Evangelist expresses his
awareness of material he has not used. In every instance, Matthew at that point has the material, and it is intensively Jewish and Palestinian; whereas, in all but one, Luke has no material, but its language is smoother than Mark's.

    At a number of other places the Second Evangelist men-
tions teaching without giving it, and at these points Matthew
too lacks the teaching; so does Luke, with the possible exception of Luke 4:16ff.:

    Mark 1:21f. corresponds in position to Matt 4:12ff., viz.,
Matthew's extended Jewish note about Capernaum. But Mark 1:22
is like Matt 7:29, "he taught them as having authority, and not
as the scribes." In Mark the latter is quite out of context.
It appears to be a further sign that the Second Evangelist knew
the Sermon on the Mount which, in its earlier "K" form, would
often have been too Jewish for his purpose.

    At three points, the Matthean parallel likewise mentions
teaching without giving it: Mark 1:39 = Matt 4:23; Mark 6:2 =
Matt 13:54; Mark 6:6 = Matt 9:35 where Matthew has "healing"
too. Only the first of these has a Lukan parallel (Luke 4:44).
As to the second, Luke 4:16ff. is a very different story from
that of Matt 13:54ff.; Mark 6:1ff.

    Twice, where Mark mentions teaching without giving it,
Matthew has healing only: Mark 6:34 = Matt 14:14 (Luke 9:11,
teaching and healing); Mark 10:1 = Matt 19:2. In these Matthean passages, as also at Matt 9:35, we perhaps have the hand
of the final Matthean redactor.

    In none of the above passages does the Second Evangelist
imply that he has or has seen the missing material. Hence,
with the exception of Mark 1:21f., these cases are on a different footing from the thirteen previously discussed: for these,
the Grundschrift itself seems to have lacked the material.

    In 1953 I remarked how, when the Second Evangelist con-
denses, not totally omits, what is before him, he often resorts
to the verb erxato. (Luke, who has a penchant for that same
verb, seldom has it where Mark does.) To this general remark
should be added one from H. B. Swete, that when the Second Evangelist is consciously omitting material, he drops his favorite euthus.[14]

4. <u>Gaps in the Second Gospel, Not Acknowledged</u>. The
Second Gospel has other gaps and awkward transitions. One of
these (10:46) was noticed above, and several in the 1953 study:
1:1-2; 5:42-43; 11:33-12:1; 14:47-48'. There are still others:

Mark 1:13-14 leaps from the temptation to the Galilean
mission. So does Matt 4:11-12, while Luke 4:13-14 is but
slightly smoother. But Matt 23:37 and Acts 1:21f. allude to a
Judean ministry during that interval, while Luke and John refer
to it frequently. Only the Second Gospel ignores it altogether.

Mark 3:21-22 leaps from the "friends" who thought Jesus
crazy, to "scribes from Jerusalem." All these appear only in
Mark at this point. Further, and for no apparent reason <u>here</u>,
the scribes accuse Jesus of being in league with Beelzebub.
That sounds like the conclusion of Matt 9:32-34, a passage the
Second Evangelist had good reason to leave out.

5. <u>Anomalies in the Theory of Markan Priority</u>. To maintain the priority of Mark, in the face of all this evidence,
one must have recourse to a large set of assumptions. In fact,
most of us have heard or read most of the following, though perhaps not so baldly put:

Impatience with Jerusalem Church leadership was early;
cordiality toward it was late.

Neglecting or erring about the Hebrew Bible was early;
adherence to it was late.

Explaining Judaism to readers was early; assuming they
were familiar with Judaism (<u>a fortiori</u> were themselves Palestinian Jews) was late.

Ignorance of Palestine and of Jerusalem was early; acquaintance with these was late.

When Mark is more wordy than Matthew, <u>Matthew has short-
ened</u>; when Mark is less wordy than Matthew, <u>Matthew has added</u>.

Patristic tradition need not be explained. If it disagrees with the hypothesis, it may be disregarded. If the fathers erred, it is not necessary to inquire what led them a-
stray.

Such assumptions, whether explicit or, far more often, un-
stated, ought never to go unchallenged.

In particular, when <u>often</u> canonical Mark looks prior, but
<u>sometimes</u> canonical Matthew looks prior, surely it is because
<u>neither is</u>, in reality, descended from the other, but both come
from the same source, which each has handled according to his
need.

V. Can We Do Without Q?

In 1953 I argued that canonical Luke had used not the
<u>Grundschrift</u> and not canonical Matthew, but canonical Mark.

There were, first, the standard "proofs" that the Second Gospel
is in some sense a middle term between the other two: (a) Some
90% of Mark is paralleled in Matthew, some 60% in Luke. (b)
These never agree against Mark in their order, and (c) only
infrequently in their wording. Actually, as pointed out in
1953, there is an identifiable Mark-Luke vocabulary, less extensive than the Matthew-Mark one, but no less real. Further,
it was argued, the Grundschrift contained much that Luke could
have used, had he known it. Most impressive of all, Luke is
almost never able to fill Mark's awkward hiatuses, whereas in
"K" they disappear as though they had never been. The gaps
seem to have embarrassed Luke, for at these points his language
is always smoother than Mark's, as if he had sought to suture
the breaks.

I further argued that Matthew's "Q" appears as a series
of late, secondary insertions. Luke preserved more of "Q," and
adhered more closely to its content and order. However, Luke's
"Q" language fairly resembles the rest of Luke, whereas Matthew's "Q" language differs markedly from the rest of Matthew.
I concluded, as perforce one must if "Q" was an independent document, that Luke had been more willing than Matthew to adapt "Q"
to his own style.

Yet, as indicated earlier in this essay, some recent studies have left me uncomfortable. There is the wide revival of
the Griesbach hypothesis, as instanced by a conference in Eng-
land in the Summer of 1979. There are the scores of places
where Mark looks like a conflation of Matthew and Luke. There
is Robert L. Lindsey's strongly argued case for the priority of
Luke.[15] William R. Farmer has shown how, when form historians
seek out the most primitive traditions, they nearly always turn
not to Mark but to the Matthean or the Lukan Sondergut.[16] There
are Austin Farrer's and H. Palmer's rather philosophical objections to "Q;" their arguments are to be discussed at another
point in our program. There is my own recognition, the significance of which I was slow to perceive, that Luke's "Q" merges
well, both structurally and linguistically, into the rest of
Luke's Gospel, while far less well into Matthew's.

Here one comes on an intriguing parallel, between what B.
H. Streeter said about Luke in 1924,[17] and what I said about Matthew in 1953:

Streeter	Parker
Luke's "Q" and "L" materials were in prior unity,	Matthew's "Markan" and "M" materials were in prior unity,
whereas Luke's "Markan" matter appears always to be subordinate, like something added.	whereas Matthew's "Q" matter appears foreign in language and content, like something added.
When Luke's "Markan" material is erased,	When Matthew's "Q" material is lifted out,
the remainder reads smoothly,	the remainder reads smoothly,

Streeter, cont'd	Parker, cont'd
as if it were a complete Gospel.	though with a different aspect.
That earlier Gospel may be designated Proto-Luke.	That prior Gospel may be designated Proto-Matthew.

To my shame, I did not notice the parallel until just the other day.

To be sure, there are differences. The final redactor of Luke was probably Luke himself, whereas the final redactor of Matthew was probably somebody else. Also we have, from the Second Evangelist, a great excerpt out of Proto-Matthew; but no ancient writer has left us a "Q" excerpt. These very differences might blind us--they had blinded me--to a reality: <u>In Matthew, the "Markan" material looks integral, the "Q" like a foreign intrusion. In Luke, the "Q" material looks integral, the "Markan" like a foreign intrusion.</u>

This could have some startling implications. First, we might conclude that neither "Q" nor "L" ever existed by itself; that <u>"Q" was just those portions of Proto-Luke</u> (or of Luke?) <u>that appealed to the final redactor of Matthew.</u> Second, we should have indeed a Two-Document Hypothesis, but the Two would be Proto-Matthew and Proto-Luke.

To make room for canonical Mark, the resulting diagram will be a trifle less neat than some. Also it might be better to leave open for the nonce the question, whether the Second Evangelist drew upon the Lukan material; hence that line is dotted. The resulting diagram might look like this:

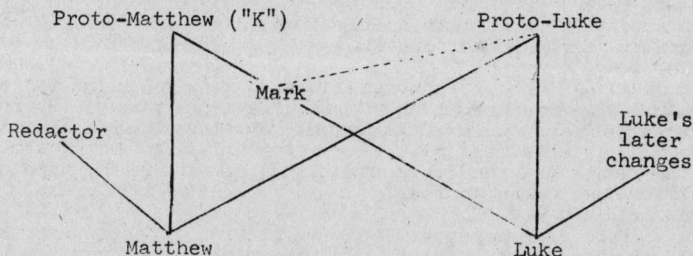

At times this solution strikes me as quite wild. At times it seems to make sense. It posits only two source documents, both of them first editions of existing books. After all, it is not very "wild" to think that a Gospel went through successive editions. That had occurred often in OT literature, and with far greater complexity, as in Esther, Jeremiah, Daniel. Probably it occurred also in other NT literature, e.g., Revelation, the Fourth Gospel,[18] perhaps the Thessalonian correspondence.

Notice, also, that this would give to Proto-Luke a vastly

more definitive role than has hitherto been postulated. That, to my mind, would be eminently fitting. (But it does not identify the "many" who, Luke 1:1 says, had written before him.)

Notice, finally, that this diagram brings together much from the findings of Griesbach, and Streeter, and some of us who came after. That too, I submit, is not unfitting.

VI. Conclusion

Whatever be thought of the right side of the above diagram, it is the left side for which I have most heartily contended. The revisions, suggested in the present pages, do not alter the main thesis.

That left side, the so-called "K" hypothesis, offers what seem to me to be seven important advantages:

1. It explains the peculiarities of Matthean vocabulary and style.

2. It corresponds to clear features of Matthean structure.

3. It corresponds to equally clear, but otherwise tantalizing, features of Second Gospel structure.

4. It accounts for the content, that is, if you will, the Redaktionsgeschichte of the First and Second Gospels.

5. It shows how inevitable it was that the First Gospel should bear the name of Matthew.

6. It fits, more nearly than any other theory I know, what the early fathers said.

7. A further boon came home to me with great force when, recently, I was preparing a small, laymen's commentary on the Gospel of Matthew.[19] This Gospel contains passage after passage that, for centuries, have seemed to Christians intricate, even inscrutable. I found, to my delight, that the "K" hypothesis really does untangle them!

This essay opened with a salutation to persons present. Let it close with a salutation to one now gone from us. In the same years when I was working on The Gospel Before Mark, the eminent Dominican scholar Léon Vaganay was preparing his monumental Le Problème Synoptique.[20] Neither of us knew of the other's labors, until we saw ourselves reviewed jointly in the European press. Simultaneously, independently, and by routes so different that they cannot be merged, we had reached nearly identical conclusions about Mark, and Matthew, and their common parent. There ensued first a correspondence, then a visit to Lyons, and thereafter a warm and, to me, marvellously supportive friendship. Should The Gospel Before Mark ever come forth in new dress and statement, one final change it must have. It must speak good of Canon Vaganay.

Footnotes

1   <u>The Gospel Before Mark</u> (Chicago, 1953).

2   This accusation continued into the Tannaitic period of the Talmud. Cf. b. Sanh. 43a; 107b.

3   "Mark, Acts, and Galilean Christianity," NTS, 16 (1970), 295-304; "When Acts Sides with John," <u>Understanding the Sacred Text</u>, J. Reumann, ed. (Valley Forge, 1972), 203-215; "The Kinship of John and Acts," <u>Christianity, Judaism and Other Greco-Roman Cults</u>, J. Neusner, ed. (Leiden, 1975), 187-205; "How They Looked at Jesus," <u>Saint Luke's Journal of Theology</u>, XIX (1975), 67-77.

4   In an article in <u>Expository Times</u>, lxiv (1953), 283ff. See also, by the same author, <u>The Acts of the Apostles</u> (New York, 1957), 12f. and attendant references.

5   In, respectively, <u>NovTest</u> 10 (1968), 95-147; HTR 64 (1971), 59-78.

6   <u>Clement of Alexandria and a Secret Gospel of Mark</u> (Cambridge, Mass., 1973); cf. especially pp. 188-192f.

7   "The Authorship of the Second Gospel," <u>Perspectives in Religious Studies</u> V, no. 1 (1978), 4-9.

8   Josephus, <u>Ant</u>. XV.v.4.

9   <u>Ant</u>. XVIII.v.2.

10   Cf. W. Wrede, <u>Das Messiasgeheimnis in den Evangelien</u> (Göttingen, 1901; 2d ed. 1913).

11   Cf. O. Weinreich, <u>Tübinger Beiträge zur Altertumswissenschaft</u> (1929), 330ff.

12   Unless, what Mark does not say, the words were directed against Herodias. Compare the words of John the Baptist at Matt 14:4; Mark 6:18.

13   On Markan theology I am particularly indebted to some recent, richly valuable studies by Paul J. Achtemeier, most of which have yet to be published.

14   <u>The Gospel According to St. Mark</u> (London, 3d ed. 1909), lviiif.

15   "A Modified Two-Document Theory of Synoptic Dependence and Interdependence," <u>NovTest</u> (1963), 239-265. My own acquaintance with Lindsey's work comes largely from personal correspondence and conversations, and from two or three articles in the 1969 <u>Jerusalem Post</u>.

16   "The Two-Document Hypothesis as a Methodological Criterion in Synoptic Research," an unpublished address delivered
at Heidelberg University, July 13, 1965.

17   The Four Gospels (London, 1924; 2d ed. 1930).

18   Cf. Pierson Parker, "Two Editions of John," JBL, LXXIX
(1956), 303-314.

19   Good News in Matthew (London, 1976).

20   Paris, 1954.

VIRGINS, WIDOWS, AND PAUL IN SECOND CENTURY ASIA MINOR

Dennis MacDonald
Goshen College

In Christian Asia Minor those who thought women should be permitted to teach and those who did not both appealed to Paul for support. The weapons of this ecclesiastical battle were not primarily differing interpretations of Paul's letters, but the transmission of popular stories about Paul on the one hand, and the creation of pseudo-Pauline letters on the other. To be specific, the Pastoral Epistles, probably from mid-second century Asia Minor,[1] apparently were written to refute an oral tradition in which Paul commissioned a woman to teach. If we can show that this was indeed one of the motivations for the writing of the Pastorals, we shall have made a contribution not only to our understanding of the Pastorals themselves, but also of those Asian communities where Paul's name was used to sanction these competing social norms. Our procedure will be to analyze (1) the use of stories about Paul in Asia Minor to legitimate women teachers, and (2) the objections to these stories in the Pastorals.

The Female Storytellers of Asia Minor

Tertullian wrote:

> But if they claim writings which are wrongly inscribed with Paul's name--I mean the example of Thecla--in support of women's freedom to teach and baptize, let them know that a presbyter in Asia, who put together that book, heaping up a narrative as it were from his own materials under Paul's name, when after conviction he confessed that he had done it from love of Paul, resigned his position.[2]

The book referred to here almost certainly is the Acts of Paul as it has been reconstructed by Carl Schmidt and others.[3] According to the AP, Thecla had refused to marry Thamyris, a wealthy Iconian, because she had embraced Paul's ascetic message. The local governor condemned her to the pyre for not marrying Thamyris, but she was rescued by a hailstorm. Another frustrated lover brought her to a governor in Antioch of Pisidia, who condemned her to the beasts. Again she was rescued, but only after she had baptized herself in a pool of ferocious (?) seals. When she found Paul again, he commissioned her to teach and provide for the poor.

Tertullian claims the Thecla story was created by the author of the AP, but no doubt this Asian presbyter had simply appropriated the story from local oral traditions. For example, the story speaks of a Pontic queen named Tryphaena, a contemporary of Paul and a distant relative to the reigning Claudians.[4] It is quite unlikely that a story about her would have been created de novo late in the second century, for as far as we can tell, she was an insignificant local figure: were it not for a few coins, we would not know she existed. Furthermore, Jerome, Eusebius, Athanasius, Methodius, Gregory of Nazianzus, Gregory of Nyssa, and Theodore of Mopsuestia all mention Thecla, but never in the context of a reference to the AP.[5] Apparently they knew of her from oral tradition.

Our claim that the Asian presbyter appropriated the story from local tradition is supported from other evidence which indicates that in Asia Minor (1) women did in fact exercise ecclesiastical authority, (2) women of the past, like Thecla, were important in ecclesiastical tradition, and (3) women were ecclesiastical storytellers. Our purpose is to show that the situation Tertullian described probably pertained to Asia Minor and that it was not an isolated incident.

Women in Ecclesiastical Authority

As far as we can tell, women exercised more ecclesiastical authority in Asia Minor than anywhere else in the early church. If, as many scholars have suggested, the last chapter of Romans was originally Paul's letter of recommendation to Ephesus on behalf of the Cenchrean deacon Phoebe,[6] the Ephesian church not only hosted this female travelling deacon, but also included a female apostle (Junia; 16:7), several female church workers (Priscilla, Mary, Tryphaena, Tryphosa, and Persis; vss 3,6,12), and other women dear to the apostle (the mother of Rufus, the sister of Nereus, and Julia; vss 13,15). But even if Romans 16 were not originally destined for Ephesus, we still have ample evidence of women in ministry in Asia Minor. Priscilla and her husband Aquila hosted a house church in Ephesus (1 Cor 16:19; cf. Acts 18:2,18,26). The virgin daughters of Philip the Evangelist (Acts 21:8-9) moved to Hierapolis with their father where they continued their prophetic ministry.[7] Pliny the Younger (ca. 112) wrote to Trajan that he received his information about the rites of the Christians in Bithynia from two slave women who were Christian officials (ministrae);[8] Miltiades (ca. 160) wrote about the influence of Ammia of Philadelphia, whom he listed among "those who prophesied in the New Testament period";[9] and Firmillian, bishop of Caesarea in Cappadocia (ca. 260), wrote about a woman there who baptized and performed the Eucharist.[10] Furthermore, several Greek inscriptions in Asia Minor contain the names of deaconesses.[11]

Women also were influential in less "orthodox" Asia Minor Christian communities. John the Prophet scolded the church at Thyatira for having tolerated "that Jezebel, the woman who calls herself a prophetess, whose teaching misleads", and who had a sizeable following (Rev 2:18-25). Of course, the Montanist prophetesses Priscilla and Maximilla exercised extraordinary influence in Asia Minor and elsewhere. Epiphanius says that a prophetess named Quintilla established a sect in Pepuza, Phrygia, in which women were "bishops, presbyters, and the rest, as if there were no difference in nature. 'For in Christ Jesus there is no male and female.'"[12] Either Quintilla or Priscilla --Epiphanius was not sure which--saw Christ in the form of a woman, who lay beside her, endowed her with wisdom, and revealed mysteries to her.[13]

Furthermore, we also have evidence that early in the second century or even in the first many Asian churches subsidized the order of widows. According to Acts 6:1, the earliest Christians maintained widows out of a common fund. Later, widows were expected to pray and care for the needs of the community in return for their support. With these new responsibilities came qualifications for enrollment in the order, such as a good reputation and a pledge to perpetual celibacy. In his letter to the Smyrneans (ca. 107), Ignatius shows clearly that the order of widows flourished in that Asian city, and that some

women there had been admitted into the order who had never married: "I greet the houses of my brothers with their wives and
children, and the virgins who are called 'widows.'"[14] Tertullian also knew of a teenaged woman that an Asian bishop had enrolled with the widows, but, unlike Ignatius, he was appalled
by it.[15]

Devotion to the ascetic life is also prominent in the
Thecla legend: Thecla rejected the amours of Thamyris and
Alexander in order to follow Paul, and was thus considered
worthy to teach the Word of God. Celibacy might have been a
prerequisite for women teachers and prophets: most of the women
known to have ministered in Asia Minor churches were celibate, and perhaps were members of this order of virgins-widows.
The two daughters of Philip who lived in Hierapolis died as
virgins.[16] Priscilla and Maximilla deserted their husbands
from the moment they received prophetic inspiration, and Priscilla thereafter was called a virgin.[17] Quintilla and the
Quintillian clergy were probably celibate, for Epiphanius says
their assemblies often commenced with a procession of "seven
virgins dressed in white . . . carrying lamps, having come in
to prophesy to the people," and who wept, "lamenting human
life."[18] In many contemporary sources this lamentation for human life was attended by asceticism designed to break the chain
of birth.[19]

Women in Ecclesiastical Tradition

Further evidence that women were influential in Christian
Asia Minor comes from the frequent references to holy women of
the past, like Thecla. For example, Priscilla and Maximilla
justified their prophetic office by referring to Ammia of Philadelphia and the daughters of Philip.[20] Likewise, Quintillians
justified their female clergy by appealing to precedence in the
daughters of Philip, in Miriam, Moses' prophesying sister, and
even in Eve, since she was the first to eat of the tree of knowledge.[21]

Epiphanius says that the Nicolaitans, mentioned in the
Apocalypse in connection with Ephesus and Pergamum, valued a
book of Norea,Noah's wife or daughter-in-law.[22] Unfortunately,
Epiphanius is notoriously unreliable when he speaks of heretics
in his own day, not to mention those in the first century; nonetheless, we need not reject his testimony prima facie. Thanks
to the discovery at Nag Hammadi, we now possess two documents
in which Norea is the revealor,[23] and in another we find references to "the First Book (or, Logos) of Noraia" that lists the
feminine names of the archons.[24] Irenaeus, Tertullian, and Clement of Alexandria all called the Nicolaitans Gnostics, and now
that we know of at least three Gnostic books in which Norea is
the revealor, it would appear that the Nicolaitans might well
have used such a book.[25]

Be that as it may, Hippolytus of Rome says the Naassenes
or Ophites in Phrygia claimed to have received their doctrines
from Mariamne, the sister of Philip the Apostle.[26] The references to her in the Sophia of Jesus Christ, which probably originated in Ophite circles,[27] imply that she received secret re-
velations. Apparently the author of the Acts of Philip wanted
to snatch Mariamne away from these Gnostics and give her lodging
in his own theological camp, for according to his story, she accompanied her brother to Hierapolis in order to refute the

Ophites.[28]

When this evidence is added Tertullian's allusion to the
Asian Thecla legend, we may conclude that (1) traditions about
women were told in second century Asia Minor by communities with
differing theologies (i.e., Ophites, Montanists, Quintillians,
and the "Orthodox"), (2) traditions about women were sometimes
used to legitimate women prophets and teachers(i.e., traditions
about Eve, Miriam, Thecla, Ammia, and the daughters of Philip),
and (3) sometimes the traditions were so used by women themselves (i.e., Priscilla, Maximilla, and the Quintillians). In
fact, women in Asia Minor were important tradents of oral narrative.

Women as Ecclesiastical Storytellers

Although all people tell stories, none tell them better
or more frequently than the unlettered. Alex Haley's Roots has
chiseled into our consciousness the vitality of Afro-American
traditional stories, but such storytelling is characteristic of
illiterate or semi-literate peoples everywhere. In fact, studies of oral narratives in modern Yugoslavia have shown that literacy itself can corrupt the storyteller's craft, and that the
gap between literate and oral cultures within the same society
often is wide.[29] Of course, women in the ancient world were
for the most part illiterate, and Greek authors frequently mention women as storytellers (from them we have the phrase "old
wives' tale").[30] Today in Turkey, women are still the primary
bearers of oral narrative.[31] (Among their stories are some
about Khoja girls, or female Muslim priests--there are no female
Muslim priests!) But we need not appeal to analogies outside
of second century Asia Minor to establish the importance of
oral stories there.

Papias, the bishop of Hierapolis (d. ca. 130), wrote
five books on the sayings of Jesus using oral tradition as his
primary source; he recorded the commandments of the Lord as they
had been repeated by the faithful.[32] He also tells us that:

> if ever anyone came who had followed the presbyters, I
> enquired into the words of the presbyters, what Andrew or
> Philip or Thomas or James or John or Matthew, or any
> other of the Lords's disciples, were saying. For I did
> not suppose that information from books would help me so
> much as the word of a living and surviving voice.[33]

Among Papias' living voices were those of the virgin daughters
of Philip who also lived in Hierapolis. One of their stories
told of the raising to life of the mother of Manaemus--notice,
the subject is a woman.[34] Perhaps they also told Papias the
story of "a woman who was accused before the Lord of many sins,
which," says Eusebius, "the Gospel according to the Hebrews contains."[35] Presumably this is the story of the adulterous woman
which appears in some texts of the Fourth Gospel between 7:52
and 8:12, and in which Jesus defends the woman against her male
accusers. In any case, Papias apparently knew the story only
in its oral form.

Furthermore, the contents of the Thecla legend--as well
as Tertullian's reference--suggest it was told primarily by
women. Everyone who reads the Thecla story in the AP is struck
by its female imagery and preoccupation. Many of the primary

characters are women: Thecla, Theocleia (her mother), and Tryphaena. Paul's followers are primarily "women and virgins,"[36]
and the crowds claim he had corrupted the women of Iconium.[37]
Notice also the female preoccupation in the following précis of
one section.[38]

> In Antioch of Pisidia, Thecla defended herself against
> the violent embraces of an official, whom the local gov-
> ernor appeased by condemning Thecla to the beasts--in
> spite of the protests of the Antiochean women. When
> Thecla asked to be kept pure from men until the day of
> her execution, she was entrusted to the house of Queen
> Tryphaena, and was escorted there by crying women. While
> with Tryphaena, Thecla offered a prayer for the salvation
> of Tryphaena's deceased daughter. Although Tryphaena and
> the other women again protested the injustice, the sol-
> diers finally took Thecla to the theatre where wild
> beasts were released against her. Then a "fierce lion-
> ess ran to her and lay down at her feet. And the crowd
> of women raised a great shout." A bear ran upon Thecla
> and the lioness killed it. "And the women mourned the
> more, since the lioness which helped her was dead." When
> more beasts were released against her, "the women threw
> petals, others nard, others cassia, others amomum, so
> that there was an abundance of perfumes. And all the
> beasts let loose were over-powered as if by sleep."
> While other means of execution were being prepared, Try-
> phaena fainted. Thinking she had died and fearing im-
> perial reprisals for the death of this member of the
> royal family, the authorities released Thecla to her
> cheering sisters. Tryphaena, revived, received her once
> again into her house, and soon the majority of the maid-
> servants were converted.

If the contents of any early Christian story suggest its tellers were women, this is it. And if the Thecla story were told
primarily by women, it is possible that other stories in the AP
were also told by women.

In a forthcoming book I show that three sections of the
AP share identical narrative patterns and oral conventions as
these have been described by modern folklorists. These sections
are (1) the Thecla section (ch. 3), (2) the Ephesian section,
which contains the story of Paul and the Baptized Lion (ch. 7,
and the appendix in New Testament Apocrypha, 2. 387-390), and
(3) the martyrdom section (chs. 9-11). Because these sections
are so structurally similar--and dissimilar from the rest of
the AP--it is likely that they were transmitted in the same
storytelling tradition, told by the same storytellers. Of
course, by itself this observation does not prove the stories
were told by women, but there are other reasons for identifying
the Ephesian and martyrdom sections of the AP with women storytellers.

Like the Thecla section, the Ephesus section is dominated
by Paul's female companions: he stays with Aquila and Priscilla in Ephesus; he tells how he had travelled with the widow
Lemma and her daughter Ammia (of Philadelphia?), who had a following in Ephesus; he is persecuted because he converted Procla
and her household; and he is visited in prison by Eubula and
Artemilla against the wishes of their husbands. Here too, as
in the Thecla section, Paul's primary antagonists are men--

especially jealous husbands--and he is saved by means of a hailstorm and a friendly lion.

In the martyrdom section, we find a reference to Mary,
the mother of Jesus, and to a respected prophetess named Myrta;
otherwise, the story is entirely about men. Fortunately, however, we can relate this section to female storytellers by a
curious external reference. According to this section of the
AP, Paul is brought before Nero for judgment, and during the
hearing Barsabas Justus and several others in Nero's guard declare that they too are soldiers of Paul's King. Nero orders
these traitors executed along with the other Christians, but
when the Romans complain about the many deaths of their fellow
citizens, Nero relents. Barsabas Justus and his friends are
released. We are not told by what good fortune Barsabas was
spared while so many others were killed; perhaps this is simply
an inconsistency characteristic of oral narrative and of which
there are several in the AP. But it would also seem possible
that sometimes the story was told with an explanation of Bar-
sabus' good fortune. Eusebius says that the daughters of
Philip told Papias about a certain Barsabas Justus, who was
forced to drink poison, and was miraculously saved from its
effects.[39] This corresponds perfectly to the AP story, for
death by poison was never used for executing common Christians:
it apparently was reserved for Roman officials accused of mal-
feasance or treason.[40] By itself this intriguing connection
between the daughters of Philip and stories about Paul is inconclusive. But when one recognizes that the sections sharing
identical narrative structures not shared with the rest of the
AP are the very sections for which there is other evidence for
linking them with women storytellers, the connection becomes
quite plausible.

Perhaps we should now back away from our mosaic of frag-
mentary references and look at the larger picture. It is clear
that women taught in Asia Minor congregations, and that their
teaching was apparently confined to oral communication. As far
as we know, we possess not one single word written by them, but
we know that many of them prophesied and told holy stories.
Many of these women teachers were celibate, and at least one of
their stories praised the virtues of virginity. Perhaps we
should interpret this virginity as a rebellion--conscious or
unconscious--against male domination. Perhaps it symbolized
not only moral purity, but independence, dedication to a calling, and criticism of conjugal society. Be that as it may,
they told stories about Paul to support their asceticism and
ministries.

On the other hand, the ecclesiastical leadership in Asia
Minor was predominantly male, not dogmatically ascetic, and
more literate. This observation itself suggests there might
have been conflicts there between female and male leadership,
between celibacy and matrimony, between orality and literacy.
But the Pastoral Epistles (PE) prove beyond reasonable doubt
that such conflicts did in fact exist, for the author of the PE
knew of these celibate women teachers and their stories, and he
wrote in Paul's name to silence them.

The Male Story Squelcher of Asia Minor

Our claim that the PE are pseudonyms written to refute the depiction of Paul in local oral traditions does not mean that everything in them is best explained in this way (although much is), for the author's intentions no doubt were quite varied and complex. Nor are we saying that the author objected to every depiction of Paul in the tradition, or that the only depiction to which he objected was that related to women teachers. In fact, we shall see that at many points he agreed, and at many others he disagreed. Furthermore, we do not mean that the author knew of the stories in the form we now have them in the AP, for this would be to ignore the flexibility and vitality characteristic of oral narratives. Our claim is simply that one of the author's motivations for writing in Paul's name was to "correct" a living oral tradition about Paul, a tradition which ultimately was incorporated into the Thecla, Ephesus, and martyrdom sections of the AP.

No doubt the first response of many readers will be incredulity, and not just of those who think Paul himself wrote the PE. Those who have recognized the relationships between the PE and the AP have almost all claimed that the AP knew of the PE, but there is no necessary chronological reason for it. The PE are not externally attested until the second half of the second century, and even if the AP were composed late in the second century--that is, a few years before Tertullian's reference to it--the stories themselves, if traditional, might well have been told much earlier. Furthermore, an analysis of the relationships between the AP and the PE will demonstrate that the PE knew of these traditions.

Knowledge of Oral Traditions about Paul

According to the AP, Paul's host in Iconium was Onesiphorus and his family, who remained loyal to the Apostle even in his imprisonment (3,2-25). The only other place in all of early Christian literature that we find Onesiphorus mentioned is in the PE.[41] 2 Tim 1:15-18 reads:

> You are aware that all who are in Asia turned away from me, and among them Phygelus and Hermogenes. May the Lord grant mercy to the household of Onesiphorus, for he often refreshed me; he was not ashamed of my chains, but when he arrived in Rome he searched for me eagerly and found me--may the Lord grant him to find mercy from the Lord on that Day--and you well know all the service he rendered at Ephesus.

Presumably, his readers, like himself, had known of the service of Onesiphorus via oral tradition.

In contrast to Onesiphorus' hospitality, the passage above mentions Hermogenes, who turned away from Paul in Asia. Similarly, 2 Tim 4:10 mentions a certain Demas, who, "in love with this present world," had deserted Paul. The only other place one finds Hermogenes mentioned is in the AP where he and Demas are depicted as Paul's travel companions to Iconium, but who, when bribed, betrayed him (3,1-16). This fits the references in the PE precisely. Furthermore, even though Demas is also mentioned in Phlm 24 and Col 4:14, it is only in the AP and the PE that he is depicted as a deserter. Both the AP and

the PE also complain about an Alexander.[42]   In light of the
close connections between these documents, the reference to
Paul's deliverance from the lion's mouth in 2 Tim 4:17 would
seem to be an allusion to the story of Paul's deliverance from
the baptized lion in the AP, and not a mere metaphor, as is
probably the case with a similar reference in 1 Cor 15:32.

In 2 Tim 3:10-11 we find another possible connection with
the stories in the AP.

> Now you have observed my teaching, my conduct, my aim in
> life, my faith, my patience, my love, my steadfastness,
> my persecutions, my sufferings, what befell me at Antioch,
> at Iconium and at Lystra, what persecutions I endured;
> yet from them all the Lord rescued me.

The Thecla section begins with Paul's flight from a persecution
in Antioch, and then narrates his persecution and rescue in Iconium, and his journey toward Lystra. The canonical Acts also
mentions persecutions and deliverances at Antioch, Iconium and
Lystra (13:44-14:23), but these stories too may be dependent on
variant oral traditions.[43] In any case, there is little evidence otherwise of the author's knowledge of the canonical Acts
in the PE, and much evidence of his knowledge of the oral traditions about Paul.

Opposition to Oral Traditions about Paul

More striking than the similarities between the AP and the
PE are the differences. For example, in the AP Paul robs
Thamyris of his betrothed, and Hieronymos of his wife. For
good reason, then, Paul was accused of upsetting households and
of leading women astray (3,13-15). But in the PE, Paul de-
nounces this very practice, for he rejects those who "make
their way into households and capture weak women, burdened with
sins and swayed by various impulses," like Thecla (2 Tim 3:6-7),
and against those who are "upsetting whole families" (Tit 1:11).
Furthermore, in 1 Tim 4:3 we find a rejection of "those who forbid people to marry and to eat foods which God created to be received with thanksgiving," but in the AP it is Paul himself who
forbids marriage and who eats only vegetarian meals (3,25).
Wine too is rejected in the AP--even the Eucharist consists of
bread and water (ch. 7)--but in 1 Tim 5:23 Paul tells Timothy:
"No longer drink only water, but use a little wine for the sake
of your stomach."

In this context also we must re-examine the scholarly consensus on 2 Tim 2:17-18, where the author warns against those
who claimed the resurrection had already taken place. This is
usually interpreted as a Gnostic-like claim that the soul puts
off the body when it receives gnosis, or when the initiate is
baptized. Of course, we must agree that our author knew and opposed Gnosticism (e.g., 1 Tim 6:20), but if the primary point
of comparison is the oral tradition, another interpretation
would seem more likely. In the Thecla section of the AP Paul
says that only those who are sexually pure will be raised (3,5
and 12), but in refuting him, Demas and Hermogenes argue that
they had already been raised, not through gnosis or baptism,
but "in the children we have" (3,14).

Curiously enough, even though the PE agree with Paul
against Demas and Hermogenes that the resurrection had not yet

taken place, they seem to agree with Demas and Hermogenes against Paul that salvation is contingent on bearing children, at least for women. We find this expressed in the following passage, in which the contrast between the AP and the PE is perhaps the most pronounced.

> Let a woman learn in silence with all submissiveness. I permit no woman to teach or to have authority over men; she is to keep silent. For Adam was formed first, then Eve; and Adam was not deceived, but the woman was deceived and became a transgressor. Yet woman will be saved through bearing children, if she continues in faith and love and holiness, with modesty (1 Tim 2:11-15).

Whereas the tradition said Paul commissioned a woman to teach, here he forbids it. Whereas the tradition said Paul told women that only those who kept themselves pure would participate in the resurrection, here he says women will be saved through bearing children. He would silence women from teaching in the churches, and have them sing lullabies in the nurseries. He had other plans for the older women.

Opposition to the Storytellers

Apparently the author also wanted to curtail the influence of some of the storytellers by limiting the number of women enrolled as widows. In 1 Tim 5:3-16, it is clear that, in the communities from which the PE came, (1) women in the order of "widows" included the young as well as the old;[44] (2) they had pledged themselves to celibacy;[45] (3) they were supported by the community at large;[46] and (4) they were responsible for intercessory prayer, acts of mercy, and visitation.[47] But the author wanted to decimate the office by denying eligibility to any widow under sixty years of age, to any whose character was questionable, and to any who could have found support from relatives or friends.[48]

The author gives three reasons for his limitations of the order: (1) the church is financially burdened; (2) some of the younger widows have broken their pledge to celibacy; and (3) some of the widows are going from house to house saying things they should not. When one examines each of these objections individually, it appears that the author's primary objection was to their itinerant communication.

(1) Three times--once at the beginning, once at the end, and once in the middle--we find almost identical formulae, each of which contains commands for the families or friends to assume economic care of the widows.

> If any widow has children or grandchildren, let them first learn their religious duty to their own family and make some return to their parents; for this is acceptable in the sight of God (vs. 4; the "religious duty" probably refers to the Fifth Commandment, Ex. 20:12).

> If anyone does not provide for his relatives, and especially for his own family, he has disowned the faith and is worse than an unbeliever (vs 8).

> If any believing woman has widows, let her assist them; let not the church be burdened, so that it may assist

those who are true widows (vs 16).

In each case, the conditional sentences are present simple conditions, which construction implies that those in the community
were in fact not caring for the widows in their own families,
while the community at large was. Furthermore, the most natural
reading of vs. 16 is to take the "believing woman" who "has widows" as a woman who kept "widows" in her home, and who received
financial assistance for doing so from the church. That such
widow-houses did in fact exist is well attested.[49]

In spite of the request that the church be relieved of
financial responsibility for the widows, it is unlikely that
the author's primary objection to the office was economic.
Notice that only in vs. 16 is it explicitly stated that the
church's budget was burdened. In the first two passages the
motivation was not economic but religious: it is a "religious
duty" to provide for one's own (vs 4); one has "disowned the
faith and is worse than an unbeliever" if he or she does not
provide for relatives (vs 8). Furthermore, it would appear
that the communities addressed in the Pastorals were relatively
well-to-do. Rich people and slave owners who profited from the
work of their believing slaves were members of the community
(1 Tim 6:1-11, 17-19). Notice also that immediately after this
passage on widows--with its alleged concern for the budget--we
find:

> Let the elders who rule well be considered worthy of
> double pay (διπλῆς τιμῆς), especially those who labor in
> preaching and teaching, for the scripture says, "You shall
> not muzzle an ox when it is treading out the grain," and,
> "the laborer deserves his wages" (5:17-18; the quotations
> are from Dt 25:4 and perhaps 24:15).

The author would pay the elders double and the widows less. We
must probe deeper if we are to understand why the widows were
considered a liability.

(2) Apparently some younger "widows" who had made a pledge
of chastity to Christ had later desired to marry, and therefore,
in the author's opinion, had incurred judgment (vss 11-12). His
objection is not to the marriage as such--which he himself com-
mends to the younger "widows"--but to the violation of a vow.
No doubt this was a problem for the widows, as it has been for
many ascetic orders, whether ancient or modern, male or female.
Nonetheless, there is more to his objection than appears at first
sight.

Notice that the author does not say the young "widows" desire to remarry, it simply says to marry (vss 12 and 14). Furthermore, the author several times seems to prohibit second mar-
riages; in fact, in this very context it says the "widow" must
have been the wife of only one husband (vs 9). This would suggest that perhaps these young "widows" were not actually widows
at all, like the virgin-widows known to Ignatius and Tertullian.
Surely this was in fact the case. The author says the community
should support only "true widows" (αἱ ὄντως χῆραι), which almost
all commentators have taken to mean those widows in the order in
contrast to other widows in the congregation. This interpretation would seem well girded by vs 16, which reads: "If some believing woman has widows, let her care for them, and do not let

the church be burdened, in order that it might care for the
true widows." But it is also possible to take the "true widow"
as one who in fact was a widow, in contrast to an unmarried
woman enrolled in the order. In support of this interpretation
is not only the author's command that young "widows" marry,
even though he objects to remarriage, but also his insistence
that the true widow is one who has been left alone (ἡ δὲ ὄντως
χήρα καὶ μεμονωμένη, vs 5), one who has indeed been a wife (vs
9). Furthermore, the true widow must have demonstrated her
abilities in child-rearing and in domestic hospitality (vs 10).
It would appear then that the reference to "the true widows" in
vs 16 is not primarily intended to distinguish between those in
the order of widows and the other widows in the community, but
to reaffirm that only women who have in fact been widowed are
eligible for support. In any case it would also appear that
this breach of the pledge by young widows probably was not the
author's primary objection to the order, because it does not
explain his insistence that even the older widows be taken from
the roll if they can find other support.

(3) The author complains that some widows "also learn to
be idle when they make house calls, and not only to be idle,
but also to be trivia peddlers (φλύαροι) and busybodies, speaking what is not acceptable" (λαλοῦσαι τὰ μὴ δέοντα,vs 13). Perhaps here we find the author's deepest irritations with the wid-
ows--at least it would explain the polymorphous limitations he
placed on the enrollment. Some of the widows in their house
calls have been transmitters of communication objectionable to
our author. Unfortunately, we are not told the content of this
communication, but surely it was not heresy--say, Gnostic or
Marcionite--or the author certainly would have raised this objection and excluded them not only from the order of widows,
but from the fellowship as well, since that is frequently his
solution for theological opposition.[50]

I suggest that the author here is attempting to silence
not only the content of the oral tradition, but its tradents as
well. 1 Timothy begins with Paul's reminder to Timothy that he
had left the young bishop in Ephesus (!) to admonish the Ephesi-
ans not to occupy themselves with μῦθοι, or stories (vss 3-4).
For some have swerved from the faith and "have wandered away
into idle talk, desiring to be teachers" (vss 6-7). Unfortunately, the genders of the Greek words here do not indicate the
genders of these storytellers, for the relevant words simply
agree with the derived forms of τὶς (vss 3 and 6), which can be
either masculine or feminine. But perhaps the gender of these
storytellers is revealed in 1 Tim 4:7 in the sentence: τοὺς δὲ
βεβήλους καὶ γραώδεις μύθους παραιτοῦ, which should be translated: "And reject the profane stories told by old women."
Notice also that this reference to old women's tales is in the
context of a discussion of those who forbid marriage (4:1-5).
In Tit 2:3-5 Paul admonishes the old women not to be slanderers,
but "to teach what is good, and so train the young women to
love their husbands and children, to be sensible, chaste, domestic, kind, and submissive to their husbands."

Conclusion

If the thrust of our argument has been correct, it would
appear that the author of the PE, like Tertullian, objected to
the depiction of Paul in Asian oral tradition, and the use of

that tradition to legitimate women teachers. His strategy was to foist these letters onto Paul, which--if accepted as Pauline --would forever "correct" the tradition and help to silence the storytellers. That is, not only does the Paul of the PE explicitly disagree with the Paul in the AP about celibacy, women teachers, and the use of wine and meat, he also muzzles the storytellers by telling Timothy and Titus to avoid stories told by old women, to prohibit women teachers, and to reduce the order of virgins-widows to a vestige.

He worked hard and well at making the letters appear Pauline. Over and over again he interspersed autobiographical allusions: references to experiences and people and cities traditionally identified with Paul. He even included rather moving descriptions of Paul's feelings soon before his death (2 Tim 4:6-18).

He succeeded. Almost all later discussions about eligibility for enrollment with the "widows" follow the advice of this Pseudo-Paul, such as those discussions in Tertullian, Clement of Alexandria, Origen, Hippolytus, and Didascalia Apostolorum, the Apostolic Constitutions, and the Ecclesiastical Canons of the Apostles. Furthermore, the polemical pseudonymity of the PE has deceived the majority of readers even to our own day. By making the PE canonical, the early church decided against women teaching, and prejudiced the interpretation of Paul for almost two millenia. This is not a plea for canonizing the AP or its depiction of Paul; it is a plea for removing the PE from our interpretations of Paul, and for placing them in the context of the controversies raging in second century Asia Minor where they belong.

Finally, let me give my thanks first to the unknown presbyter of Asia who lost his title and ecclesiastical authority for having written down these unpopular popular stories, and second, to the unknown scribes of many centuries who transferred the story of Thecla to ever newer papyri. Without them this paper would have been impossible.

NOTES

[1]Although Hans von Campenhausen has failed to convince many that the author of the Pastorals was Polycarp, he has shown that the ecclesiastical situation, the proto-Catholic bias, and the use of tradition in the Pastorals are strikingly similar to those in Smyrna in the mid-second century (Polykarp von Smyrna und die Pastoralbriefe /Sitzungsberichte der Heidelberger Akademie der Wissenschaft. Philosophisch-Historische Klasse; Heidelberg: Carl Winter, 1951/, also in Aus der Frühzeit des Christentums /Tübingen: J.C.B. Mohr (Paul Siebeck), 1963/ 197-252).

[2]De baptismo I, 17, as quoted in A New Eusebius: Documents Illustrative of the History of the Church to A.D. 337 (ed. J. Stevenson; London: S.P.C.K., 1957) 184.

[3]Acta Pauli aus der Heidelberger koptischen Papyrushandschrift nr. 1 (Hildesheim: Georg Olms Verlagsbuchhandlung, 1965; 1965; reprint of the second edition, Leipzig: J. C. Hinrichs, 1905), and Πράξεις Παύλου: Acta Pauli nach dem Papyrus der Hamburger Staats-und Universitäts-Bibliothek (with the help of

Wilhelm Schubart; Glückstadt and Hamburg: J.J. Augustin, 1936).
ET available in New Testament Apocrypha (ed. Edgar Hennecke and
Wilhelm Schneemelcher; trans. R. McL. Wilson; Philadelphia:
Westminster Press, 1965) 2. 352-390.

[4]William M. Ramsay, "The Acts of Paul and Thekla," in The
Church in the Roman Empire before A.D. 170 (Grand Rapids: Baker
Book House, 1954) 382-389.

[5]See the article on Thecla by John Gwynn in The Dictionary of Christian Biography (London: John Murray, 1887) 4. 886-
892. Gregory of Nazianzus says he visited a monastery bearing
her name in Seleucia in about 375 CE, and there is ample literary evidence for a Thecla cult in the fourth century (H. Lec-
lerq, "Thecla" in Dictionnaire d'archéologie et de liturgie
/Paris: Librairie Letouzey et Ané, 1953/ 15. 2225-2235, and the
entry for Thecla in Bibliotheca Hagiographica Graeca /third edition ed. François Halken; Bruxelles: Societé des Bollandistes,
1957/ 2. 267-269).

[6]The arguments for an Ephesian destination are as follows:
(1) letters of recommendation were common in Pauline circles
(e.g., Acts 18:27; 2 Cor 3:1-3; 8:16-23), (2) vss 30-33 of chapter 15, which include a benediction and a final Amen, appear to
be the end of a letter, (3) the admonition in 16:17-20 that the
recipients avoid those who were creating dissensions seems to
be unrelated to anything in the rest of Romans, and it has an
authoritarian spirit unlike that in the rest of the book, (4)
Paul probably would not have addressed so many people with intimate greetings in a letter to a church he had never visited, (5)
Aquila and Priscilla, mentioned in vss 3-4, were last mentioned
in connection with Ephesus (1 Cor 16:19; cf. Acts 18:24-26), and
(6) in vs 5 Epaenetus is called the first convert in Asia.

[7]Eusebius, HE 3, 31, 3, quoting a letter of Polycrates of
Ephesus ,to Victor of Rome (cf. 3,39,8-10). See also HE 3, 31, 4,
where Eusebius also quotes from a work of Gaius against Proclus
to confirm the witness of Polycrates. For a good discussion of
the confusion of Philip the Evangelist with Philip the Apostle
see P. Corssen, "Die Töchter des Philippus," ZNW 2 (1901) 289-
299.

[8]Pliny, Letters 10, 96, 8.

[9]Quoted by Apollinarius of Hierapolis in Eusebius, HE 5,
17, 2-4.

[10]Cyprian, Ep. 74, 10 and 11.

[11]Nunes, Strateges, Pribus, and Matrona in Eastern Phrygia
(at Axylos); Masa, Aurelia Faustina, Paula, and Timothea in
Cilicia (at Laodicea Combusta and Korykos); Arete in Caria (at
Aphrodisias); and Elaphia in Nevinne. See Roger Gryson, The
Ministry of Women in the Early Church (trans. Jean Laporte and
Mary Louise Hall; Collegeville, Minn.: The Liturgical Press,
1976) 90-91.

[12]Panarion, heresy 49, 2, quoting Gal 3:28.

[13]Ibid., heresy 49, 1.

[14]Smyrn. 13:1.

[15]"In a certain place a virgin of less than twenty years of age has been placed in the order of widows" (De virginibus velandis, ch. 9, ANCL). This "certain place" undoubtedly was in Asia Minor. Before writing this Latin treatise Tertullian had already gone to the trouble of writing one in Greek, which certainly suggests that the objectionable practice of not veiling virgins obtained in the Greek East. But Greece was not the place, for he says explicitly that all adult Greek women wore veils, even in Corinth (ch. 8). Furthermore, the congregations where virgins were not veiled were founded by "apostles and apostolic people" (ch. 2).

Tertullian called this virgin-widow a monstrosity. This attitude, so unlike Ignatius', probably reflects the different way African churches supported single women. African (and Syrian) churches had a separate order of virgins, but there was no such distinction in Asia Minor. Needy women who had taken the pledge to celibacy were simply enrolled with the widows and shared their title.

[16]Eusebius, HE 3, 31, 3.

[17]Ibid., 3, 18, 3.

[18]Panarion, heresy 49, 2.

[19]Marcion, Julius Cassianus, the Gospel of the Egyptians (in Clement of Alexandria), the Gospel of Thomas, the Acts of Thomas, and the Gospel of Philip to name a few.

[20]Eusebius, HE 5, 17, 4, and Origen's fragment on 1 Cor #74 published in JTS 10 (1908-9) 41-42.

[21]Epiphanius, Panarion, heresy 49, 2.

[22]Ibid., heresy 26, 1, 3; cf. Philaster of Brescia, Liber de haeresibus 33, 3. Nicolaitans are mentioned in Rev 2:6 and 15.

[23]The Hypostasis of the Archons and the Thought of Norea.

[24]CG II, 102, 10-11, and 24-25.

[25]Of course, Gnostics frequently venerated women revealors, and not only in Asia Minor, e.g., see Origen, Contra Celsum 5, 62.

[26]Ref. 5, 7, 1.

[27]According to Douglas M. Parrott in The Nag Hammadi Library In English (ed. James M. Robinson; San Francisco: Harper and Row, 1977) 207.

[28]Acts of Philip 9, 107-129.

[29]Albert B. Lord, The Singer of Tales (Harvard Studies in Comparative Literature 24; Cambridge, Mass.: Harvard University Press, 1960; reprint New York: Atheneum, 1978) 124-138.

[30]For example, see Plato, Republic I, 350E; II, 377C; Gorgias 527A; Theaetetus 176B; and Strabo, Geography I, 2, 3, C 16.

31According to Pertev Naili Boratav, <u>Zaman Zaman Ichinde</u> (Istanbul: Remzi Kitabevi 1958) 14-15, quoted by Warren S. Walker and Ahmet E. Uysal in <u>Tales Alive in Turkey</u> (Cambridge, Mass.: Harvard University Press, 1966) 2.

32Eusebius, <u>HE</u> 3, 39, 3.

33<u>Ibid</u>., 3, 39, 4.

34According to the Epitome of Philip of Side (<u>TU</u> v. 2, 170); cf. Eusebius, <u>HE</u> 3, 39, 9.

35<u>HE</u> 3, 39, 17.

36Chapter 7.

37Chapter 15.

38The précis is of chapters 26-39.

39<u>HE</u> 3, 39, 9.

40See for example Ignatius' lists of kinds of execution in Rom 5:3 and Smyrn 4:2. I have read through Herbert Musurillo's <u>Acts of the Christian Martyrs: Introduction, Texts and Translations</u> (London: Oxford University Press, 1972), and I have not found a single reference to death by poison. In the <u>Acts of John</u> we find the Apostle willingly submitting to a trial by ordeal which involved drinking poison, and in which John was spared. Notice, however, that the poison was not given John forcibly; he willingly took it to prove God's ability to do wonder through him (ch. 20).
  As Eusebius knew, a Barsabas Justus also appears in the Acts of the Apostles as a member of the Palestinian church, and was one of the two men eligible to occupy Judas' place among the twelve (1:21-26; cf. 15:22). Since it is unlikely that there were two people with the same name, one in Palestine and one in Rome, it would appear that the tradition simply used the same name in different stories.

412 Tim 1:15-18 and 4:19.

422 Tim 4:15-16; AP 3, 26-35.

43According to Ernst Haenchen, <u>The Acts of the Apostles: A Commentary</u> (trans. Bernard Noble and Gerald Shinn, under the supervision of Hugh Anderson, and with the translation revised by R. McL. Wilson; Philadelphia: Westminster, 1971) 433.

441 Tim 5:11.

451 Tim 5:12.

461 Tim 5:3, 8, 16.

471 Tim 5:5, 13.

481 Tim 5:4, 8, 9, 10 and 16.

[49]The Acts of Peter mention a Marcellus who supported widows in his home (21,22,28,29). Hermas mentions a certain Grapte who was responsible for widows and orphans (Vis. 2,4,3), and Eleusis of Cyzikus (fourth cent.) established houses for widows and virgins (Sozomenus, Hist. Eccl. V,15,5). Notice also that Tabitha in Acts 9:36-42 belonged to a circle of widows whom she had supplied with garments.

[50]1 Tim 1:20 (6:3-5); 2 Tim 4:14-15; Tit 3:8-11.

"THIS IS A HARD SAYING;

WHO CAN BE A LISTENER TO IT?"

THE CREATION OF THE READER IN JOHN 6

Gary Phillips

College of the Holy Cross

PRÉCIS

The purpose of this essay is to describe and explain John 6 in light of its discoursive structure(s). Our approach is macro-textual and not concerned with an exhaustive analysis of the syntactic and semantic structures of individual pericopaes in John 6. Rather the attention is placed upon the text's *PRAGMATIC* features. One of these pragmatic structures we can label the *enunciative structure*.

One reason for this particular approach isthe need to begin redressing the syntactic and semantic imbalance in the structural study of texts by focussing upon text pragmatic and text macro-structures. Prevailing conditions in the structural market place favor text syntactics and text semantics at a micro-level (the pericopae as opposed to the larger texual unit). Often as not this involves a methodological choice reflecting a static conception of text, a position which is counter to the view of text as a particular kind of discoursive event.

Our approach assumes a dynamic view of text à la Ricoeur. Text is a discourse that presupposes a speaker, a world and a vis-à-vis. Text is a discoursive work, a linguistic productivity in which there is reference forward to an extra-linguistic reality, backward to a speaker and a communicative relationship with a listener. One way of describing the "discoursive" structure of John 6, which is critical to a comprehension of the text's meaning effect, is in terms of the linguistic categories applied to the study of enunciation (*énonciation*): discourse/discourse content : : enunciation/utterance.

John 6 presents an excellent text for enunciative analysis for reasons important to traditional *and* structural criticism. Identified as John's "Bread of Life Discourse", the chapter is separated by traditional exegesis into narrative and discourse parts. In the process the chapter's overall coherence and organization is obscured if not lost. Either the narrative parts (the Multiplication of Bread and Walk on Water) illustrate the discourse part or the discourse expands and develops the narrative section in verbal form. It should be noted that the distinction between narrative and discourse is not absolute: important discourse is to be found at several points in the more-or-less narrative verses (6:1-21). On the other hand structural exegesis tends for the most part to work with small text units of a narrative character and lacks the

means for taking into account the text's pragmatic dimension
and its importance for an understanding the text's meaning
effect. The tendency to ignore the pragmatic domain is endemic
to the transformational models used by structural exegetes. An
analysis sensitive to discourse structure can speak to the
interests and needs of both methodological approaches.

Through a description of the discoursive structure of
John 6 in enunciative terms we can account for the *event quality* or performative nature of John 6 as text. The manner in
which the text "acts" or "works" is to be seen in the way it
creates a textual world and specific speaker/listener roles
to populate that textual space. The nature and function of
these discoursive roles is dictated by the relationship between text (text enunciation), narration (narrator's enunciation) and narrated events (character enunciation). Each of
these enunciative levels of the text may be described as a
distinct discoursive level which means each has its own
enunciative subject, temporal, spatial and modal coordinates.
A unique aspect of John 6's meaning effect has to do with the
interpenetration (*imbrication*) of the discoursive roles at
each of these levels. Interpenetration of discourse by narrative personages, the narrator and narratee and reader explains
the metaphorical (paradigmatic) process which allows the implied reader to "enter" the world of the text as one of Jesus'
discoursive partners, a "you" in dialog with Jesus. It is the
written text however which is responsible for fashioning its
readership through the narrativization of the text/reader
discourse *as* the narration of Jesus engaged in different modes
of discourse.

The implied reader's discourse with the text is in an
iconic relation to the discourse that takes place within the
text. This textual effect is created by the narrator's (the
manifestation of the implied author) manipulation of the narratee. By presenting a series of different verbal encounters
with Jesus the narratee is brought (1) to an understanding of
Jesus' nature as *Speaker* of words of life (6:63) and (2) to a
perception of who is able to be a *Listener* to him. It is in this
fashion that the text determines who will be reader.

DISCOURSE AND ENUNCIATION

Eugene Nida defines discourse as a "specimen of linguistic material displaying structural and semantic coherence, unity
and completeness, and conveying a message." All discourse
displays eight kinds of universal features: two relate to the
discourse as a whole (markers of beginning and end; transitional
markers of internal divisions of the whole discourse); three
relate to the events contained within the discourse (markers
of temporal relations, spatial relations and logical relations);
two relate to objects within the discourse (identification of
discourse participants; devices that highlight or background
the mode of discoursive participation); and one relates to the
author (markers of attitude or point of view).

The enunciative structure refers (1) to that set of
semiotic conditions of communication which is responsible for
the production of a given text or message; the enunciative
structure *conditions* the text as a particular type of discoursive event. Each and every utterance presupposes an enunciation
whose presence is manifested through a variety of indicial
signs within that utterance. The enunciative structure also
functions as a mediator between the virtual structures of the

text and the realized form that that text assumes. The enunciative structure _mediates_ between competence and performance in the production of text and is thus instrumental in insuring the _mise en discours_ of the text.

Nida's discourse universals may be coorelatedwith the four fundamental conditions of enunciation: those of subject, time, space and modality. The network of these four conditions constitutes the enunciative structure and the very possibility of producing text as discourse. Each and every instance of discourse belongs to an enunciative _context_ or situation of discourse. Thus the discoursive situation can be characterized in light of the indices of enunciation: of subject (personal pronouns "I" and "you", "we"; of time (temporal adverbs, verbal tense markers); of space (proximal and distal demonstrative pronouns; and of modality (evaluative adjectives, adverbs, rhetorical devices, verbal mood).

No two languages or texts make use of the same discoursive features to express these fundamental enunciative conditions. Rather each language and text has its own complex network of constraints in relation with its semiotactic classes (that aspect of the linguistic context pertaining to the meaning of terms surrounding a given term). The semiotactic context acts with the syntax to select the most appropriate meaning for each word; both together regulate the discoursive combination possible. In other words the text's discoursive structure cooperates with its semantic and syntactic constraints to ground the text in a particular context, in relation to a speaker/listener and a vis-à-vis. The pragmatic constraints which make the text discourse are finally inseparable from syntactic and semantic structures of the text.

SEGMENTATION OF THE TEXT : THE NARRATED EVENTS

The text proposes a criterion for segmentation in its manner of highlighting Jesus' discourse. We shall look for an organization of the text in terms of the discoursive exchanges between Jesus and other personages at the level of narrated events. Jesus is portrayed in discourse with the following figures:

Discourse #	Verses	Personage(s)
1	6:1-13	Philip, Andrew, disciples
2	6:14-15	crowd
3	6:16-21	his disciples
4	6:22-40	crowd
5	6:41-58	Jews
6	6:59-65	many disciples
7	6:66-71	Simon Peter, Twelve

Jesus engages two types of discoursive partners: small groups with specified spokespersons and larger groups with unspecified speakers. The chapter presents the discourses in a chiastic patter: small group/large group/large group/small group. The significance of the chiastic movement is apparent when considering the narrator-narratee discourse. The segmentation of the text in terms of discoursive contexts is supported further by the _inclusio_ of 6:1-13 and 66-71. The common elements include reference to Simon Peter, the disciples, the Twelve (disciples, baskets) and the parallel insertion of the narrator's voice ("This he said to test him; Jesus himself knew what he meantto do"; "He meant Judas, son of Simon Iscariot. He it was who would betray him, and he was one of the Twelve").

In the text's first discourse (*Dis1*) Jesus is marked spatially "on the farther shore of the Sea of Galilee", specifically on a "hill-side"; temporally, "near the time of the Passover"; the discursive partners are Jesus ("we"), Philip, Andrew and his disciples ("we"); the modality is given by the narrator, to "test". In this exchange Jesus clearly directs the flow of the discourse with his inclusive question, "Where are *we* to buy bread to feed these people?". The question however is not directly answered; neither the location (πόθεν) nor the identity and the source of the bread is mentioned in Philip's and Andrew's responses.

In *Dis2* the subject conditions change. It is the people who speak , however discourse with Jesus never occurs: (1) the people speak to themselves; (2) Jesus is reduced to a non-discursive role (third person); and (3) most importantly Jesus refuses to speak by going away. The people acclaim Jesus"the Prophet that was to come into the world" as a response to what has transpired immediately before. But Jesus refuses this identity at this time and for this reason: the people rightly identify Jesus as prophet but for the wrong reasons. Only after Jesus reinterprets the Scriptures and teaches is the identity of Jesus fully unmasked (6:51). Jesus is prophet in *Word* and *Deed*. With respect to the modality of their discourse it is rejected for reasons of improper illocutionary force. The underlying intention on the people's part is to "proclaim him king" and not to come and listen.

The enunciative context of *Dis3* is very different--a contrast to the people's remark immediately preceding. The discursive partners are Jesus ("I") and his disciples. The disciples are the implicit "you" of "do not be afraid" (6:20). Spatially both are "on the sea"; temporally it is "after nightfall"; the modality of the discourse, comfort. There is an immediate juxtaposition in Jesus' refusal to respond to people's acclaim and the disciples' terrified silence (compare Matthew 14:27; Mark 6:49). Jesus is the speaker "I" with power and the disciples are the wordless discursive partner able after Jesus' word to complete their trip in a fashion similar to the discursive behavior of the disciples in the feeding of the crowd at the conclusion of *Dis1* where they are also empowered and complete their task: ("Jesus gave thanks and distributed . . . "; "he called out , . . and immediately the boat reached land").

Dis4 is complex. Made up of four parts,we shall plot the course of the discourse. The discursive partners are Jesus and the crowd. Except possibly for the second exchange (6:28-29) the crowd does not assume an enunciatee role ("you") in relation to Jesus ("I"); the crowd consistently speaks as "I". Spatially the location is the synagogue in Capernaum (6:59). Temporally it is the "next morning" after the multiplication of bread and crossing of the sea. The "true" modality is to seek to have Jesus provide perishable food (6:25). However Jesus challenges the crowd's intention. They are neither concerned with Jesus' location or status nor with expressing their real discursive intention ("Rabbi . . . when did you come here?"). The illocutionary force of their comment in this initial exchange is exposed in 6:26: to have Jesus provide perishable food. In Jesus' counter his powers of discernment are revealed. As he takes charge of the discourse the inadequacy of their quest is connected with the improper identification of Jesus (6:14). Jesus redefines the object of their quest: "food that lasts, the food of eternal life" instead of "perishable food". In the second exchange the crowd counters with a question with a different illocutionary force. The object of their search remains the same though their role in securing the food has been altered: what are *they* to do? Jesus' response is an imperative and repeats his first comment though in different form: "believe in the one whom he [God] has sent" (6:29). Jesus through his conversation with the crowd has begun to reveal his identity as the bread that does not perish. At a third moment the crowd demands an example of a believable sign and appeals to Scripture and the episode of manna in the desert (Exodus 16:14). The same dynamic asserts itself here as before. Jesus takes charge of the discourse and corrects the crowd's understanding of Scripture: the subject is not Moses but the Father who worked both then (ἔδωκεν) and now (δίδωσιν) to provide food. Jesus' response to the demand for bread à la Moses shifts the temporal circumstance from the past to the present: his Father presently gives the bread. Thus Jesus' response becomes the *sign par excellence*.

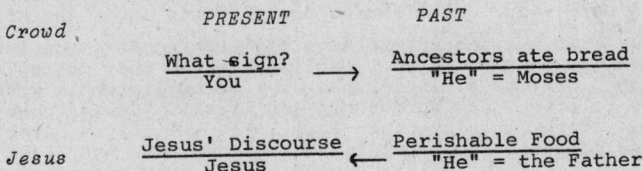

	PRESENT	PAST
Crowd	What sign? / You	Ancestors ate bread / "He" = Moses
Jesus	Jesus' Discourse / Jesus	Perishable Food / "He" = the Father

In the fourth exchange the crowd demands once again that Jesus provide bread on the analogy with Moses that Jesus has already shown incorrect. Finally they ask for what is implied in 6:30 and underlying 6:25: provide bread. Jesus' response is further self-identification (6:20). Apparently Jesus' correction of the crowd's use of Scripture and his metaphorical equation go unheard, or at least are misunderstood. The crowd's inability to read Scripture is matched only by their inability to listen to what Jesus is saying to them: namely that his word is life sustaining as it was for the disciples on the sea ("It is I" = "I am the bread of life"; "ἐγώ εἰμι"="ἐγώ εἰμι ὁ ἄρτος τῆς ζωῆς").

In the next discursive context (*Dis5*) the major enunciative change is in the identification of the enunciative partner (the Jews). Is it the case that there is a progressive identification of a discoursive partner as there is a progressive identification of Jesus? As in the case of Jesus' non-discourse with the people in *Dis2* there is no exchange in Jesus' conversation with the Jews. The Jews talk only among themselves. Jesus is not a discoursive "you" but a non-discoursive "he" (6:42). In one sense we could say that discourse with the Jews ends before it begins, for in order to have dialog with Jesus he must be credited as an enunciatee, a "you". Jesus' displacement from the Jew's discourse is significant in view of the reference made to him: namely Jesus' own words quoted by the Jews to one another ("I have come down from heaven", 6:42). The discoursive equation of Jews with crowd is strengthened by the parallel between Scriptural misunderstanding (6:31) and decontextualizing of Jesus' remarks. The same attitude toward Jesus' words prevails. There is great irony in the *mouthing of Jesus' words* and the failure to recognize it as "food that lasts". They "eat" the imperishable food but cannot"stomach" it (6:60) like the "many disciples" who similarly refuse Jesus'

words as life sustaining. One must do more than simply
utter Jesus' words in order to become a discoursive partner; one
must give those words a certain illocutionary force. Even
discoursive partners can betray Jesus (6:70-71).

Jesus responds with an imperative and an instruction.
By quoting Isaiah the Prophet (54:13) Jesus speaks through
Isaiah's words: "And they shall all be taught by God" (6:45).
The enunciator Jesus and the enunciator Isaiah merge. The
prophet's words are absorbed within Jesus' discourse thereby
attributing authority to Jesus' words and confirming the
reason for seeking out conversation with Jesus: to come and be
taught. It is plain from the Jews "murmuring" that they have
not and are not listening either to Scripture or Jesus' own
words. They too have not come to engage Jesus in discourse.

However that is not the end of it. Jesus continues the
defining process already begun. He is "the bread that comes
down from heaven". Now that the Scriptures are taken up into
Jesus' discourse they are given a true interpretation: to
consume Jesus as the bread of life is to come and listen to
his word about God. Eating Jesus' words is eating his flesh.

In the second exchange of *Dis5* the Jews continue to
speak to one another. This time however they do not speak
Jesus' own words. Still the Jews do not listen to what Jesus
has to offer: his word about God (6:45). Jesus' power response
("In truth, in very truth I tell you . . .") is directed to
non-listeners and non-believers. They have not heard the
Scriptures from the start even though they possessed the
Scriptures as a verbal sign and Jesus' own words as an inter-
pretant of that sign. Had they listened to him from the
beginning they would have realized who Jesus was when he said
"Where are we to buy bread to feed these people?" (6:5).

In *Dis6* the spatial location remains the same (the syna-
goguein Capernaum). Temporally it is   *after* Jesus' discourse with the Jews. The discoursive partners have changed
to "many of his disciples" and Jesus; the modality of the
disciple's comments is rejection, disbelief. Like the people
and Jews before them the disciples speak to themselves. Jesus
is relegated to a non-discoursive role which he rejects (6:62).
Jesus addresses a series of questions to them for which there
is no reply. Jesus identifies his words (6:64) as spirit, as
life sustaining (6:63). And as the people and the Jews have
come to Jesus for the wrong reasons, so many of his disciples
have not really come to him to listen. His words are not
digestible ("This is more than we can stomach! Why listen to
such *talk*?", 6:60). Rejecting Jesus' words is the same as
saying the food that lasts cannot be consumed!

In *Dis7* the enunciative roles are filled by Jesus and
Simon Peter for the Twelve. Temporally it is "from that time
on". Spatially the discourse is with Jesus ("Lord, to whom
shall we go? Your words are words of eternal life", 6:68).
Again the modality is testing. In Simon Peter's response Jesus
is identified as the Holy One of God, that is as a prophet
(cf. II Kings 4:9). And this is done significantly in associating Jesus with the word. It is proper now to identify Jesus
in this way because of what he *says* and *does*. The text ends with
a question (6:70) for which there is no reply; it is addressed
to a "you" which we will identify jointly as the Twelve and the
narratee of the text. This final question applies to the
discoursive partners at the levels of narrated events and of
narration. Quite appropriately then it brings the text to a

close at the narrated events level and opens it up for the
narratee and implied reader of the text. For the latter two
the conversation is only beginning.

NARRATIONAL LEVEL

The relation of mutual implication between *énonciation*
and *énoncé* is important in explaining discourse at the level of
the narrator's activity. The narrated events (*énoncés* or
utterances) of John 6 call for a narrational uttering (*énonciation*). In precisely the same way the narration of the text
(*énonciation énoncé*) itself presupposes a textual enunciation.
On the narrational level the narrator (enunciator) and narratee
(enunciatee) are conditioned with respect to time, space and
modality. In traditional exegetical terms the narrator is
identified as the Fourth Evangelist and the narratee the
Gospel audience. However, the discoursive roles of narrator
and narratee are textual *constructs*; they are *intratextual
realities* distinct from Scriptive Author and Scriptive Reader
which we will consider in the next section of our essay.

Defining narrational discourse in enunciative terms
permits us to give a functional as opposed to ontological description of the narrator's part in the text's creation of meaning. By focussing upon the narrational roles we shall identify
the way in which the enunciator-narrator controls the flow of
narrated events in his/her discourse. This will additionally
expose the valuation that the events and existents of the
narrated level receive at the hand of the narrator and reveal
the manipulation of the narratee's understanding of the narrated
events.

The narrator's presence/absence is discernible in a
number of ways in John 6. Markers of the presence of narrational discourse signal diegetic shifts in the reader's movement from
level to level of the text. These "shifters" may take an overt
or covert form. Overt shifters, for example, signal a *distance*
between textual levels as is seen in "Some time later Jesus with-
drew to the farther shore of the sea of Galilee (or Tiberias),
and . . . " (6:1). A temporal distance is indicated through the
use of demonstrative (ταῦτα) and the aorist tense (ἀπῆλθεν).
The reference in 6:1 is backward in time to Jesus' miraculous
and discoursive activity in Jerusalem (Chapter 5). Markers of
this sort indicate the temporal situation of the narrator's
discourse as being anterior to the time of the narrated events.
The absence however of overt signals of the narrator's presence
does not mean an absence of the narrator. Effacement of narration (a good example is the "narrative" material in 6:16-21)
is a narrational technique for presenting the narrated events
in a certain fashion, that usually being to create a stronger
sense of objectivity, hence realism and truth. Important
markers of diegetic shift in John 6 are found in 6:41 ("At this
the Jews began to murmur disapprovingly because he said . . . "),
6:52 ("This led to a fierce dispute among the Jews."), 6:59
("This was spoken in synagogue when Jesus was teaching in capernaum.") and 6:66 ("From that time on . . . .").

Other markers of the narrator's discourse with the
narratee take on an explanatory character: 6:1 ("(of Tiberias)"),
6:4 ("the great Jewish festival"), 6:4 ("Jesus said . . ."),
6:6 ("This he said to test him; Jesus himself knew what he meant
to do"), 6:22 (Jesus, they knew, had not embarked with his disciples"), 6:64 ("For Jesus knew all along who were without faith

and who was to betray him"), 6:71 ("He meant Judas . . . ."). The function of the presence of markers such as these is to inform the narratee of certain "facts" by letting the narratee in on the "true" meaning of particular narrated events. Through a progressive unfolding of the narrated events the narratee's understanding is molded and defined as well. Just as Jesus' identity is revealed through progressive discursive encounters at the level of narrated events, so also is the role of the narratee formed in discourse with the narrator.

An important characteristic of the narration of John 6 is the shifting that takes place between past and present, narrative and discourse. Regular movement from one temporality to the other accentuates the anteriority of the narrator/narratee vis-à-vis the narrated events: for example, 6:25 ("they said" in the middle of a direct quotation) and 6:64b ("for Jesus knew . . .So he said . . ." which breaks apart one of Jesus' responses). At the same time the juxtaposition of narrative and direct quotation gives the effect of interpenetration of narrational discourse with the discourse at the level of narrated events. This becomes a useful tool for the narrator/implied author of John 6 who desires for there to be a discursive overlap among the levels of the text. The narrator can thus enter the text as a discursive partner to Jesus and remain the narratee speaking/listening to the narrator.

The first clue as to the narrator's discursive intent is found in the first words of Jesus in *Dis1*: "Where are *we* to buy bread to feed these people?" The inclusive first person pronoun "we" functions as an enunciative indice of the disciples and Jesus as well as the narratee and narrator. Discursive interpenetration constitutes this a question at both discursive levels. Moreover the narrator's interpretative remark in 6:6 draws the narratee's attention to the question and effectively signals the narrational task ahead. The stage is set for a search through various discoursive contexts for an adequate *speaking* model. After the narrator presents the narratee with the examples of Philip and Andrew, the people, the silent disciples, the crowd, the Jews, Jesus' many disciples and Simon Peter for the Twelve the narratee is led to select the "true" discoursive model. This narrational process and the narratee's corresponding "growth in comprehension" are performative acts: the end is obtained for both narrator and narratee through the very act of entering the text as discoursive partners.

The narrator's task is to direct the narratee to a "right" selection of discoursive role. By leading the narratee through a series of seven discoursive exchanges at the level of narrated events the narrator constructs a "stance" or point of view from which to evaluate and select the right discoursive role; this means at the same time choosing the right illocutionary force with which to speak: to express doubt, to proclaim Jesus King, to secure perishable food, to express doubt about Jesus' words or to express belief in Jesus' words.

The narrator's point of view is alligned with Jesus' discoursive "I". When Jesus interacts with the various narrative personages, the narrator does as well (and by implication the narratee). At the narrative events level Jesus' discourse progressively identifies and defines the speaker, Jesus. In *Dis1* Philip and Andrew are questioned about the source of bread for the crowd. Their response is off the mark because they have

not discerned what is true but does not appear so about Jesus:
namely that Jesus' words are food (6:63). What appears to be
food is not: that is perishable food. The narrator is interested in doing more than recoding "food" into "words"; it is
a quest to instruct a narratee in properly answering Jesus
(a test). The search is on for a right narratee-listener.

That the search has commenced is confirmed in the second
discourse (*Dis2*), or rather lack of discourse! The crowd's
affirmation is met with Jesus' silence. The narratee's comprehension of the one-way conversation is further explained
by the narrator who reveals the illocutionary force of the
discoursive statement ("they meant to come and seize him to
proclaim him king", 6:15).

Jesus' words in *Dis3* are uni-directional, however the
illocutionary force is different from *Dis1*. In 6:20 Jesus
wants to both comfort the disciples and provide a self-identification. In contrast to the crowd's response the disciple's
behavior is acceptable. Juxtaposition of the disciples' silence
and Jesus' silence in the preceding discourse suggests a paradigmatic relationship between Jesus' and his disciples' discoursive behavior, a paradigmatic relation that functions between
the personage Jesus and the narratee, and ultimately the narratee and implied reader of the text, with respect to the identification of Jesus in light of his multiplication of bread. Jesus
is <u>not</u> prophet for this reason. Who is he then? The other
side of the search for a right discursive partner is a true
identification of Jesus. The narrator has begun to answer this
latter question by answering his *own* question in 6:5: Who?
Where? the bread. The answer: "It is I" and approaching the
disciples on the sea (*speaking*).

Dis4 presents a four stage discourse and another discoursive model in which "true" discourse with Jesus is still
lacking. First, far from being a discourse the exchange is
merely a repetition of question and counter statement with
no movement in the conversation. The crowd does not listen;
it refuses to give up the enunciative "I" to take on the "you"
proposed by Jesus. Secondly, because the crowd does not listen
it is unable to recognize food when it hears it. The narratee
is led to evaluate this way of conversing negatively.

Crowd's Question	Jesus' Response
When did you come here? (6:25)	You did not come for me but for bread (6:26)
What work do we do to obtain food? (6:28)	Believe in this bread (6:29)
What sign can you give? Moses gave bread. (6:30-31)	The Father not Moses gave it. He gives it now (6:32)
Give us bread (6:35)	Take it; here it is (6:35)

The narrator next juxtaposes the "Jews" and the "crowd".
As far as the narratee is concerned the enunciative subject
of *Dis5* could be crowd-Jews and later in *Dis6* crowd-Jews-many
disciples. The narrator presents the Jews <u>as if</u> in discourse
with Jesus. But the possibility of conversation is even more
remote than before by their speaking to one another and re-
ducing Jesus to a non-discoursive role. After explaining the
cause of the Jews unrest (6:41), Jesus is seemingly identified
(6:42): they know his father and mother. Quite ironically the
Jews mouth Jesus' own words and <u>unknowingly</u> possess imperishable

food (his words) though this is not what they seek. Jesus
counters by *teaching*. He appeals to Scripture in a way that
(1) recalls the crowd's acclaim of Jesus as king (6:14) now
explained in terms of teaching and (2) refers anaphorically to
the crowd's mistaken interpretation of Moses, manna and the
food that comes from God. Jesus reinterprets metaphorically
and expands the ἐγώ εἰμι of 6:20 and ἐγώ εἰμι ὁ ἄρτος τῆς ζωῆς
of 6:35. In 6:45 the narrator equates coming and *eating* with
coming and *listening*. However the narrator does not shift
from a gustatory to an auditory code; rather there is a
broadening and developing of the gustatory description of
Jesus to include the necessary auditory dimension: in order
to *eat* Jesus' words (*to speak*) it is necessary to *listen*
to his words. The identification of the speaker brings
with it an identification of the listener. Note importantly
that the vivid language regarding eating follows upon this
discourse with its teaching illocutionary force (cf. possibly
Isaiah 54:31, Jeremiah 31:33-34): the narrator says through
the arrangement of materials that listening precedes speaking.

At the level of narrated events the text moves progressively closer to an identification of Jesus (by way of the
Scriptures) as true food and as prophet of the Scriptural word.
At the same time there is a progressive deterioration in discoursive relations. The identity of Jesus and his listeners'
identity are revealed in inverse proportion to one another.
This is part of the narrator's narrative strategy vis-à-vis
the narratee. The greater the clarity regarding Jesus' identity
the more pronounced the absence up through this point in the
narrative of an adequate discoursive partner : the enunciator
Jesus ("I") comes into focus; the enunciatee narratee ("you")
fades.

Progressive Identification of Jesus

ἐγώ εἰμι   (6:20)
ἐγώ εἰμι ὁ ἄρτος τῆς ζωῆς   (6:34)
ἐγώ εἰμι ὁ ἄρτος ὁ ζῶν ὁ ἐκ τοῦ οὐρανοῦ   (6:51)

Degenerating Discoursive Relation

personage	*discourse flow*
Philip, Andrew	connected in both directions
crowd	disconnected in both directions
Jews	disconnected in one direction

The narrator's presence is marked forcefully beginning
6:59. The narratee immediately senses the final discourse
to be directed to him/her. The narrative has moved chiastically
from discourse with disciples to discourse with crowd to discourse with Jews and back to discourse with disciples. Dis-
coursively the movement has been from speaking (in a certain
fashion) to refusal to listen (6:60).

The narratee enters the narration overtly in 6:66: a
plural "you" (ὑμεῖς) responded to by a singular Simon Peter.
In addition the temporal deictic ἐκ τούτου creates the impression of a great temporal distance between the narrational
discourse and the narrated events. It is as if Jesus the personage is distancized from the abortive discourses in 6:1-65
and now turns to the Twelve-Simon Peter and speaks in an enunciative time contemporaneous with the narrational enunciation.
At the same time *Dis7* effectively concludes the narrated events.

Jesus' initial question in 6:8 is now answered: the where of
the food (Jesus) and the what of the food (Jesus' word).
Location and identity of content are made clear. Jesus and
Simon Peter converse. Simon Peter is presented to the narratee as *the* disciple who accepts and properly fills the listening
post. Simon Peter is the narratee's model.

With the affirmation by Simon Peter and the use of the
emphatic ἡμεῖς the narratee's association with Simon Peter is
made enunciatively complete. However the narrator is not
finished; he gives the narration one final twist. Jesus identifies himself as the one who chooses the ὑμεῖς at the level of
narrated events (Simon Peter, the Twelve) and at the level of
narration (the narratee). On the one hand the testing procedure is complete when the narratee adopts Simon Peter as a
discoursive model and enters Simon's own discourse. On the
other hand the selection of listener has already been made. We
could almost say that the discourse has chosen its listener.

CREATING A READER: THE TEXT'S WORK

It is at the third discoursive level (textual enunciation) that we come to the intersecting point of the intra- and
extra-textual domains. The exchange between text and scriptive
reader occurs through the production of the implied author and
implied reader roles. In contrast to the scriptive author--the
historical enunciator of the text--the implied author is that
structural principle which invests the textual world with its
particular values (semantic universe); the implied author is
the one responsible for producing the narrational discourse and
the semantic norms grounding the text. Unlike the narrator who
has a voice, the implied author stays silent, constructed only
indirectly by the implied reader.

The implied reader is the discoursive role immanent to
the enunciation of the text. It is a discoursive role that
can be filled by a scriptive reader who contracts to enter into
dialog with the implied author/narrator. In order to become an
implied reader the scriptive reader must agree to become the
enunciatee of the text and thus to accept the value structures
which the implied author proposes for the world of the text as
it is reflected and refracted through the text's narration and
narrated events. Once the contract is accepted the implied
reader goes on line and enters into discourse with the text.

The work of John 6 as text is, in part, the performative
act of fabricating its reader/listener. As a unique sort of
speech act, the text establishes a world which functions as a
context, a world of reference, wherein dialog between text/
implied author/narrator/Jesus and scriptive reader/implied
reader/narratee and Simon Peter may occur. With the distanci-
ation of the scriptive author the text (*Jesus' Word*) assumes
the enunciator's role as *Speaker* and establishes the guidelines
which make *Listening* possible. The text is at work suggesting
its own segmentation and fashioning its proper reader.

By means of the narrative technique of narrating Jesus'
discourse John 6 shows how it is possible to have discourse
with Jesus distanciated and displaced by the *WORD*. Reader,
narratee and personage merge. The textual world in which Jesus
as prophetic source of the *WORD (SCRIPTURE)* that sustains life
(in search of an ear to hear) becomes an icon of the reader's,
own world, a world where Jesus is not to be found, yet a world
where discourse remains a possibility.

A final word concerning the *eucharistic* character of
John 6. Our text preserves the words it takes to eat and live:
in the discourse of a discourse of a discourse. It is in this
way that John 6 functions as Scripture, nourishing the reader
in the same way that Isaiah's words nourish Jesus' own discourse. John 6 as Jesus' word preserves a place (πόθεν) where
the reader can come and feast upon the *WORD*. For us as readers
there is but words, however words in abundance (6:13). Though
Jesus is displaced by the text of his words the possibility is
preserved for those who can listen/eat Jesus' words/bread. We
need only the stomach to listen.

NOTES

[1]Paul Ricoeur, *Interpretation Theory. Discourse and
the Surplus of Meaning* (Fort Worth: Texas Christian University
Press, 1976), Chapter 1.

[2]Eugene Nida and Charles Taber, *The Theory and Practice
of Translation* (Leiden: E.J. Brill, 1969), p. 200.

IT IS WRITTEN

A STRUCTURALIST ANALYSIS OF JOHN 6

John Dominic Crossan

DePaul University

> If it recedes one day, leaving behind its works and signs on the
> shores of our civilization, the structuralist invasion might be-
> come a question for the historian of ideas, or perhaps even an
> object. But the historian would be deceived if he came to this
> pass: by the very act of considering the structuralist invasion
> as an object he would forget its meaning and would forget that
> what is at stake, first of all, is an adventure of vision, a con-
> version of the way of putting questions to any object posed before
> us, to historical objects -- his own -- in particular. And, un-
> expectedly among these, the literary object.
>
> Jacques Derrida[1]

The subject of this article needs two immediate qualifications. First, it concerns only a smaller unit, John 6, within
a larger unit, the gospel of John, and thus it must be considered at best a *first probe*, to be corrected by, even if also
corrective of any fuller work on the larger text. Second, the
subtitle should be read in the light of the epigraph. The
essay is "an adventure of vision," an exercise in structuralist
imagination rather than the detailed application of a deduc-
tive method and the precise application of a metatextual vocabulary. I have tried quite deliberately to keep the metatextual terminoloy to an absolute minimum and to use or create
only what this present text seemed to demand.

What would one see if one took John 6 as a unity and
officially omitted any historical questioning of the text?
What would happen if one attempted by looking at *how* the text
means to see *what* the text means? An historical vision could
legitimately explain disjunctions in terms of sources and re-
dactions, of additions appended by an initial author, an inter-
mediate redactor, or even a final editor. But a structuralist
vision will want to know, even granting all that is true, how
did such an appender add it here rather than there, now rather
than earlier or later? The adventure of vision is to see John
6 as a whole and to study how it holds together as such.

I. UNITY

John 6 may be taken an an integrated whole for both external and internal reasons.

A. EXTERNAL INDICES OF UNITY

John 6:1 contains the phrase, "*After this Jesus* went to
the other side of the Sea of *Galilee*" and John 7:1 repeats most
of this with, "*After this Jesus* went about in *Galilee*."

B. INTERNAL INDICES OF UNITY

There are three internal indications of unity, in terms
of theme, frame, and structure.

1. Theme. The general theme of "bread" appears as early as
6:5 and as late as 6:58 and thus dominates the chapter.

198

2. Frame. There is a precise inclusion between the handling of the Disciples in 6:1-15 and the Twelve in 6:67-71:

The Disciples (6:1-15)   *The Twelve (6:67-71)*

The Disciples (6:3)   The Twelve (6:67)
  Philip (6:5,7)   Simon Peter (6:68)
  Andrew (6:8)   Judas (6:71a)
The Disciples (6:12)   The Twelve (6:70,71b)

Granted these general frames, one might also draw attention to (1) Jesus' foreknowledge in 6:6 and again in 6:64,71; and (2) the mention of Simon Peter in 6:8 and 6:68.

3. Structure. There is a general parallel structure within the chapter:
   (1) Jesus and Crowds   6:1-15   6:22-59
   (2) Jesus and Disciples   6:16-21   6:60-71

The first column of verses is primarily Jesus' deeds for the Crowds or Disciples while the second column is primarily his words to the Crowds or Disciples.

There is thus sufficient indications of unity within John 6 to render valid its study within the overall unity of the gospel of John.

II. TIME

The text is broken up by several temporal indices. These may be distinguished as internal and external ones.

A. INTERNAL INDICES OF TIME

The internal indices differentiate the text into:
(1) 6:1-15. The *first day* is specified directly by the following two indices.
(2) 6:16-21. The *night* is specified directly by "when evening came" (6:16) and "it was now dark" (6:17).
(3) 6:22-71. The *second day* is specified directly by "on the next day" (6:22).

B. EXTERNAL INDICES OF TIME

There is also a single temporal index linking the text with an external situation. This is given directly and explicitly by, "Now the Passover, the feast of the Jews, was at hand" (6:4).

Three points may be noted immediately concerning this phrase. It is displaced, disconnected, and disassociated within its context.
(1) Displacement. It is quite common to start a narrative with a temporal and spatial index. The standard opening is: "Once upon a time in a land far away." In the present case the order is spatial (6:1) followed by temporal (6:4). This is exactly the same sequence given in the external indices of inclusion for the text (see IA above), when one compares 6:1,4 with 7: 1-2: "After this Jesus went about in Galilee; he would not go about in Judea, because the Jews sought to kill him [*space*]. Now the Jews' feast of Tabernacles was at hand [*time*]."
My present point is not, however, the spatial and temporal sequence but rather the fact that the spatial index is given in 6:1, the story gets underway in 6:2-3, and only then, almost as an interruption, is the temporal index cited in 6:4.

One expects its position to be immediately after 6:1 rather
than after 6:3.
(2) Disconnection. The feast of Passover is said to be "at
hand." Thereafter, throughout John 6, one waits in vain for
some connection between this statement, vague as it is, and
the feast of Passover itself. This is what happens in the three
other places where John declares a feast to be "at hand: (a) 2;
13 leads into 2:23; (b) 7:2 connects with 7:8,10,11,14,37; and
(c) 11:55 continues with 12:1; 13:1,29; 18:28,39; 19:14,31,42.
After 6:4, however, there is no further mention of the Passover
whose nearness has just been noted.
(3) Disassociation. The second half of the sentence in 6:4b,
"the feast of the Jews," indicates that (a) the implied readers are "not-Jews" but (2) leaves open whether the implied
writer is "Jew" or "not-Jew." (For example: "It was Thanksgiving, a holiday for Americans," is being said to non-
Americans by either an American or non-American).

III. SPACE

The text is divided spatially by indices which are more
complicated than the temporal ones. These may be designated as
general and specific internal indices as well as external ones.

A. GENERAL INTERNAL INDICES OF SPACE

The text is broken up as follows by these indices. It
should be noted that the divisions are close to but not identical with the previous temporal divisions.
(1) 6:1-15. The *first land* is specified directly by "to the
other side of the Sea of Galilee" (6:1).
(2) 6:16-24. The *sea* is specified directly by the repeated mentions of "sea" (6:1,16,17,18,19,22,25).
(3) 6:25-71. The *second land* is specified directly, first for
Jesus and the Disciples by "at the land" (6:21), and then for
the Crowds by "got into the boats and went to Capernaum"
(6:24). In 6:22 there is a counterpoint to the same phrase
in 6:1 ("the other side of the sea").

B. SPECIFIC INTERNAL INDICES OF SPACE

Each of the three spatial contexts has been organized
or centered around a specific phenomenon, respectively, a
mountain, a boat or boats, and a synagogue.
(1) 6:1-15 (first land: mountain). The scene opens with Jesus
located positively εἰς τὸ ὄρος (6:3). It concludes with Jesus
located, again positively, in the same place, πάλιν εἰς τὸ ὄρος
(6:15). It is only because of these positive frames that one
presumes, negatively, that the central event tales place *not on
the mountain*. There is thus a triple sequence of on (6:3), off
(6:5-14), and on the mountain (6:15).
(2) 6:16-21 (sea: single boat). This boat receives a treatment
somewhat similar to that of the mountain. There is again a
triple sequence of inside (6:16-18), outside (6:19-20), and inside the boat (6:21).
(3) 6:22-24 (sea: multiple boats). This unit is simpler than
the preceding one. It has a double sequence of being without
(6:22) and then with boats (6:23-24). But this whole incident
both separates absolutely what happens between Jesus and the
Disciples in the between-time and between-space of 6:16-21 from
what happens to the Crowds on the same sea. They do not exper-

perience the combination of both outside-time (the night between the two days) and also outside-space (the sea between the
two lands) during which Jesus proclaims to the Disciples his
outside-grammar revelation: "I AM" (6:20).

(4) 6:25-71 (second land: synagogue). Once again this unit is
simpler than the initial two sections. There is only a double
sequence and even this must be considered implicit and indirect. The dialogue of 6:25-58 concludes with, "This he said
in the synagogue" (6:59a). The dialogue which then ensues in
6:60-71 is unspecified with regard to space but one presumes
negatively, that it is *not in the synagogue*. Hence, presumably,
a double sequence of inside (6:25-59) and outside the synagogue
(6:60-71).

C. EXTERNAL INDICES OF SPACE

Those internal indices connect, to some extent, with
these external ones.

The first land and its mountain are specified but negatively as being "on the other side of the Sea of Galilee, which
is the Sea of Tiberias" (6:1). This also specifies, and positively, the sea between the two lands. But it is the second
land and its synagogue which is specified most explicitly and
positively. The scene is set in Capernaum (6:17,21,24) and is
centered around "the synagogue, as he taught at Capernaum"
(6:59b).

IV. NARRATIVE

The terms Narrative and Discourse distinguish between
deeds and *words* within the text. The normal line between Narrative and Discourse is indicated by the quotation mark. I do
not intend any other more profound differentiation at the moment.[2]

A second distinction is that between Actant and Action.
Actants are the personae who cause cerian effects, or Actions,
within the text.

A. NARRATIVE ACTANTS

(1) 6:1-15. Between the external index of space in 6:1 and the
external index of time in 6:4, the three major Narrative Actants
are introduced, separately and pointedly.

(a) Jesus is introduced first in 6:1, as if he was
crossing the sea by himself ("Jesus went"), although, of course,
the Disciples are with him. But the principal Narrative Actant
may be appropriately introduced first and alone.

(b) Crowds are introduced in second place in 6:2, and
they have "followed him."

(c) Disciples finally appear in 6:3 and they are simply
"with" Jesus.

Later, with a deliberateness similar to their introduction in 6:1-3, the three Narrative Actants separate and go their
different ways in 6:15-16.

(2) 6:16-21. Only two Narrative Actants reappear here; the
Disciples alone (6:16-18), then Jesus and the Disciples (6:19-
21).

(3) 6:22-24. Although the other two Narrative Actants are mentioned (6:22,24), the Crowds are alone in this unit.

(4) 6:25-59. The Disciples are *textually* absent, with only Jesus
and the Crowds explicitly mentioned. It is clear from 6:60, of

course, that the Disciples were actually present throughout
6:25-59.

But there is a strange development between 6:25-40 and
6:41-59. Prior to 6:25-40 the Crowds have been frequently
identified with various terms (6:2,5,10a,10b,14,22,24). That
is, four times in 6:1-15 and twice in 6:22-24. Now, suddenly,
they become nameless. Throughout the fairly long section in
6:25-40 they are identified only indirectly, remaining hidden
behind such words as "they" or "them." But, again suddenly,
they are termed "the Jews" in 6:41 and 6:52 and it is "the
Jews" who speak with Jesus throughout 6:41-59. The Crowds of
6:1-40 become "the Jews" of 6:41-59.
(5) 6:60-71. Once again only two Narrative Actants are textually present, but now it is Jesus and the Disciples.

But a similar strange development takes place between
6:60-66 and 6:67-71 as previously between 6:1-40 and 6:41-59.
In 6:60-66 the Disciples are named three times (6:60,61,66).
Then in 6:67-71 there appears a group not heretofore either
distinguished or named. And as with the Disciples in 6:60-66,
so now this new group, the Twelve, are named three times once
they appear (6:67,70,71).

B. NARRATIVE ACTIONS

There are two main Narrative Actions to be considered
in the text: Moving and Feeding.

1. Narrative Moving

In discussing Space and Time, the phenomenon of Moving
was already evident. But here I wish to distinguish between
Moving in terms of Space and Moving in terms of Narrative
Actants.

(1) Narrative Moving and Space

In terms of Space the Moving is rather homogeneous.
First, Jesus explicitly (6:1), the Disciples implicitly (6:3),
and the Crowds explicitly (6:2,5), "went to the other side of
the Sea of Galilee" (6:1). So also, again with Jesus and the
Disciples in first place (6:17,21), and the Crowds in second
place (6:24), there is a recrossing of the sea to Capernaum.

(2) Narrative Moving and Narrative Actants

But Moving is much more significant not just in terms
of who is Moving to where but in terms of who is Moving to
which other Narrative Actant.

(a) Jesus and the Disciples

Coming. Jesus comes to the Disciples but the Disciples do not come to Jesus. Thus, Jesus comes to the Disciples
in 6:16-21 and this advent is emphasized by the rather awkward
comment in 6:17b. After having noted that the Disciples had embarked, it is then said that Jesus had not arrived. "When
evening came, his disciples went down to the sea, got into a
boat, and started across the sea to Capernaum. It was now dark,
and Jesus had not yet come to them" (6:16-17). It should be
noted that when Jesus comes to them in 6:21 they are
immediately where they want to be. The Disciples, on the other
hand, never come to Jesus; they are always sinply there (6:3).
Compare, in contrast, Mark 6:35 with John 6:5.

Going. Jesus leaves the Disciples in 6:15. Although
the primary withdrawal here is from the Crowds, the terminal
presence of Jesus on the mountain alone (6:15) reflects back on

the initial one on the mountain with his disciples (6:3). So
also do the Disciples leave Jesus in 6:16 (compare, in contrast, Mark 6:45), and (some of) the Disciples leave him in
6:66.

(b) Jesus and the Crowds

Coming. Jesus never comes to the Crowds. It is twice
stressed, most emphatically, that they come after him. They move
after him, first in 6:2 ("a multitude followed him") and 6:5
("a multitude was coming to him"), and again later in 6:22-25
("seeking" in 6:24, "found" in 6:25). Thus, once on each day
and once on each land, the Crowds move after Jesus. Compare,
for contrast, Mark 6:33-34 with John 6:2,5, and note that the
Crowds precede Jesus in Mark so that he comes to them.

Going. Jesus, of course, leaves the Crowds in 6:15.
It would also seem that he is leaving them, textually, in 6:59.
But nowhere in the text are the Crowds explicitly described as
Moving away from Jesus.

In summary: Jesus never comes to the Crowds but they
always come to him; Jesus comes to the Disciples and they
never come to him; Jesus leaves them both but the Disciples
and not the Crowds leave him.

2. Narrative Feeding

The Narrative Action of Feeding in 6:1-15 is totally
dominated by Jesus. In terms of Action, he himself distributes
the food in 6:11, in contrast, for example, with Mark 6:41
where the Disciples do this.

3. Narrative Moving and Narrative Feeding

The twin Narrative Actions are closely linked together
in that the Crowds come to Jesus, the Feeding ensues, then
Jesus and the Disciples leave, and the Crowds follow. Thus the
feeding is at the center of the Moving and the Moving is to
and from the Feeding.

V. DISCOURSE

The simplest reading of the text reveals how the predominance of Narrative in 6:1-21 gives way to the predominance
of Discourse in 6:22-71. But before turning attention to that
situation, it will be useful to study the interaction of
Narrative and Discourse in 6:1-24.

A. NARRATIVE AND DISCOURSE

(1) 6:1-15. In this unit there is a section of Discourse (6:
5-10) framed by two Narrative sections (6:1-4,11-15). The
Narrative is quite conceivable by itself, as if one read from
6:1-4 into 6:11-15. But the interaction of Narrative and Discourse in this small unit of 6:1-15 effects certain very significant results.

(a) The Discourse in 6:5 stresses, just as did the
Narrative in 6:11, the complete dominance of Jesus over this
entire event. Compare, in contrast, Mark 6:35, where the
Disciples initiate the Discourse.

(b) The Discourse here establishes the pattern of (i) a
dialogue composed of (ii) questions which (iii) are not really
answered. This will be much more important in 6:25-71.

(c) The predominance of Narrative over Discourse in 6:
1-15 prepares the way for the opposite situation in 6:25-71.

(d) In 6:5-10 the three Narrative Actants become Discourse Actants, that is, they talk about themselves. Thus in 6:5 Jesus asks the Disciples about the Crowds: "How are *we* to buy bread, so that *these* people may eat?" This will also be of future importance.

(e) The Discourse between Jesus and the Disciples in 6:5-10 contains a single Discourse Actant who, unlike the preceding case, is never a Narrative Actant. Yet this Discourse Actant is the necessary basis for the continuance of both Narrative and Discourse. In 6:8 Andrew says, "There is a lad here who has five barley loaves and two fish." When one notices that this Discourse Actant is absent in Mark 6:38, one might well wonder if it has a function here in John. At very least, it is a first alert to the possibility of Discourse Actants who are not Narrative Actants, who appear only in the Discourse and yet on whom the whole Narrative and Discourse may depend.
(2) 6:16-21. In this unit there is again Discourse (unanswered dialogue) in 6:20 within Narrative frames in 6:16-19 and 6:21. Once again the Narrative is conceivable without the Discourse and once again Narrative Actants cross the quotation marks to become Discourse Actants. Jesus talks about himself to the Disciples and about them to themselves.

But now, in contrast to 6:1-15, the Discourse is extremely important. In Mark 6:49-50 the frightened disciples "thought it was a ghost, and cried out; for they all saw him, and were terrified." In such a situation the phrase ἐγώ εἰμι may well be translated by the reassuring,"It is I." But not so in John where there is no mention of non-recognition. There is, of course, fear which is the proper response of numinous awe. In such a context, then, the phrase must be given full transcendental value. Given absolutely, without any qualification or addition, it breaks the rules of grammar and must be taken precisely as such a breach. Jesus says: I AM.

B. NARRATIVE ACTANTS AND DISCOURSE ACTANTS

A distinction was noted above between Narrative-Discourse Actants and pure Discourse Actants, between Actants appearing in both Narrative and Discourse and those appearing only in Discourse. These latter now require further study.

1. The Presence of Discourse Actants

The following are the major Discourse Actants to be noted in 6:25-71.
(1) Jesus introduces God under various titles. The first mention is of "God the Father" (6:27) and thereafter one finds "God" (6:29,33,46), "my Father" (6:32,40), "the Father" (6:37,44,45,46 twice,57,65), "the living Father" (6:57), and "Him Who Sent Me" (6:38,39).
The Crowds refer to God, once as "God" (6:28) and once as "He" (6:31).
The Disciples do not mention any Discourse Actant but the Twelve mention God in addressing Jesus as "the Holy One of God" (6:69).
(2) Jesus speaks of the "Son of Man," once to the Crowds, once to "the Jews," and once to the Disciples (6:27,53,62). He also refers to "Him Whom He Has Sent" (6:29), and to "the Son" (6:40).
There are no such references for either Crowds or Disciples, but the Twelve address Jesus as "the Holy One of God" (6:69).

(3) Jesus refers to "Moses" (6:32), "the prophets" (6:45), and "your fathers" (6:49). The Crowds also refer to "our fathers" (6:31).

The Crowds refer to the parents of Jesus: "Jesus, the son of Joseph, whose father and mother we know" (6:42).

(4) Finally, and most importantly, there is a group designated repeatedly by Jesus, and nobody else, with such expressions as (a) "he who ..." (6:35,47), or (b) "all who ..." (6:37,39,40, 45), or (c) "anyone who ..." (6:50,51), or "no one ... unless ..." (6:44,65).

2. The Dominance of Discourse Actants

There are two facets to this domination. First, once certain Discourse Actants appear they dominate not only the succeeding Discourse but even the preceding Narrative as well. These Discourse Actants *absorb* and *consume* (the verbs are not innocently chosen) the Narrative Actants themselves. Second, the apparent exception to that generality is Jesus. In this case all the mediator Discourse Actants are absorbed along with the Narrative Actant Jesus into the Narrative-Discourse Actant, the "I" of Jesus. Here it is this Narrative-Discourse Actant which continues to dominate the text and which *absorbs* and *consumes* the Narrative Actant Jesus himself.

(1) God. The domination of this Discourse Actant over the entire text, both Narrative and Discourse, will be discussed below under C.

(2) Jesus. After the supreme and unqualified revelation of "I AM" in 6:20, it is not very surprising that the "I" of Jesus should dominate the Discourse. This is effected in two ways. First, of course, only Jesus uses "I" within the Discourse. The Disciples/Twelve (6:68-69) and the Crowds (6:28,30,34,52) use "we." Second, and more important, all other mediating Discourse Actants are absorbed into this "I" of Jesus. Thus anything said of Discourse Actants such as "Son of Man," or "Son," or "Him Who He Has Sent" is repeated also in terms of the "I" of Jesus, with one very important exception:

(a) Son of Man. In 6:27 it is the "Son of Man" who "will give" them "the food which endures for eternal life." But in 6:50-51, "I shall give" (51) this bread "that a man may eat of it and not die" (50). Again, what is said of the "Son of Man" in 6:53 is repeated of the "I" of Jesus in 6:54: "unless you eat the flesh of the Son of man and drink his blood, you have no life in you; he who eats my flesh and drinks my blood has eternal life."

(b) Son. In 6:40 it is a question of "every one who sees the Son and believes in him ..." But in 6:36, "you have seen me and yet do not believe."

(c) The Sent One. In 6:29 Jesus refers to "him whom he has sent" but in 6:38 it is a case of "him who sent me."

(d) Finally, there is the statement in 6:62, "What if you were to see the Son of man ascending where he was before?" Nowhere in John 6 is there any mention of the "I" of Jesus ascending to heaven. This leaves an unfulfilled expectation reminding us that John 6 is part of a wider unity and 6:62 will be repeated in terms of the "I" of Jesus only much later in 20:17: "I am ascending to my Father."

In summary, then, the Narrative Actant Jesus and also the mediator Discourse Actants such as "Son of Man," "Son," and "Sent One," are absorbed into and consumed by the Narrative-

Discourse Actant, the "I" of Jesus.
(3) The Crowds & "The Jews." One could imagine three types of
pronominal interaction within Discourse:
   (a) "I-You": speaker and hearer interact as reciproca-
ting "I" and "You" in their mutual Discourse.
   (b) "I-He": speaker interacts reciprocally with another
than the hearer in his own Discourse.
   (c) "You-He": speaker has the hearer ("you") and another
("he") interact reciprocally in his own Discourse
   In the light of these possibilities, there is a very
strange change between Jesus' dialogue with the unspecified
Crowds in 6:25-34 and the specified "Jews" in 6:35-38.
   In dialogue with the Crowds (a) there is not a single
instance of I-He" Discourse but (b) "I-You" (6:26,30,32a,34)
and (c) "You-He" (6:27,29,32 twice) are about evenly distributed. Note, for example, how 6:26 ("I-You") shifts to 6:27
("You-He"), or again how 6:32a ("I-You") moves to 6:32b ("You-
He").
   But in dialogue with "the Jews" all this changes com-
pletely. (a) Now "I-He" dominates completely (6:35b,37,38,39,
40,44,45b,54,56,57) so that (b) only three uses of "I-You"
(6:36,47a,53a) and (c) only one use of "You-He" appear (6:53b).
Note, for example, how 6:53-54 move from "I-You" (53a) to
"You-He" (53b) to "I-He" (54).
   This means, in summary, that the "You" of the Crowds/
"Jews" disappears almost completely. It is displaced and absorbed by the reiterated mentions of the new Discourse Actant,
"He who ..." (see B1[4] above).
(4) The Disciples. There is a rather similar development in
the case of the Disciples. Although there is no such sheer
numerical predominance of "I-He" as previously in 6:25-59
for the Crowds and "the Jews," it is clear, in 6:60-66, that
(a) "I-He" gets the last word in 6:65b ("no one can come to
me unless it is granted him by the Father") despite about
even usage of (b) "I-You" (6:63,65a) and (c) "You-He" (6:62).
   Like the Crowds and "the Jews," the departing Disciples
lose their "You" into "He who ... ("no one ... unless ...)
(5) The Twelve. In 6:67-71 the dialogue is exclusively "I-
You" with nothing of either "I-He" or "You-He." But I am not
inclined to read this as a terminal exaltation of "I-You"
over the other forms of dialogue in John 6. First, there is
the evident and supreme approbation contained in the reiterated "I-He" expressions noted above. Second, there is the fact
that 6:67-71 is very deliberately open to the future of the
gospel as a whole. This derives not only from the instability
effected by the positive and negative poles of "Simon Peter"
in 6:68 and "Judas the son of Simon Iscariot" in 6:71, but
also from the fact that, at this stage, we do not know what it
might mean "to betray him."
   In conclusion, then, the Narrative-Discourse Actant, the
"I" of Jesus has taken over the Discourse completely but the
most important recipient of this dialogue is "I-He" so that
it is the "He who ..." that is the counterpart of the "I" of
Jesus.

C. NARRATIVE ACTIONS AND DISCOURSE ACTIONS

   A very similar process takes place between Narrative
and Discourse Actions as that just seen for Narrative and Discourse Actants.

1. The Presence of Discourse Actions

There were two Narrative Actions considered earlier: Moving and Feeding. In the Discourse two new Discourse Actions are introduced. But these are not new in the way that the added Discourse Actants (God, Son of Man, etc.) were new, that is, not previously mentioned in the Narrative. They are new because they are the transcendental equivalents of the earlier Narrative Actions of Moving and Feeding. The Discourse Actions are transcendental Moving and transcendental Feeding. But, as with the Discourse Actants, once these Discourse Actions are introduced they dominate both the Narrative and the Discourse by absorbing and consuming the Narrative Actions within themselves.

(1) Narrative Moving and Discourse Moving

In discussing the Narrative Action of Moving above, I distinguished between Moving in Space and Moving between Actants. So also here with Discourse Moving.

(a) Discourse Moving in Space

Narrative Moving in Space was rather uniform: Jesus and the Disciples (6:1-3), and then the Crowds (6:2,5) crossed the sea; the Disciples and Jesus (6:16-21), and the the Crowds (6:22-25) crossed it back again.

But the new Discourse Moving separates Jesus from all the others, intersecting, as it were, all such horizontal movements with its own radical verticality. This Discourse Moving involves Jesus' descending and reascending back to heaven:

descending: 6:33,38,41,42,50,51,58 (see also 46)
reascending: 6:62

This then becomes the primary Moving and it overshadows completely any geographical movements by Jesus or the others.

(b) Discourse Moving among Actants

In similar fashion another and superior Moving subsumes the movements of either Crowds to Jesus or of Jesus to the Disciples. Any Moving to Jesus must be a "coming" (6:35-37,44, 65) which is "given" (6:37,39) or "drawn" (6:44) or "granted" (6:65) by God. Only one who has "heard and learned from the Father comes to me" (6:45). Even more significantly, not even a choice by Jesus himself precludes this imperative: "Did I not choose you, the twelve, and one of you is a devil?" (6:70). Neither the Crowds' coming to Jesus nor Jesus' coming to the Disciples is what counts since all such Narrative Moving is controlled absolutely by a far more profound and transcendental Discourse Moving.

(2) Narrative Feeding and Discourse Feeding

The second major Narrative Action was Feeding. As one moves into Discourse one is prepared for a rather obvious parallel between feeding an teaching, between bread and revelation. This would be an obvious development of 6:1-15 (feeding, bread) and 6:16-21 (teaching, revelation). One is quite prepared for a relationship between Narrative and Discourse along the following lines. In Narrative: (a) Source of Food, (b) Feeder, (c) Feeding, (d) Food, (e) Consumption of Food, (f) Consumer, (g) Bodily Life, will beget a parallelism in Discourse of: (a') Source of Revelation, (b') Revealer, (c') Revealing, (d') Revelation, (e') Belief, (f') Believer, (g')

Eternal Life. But this is not at all what happens. Still, what
does happen is in complete continuity with the fundamental process whereby Discourse has been steadily absorbing and consuming the Narrative and where the only Narrative element (Actants
and Actions) not already thus consumed is the Narrative-
Discourse Actant, the "I" of Jesus. But it would be impossible
to emphasize too much the paradoxical nature of this final
consumption since it is the "I" of Jesus that demands that the
"I" be consumed. Thus even, or especially, here the absolute
and unqualified "I AM" of 6:20 is still dominant, even over
"I AM to be consumed" in 6:51-58.

The steps of the process whereby the Feeder becomes the
Food are both deliberate and obvious:

(a) The first step is 6:25-34 and the message is sooth-
ingly acceptable. God will give you the true bread from heaven
which insures eternal life. What can anyone respond but: "Lord,
give us this bread always" (6:34).

(b) The second step is 6:35-48 (in a giant chiasm between 6:35a and 6:48 with the center at 6:42a) and now the
Discourse turns problematic but not yet as problematic as it
will be later. This bread is now identified with the "I" of
Jesus. Feeder and Food are equated. The response now is murmuring and questioning (6:41-42). But the situation is not yet
desperate. At this point it is still possible to hear Jesus
metaphorically. If he is heavenly bread, one could see it as
a metaphorical expression that he is not only Revealer (Feeder)
but Revelation (Food). The call for *consumption* would still be
metaphorical and would mean *acceptance* of the Revealer as the
Revelation.

(c) The third step is in 6:49-58 and it may be summarized as follows:

```
6:49-50    Bread/Eat
6:51-52    I/Bread/Eat/My Flesh
6:53-56            Eat/Flesh//Drink/Blood [four times]
6:57       I/    /Eat/Me
6:58       Bread/Eat
```

The outer frames of 6:49-50 and 6:58 do not really go beyond
the development of the second step in 6:35-48. The next inner
frames of 6:51-52 and 6:57 already bo beyond this by insisting
outside metaphorical tolerances that the bread, which is Jesus,
must be *eaten*. But it is the inner core of 6:53-56 that makes
it clear that something beyond metaphor is happening. In a
formulaic, hypnotic, and almost rhapsodic repetition the
phrases, Eat/Flesh//Drink/Blood, move the Discourse beyond any
interpretation in terms of merely *accepting* (eating) the Revealer.

I would summarize the total development so far as follows:

```
6:25-34    Bread
6:35-48    I/Bread
6:49-58    I/Bread/Eat Me
```

Eat/My Flesh//Drink/My Blood

Two questions must now be asked. First, what is the meaning of this fourfold repetition of Eat/Flesh//Drink/Blood. Second, why is it placed precisely here in John 6?

The language of 6:49-58 is explicable only in terms of
eucharistic formulae known from outside this chapter but it is

even more startling than the similar formulaic repetitions in
1 Cor 11:27-29 (eat/bread//drink/cup). This furnishes four main
points: it is formulaic eucharistic language; it is extremely
more *realistic* than is usual elsewhere for such formulae; it
is addressed to the murmuring and debating Crowds/"Jews"; it is
not reacted to by them but by the Disciples among whom it
causes a division (6:60-66).

It is the reaction of the Disciples that must come
first in interpretation since John omits here any reaction
from the Crowds/"Jews." To the murmuring Disciples Jesus says:
"'Do you take offense at this? Then what if you were to see
the Son of man ascending where he was before?'" (6:61b-62).
At first glance the logic of this question is not very compelling. If one presumes that *ascension* means some sort of great
triumphant manifestation, then belief would be rendered easier
rather than harder by witnessing it. But if ascension means
crucifixion, then the logic is clarified. So also is the basic
meaning of 6:51-58. Jesus is announcing there that to accept
him is to accept the one who must die, who must die by the
violent separation of body and blood, that is, as we shall only
know later, by crucifixion. But it is also to insist that such
acceptance is the only way that acceptance will ever after be
possible. In other words: I am always the one to be consumed.
Hence, of course, the double mention of betrayal (6:64,70-71)
follows the mention of crucifixion-ascension (6:62).

Thus the primary function of the eucharistic language
is to indicate a split in eucharistic understanding, that is,
in the permanent acceptance of crucifixion, among the Disciples.
Jesus must always be accepted as the Crucified One. What the
alternative to crucifixion-eucharist might be is not indicated
within this chapter (parousis-eucharist?).

But the unit in 6:51-58 is expressly addressed to the
Crowds/"Jews" who do not react to it after 6:59 while the
Disciples to whom it is not specifically addressed are the ones
who respond to it, both negatively and positively. For John
"the Jews" are those who will deny and reject the divine necessity of this crucifixional destiny and by so doing render it
inevitable. *The supreme irony is that, for John, those who
reject crucifixion theoretically will thereby effect it poli-
tically.* Hence, although addressed to "the Jews," their final
reaction is not recorded yet. But it is reacted to immediately
by some of the Disciples now because even though they will not
effect the crucifixion, they will deny its permanent and endur-
ing, that is, its eucharistic necessity.

VI. SCRIPT

This final section will, first, sum up what has happened
so far, and, second, draw attention to what is the most obvious
facet of the text and therefore is almost always overlooked: *it
is written.*

A. TIME, SPACE, NARRATIVE, DISCOURSE

John 6 is not just composed of a simple balance of Narrative (6:1-24) whose physicality symbolizes what the succeeding
Discourse (6:25-71) renders spiritual and transcendental. It is
characterized by layers of text whose successive levels dominate
and absorb the previous ones. In view of the text's dominant
motif of *eating* it seems necessary to characterize this process

as *consumption*.

There exists first of all the consumption of the Time, Space, Narrative, and Discourse of the Jewish Passover experience by the Time, Space, Narrative, and Discourse of a universal "Passover" phenomenon. Thus the Time of 6:4 is universalized into day-night-day and the Space sequence of crossing the sea, ascending and descending the mountain, and entering the synagogue is negated by having the sea recrossed, the mountain reascended, and the synagogue exited. The Narrative of the Feeding is 6:1-15 transcends the Exodus feeding stories as the Dialogue makes explicit in 6:31-33,49,58. And now the murmuring of the Crowds or Disciples is not about the Narrative on Feeding as it was during the Exodus but about the very Discourse itself (6:41,52,60-61).

There is also, however, the consumption of the Time, Space, and Narrative of this universalized "Passover" by the Discourse which accompanies them.

Most specifically there is the consumption of the text's receiver within the collectivity of the "He Who ..."

Finally, and most importantly, there is the consumption *by* the text's receiver (as "He Who ...") *of* the "I" of Jesus, whose absolute "I AM" (6:20) will nevertheless transcend both "I am the bread" (6:35,48,51a) and "I am to be consumed" (6: 51b-57).

B. IT IS WRITTEN

The Crowds, representing the Jewish Passover experience, and Jesus, advocating its transcendence, both invoke the biblical writings as support. In 6:31 the Crowds, talking of physical feeding, say: "*It is written*, 'He gave them bread from heaven to eat.'" And in 6:45 Jesus, speaking of spiritual feeding, says: "*It is written* in the prophets, 'And they shall all be taught by God.'" Thus the twin poles of the Discourse alike appeal to "it is written."

This central and double appeal to Scripture, and thus to *script*, force us to face what we are carefully avoiding in studying this "oral" Discourse, namely, the most obvious and therefore invisible fact about the Narrative and Discourse in John 6: *it is written*. Peter is absolutely correct in saying to Jesus:"'You have the words of eternal life'" (6:68b) but we, the readers, know them only as written, as script, and we know even Peter's oral confession only as written, as script.

At this point I am beginning to glimpse a question which renders the laborious structuralist analysis at least personally worthwhile because it has unearthed a heremeneutical issue which historical analysis did not and presumably could not uncover.

Is it of any significance that we read John 6 as *script* rather than see and hear "it" happen as event? When John 1:14 says that "the Word became flesh" and John 6:63 adds that "the flesh is of no avail," should we conclude that the Word of God became flesh and voice in order finally to become script: "the Word became script"? There, presumably, is the hermeneutical heart: is the Word of God oral or scribal or both, and, if both, are there differences and hierarchies to be maintained within that answer? Or does the Word of God have a history wherein it was originally oral and thence became scribal and what differences and hierarchies exist between such stages: oral (lost forever?), oral-scribal, and pure scribal? And is that the end of such an historical development?

At this point we can sense the questions reaching out
to envelop our contemporary selves. Does it make any difference that I am asking these questions in script and you are
reading them from script and how can we either ask or answer
them without inevitable paradox? How could we proclaim in
script the primacy of orality?

But in raising these questions I recognize that I am far
from being alone. For this precise problem there is already,[3]

> a community of the question, therefore, within that
> fragile moment when the question is not yet deter-
> mined enough for the hypocrisy of an answer to have
> already initiated itself beneath the mask of the
> question, and not yet determined enough for its
> voice to have been already and fraudulently articulated
> within the very syntax of the question. A community
> of decision, of initiative, of absolute initiality,
> but also a threatened community, in which the ques-
> tion has not yet found the language it has decided
> to seek, is not yet sure of its own possibility
> within the community. A community of the question
> about the possibility of the question.

The brilliant polarities of the community of this question are
represented by the writings of Walter Ong[4] and Jacques Derrida[5].
Ong argues for the primacy of oral over scribal communication
basing himself primarily on the historical primordiality of
speech over script in both the species and the child. This is,
however, a very dangerous argument since logically it would
give an even more elevated and primordial value to the gurgle
and the grunt. It is also anomalous that Ong never seems at
all self-conscious in *writing* about the primacy of orality
or even in citing the scripted Scriptures in support of this
primordiality. Derrida, who has the advantage of a single word,
écriture, meaning both writing and Scripture, argues for the
philosophic primordiality of *écriture* since script reveals more
fully, openly, and honestly the absence and deferment at the
heart of the sign, of all signs of course, but which the presence of the speaker disguises in oral conversation while the
absence of the writer proclaims it in scribal dialogue.

Holding, for here and now, the discussion exclusively
to oral and scribal communication and bracketing the far more
compelling problem of electronic communication (of Derrida one
must ask: does the videotape of a dead lover reveal presence
or absence, or does it, by intensifying the illusion of presence, intensify even more devastatingly the experience of absence?), I find that John 6 seems more adequately understood
through Derrida than through Ong, and for two reasons.

First, if the "words" of Jesus are a mystery of spirit
and life (6:63b,68), wherein what must always be consumed must
always be there to be consumed anew, does this not apply more
to the scribal than the oral Word of God?

Second, the Discourse in John 6 is in dialogue format
and the dialogue is one of question and answer. What could be
more oral than question and answer since questioner and answer-
er must be mutually present to one another? But these questions
in John 6 seem to receive non-answers or pseudo-answers. I
think this is empirically verifiable since if one lined up all
the questions in one column and all their answers in another,

juggled column, one could hardly line them up properly without prior knowledge of John 6. Here is the list of questions and "answers" in John 6:

Question	Answer	Non-Answer	Counter-Question
6:5		6:7	
6:9		6:10	
6:25		6:26	
6:28	6:29		
6:30(two)		6:32-33(?)	
6:42(two)		6:43	
6:52		6:53	
6:60			6:61-62(two)
6:67	6:68b-9		6:68a
6:70			

There are twelve questions of which only two receive real answers; eight receive non-ansers; two receive counter-questions; and one, the final word of Jesus, is a question which, in receiving no answer, terminates the Discourse. In authentic oral dialogue such "answers" would soon generate protest and demands for real answers.

Thus John 6 creates the illusion of orality and the entire Discourse proceeds through questions and pseudo-answers. The one exception is, of course, the "I AM; do not be afraid" of 6:20, but that is an exception to everything, and even that is now script and only script. Tentatively, then, John 6 moves towards this: the Word of God is script.

C. SCRIPT AND ETERNAL LIFE

Throughout 6:25-71 Jesus promises both eternal life and a raising up on the last day. "Life" is mentioned in 6:33,35,48, 51,53,57,63; "eternal life" in 6:27,47,51,58,68; "raising up" in 6:39,44; and the last two terms are combined together in 6:40,54. Read together the promise is of eternal life here and now immediately as well as the promise that death will not effect the individual believer who will be raised up on the individual's last day. As used in John 6, it does not seem possible that "the last day" could refer specifically to a cosmic eschaton, else the believer would have to be "dead" for the period before its advent. But that, of course, would require further discussion in the light of the entire gospel.

But the far more important point to be noted is how the Discourse Actants are reflected in this promise. It is *never* said to anyone in John 6 by Jesus: "if *you* believe, eat, drink, etc. ... *I* will give *you* eternal life and *I* will raise *you* up on the last day." As noted before, the Discourse "I" of Jesus subsumes all other titles and even Jesus himself, but the recipients of eternal life are not a "you" but a "he who."

And all of this endures only in script, for us here and now it endures only in script. In script, then, the Discourse "I" of Jesus remains eternally but the believer, even in script, obtains eternal life not as a personal "you" but within the community of a "he who ..." In the words of the script, "As the living Father sent *me*, and *I* live because of the Father, so *he who* eats me will *live because of me*" (6:57).

D. GATHERING THE FRAGMENTS

I have held until last one unit of text not previously discussed but singularly striking in its emphasis. "And when

212

they had eaten their fill, he told his disciples, 'Gather up
the fragments left, over, that nothing may be lost.' So they
gathered them up and filled twelve baskets with fragments from
the five barley loaves, left by those who had eaten" (6:12-13).
It is useful at this point, as so often throughout this paper,
to keep an eye on Mark, not in terms of sources but simply as
a variation on the same story. Mark 6:41b-43 says: "and he
divided the two fish among them all. And they all ate and were
satisfied. And *they* took up twelve baskets full of broken
pieces and of the fish." Note the vagueness of Mark's *they*.
Thus John is very different from Mark in that he has: (1) an
explicit command from Jesus to gather the fragments; (2) the
command is explicitly to his disciples; (3) the reason is also
given by Jesus: "that nothing may be lost"; (4) the disciples
explicitly gather only the bread and not the fish. But there
is something even more striking in John and that is the way
these "twelve baskets" at the start of the chapter in 6:13
force a linkage with the previously unmentioned "twelve"
disciples at the end of the text in 6:67-71. One therefore
presumes that there is one basket for each of the twelve
disciples who stay with Jesus after the others depart.

It is impossible to read the text of John, whatever
about Mark, in terms of respect for either the pastoral site
or the divine gift. The former would demand even greater concern for the fish fragments and the latter would demand at
least equal care for both. It is only of the bread that nothing must be lost, and the bread, with the fish quietly for-
gotten, becomes the Discourse "I" of Jesus. It is, then, the
fragments of Jesus which must be gathered so that nothing may
be lost.

Once again, and finally, the scripted text reaches out
to envelop the reader. John 6 is "fragments ... left by those
who have eaten." But Jesus must always come to us as of old,
by the lakeside, that is, in fragments. The fragments will
have to be gathered anew by those who consider themselves
disciples and there will be not only multiple fragments but
even multiple baskets. And among those baskets will be the
basket of the one who must betray. It may be possible to
distinguish them, however, in that the basket of the one who
must betray will always be single and univocal while those
of the others will have to be multiple and plural.

NOTES
[1]Jacques Derrida, "Force et Signification," *Critique*,
193-94 (June-July, 1963) was the opening essay in his
L'écriture et la différence (Paris: Seuil, 1967), a collection
of essays all, save one, published separately during 1963-
1966. The collection has been translated by Alan Bass as
Writing and Difference (Chicago: University of Chicago Press,
1978), and this opening essay, "Force and Signification"
(pp. 3-30) has been reprinted in *Structuralist Review*, 1,2
(Winter, 1978), pp. 13-54. My quotation is that essay's opening sentences. See Robert Detweiler, *Story, Sign, and Self*.
Philadelphia: Fortress Press/Missoula, MT: Scholars Press,1978.
[2]I am aware that the terms Narrative (deeds) and Discourse (words) are not entirely satisfactory. They may cause
confusion with the much more technical distinctions between
Story (the content, the what) and Discourse (the expression,

the how) suggested by Seymour Chatman, *Story and Discourse: Narrative Structure in Fiction and Film* (Ithaca, NY: Cornell University Press, 1978). I have not been able to adapt Chatman's excellent categories to John 6 (although it may well be possible to do so with future study) primarily because of the very special relationship between what Jesus does (my Narrative) and what Jesus says (my Discourse) in John 6. But, for future reference, see Chatman's section on (his term) "Discourse" (pp. 146-262) and especially his comment that, "When we know more about textual and semantic analysis, it may be possible to develop viable taxonomies of dialogue types" (p. 177). He cites Maurice Blanchot's three-way distinction of dialogue, exemplified from Malraux, James, and Kafka, and notes that, "Kafka's characters, for their part, are doomed forever to talk at cross purposes, past each other" (p. 178).

[3]Jacques Derrida, *Writing and Difference*, p. 80. See also pp. 292-93.

[4]Walter J. Ong, *The Presence of the Word* (New Haven, CT: Yale University Press, 1967); *Rhetoric, Romance, and Technology* (Ithaca, NY: Cornell University Press, 1971); *Interfaces of the Word* (Ithaca, NY: Cornell University Press, 1977). A magnificent section of that last book, pp. 230-71, has been reprinted as "Maranatha: Death and Life in the Text of the Book," *JAAR*, 45 (December, 1977), pp. 419-49.

[5]Besides the collection noted in the first footnote above, see also, "White Mythology: Metaphor in the Text of Philosophy," *New Literary History*, 6 (1974), pp. 5-74; and *Of Grammatology*, trans. by Gayatri Chakravorty Spivak (Baltimore, MD: The Johns Hopkins University Press, 1976).

THE AGREEMENTS THAT EXIST BETWEEN LUKE AND JOHN

F. Lamar Cribbs

The First United Methodist Church, Rocky Ford, Colo.

Until quite recently, St. John was considered by most in-
terpreters as a gospel that was not composed until after the
three Synoptic Gospels had all been completed and were becoming
known.[1] Thus it was not only frequently asserted that the
fourth evangelist was acquainted with and dependent upon one or
more of the Synoptics,[2] but different writers had also urged
that John (I use this term as only a traditional way of referring to the author) seemingly wrote his gospel in order to supplement,[3] correct,[4] or interpret[5] the material found in these
earlier gospels.

However, in 1938 P. Gardner-Smith produced an important
monograph[6] that seriously questioned the prevailing critical
opinion that John had used (or had been influenced by) the
Synoptics in the writing of his gospel.[7] This thesis of
Johannine independence has been supported and developed in
recent years by an increasing number of writers (e.g., E. R.
Goodenough, B. Noack, R. Bultmann, E. Haenchen, I. Buse, C. H.
Dodd, B. M. V. van Iersel, D. Moody Smith, Jr., Frederick H.
Borsch, Raymond E. Brown)[8] who have urged in various ways that
the evidence gained from a comparative study of John and the
Synoptics does not support the theory of Johannine dependence
upon the Synoptic Gospels.[9] Certainly this judgment has never
been even nearly unanimous, and several recent writers (e.g.,
C. K. Barrett, E. K. Lee, A. Mendner, John A. Bailey, J.
Blinzler)[10] have strongly urged that John knew and was influenced by the Synoptics (esp. Mark and Luke). On the other
hand, several of the most recent writers on John (e.g., J. N.
Sanders, R. Schnackenburg, R. T. Fortna, L. Morris, A. Wind,
Charles H. H. Scobie, James M. Robinson)[11] have all argued in
favor of Johannine independence of the Synoptics. Thus even
though there exists no real consensus on this question, there
nevertheless now exist a considerable number of scholars who
think that John was not dependent upon any of the Synoptics
when he composed his Gospel.[12]

Yet while the scarcity of close verbal/factual/conceptual
parallels between John and Matthew/Mark[13] would seem to justify
the skepticism that exists among many writers today with regard
to there being any direct literary relationship between the
Gospels of John and Matthew/Mark,[14] the same judgment would not
appear to be valid with relationship to the Gospels of Luke and
John (cf. below). Thus while John contains relatively few
verbal/factual agreements[15] with Matthew[16] and Mark,[17] several
recent comparative studies of Luke and John "have disclosed
the existence of a considerably larger number of verbal parallels between these two Gospels than had heretofore generally
been recognized."[18] Let just four examples from these recent
Lukan/Johannine studies suffice to illustrate this point. In
1951, E. Osty in his examination of the Lukan/Johannine passion
narratives identified over forty Lukan agreements with John in
these narratives alone.[19] Then Pierson Parker, in his study of

"Luke and the Fourth Evangelist," observed that John's "sharings with the Third Evangelist are enormous in their number and range" and that "John agrees with Luke alone five times as often as with Matthew alone, or with the Second Gospel alone."[20] Similarly, Raymond E. Brown has written that the Lukan/Johannine parallels occur "both in minute details and in the broad sweep of narrative and ideas,"[21] with some of these parallels being "too precise to be accidental."[22] Then Edwin D. Freed and Russell B. Hunt, in their recent study in the JBL, have observed that "when Luke shares a pericope with all three co-evangelists, in all but one instance (the cleansing of the temple) he agrees with John against Mark and Matthew in important details" (cf. esp. their chart immediately following this statement in which they list over twenty major factual agreements of Luke with John against both Mark and Matthew).[23]

These studies have disclosed that a considerable number of verbal/factual/conceptual agreements seem to exist between the Gospels of Luke and John. Following is a summary of some of the basic types of agreements that are to be found in a comparative study of these two gospels.

* There exist about sixty verbal parallels between Luke and John (cf. below, esp. Sec. I), some of which exhibit almost verbatim agreement between these two evangelists.[24]

* While Luke exhibits a few more verbal parallels with Matthew and Mark in the twenty-four pericopes that he shares with all three of his co-evangelists[25] than he does with John,[26] in individual verses the percentage of verbal agreement between Luke and John is often quite comparable to the degree of verbal agreement that exists between many of Luke's parallels with Matthew and Mark (cf. below, esp. Sections I-B and I-C).[27]

* In the 143 verses that comprise "the quadruple tradition" (the twenty-four pericopes that Luke shares with all three of his co-evangelists) there exist some forty-five instances in which Luke agrees with the information found in John (or vice versa) rather than with the differing data that is to be found in Matthew/Mark[28] as well as some thirty additional instances in which Luke and John agree in the omitting of important data that is to be found in the comparable passages of the first two gospels.[29]

* Although Luke agrees with the Matthean/Markan order of events with remarkable precision through most of the triple tradition (cf. below, esp. Sec. III),[30] in the twenty-four pericopes that Luke shares with all three of his co-evangelists there exist some twenty instances in which Luke seems to be in agreement with the Johannine order of events (or vice versa)[31] rather than with the differing order of events that is to be found in the comparable passages in both Matthew and Mark.[32]

* In addition to the sixty/sixty-five verbal parallels[33] that exist between Luke and John, there also exist some twenty-five verbal resemblances between these two gospels that contain wording, phrasing, or concepts that are lacking in the first two gospels (cf. below, esp. Sec. I-E).

* There also exists a considerable number of concepts, terms, and phrases that in the NT are to be found only or

mainly in the Lukan and the Johannine writings.[34]

  * The vast preponderance of the Lukan/Johannine agreements
(e.g., all but six of the close Lukan/Johannine verbal parallels, most of their sequential agreements, and over 80% of
their factual agreements) occur between their respective
passion/resurrection narratives. Indeed, in certain sections
of his passion narrative (cf. esp. Luke 22:31-35,47-50,54-59,
66-71; 23:1-25,32-33,52-56; 24:1-11; and parr.) Luke shares
almost as many of his words with John as he does with either
Matthew or Mark (cf. below, esp. Sec. IV) so that a comparative examination of the passion narratives of Luke and John
would seem to be of considerable importance in any attempt to
explain the possible relationships that may exist between these
two gospels.

  All of the foregoing considerations suggest that these
Lukan/Johannine agreements comprise an area of NT study that
needs considerable investigation and discussion.[35] Indeed,
it seems to us that the extent and preciseness of many of
these verbal/factual/sequential/conceptual agreements suggest
that some type of relationship exists between Luke and John.
Certainly, many explanations for these Lukan/Johannine parallels remain possible (e.g., John may have known Luke,[36] John
may have known the traditions that lie back of Luke,[37] John
and Luke may have been acquainted with the same or similar
oral/written traditions,[38] Luke may have been acquainted
with the sources or traditions that lie back of John,[39] Luke
may have known some early form of Johannine thought,[40] Luke
may have been acquainted with some early form of John[41]),
with not all of these options being "necessarily mutually
exclusive."[42] Any analysis of these Lukan/Johannine parallels thus needs to give careful consideration to the number
and exactness of the agreements that exist between Luke and
John as well as to observe the differences that exist between
these two gospels in the pericopes that they have in common.
As Samuel Sandmel has written:

> I am not denying that literary parallels and literary
> influence, in the form of source and derivation, exist.
> . . . However, I am speaking words of caution about
> exaggerations about the parallels and about source and
> derivation. . . . Thus, in the case of passages in
> Samuel-Kings and Chronicles, the concession that paral-
> lel passages do exist falls short of determining
> whether the Chronicler borrowed from the author of
> Samuel-Kings, or vice-versa. That determination rests
> on inherent probabilities which emerge from close
> study.[43]

  The purpose of this study will thus be quite limited. That
is, rather than arguing in support of some particular solution
to the Lukan/Johannine question, we will herein attempt to make
a rather comprehensive presentation of the various Lukan/Johan-
nine agreements so that we can have a more adequate basis for
approaching the question of dependence/independence. Hence in
this paper we shall first attempt to give a rather definitive
enumeration of the different types of agreements (e.g. verbal
parallels, verbal resemblances, factual agreements common only
to Luke and John, sequential agreements between only Luke and
John, conceptual agreements common only to Luke and John in the

NT) that exist between Luke and John, after which we will examine in detail three selected Lukan/Johannine pericopes from
their passion/resurrection narratives (i.e., Luke 22:31-34/
John 13:36-38; Luke 23:20-23/John 19:6-15; Luke 24:36-43/John
20:19-29) that contain a considerable number of verbal/factual/
sequential agreements between these two gospels. We shall then
conclude this study by suggesting that these various Lukan/
Johannine parallels indicate that some type of literary relationship seems to exist between the Gospels of Luke and John.

I. VERBAL PARALLELS SHARED BY LUKE AND JOHN

Statistical analysis (esp. with regard to the extent and
percentage of verbal agreement) has historically been recognized as an important factor in source criticism by many
writers (e.g., J. C. Hawkins, B. S. Easton, B. H. Streeter,
V. Taylor, P. Parker, A. M. Perry, A. M. Honore, R. Morgenthaler).[44] Thus the high percentage of verbal agreement that
exists between Matthew, Mark, and Luke has persuaded most inter-
preters that some kind of direct relationship must exist among
these three gospels. As Stephen Neill has written:

> The resemblances between the Gospels in Greek are at
> points so close as to be inexplicable, unless there
> was some kind of literary dependence between them after
> some part at least of the Gospel material had been
> written down, and written down in Greek.[45]

For example, if the eighty-two pericopes that comprise the triple
tradition are considered as a whole, then it will be found that
Matthew shares about 55-57% of his words in these pericopes with
Mark, and Luke shares about 45-47% of his words in these same
pericopes with Mark.[46] However, if just the pre-passion pericopes from the triple tradition are compared, it will be found
that Luke's average verbal agreement with Mark in these sixty-
one pericopes is much higher (averaging 54-56%)[47] than it is in
the last three chapters of his gospel (where it averages only
about 26%).[48] As Vincent Taylor has observed:

> The percentage of Markan words in Lk. iv. 31-44 is
> 52, in Lk. v. 12 - vi. 11 it is 53.6, and there are
> similar percentages in Lk. viii. 4 - ix. 50 and Lk.
> xviii. 15-43, where it rises to 68.[49]

On the other hand, Luke's average verbal agreement with Matthew in the triple tradition is considerably lower (averaging
about 42% in his pre-passion narratives and about 22% in his
passion narratives) than is his average agreement with Mark in
these same pericopes.[50] Contrariwise, Luke's verbal agreement
with Matthew in the double tradition is much higher (averaging
about 60%) than is Luke's average agreement with Matthew in the
triple tradition (where it averages only about 37-38%).[51] However, it should be observed that much of the material in the
double tradition consists of the words of Jesus, and as Joseph
B. Tyson has observed, "It can be shown that there is a generally higher rate of agreement in reports of Jesus' teaching
than in other categories of material."[52] Indeed, if the 'sayings pericopes' from the double tradition (e.g., Luke 6:27-38;
7:24-35; 11:29-52; 12:22-34; 14:15-24; and parr.) are compared
with 'sayings pericopes' from the triple tradition (e.g., Luke
5:33-39; 9:20-27; 18:18-33; 20:1-18,27-44; and parr.), the
rate of verbal agreement between the synoptists in both tradi-

tions would be found to be quite comparable.[53] Thus there
exist extensive close verbal agreements between all the synoptists (Matthew with Mark, Luke with Mark, Luke with Matthew)
in many sections of their gospels, a phenomenon which suggests
(whatever our own view of the synoptic problem may be)[54] that
either some kind of direct relationship exists between these
gospels or that all three of these evangelists were dependent
upon a common written source.[55]

However, when John is compared with the Synoptics it is to
be found that no such extensive parallelism exists between
these gospels as exists among Matthew, Mark, and Luke. Indeed,
it "has been estimated that only ca. 8% of its material is paralleled in any of the Synoptics."[56] Thus when John is examined
it is to be observed that the fourth evangelist shares just
twenty-four pericopes (i.e., 1:19-23,24-28,32-34; 2:14-18;
6:1-14,66-71; 12:1-8,12-19; 13:1-20,21-30,36-38; 18:1-2,3-12,
15-18,19-23,25-27,28-38,39-40; 19:1-3,6-16,17-22,23-27,28-30,
38-42; 20:1-18) with all three of his co-evangelists in somewhat comparable form, one additional pericope (6:16-21) with
Matthew/Mark, one pericope (4:46-54) with Matthew/Luke, and
three other pericopes (19:4-5; 20:19-29; 21:1-14) with Luke
only as well as certain individual sayings with one or more of
the synoptists.[57]

When John is compared with the first two gospels only, it
is to be noticed that not only are John's verbal agreements
with Matthew/Mark (except for seven sayings John shares with
all three of his co-evangelists - cf. below)[58] limited almost
entirely to just seven pericopes (i.e., the Baptist's proclamation, the feeding of the five thousand, Jesus' walking on
the sea, the anointing, the entry, the last supper, the mocking
of Jesus by the soldiers), but that John's parallels with
Matthew/Mark are also both quite infrequent[59] and imprecise.[60]

Contrariwise, when John is compared with Luke it is to be
found that John exhibits verbal parallels in every one of the
twenty-eight pericopes they have in common (except for the
pericope describing Jesus' cleansing of the temple), with some
of the Lukan/Johannine passion parallels being especially quite
close. Thus S. I. Buse has observed that while the passion
agreements between Matthew and John are neither frequent nor
decisive, those between Luke and John in these same passion
narratives are both numerous and quite precise.[61] Similarly,
J. N. Sanders has written that there exist "clear contacts"
between Luke 24:33-43 and John 20:19-29 even if vss. 24:36b
and 24:40 were not part "of the original text of Luke."[62] It
is therefore to be observed that the passion/resurrection narratives of Luke in particular exhibit a considerable number of
close verbal agreements with the comparable sections of the
Johannine narrative.[63] Hence an examination of the Lukan/Johan-
nine verbal parallels would seem to be of considerable importance in any attempt to discover if some kind of relationship
could possibly exist between the Gospels of Luke and John.[64]

A comparison and analysis of the various verbal agreements
that exist between Luke and John would seem to justify the
following observations.

(A). There exist at least sixty verbal parallels between
Luke and John, with over thirty of them exhibiting quite close
verbal agreement between these two evangelists. Following is

220

a chart illustrating many of the close verbal parallels that
exist between these two gospels (in this chart we will use a
double underline to indicate exact verbal agreement between
these two gospels and a single underline to indicate the
usage of a comparable form of the same basic Greek word by
both Luke and John).

CHART I

A CHART OF THE LUKAN/JOHANNINE CLOSE VERBAL PARALLELS[65]

St. Luke	St. John
John answered them all (3:16a)	John answered them (1:26a)
"I baptize you with water" (3:16b)	"I baptize with water" (1:26b)
"The thong of whose sandals I am not fit to untie (3:16d)	"The thong of whose sandal I am not worthy to untie (1:27b)
And they said, "Is this not Joseph's son?" (4:22b)	They said, "Is this not Jesus, the son of Joseph?" (6:42a)
And anointed them with the ointment (7:38e)	And anointed the feet of Jesus (12:3b)
And wiped them with her hair (7:44d; cf. also 7:38c)	And wiped his feet with her hair (12:3c)
The crowds . . . followed him (9:11a)	A multitude followed him (6:2a)
They saw his glory (9:32c)	He saw his glory (12:41b)
"Blessed is the king who comes in the name of the Lord" (19:38a)	Blessed is he who comes in the name of the Lord, even the King of Israel" (12:13b)
Then Satan entered into Judas (22:3a)	Satan entered into him (13:27b)
"I tell you, Peter, the cock will not crow this day, until you three times deny that you know me" (22:34)	"I say to you, the cock will not crow, till you have denied me three times" (13:38b)
And one of them struck the slave of the high priest and cut off his right ear (22:50)	Then Simon Peter . . . struck the high priest's slave and cut off his right ear (18:10)
"You also are one of them" (22:58c)	"Are you not also one of his disciples" (18:25b)
"Man, I am not" (22:58c)	"I am not" (18:25c)
"If you are the Christ, tell us" (22:67a)	"If you are the Christ, tell us plainly" (10:24c)
But he said to them, "If I tell you, you will not believe" (22:67b)	Jesus answered them, "I told you, and you do not believe" (10:25a)
"You say that I am" (22:70b)	"You say that I am a king" (18:37b)
"I find no crime in this man" (22:4b)	"I find no crime in him" (18:38c)

St. Luke	St. John
But they all cried out together (23:18a)	They cried out again (18:40a)
"Away with this man" (23:18b)	"Not this man . . . . Away with him" (18:40b; 19:15a)
Pilate . . . , desiring to release Jesus (23:20)	Pilate sought to release him (19:12)
But they shouted out, "Crucify, crucify him" (23:21)	They cried out, "Crucify him, crucify him" (19:6b)
"I have found in him no crime deserving death" (23:22c)	"For I find no crime in him" (19:6c)
But they were urgent, demanding with loud cries that he should be crucified (23:23)	They cried out . . . , "Crucify him" (19:15a)
. . . to the place which is called the skull (23:33a)	. . . to the place called the place of a skull (19:17b)
There they crucified him (23:33b)	There they crucified him (19:18a)
Where no one had ever yet been laid (23:53c)	Where no one had ever been laid (19:41c)
But on the first day of the week (24:1a)	Now on the first day of the week (20:1a)
And they found the stone rolled away from the tomb (24:2)	And saw that the stone had been taken away from the tomb (20:1d)
But Peter rose and ran to the tomb (24:12a)	Peter then came out with the other disciple, and they went toward the tomb. They both ran . . . . (20:3-4a)
Stooping and looking in, he saw the linen cloths by themselves (24:12b)	And stooping to look in, he saw the linen cloths lying there (20:5a)
Jesus himself stood among them (24:36a)	Jesus came and stood among them (20:19c)
And he said to them, "Peace be with you" (24:36b)	And said to them, "Peace be with you" (20:19d)
"See my hands" (24:39a)	"See my hands" (20:27b)
And when he said this, he showed them his hands and his feet (24:40)	When he had said this, he showed them his hands and his side (20:20)

A survey of these Lukan/Johannine parallels discloses that verbal agreements exist between these two gospels at virtually every place where overlaps between the Lukan and the Johannine traditions occur. Indeed, if such verbal agreements as Luke 5:5a/John 21:3d, Luke 7:2c/John 4:47c,[66] Luke 7:3c/John 4:47b, Luke 22:39/John 18:1b-2, and Luke 23:9b/John 19:9c are included, then Luke exhibits verbal agreements with John (or vice versa) in all but one (Luke 19:45-46/John 2:14-17)[67] of

the twenty-eight pericopes that Luke shares with John.68 Some
of these Lukan/Johannine parallels are quite close (cf. esp.
Luke 3:16/John 1:26-27; Luke 19:38a/John 12:13b; Luke 22:34/
John 13:38b; Luke 22:50/John 18:10; Luke 22:67a/John 10:24c;
Luke 23:4b/John 18:38c/ Luke 23:53c/John 19:41c/ Luke 24:1a/
John 20:1a; Luke 24:36/John 20:19) and in individual verses
in the twenty-four pericopes that comprise "the quadruple
tradition" Luke exhibits a degree of verbal agreement with
John that is sometimes quite comparable to the percentage of
verbal agreement that often exists between Luke and Matthew/
Mark in these same pericopes. This is not to assume a
particular solution for either the synoptic problem69 or the
Lukan/Johannine question, but only to observe that the percentage of verbal agreement that exists in certain pericopes between Luke and John is sometimes quite comparable to the degree
of agreement that exists between Luke and Matthew/Mark in these
same passages. Thus if Luke shares eleven words out of
fourteen with Mark at 22:19, thirteen out of eighteen at 22:22,
eight out of sixteen at 22:34, ten out of seventeen at 22:50,
eleven out of nineteen at 23:26, and eight out of twelve at
23:53a, it can also be observed that Luke shares eight words
out of nine with John at 19:38a, nine out of sixteen at 22:34,
eleven out of seventeen at 22:50, twelve out of seventeen at
22:67, ten out of seventeen at 23:4, nine out of fifteen at
23:16-18, and four out of six at 23:53b.

(B). There are seven "sayings" found in all four of our
gospels, but with the exception of Pilate's opening question
to Jesus (which occurs in verbatim form in all four accounts)70
the form of the saying found in John seems to be closer to the
Lukan form (or vice versa) than it is to either Matthew or
Mark. Following is a comparison of the form in which these
six "sayings" occur in our several gospels (to simplify the
chart, only the Matthean, Lukan, and the Johannine forms of
each saying will be given; the Markan variations from the
Matthean form will be placed in parentheses within the Matthean wording of each saying). In this chart a single underline will be placed under the Matthean/Markan material lacking
in both Luke and John while a double underline will be placed
under those words common to Luke and John but which are lacking
(or found in a different form) in both Matthew and Mark.

CHART II

A COMPARISON OF THOSE SAYINGS FOUND IN ALL FOUR OF OUR GOSPELS

Matthew/Mark	Luke	John
Whose sandals (Mark has 'the thong of whose sandals') I am not fit to carry (Mark has 'to stoop down and untie) (Matt 3:11c/Mark 1:7c)	The thong of whose sandals I am not fit to untie (3:16d)	The thong of whose sandal I am not worthy to untie (1:27b)
Is not this the carpenter's son (Mark has 'the carpenter')? (Matt 13:55/Mark 6:3)	Is not this Joseph's son? (4:22c)	Is not this Jesus, the son of Joseph? (6:42a)

Matthew/Mark	Luke	John
Hosanna to the Son of David (Mark here has just 'Hosanna')! Blessed is he who comes in the name of the Lord (Mark adds 'Blessed is the kingdom of our father David that is coming')! (Matt 21:9b/Mark 11:9b)	Blessed is the King who comes in the name of the Lord! (19:38a)	Hosanna! Blessed is he who comes in the name of the Lord, even the King of Israel! (12:13b)
Truly, I say to you, this very night, before the cock crows (Mark adds 'twice'), you will deny me three times. (Matt 26:34/Mark 14:30)	I tell you, Peter, the cock will not crow this day, until you three times deny that you know me. (22:34)	Truly, truly, I say to you, the cock will not crow, till you have denied me three times. (13:38b)
One of those who were with Jesus (Mark has 'who stood by') . . . drew his sword, and struck the slave of the high priest, and cut off his ear. (Matt 26:51/Mark 14:47)	And one of them struck the slave of the high priest and cut off his right ear. (22:50)	Then Simon Peter . . . drew it (his sword) and struck the high priest's slave and cut off his right ear. (18:10a)
They all said (Mark has 'And they cried out again'), 'Let him be crucified' (Mark has 'Crucify him'). (Matt 27:22/Mark 15:13)	But they shouted out, 'Crucify, crucify him!' (23:21)	They cried out, 'Crucify him, crucify him!' (19:6b)

The above chart not only exhibits the relatively high degree of verbal agreement that exists between Luke and John in their versions of these sayings (ranging from 57% for Luke 22:21/John 19:6b to over 80% for Luke 19:38a/John 12:13b), but it also discloses that these six Lukan/Johannine passages share certain traits (e.g., Jesus is "the son of Joseph," the proclamation of Jesus as "King," the double cry, "Crucify, crucify") that are lacking in the parallel passages in both Matthew and Mark. Contrariwise, certain features found in the Matthean and/or Markan versions of these sayings are lacking in both Luke and John. Let just two examples suffice to illustrate this phenomenon:

(1) Luke 3:16d/John 1:27b. The verbal agreement between Luke and John in this passage is quite close. Thus nine of the ten words found in Luke 3:16d have a parallel in John 1:27b while nine of the eleven words found in John have a parallel in Luke. Luke does agree with Matt 3:11c and Mark 1:7c against John 1:27b in his use of "fit" instead of "worthy" as well as in his use of the plural form of "sandal" rather than the singular.[71] On the other hand, Luke's version of this saying ("the thong of whose sandals I am not fit to untie") is closest to the Johannine form for Matthew/Mark have distinct divergences from the form found in Luke and John (Matt 3:11c has "carry his sandals" and Mark 1:7c has "stoop down and untie").[72] Moreover, in both Luke and John this phrase

is the <u>fourth phrase</u> in their versions of John's proclamation (cf. below, Sec. III) while both Luke (3:16) and John (1:26-27) also place this proclamation right after some speculation as to whether or not the Baptist might be the Messiah (cf. Luke 3:15/John 1:19-25).

(2). <u>Luke 19:38a/John 12:13b</u>. The verbal agreement between Luke's version of the crowd's acclamation (Εὐλογημένος ὁ ἐρχόμενος, ὁ Βασιλεὺς ἐν ὀνόματι Κυρίου) and John's (Εὐλογημένος ὁ ἐρχόμενος ἐν ὀνόματι Κυρίου, καὶ ὁ Βασιλεὺς τοῦ Ἰσραὴλ) is seemingly quite close. Thus all eight of Luke's words in 19:38a have a parallel in John 12:13b while John shares eight of the eleven words found in his version of this saying with Luke. Contrariwise, Matthew 21:9b and Mark 11:9b-10 share only about half of their words with Luke 19:38a (Matthew here shares eight out of fourteen words with Luke while Mark shares just eight words out of nineteen) and contain certain material (e.g., Matthew's "Hosanna to the son of David" and Mark's "Blessed is the kingdom of our father David that is coming") that have no parallel in either Luke or John. Thus both Luke and John lack the Matthean/Markan references to David and agree that the "multitude"/"crowd" had acclaimed Jesus as their "King" on the occasion of his entry into Jerusalem.[73] Both Luke and John also place a reference to Jesus' "mighty works"/"signs" just prior to his entry into Jerusalem (cf. Luke 19:37/John 12:9-11)[74] and similarly agree in portraying the Pharisees "as reacting negatively to the acclamation"[75] in the verses immediately following this incident (cf. Luke 19:39/John 12:19). Luke 19:37-40 and John 12:9-19 thus seem to share in certain features that are lacking in both Matthew and Mark.

(C). There are also certain instances in which the degree of agreement/disagreement that exists between Luke and John <u>is quite comparable</u> to the degree of agreement/disagreement that exists between a number of Luke's parallels with Matthew/Mark. This again is not to posit a solution to either the Synoptic problem or the Lukan/Johannine question, but only to observe that some of the parallels between Luke and John <u>seem to be as close</u> as are some of the parallels that exist between Luke and Matthew/Mark. Let the following five examples serve to illustrate this phenomenon.

* John 1:26a ("John answered them") is as close to Luke 3:16a ("John answered them <u>all</u>")[76] as Mark 3:5 ("And he looked around at them")[77] is to Luke 6:10 ("And he looked around on them <u>all</u>").

* John 10:24b ("If you are the Christ, tell us <u>plainly</u>")[78] is as close to Luke 22:67a ("If you are the Christ, tell us") as Mark 8:31-32 ("And he began to teach them that the Son of man must suffer many things . . . . And he said this <u>plainly</u>") is to Luke 9:22 ("saying, the Son of man must suffer many things").

* John 12:13b ("Blessed is . . . the King <u>of Israel</u>") is as close to Luke 19:38a ("Blessed is the King") as Matt 27:42b/Mark 15:32a ("Let the Christ, the King <u>of Israel</u>") is to Luke 23:37a ("If you are the King of the Jews, save yourself").[79]

* John 18:25c ("I am not") is as close to Luke 22:58c ("<u>Man</u>, I am not") as Matt 9:2c/Mark 2:5b ("My son, your sins are forgiven") is to Luke 5:29b ("<u>Man</u>, your sins are forgiven

you").

* John 19:41c ("Where no one had ever been laid") is as close to Luke 23:53c ("Where no one had ever yet been laid") as Mark 11:2c ("on which no one has ever sat") is to Luke 19:30c ("on which no one has ever yet sat").

(D). An examination of the twenty-four pericopes found in all four of the gospels discloses the phenomenon that in at least ten of these pericopes Luke shares almost as many (or in some instances even more) of his words with John as he does with either Matthew or Mark. The following chart attempts to illustrate this situation.

CHART III

THE NUMBER OF WORDS LUKE SHARES WITH HIS THREE CO-EVANGELISTS IN CERTAIN SELECTED PERICOPES FROM THE QUADRUPLE TRADITION

Selected Passage From St. Luke	Number Of Words Used By Luke	Number Of Words Luke Shares With Matthew	Number Of Words Luke Shares With Mark	Number Of Words Luke Shares With John
3:16	33	21	23	23
22:31-34	62	11	12	15
22:50-54a	91	33	36	33
22:66-71	94	29	32	31
23:1-5	89	19	21	22
23:6-12	121	5	6	11
23:13-19	88	10	9	16
23:20-25	77	22	24	26
23:32-33	32	13	14	12
24:1-11	155	28	34	27
24:1-12	176	31	37	39

On the other hand, a comparison of the Johannine version of these pericopes with the comparable passages in the Synoptics discloses that John shares almost twice as many words with Luke in these verses as he does with either Matthew or Mark. Again let a chart illustrate this phenomenon.

CHART IV

THE NUMBER OF WORDS JOHN SHARES WITH THE SYNOPTISTS IN THESE PERICOPES

Selected Passage From St. John	Number Of Words Used By John	Number Of Words John Shares With Matthew	Number Of Words John Shares With Mark	Number Of Words John Shares With Luke
1:26-27	31	13	15	19
10:24-25a,36	50	10	9	20
13:36-38	58	13	14	18
18:10-13a	71	16	15	21
18:28-38	257	15	18	41
18:39-40	33	7	9	10
19:6-9	77	6	9	18
19:17-19	51	13	12	20
20:1-12	205	19	22	38

An examination of Chart III discloses that in five of these
ten pericopes Luke has more words in common with John than he
has with either Matthew or Mark, and in four more of these
pericopes Luke shares just one to three fewer words with John
than he does with the first two evangelists. On the other
hand, Chart IV shows that John has more words in common with
Luke in nine of these pericopes and shares about twice as many
words with Luke in four of these same pericopes as he does
with either Matthew or Mark. Moreover, an analysis of the
words John shares with his three co-evangelists reveals that
most of the words John shares with Matthew/Mark are words
that are common to all four evangelists in these pericopes.
Thus if one were to underline only the words that John has in
common with just one of his co-evangelists, it would be found
that John shares over four times as many words with Luke only
as he does with either Matthew only or Mark only.[80] Let the
following two examples suffice to illustrate this point.

(1). The Proclamation of John the Baptist. When one examines the Johannine form of this proclamation (1:26-27) it is to
be found that John contains three phrases ("John answered them,"
"I baptize with water," "the thong of whose sandal I am not
worthy to untie") that are quite close to the comparable
phrases found in Luke 3:16, and that in two of these phrases
(1:26a,27b) John stands closer to Luke than he does to either
Matthew (3:11) or Mark (1:7-8). Thus while sixteen of the
twenty words found in these three phrases in John have a parallel in Luke (and vice versa),[81] the fourth evangelist shares
just thirteen of these same twenty words with Mark and only ten
of these words with Matthew. For example, John's introductory
phrase (ἀπεκρίθη αὐτοῖς ὁ Ἰωάννης λέγων) to the
Baptist's proclamation at 1:26a would seem to be quite comparable to the words (ἀπεκρίνατο λέγων πᾶσιν ὁ
Ἰωάννης) that Luke used to introduce his version of this
proclamation at 3:16a but quite dissimilar to the introductory
phrases found in both Matt 3:7b (εἶπεν αὐτοῖς)
and Mark 1:7a (Καὶ ἐκήρυσσεν λέγων). John (1:26b)
then agrees with both Matthew (3:11a) and Luke (3:16b) against
Mark (1:8a) in making the opening phrase of John's proclamation
to be a reference to his baptism with water,[82] while the fourth
evangelist's final phrase of the Baptist's proclamation (1:27b)
is, as we have already observed, considerably closer to Luke
3:16d than it is to either Matt 3:11c or Mark 1:7c. Thus if
one were to analyze John 1:26-27 by the format developed by
E. P. Sanders, then this Johannine passage could be summarized
as follows:

John 1:26-27 contains

    10 triple agreements with Matthew, Mark, and Luke
     5 double agreements with Mark and Luke
     1 double agreement with Matthew and Mark
     2 single agreements with Matthew = 13 agreements with Matthew
    no single agreements with Mark   = 15 agreements with Mark
     4 single agreements with Luke   = 19 agreements with Luke

(2). The Barabbas Incident. The wording of John 18:40
would seem to be somewhat comparable to Luke 23:18 but quite
different from both Matt 27:20 and Mark 15:11. Thus a comparison of Luke 23:18 with John 18:40 shows that six of the eleven
words found in this Lukan verse have a parallel in John[83]

while the fourth evangelist here shares five out of nine words with Luke. Contrariwise, Matt 27:20 shares only two out of seventeen words with Luke/John while Mark 15:11 shares just three out of twelve words with these latter two evangelists. For example, the Lukan introductory phrase ("They all cried out together") would seem to be quite similar to the way John began his account of this incident ("They cried out again")[84] but quite dissimilar to the form found in both Matthew ("the chief priests . . . persuaded the people") and Mark ("the chief priests stirred up the crowd"). Moreover, the Lukan form of the response of the Jewish authorities to Pilate (Αἷρε τοῦτον, ἀπόλυσον δὲ ἡμῖν τὸν Βαραββᾶν) also seems to be somewhat comparable to the Johannine form (Μὴ τοῦτον ἀλλὰ τὸν Βαραββᾶν). The contexts in which both Luke 23:18 and John 18:40 are located also appear to be quite similar (e.g., both evangelists place an attempt by Pilate to release Jesus immediately before this incident and a description of Barabbas immediately afterwards) while both Luke 23:14-19 and John 18"38b-40 also seemingly contain the same basic sequence of events (cf. below, Sec. III).[85]

(E). In addition to these verbal parallels that exist between Luke and John, these two evangelists also seem to share in a number of other verbal resemblances including certain instances in which they are closer to each other than they are to either Matthew or Mark. Let the following chart illustrate this situation.

CHART V

THE VERBAL RESEMBLANCES THAT EXIST BETWEEN LUKE AND JOHN[86]

Matthew/Mark	Luke	John
-	Who from the beginning were eyewitnesses (1:2b)	You also are witnesses, because you have been with me from the beginning (15:27)
-	And blessed is she who believed (1:45a)	Blessed are those who have not seen and yet believe (20:29b)
Now after John was arrested (Matt 4:12/Mark 1:14)	He shut up John in prison (3:20b)	John had not yet been put in prison (3:24)
And he appointed twelve (Mark 3:14a)	And chose from them twelve (6:13b)	Did I not choose you the twelve (6:70b)
Go and tell John what you hear and see (Matt 11:4)	Go and tell John what you have seen and heard (7:22a)	He bears witness to what he has seen and heard (3:32a)
-	And he who rejects me (10:16c)	He who rejects me (12:48a)
-	He will gird himself (12:37b)	Jesus . . . girded himself (13:4c)
The chief priests . . . were seeking how to arrest him (Matt 26:4/Mark 14:1b)	The chief priests . . . were seeking how to put him to death (22:2a)	They took counsel on how to put him to death (11:53b)

Matthew/Mark	Luke	John
-	You did not lay hands on me (22:53b)	But no one laid hands on him (7:30b)
-	He was hoping to see some sign done by him (23:8c)	When the people saw the sign which he had done (6:14a)
-	And they remembered his words (24:8)	His disciples remembered that he had said this (2:22b)
-	He took the bread . . . and gave it to them (24:30)	Jesus . . . took the bread and gave it to them (21:13)
-	Have you anything here to eat? (24:41b)	Children, have you any fish? (21:5b)
-	These are my words which I spoke to you, while I was still with you (24:44a)	These things I have spoken to you, while I am still with you (14:25)
-	That everything written about me in the law of Moses and the prophets . . . must be fulfilled (24:44b)	We have found him of whom Moses in the law and also the prophets wrote (1:45b)
-	You are witnesses of these things (24:48)	This is the disciple who is bearing witness to these things (21:24a)

The above examples would therefore seem sufficient to illustrate the phenomenon that Luke and John share in a number of
verbal resemblances[87] that are lacking in Matthew/Mark. Thus
Luke and John are our only NT writers to speak of those who had
been "witnesses from the beginning" (Luke 1:2; John 15:27;
Acts 1:22), to refer to Jesus' "choosing of the twelve" (Luke
6:13; John 6:70; 13:18; 15:16,19; Acts 1:2,24), to write of
those who had attempted to "lay hands on Jesus" (Luke 20:19;
22:53; John 7:30,44), or to allude to the "seeing of signs
being done" (Luke 23:8; John 2:23; 6:2,14; Acts 8:6). A considerable number of verbal agreements/resemblances would therefore seem to exist between the Gospels of Luke and John.

II. FACTUAL INFORMATION COMMON TO LUKE AND JOHN

A comparison of the first three gospels discloses that the
Synoptics also share in a large amount of common factual material and that this parallelism often extends to even the smallest details. Thus the degree of factual agreement between the
Synoptics would seem to be especially high in the sixty-one pre-
passion pericopes that are to be found in all three of these
gospels.[88] Certainly, some factual differences do exist between
Matthew/Mark/Luke in these pericopes, although rarely do all
three synoptists present entirely contrasting information in
these sections of their gospels. So even though Matthew/Luke
sometimes agree factually against Mark (e.g., Matt 9:6/Luke
5:24, use "bed" and Mark 2:11 "pallet," Matt 9:20/Luke 8:44 have

"fringe of his garment" and Mark 5:27 "his garment," Matt
10:10/Luke 9:3 have "no staff" while Mark 6:8 has "except a
staff"), <u>Luke/Mark</u> <u>sometimes</u> <u>agree against Matthew</u> (e.g.,
Luke 5:27/Mark 2:14 have "Levi" and Matt 9:9 has "Matthew,"
Luke 8:27/Mark 5:2 have "a demoniac" and Matt 8:28 "two de-
moniacs," Luke 8:42/Mark 5:23 state that Jairus' daughter
"was dying" while Matt 9:18 asserts that she had "just died,"
Luke 18:35/Mark 10:46 have "a blind beggar" while Matt 20:30
has "two blind men"), <u>and Matthew/Mark</u> <u>sometimes agree</u>
<u>against Luke</u> (e.g., Matt 8:2/Mark 1:40 have "knelt before
him" while Luke 5:12 has "fell on his face," Matt 14:13/
Mark 6:32 depict Jesus as withdrawing "to a lonely place"
and Luke 9:10 "to a city called Bethsaida," Matt 17:1/Mark
9:2 use "after six days" while Luke 9:28 has "about eight
days after"), <u>the degree of factual agreement between the</u>
<u>first three evangelists</u> in these pre-passion pericopes from
the triple tradition <u>is nevertheless quite high</u>. Let just
one pericope from Jesus' early Galilean ministry (the healing
of a leper) suffice to illustrate this situation.

<u>FACTUAL DETAILS FOUND IN MATT 8:1-4/MARK 1:40-45/LUKE 5:12-16</u>

Matthew 8:1-4	Mark 1:40-45	Luke 5:12-16
A leper came to Jesus	A leper came to Jesus	A man full of leprosy came to Jesus
and knelt before him and asked Jesus to make him clean.	and kneeling and besought Jesus to make him clean.	and fell on his face and besought Jesus to make him clean.
Jesus then touched him saying, "I will; be clean."	Moved with pity, Jesus touched him and said, "I will; be clean."	Jesus then touched him saying, "I will; be clean."
Immediately his leprosy was cleansed.	Immediately the leprosy left him and he was made clean.	Immediately the leprosy left him
Jesus then said to him,	Jesus then sternly charged him to	Jesus then charged him
"Say nothing to anyone; but go, show yourself to the priest, and offer the gift that Moses commanded, for a proof to the people."	"say nothing to anyone; but go, show yourself to the priest, and offer for your cleansing what Moses commanded, for a proof to the people."	to tell no one; but "go and show yourself to the priest, and make an offering for your cleansing, as Moses commanded, for a proof to the people."

An analysis of other pre-passion pericopes from the triple
tradition would likewise demonstrate that despite some differences, these three evangelists tell many of the same stories in
much the same way.[89] Similarly, there exists a high degree of
factual agreement between the Synoptics in those pericopes that
are common to any two of these gospels. Thus even though those
pericopes found in only Matthew and Luke consist largely of
Jesus' teachings, the narrative material in these pericopes
exhibits quite close agreement with regard to the factual information that they contain. For example, Matt 11:2-6/Luke 7:18-
23 mention exactly the same five types of healing miracles,
Matt 11:7-19/Luke 7:24-35 give the same estimate of the life of

John the Baptist, and Matt 11:20-24/Luke 10:13-15 make reference to precisely the same five towns. Likewise, those pericopes common to just Mark and Luke[90] share in many of the same
factual traditions. Again, let one example (The Widow's Gift)
suffice to represent this situation.

Mark 12:41-44	Luke 21:1-4
Jesus watched the multitude put- ting money into the treasury. Many rich people put in large sums. And a poor widow came, and put in two copper coins.	Jesus saw the rich putting their gifts into the treasury; And he saw a poor widow put in two copper coins.
And Jesus said to his disciples, "This poor widow has put in more than all those who are contributing to the treasury. For they all contributed out of their abundance; but she out of her poverty has put in everything she had."	And Jesus said, "This poor widow has put in more than all of them; For they all contributed out of their abundance, but she out of her poverty put in all the living that she had."

It is thus to be observed that each of the Synoptics exhibits a large number of factual agreements (e.g., the same place-
names, same events described, same minute details mentioned)
with one or both of the other first three gospels in most of
the pericopes they have in common in the pre-passion sections
of their gospels. St. Luke in particular not only shares a
considerable quantity of factual data with Matthew/Mark in
these pericopes but the third evangelist also rarely disagrees
with both of the first two evangelists in passages they all
have in common prior to the beginning of his passion narrative.

When St. John is compared with the Synoptics it is to be
found that the Fourth Gospel possesses few close factual agreements with either Matthew or Mark.[91] Contrariwise, an examination of the twenty-eight pericopes common to both Luke and John
discloses that these latter two evangelists share in a substantial number of quite precise factual agreements including a
number of instances (cf. below) in which Luke and John agree
with each other against the contrasting information that is to
be found in the comparable passages of the first two gospels.
This latter phenomenon occurs with special frequency in the
Lukan/Johannine passion narratives with the many factual agreements between Luke 23:1-25 and John 18:28-19:16 against Matt
27:11-31/Mark 15:1-20 being quite noteworthy. With regard to
the factual traditions common to Luke and John, the following
related phenomena should especially be considered.

(1). Of the 176 verses found in those twenty-eight Lukan
pericopes that Luke has in common with John, there exist some
fifty verses that exhibit factual agreements with John and some
forty instances in which Luke agrees with the information found
in John (or vice versa) rather than with the differing details
that are to be found in the comparable pericopes of both Matthew
and Mark. Following is a chart listing many of these Lukan
agreements with John against Matthew/Mark.

CHART VI

A SUMMARY OF THE LUKAN/JOHANNINE FACTUAL AGREEMENTS AGAINST MATTHEW/MARK

Matthew/Mark	Luke	John
Matt 26:57 mentions only "Caiaphas"	Mentions both "Annas" and "Caiaphas" (3:2)	Mentions both "Annas" and "Caiaphas" (18:13,24)
No allusion to John the Baptist as "the Christ"	People wonder if John might be "the Christ" (3:15)	John is asked if he was "the Christ" (1:20)
No miraculous catch of fish described	A miraculous catch of fish described (5:1-11)	A miraculous catch of fish described (21:1-14)
-	They had caught nothing all night (5:5)	That night they caught nothing (21:3d)
No mention of another Judas	Mentions another Judas (6:16)	Mentions another Judas (14:22)
A woman anoints the head of Jesus (Matt 26:7/Mark 14:3)	A woman anoints the feet of Jesus (7:38)	Mary of Bethany anoints the feet of Jesus (12:3)
No mention made of the woman's hair	A woman wipes his feet with her hair (7:38c)	Mary wipes his feet with her hair (12:3b)
Two miraculous feedings	One miraculous feeding	One miraculous feeding
The people arrived at the site ahead of him (Matt 14:13/Mark 6:33)	The crowds followed him (9:11a)	A multitude followed him (6:2a)
No acclamation of Jesus as "King" by the people (Matt 21:9/Mark 11:9-10)	The Multitude hails Jesus as "King" (19:38a)	The people acclaim Jesus as the "King of Israel" (12:13b)
No mention of Pharisees in description of entry	Pharisees mentioned (19:39)	Pharisees mentioned (12:19)
No reason given for Judas' betrayal	Judas' treachery is attributed to Satan (22:3a)	Judas' treachery is attributed to Satan (13:27)
Jesus goes to a place called "Gethsemane" (Matt 26:36/Mark 13:21)	The site of Jesus' betrayal is referred to as "the place" (22:40)	The site of Jesus' betrayal is referred to as "the place" (18:2b)
No hint given that Jesus had ever gone there before	Jesus went there "as was his custom" (22:39)	Jesus had "often" been there before (18:2c)
The servant's ear is cut off (Matt 26:51/Mark 14:47)	The servant's right ear[92] is cut off (22:50)	The servant's right ear is cut off (18:10)
Peter's second accuser was a maid (Matt 26:71/Mark 14:69)	Peter's second accuser was a man (22:58)	Peter's second accuser were certain men (18:25b)
But Peter said, "I do not know the man" (Matt 26:72)	Peter's second denial was, "Man, I am not" (22:58c)	Peter's second denial was, "I am not" (18:25c)

Matthew/Mark	Luke	John
Single question about his Messiahship/Sonship (Matt 26:63/Mark 14:61)	Double question about his Messiahship/Sonship (22:67,70)	Double question about his Messiahship/Sonship (10:24,33)
No specific charges brought to Pilate	Specific charges given (23:2)	Specific charges given (18:30; 19:7,12)
-	Jesus says that he "is Christ a king" (23:2d)	He "makes himself a king" (19:12c)
One assertion by Pilate of Jesus' innocence (Matt 27:23/Mark 15:14)	Three assertions by Pilate of Jesus' innocence (23:4,14,22c)	Three assertions by Pilate of Jesus' innocence (18:38; 19:4,6)
No explicit attempts to release Jesus	Pilate "desired to release Jesus" (23:20)	Pilate "sought to release Jesus" (19:12)
-	The Jews cry, "Away with this man" (23:18)	The Jews cry, "Away with him" (19:15)
The single demand, "Crucify him" (Matt 27:22/Mark 15:13)	The double demand, "Crucify, crucify him" (23:21)	The double demand, "Crucify him, crucify him" (19:6b)
Jesus is buried "in a (new) tomb . . . hewn out of the rock" (Matt 27:60/Mark 15:46)	Jesus is buried "in a rock-hewn tomb, where no one had ever yet been laid" (23:53)	Jesus is buried "in a new tomb where no one had ever been laid" (19:41c)
The women see "an angel/ a man" at the tomb (Matt 28:2/Mark 16:5)	The women see "two men/ angels"[93] at the tomb (24:4,23)	Mary Magdalene sees "two angels" at the tomb (20:12)
No disciples go to the tomb	Some of Jesus' disciples go to the tomb (24:24)	Two of Jesus' disciples go to the tomb (20:3-7)
No Jerusalem appearances	Jesus appears to his disciples in Jerusalem on the evening of his resurrection (24:36)	Jesus appears to his disciples in Jerusalem on the evening of his resurrection (20:19)
-	Jesus said to them, "See my hands" (24:39a)	Jesus said to Thomas, "See my hands" (20:27c)
-	The disciples "disbelieved for joy"[94] (24:41a)	"Then the disciples rejoiced" (20:20b)
-	Jesus appoints them to be "witnesses of these things" (24:48)	The author is bearing "witness to these things" (21:24a)

(2). A study of those pericopes found in all four of our gospels similarly discloses that Luke and John not only lack a considerable number of events, details, and passages that are to be found in the comparable pericopes of both Matthew and Mark but that Luke/John also contain certain pericopes (e.g., Luke 22:31-34/John 13:36-38; Luke 22:47-53/John 18:3-11; Luke 22:66-71/John 18:19-24; Luke 23:33-38/John 19:17-22) in which they share in virtually the same omissions of Matthean/Markan

<u>factual</u> <u>data</u>. Following is a chart that seeks to uplift the more noteworthy of these Lukan/Johannine omissions of Matthean/ Markan material.[95]

CHART VII

<u>A</u> <u>SUMMARY</u> <u>OF</u> <u>THE</u> <u>LUKAN/JOHANNINE</u> <u>OMISSIONS</u> <u>OF</u> <u>MATTHEAN/MARKAN</u> <u>MATERIAL</u>

Event, Detail, Or Passage	Found In Both Matthew and Mark		But Lacking In Both Luke and John	
The food and dress of John the Baptist	3:4	1:6	3:3-10	1:19-28
An explicit description of the baptism of Jesus by John	3:16	1:9-10	3:18-21	1:29-34
The naming of Jesus' brothers	13:55-56	6:3	4:22-23	6:42-44
The reference to "Caesarea Philippi"	16:13	8:27	9:18-22	6:66-71
The reference to David in the crowd's acclamation of Jesus	21:9	11:10	19:37-38	12:13-15
The disciples' sorrow when Jesus told them that one of them would betray him	26:22	14:19	22:21-23	13:21-25
The disciples ask, "Is it I?"	26:22	14:19	22:22-23	13:21-25
"It would have been better for that man if he had not been born"	26:24	14:21	22:22-23	13:21-25
Jesus' prediction that all of his disciples would "fall away"	26:31	14:27	22:31-34	13:36-38
Jesus' quotation of Zech 13:7 in his prophecy of Peter's denials	26:31	14:27	22:31-34	13:36-38
Jesus' promise to go before his disciples into Galilee after his resurrection	26:32	14:28	22:31-34	13:36-38
Peter's vehement protest	26:35	14:31	22:31-34	13:36-38
The disciples' pledge of loyalty	26:35	14:31	22:31-34	13:36-38
The reference to "Gethsemane"	26:36	14:32	22:39-40	18:1-2
Judas' kiss is described as a pre-arranged signal	26:48	14:44	22:47-48	18:3-5
An explicit description of Judas' kiss of betrayal	26:49	14:45	22:47-48	18:3-6
All the disciples forsake Jesus	26:56	14:50	22:53-54	18:11-12
False witnesses testify against Jesus in his trial before the Council and the High Priest	26:59	14:56	22:66-71	18:19-24
These witnesses claim that Jesus had threatened "to destroy the temple"	26:61	14:58	22:66-71	18:19-24
The statements of the High Priest	26:62	14:60	22:66-71	18:19-24

234

Event, Detail, Or Passage	Found In Both Matthew and Mark		But Lacking In Both Luke and John	
The allusion to "coming on the clouds of heaven"	26:64	14:62	22:66-71	18:19-24
The rage of the High Priest	26:65	14:63	22:66-71	18:19-24
Jesus is accused of blasphemy	26:65	14:64	22:66-71	18:19-24
Jesus is condemned by the Council	26:66	14:64	22:66-71	18:19-24
Peter's vehement protest following the third accusation	26:74	14:71	22:59-60	18:25-26
Pilate perceives the envy of the chief priests	27:18	15:10	23:16-18	18:38-40
The chief priests persuade the crowd to ask for Barabbas instead of Jesus	27:20	15:11	23:18-19	18:39-40
Pilate responds, "Then what shall I do with Jesus?"	27:22	15:12	23:19-21	19:3-6
The soldiers spat upon Jesus and struck his head with a reed	27:30	15:19	23:10-12	19:1-3
They offered him wine to drink	27:34	15:23	23:33-34	19:16-18
Jesus is derided by those who passed by	27:39-40	15:29-30	23:35-38	19:21-30
"My God, my God, why hast thou forsaken me?"	27:46	15:34	23:44-45	19:23-30
The reference to Elijah	27:47-49	15:35-36	23:45-46	19:28-30
Joseph of Arimathea "rolled a stone against the door of the tomb"	27:60	15:46	23:53-54	19:41-42
The stone is described as being "great" or "very large"	27:60	16:4	24:1-3	20:1-2
The women are instructed to tell the disciples that Jesus was going before them into Galilee[96]	28:7	16:7	24:6-11	20:11-18

(3). Luke and John also seem to share in certain other factual/conceptual resemblances that are lacking in Matthew/Mark and exhibit certain traits that in the NT are peculiar to the Lukan and the Johannine writings. Following is a listing of some of these Lukan/Johannine resemblances.

* Certain persons (i.e., Mary and Martha, Lazarus, Annas, another Judas) are mentioned only in Luke and John.

* In both Luke (3:2; cf. also Acts 4:6) and John (18:13-24) "the high-priesthood of Annas seems to overlap that of Caiaphas."[97]

* Both Luke (9:51-56; 10:29-37; 17:11-19) and John (4:4-43) exhibit a real interest in Samaria[98] and depict Jesus and his disciples as visiting Samaria (cf. also Acts 8:4-25).

* Both Luke and John allude to Judea "far more often than do the first two gospels."[99]

* Luke and John also refer to Jerusalem much more frequently than do either Matthew or Mark[100] and exhibit special interest

in the temple.[101]

* Luke suggests (cf. e.g., 13:34; 22:39) and John (2:13; 5:1; 7:10; 12:12) explicitly asserts that Jesus had visited Jerusalem a number of times prior to the visit that resulted in his death.

* Both Luke and John assert that Jesus frequently "taught in the temple" (cf. Luke 19:47; 20:1; 21:37-38; John 7:14,28; 8:20; 10:23; 18:20).

* Only Luke (3:23; 4:22) and John (1:45; 6:42) speak of Jesus as "the son of Joseph."

* Only Luke (4:30) and John (8:59; 10:39) tell of Jesus miraculously escaping from a crowd.

* Only Luke (12:4) and John (15:14) inform us that Jesus had referred to his disciples as "my friends."

* Only Luke (24:51) and John (6:62; 16:28; 20:17) speak of Jesus' ascension (cf. also Acts 1:9-11).

* Luke (2:11) and John (4:42) are the only evangelists who apply the word "Saviour" (σωτήρ) to Jesus.

* Only Luke and John speak of Jesus' disciples as being witnesses "from the beginning"[102] (cf. Luke 1:2b; John 15:27; Acts 1:22; I John 1:1).

* Luke and John are our only NT writers to use the term "witness" in the sense of bearing testimony to Christ with any frequency.[103]

It is thus to be observed that Luke and John seemingly share in a considerable number of factual/conceptual traditions (esp. in their passion/resurrection narratives) that are lacking in the first two gospels. As Pierson Parker has written, "The fact is that Luke and John together inherited a huge fund of tradition and of ideas that was closed to the other evangelists."[104]

III. SEQUENTIAL AGREEMENTS SHARED BY LUKE AND JOHN

Numerous writers (e.g., B. H. Streeter, A. M. Perry, E. P. Sanders, J. Jeremias, A. Wickenhauser, V. Taylor, F. V. Filson) have urged that extensive agreements in the order of events between two or more documents is an important factor in determining the interrelatedness of these documents.[105] Thus the high degree of agreement between the first three gospels with regard to their order of pericopes has been a significant factor in influencing many writers to suggest that some form of literary relationship exists among these three gospels.[106] For example, seventy-three of the eighty-one pericopes that comprise the triple tradition occur in the same corresponding order in both Mark and Luke, seventy of these same pericopes occur in the same relative order in both Matthew and Mark, while sixty-two of these pericopes also occur in the same relative order in both Matthew and Luke. All of the Synoptics "have the five Galilean disputes in the same order,"[107] while the thirty pericopes found in the triple tradition between the

feeding of the five thousand (Matt 14:13/Mark 6:30/Luke 9:10)
and the Last Supper (Matt 26:19/Mark 14:16/Luke 22:13) occur
in the same corresponding order in all three of these gospels.
Moreover, all eighteen of the pericopes common to just Matthew
and Mark occur in the same relative order in both of these gospels while all six of the pericopes common to just Mark and
Luke also occur in the same order in these two gospels.
These extensive sequential agreements that exist among the
first three gospels would thus seem to indicate that the
synoptists either "used each other in some way" or were all
dependent in some manner upon some other common source or tradition.[108]

The degree of sequential agreement that exists between Mark
and Luke in most sections of their gospels would seem to be
especially quite high.[109] Thus eighteen of the first nineteen
pericopes common to both Mark and Luke (up to Jesus' calling
of the twelve) occur in the same relative sequence in both of
these gospels[110] while all fifteen pericopes found in the
Second and the Third Gospels between the Stilling of the Storm
(Mark 4:35-41/Luke 8:22-25) and the Question about Greatness
(Mark 9:33-37/Luke 9:46-48) occur in the same corresponding
order in both Mark and Luke. Similarly, all thirteen of the
miracle pericopes common to these two gospels also occur in
exactly the same sequence in both Mark and Luke.[111] Overall,
seventy-nine of the eighty-seven pericopes that are common to
Mark and Luke occur in the same corresponding order in both of
these gospels.

Moreover, this high degree of sequential agreement between
Mark and Luke extends even to the order in which events are
recorded within pericopes in the various pre-passion sections
of these two gospels. For example, the sequential agreement
between Mark 1:21-34 and Luke 4:31-41 with regard to their
order of events would seem to be quite precise. Thus both
Mark (1:21) and Luke (4:31) begin this section of their narratives by telling us that Jesus entered the synagogue in Capernaum on the sabbath and taught. Both Mark (1:22) and Luke
(4:32) then immediately inform us that the people "were aston-
ished at his teaching." Mark (1:23-26) and Luke (4:33-35)
then immediately describe the casting out of an unclean spirit
by Jesus after which they both tell us (Mark 1:27/Luke 4:36)
that the people were amazed at his power. Both Mark (1:29-31)
and Luke (4:38-39) then tell us that Jesus entered into Simon's
house and healed his mother-in-law, after which they both (cf.
Mark 1:32-34/Luke 4:40-41) inform us that at sundown "they
brought to him all who were sick" and that Jesus then healed
them and "cast out many demons."

It is thus to be observed that the sequential agreement between Mark and Luke within these three pericopes is quite exact,
and similar extensive agreements with regard to their sequence
of events occur in numerous other Markan/Lukan passages in the
pre-passion sections of their gospels (cf. e.g., Mark 1:40-
3:6/Luke 5:12-6:11; Mark 4:35-5:43/Luke 8:22-56; Mark 8:27-
9:40/Luke 9:18-50; Mark 10:13-34/Luke 18:15-34; Mark 11:27-
13:2/Luke 20:1-21:6). Contrariwise, there also exist certain
passages in Luke (e.g., 3:15-16; 5:1-11; 7:36-38; 9:10-20;
19:37-40; 22:14-34,47-57,66-70; 23:1-25,32-38,50-56; 24:1-4)
in which the Third Gospel exhibits quite a different sequence

of events from that which is to be found in the comparable
passages in both Matthew and Mark, a sequence that sometimes
places Luke in rather close agreement with the order for these
events that is to be found in the Gospel of John. Thus certain writers (e.g., J. C. Hawkins, V. Taylor, J. Jeremias)
have observed that Luke's passion narrative contains at least
fourteen "variations in order" as compared with Matthew/Mark[112]
while other recent writers (e.g., Pierson Parker, J. A. Bailey,
Raymond E. Brown, J. N. Sanders, Edwin D. Freed/Russell B.
Hunt) have noticed a number of the sequential agreements that
exist between Luke and John in these same passion narratives.[113]

When Luke and John are compared it is to be found that
these two gospels exhibit a considerable number of sequential
agreements that are lacking in the first two gospels. These
Lukan/Johannine agreements vary in type (ranging from the sequence in which individual events occur to the order in which
phrases occur in individual verses), agreements that seemingly
can be broken down into the following three basic categories.

(A). There exist some twenty-four instances in which the
Lukan/Johannine sequence of events differs from a contrasting
order for these same events that is to be found in Matthew/Mark.
The following chart will attempt to illustrate this situation.

CHART VIII

SEQUENTIAL AGREEMENTS THAT EXIST BETWEEN LUKE/JOHN AGAINST MATTHEW/MARK

Matthew/Mark	Luke	John
-	Messianic specula-tion precedes the proclamation by John the Baptist (3:15)	Messianic specula-tion precedes the proclamation by John the Baptist (1:20-25)
A crowd preceded Jesus to the site of the feed-ing of the 5000 (Matt 14:14/Mark 6:34)	A crowd followed Jesus to the site of the feeding of the 5000 (9:11)	A multitude followed Jesus to the site of the feeding of the 5000 (6:2)
Size of multitude men-tioned at end of passage (Matt 14:21/Mark 6:44)	Size of multitude men-tioned in the middle of the pericope (9:14)	Size of multitude men-tioned in the middle of the pericope (6:10)
Peter's confession fol-lows the feeding of the four thousand (Matt 16:16/Mark 8:29)	Peter's confession fol-lows the feeding of the five thousand (9:20)	Peter's confession fol-lows the feeding of the five thousand (6:69)
No mention of any miracle just prior to the Entry	Refers to Jesus' mighty works just prior to the Entry (19:37)	Refers to the raising of Lazarus just prior to the Entry (12:9)
Prophecy of the betrayal precedes the Institution (Matt 26:21/Mark 14:18)	Prophecy of the betrayal follows a sacramental meal (22:21)	Prophecy of the betrayal follows a sacramental meal (13:21)
Prophecy of the denial follows departure from the upper room (Matt 26:34/Mark 14:30)	Prophecy of the denial precedes departure from the upper room (22:34)	Prophecy of the denial precedes departure from the upper room (13:38)

Matthew/Mark	Luke	John
One question concerning his messiahship/sonship (Matt 26:63/Mark 14:61)	Question about sonship follows question about his messiahship (22:70)	Question about sonship follows question about his messiahship (10:36)
Jewish accusations follow Pilate's opening question to Jesus (Matt 27:12/Mark 15:3)	Jewish accusations precede Pilate's opening question to Jesus (23:2)	Jewish accusations precede Pilate's opening question to Jesus (18:29)
Pilate's only assertion of Jesus' innocence comes near the end of his trial before Pilate (Matt 27:23/Mark 15:14)	First assertion of Jesus' innocence comes right after Pilate's opening question (23:4)	First assertion of Jesus' innocence comes right after Pilate's opening question (18:38)
The mocking of Jesus comes after his trial before Pilate (Matt 27:27/Mark 15:14)	The mocking of Jesus comes midway in his trial before Pilate (23:6-12)	The mocking of Jesus comes midway in his trial before Pilate (19:1-3)
Only one affirmation of Jesus' innocence mentioned (Matt 27:23/Mark 15:14)	Second affirmation of Jesus' innocence follows right after the mocking (23:14)	Second affirmation of Jesus' innocence follows right after the mocking (19:4)
Barabbas mentioned before Pilate offered to release Jesus (Matt 27:16/Mark 15:7)	Barabbas not mentioned until after Pilate offered to release Jesus (23:16,18)	Barabbas not mentioned until after Pilate offered to release Jesus (18:39,40)
Barabbas described before the Jews demand that he be released (Matt 27:16/Mark 15:7)	Barabbas not described until after the Jews demand that he be released (23:19)	Barabbas not described until after the Jews demand that he be released (18:40b)
-	Third affirmation of Jesus' innocence follows right after the double demand (23:22)	Third affirmation of Jesus' innocence follows right after the double demand (19:6c)
No further attempts by Pilate to release Jesus	After this affirmation Pilate again attempts to release Jesus (23:22d)	After this affirmation Pilate again attempts to release Jesus (19:10-12)
The offering of wine immediately follows the arrival at Golgotha (Matt 27:34/Mark 15:23)	The crucifixion of Jesus follows right after their arrival at Golgotha (23:33b)	The crucifixion of Jesus follows right after their arrival at Golgotha (19:18a)
The two robbers mentioned only after the inscription is described (Matt 27:38/Mark 15:27)	The two crucified with Jesus mentioned well before the inscription (23:33c,38)	The two crucified with Jesus mentioned well before the inscription (19:18b-20)
The day of Preparation mentioned before the tomb is described (Mark 15:42)	The day of Preparation mentioned right after the tomb is described (23:54)	The day of Preparation mentioned right after the tomb is described (19:42)
The "first day of the week" referred to after the sabbath is mentioned (Matt 28:1b/Mark 16:2)	The "first day of the week" mentioned at the very beginning of the resurrection pericope (24:1a)	The "first day of the week" mentioned at the very beginning of the resurrection pericope (20:1a)

Matthew/Mark	Luke	John
No recorded appearance of Jesus to his disciples in Jerusalem	An appearance of Jesus to his disciples in Jerusalem follows right after an earlier appearance on the same day (24:36)	An appearance of Jesus to his disciples in Jerusalem follows right after an earlier appearance on the same day (20:19)
-	After he appeared, Jesus immediately showed his disciples his hands (24:39a)	After he appeared, Jesus immediately showed his disciples his hands (20:20)

(B).   In certain instances these Lukan/Johannine sequential agreements extend over several consecutive verses in which three or more distinct events are related in the same chronological order by both Luke and John. Let four examples suffice to illustrate this phenomenon.

* A significant sequential agreement seemingly exists between Luke 22:14-34 and John 13:3-38 with regard to the order in which the major events that comprise the last supper scene occur in these two gospels.[114] Thus these events are narrated in the following sequence in both Luke and John: (a) the last supper begins; (b) a sacramental act (in Luke the eucharist, in John the footwashing; (c) Jesus' prediction of Judas' betrayal; (d) the reaction of the disciples; (e) Jesus' prediction of Peter's three-fold denial; (f) their departure from the upper room. On the other hand, Matthew/Mark exhibit quite a differing order for these same events (i.e., a,c,d,b, f,e).

* Luke and John also exhibit the same sequence of events in the opening scene of Jesus' trial before Pilate. Thus the order found in Luke 23:1-4/John 18:28-38 is as follows: (a) Jesus is brought before Pilate; (b) the Jews make accusations against Jesus; (c) Pilate's opening question to Jesus; (d) Pilate's first affirmation of Jesus' innocence. Contrariwise, in Matthew/Mark the sequence for these same events is a,c,b,k.

* Although Luke places the Barabbas incident after his version of the mocking while John places it before the mocking, there nevertheless exists a remarkable agreement in sequence between Luke 23:14b-19 and John 18:38b-40. In both gospels the order of events is as follows: (a) an affirmation of Jesus' innocence; (b) Pilate's first offer to release Jesus; (c) the Jews cry out against Jesus; (d) the first mention of Barabbas; (e) a description of Barabbas. On the other hand, these events occur in quite a different order in Matthew/Mark (i.e., e,d,b,c,a).

* The events that comprise the last scene of Jesus' trial before Pilate also occur in the same relative order in both Luke and John. Thus the sequence found in Luke 23:20-23 and John 19:5-15 is as follows: (a) Pilate addresses the Jews again; (b) the Jews cry out; (c) the double demand; (d) Pilate's third affirmation of Jesus' innocence; (e) Pilate again seeks to release Jesus; (f) the Jews again demand his crucifixion. Contrariwise, in Matthew 27:22-26/Mark 15:12-15

the following sequence for this final scene is to be found:
(a) Pilate asks, "What then shall I do with Jesus?"; (b) the
Jews cry out; (c) the single demand; (d) Pilate's only affirmation of innocence; (e) the Jews again urge his crucifixion.
Thus though a basic similarity exists among all four accounts,
Luke and John would seem to be closer to each other than
either is to Matthew or Mark.

(C). Certain Lukan/Johannine passages also exhibit the
same sentence and word order within comparable pericopes. Let
three examples suffice to represent this situation.

(1) The Proclamation of John

Luke 3:16		John 1:26-27
John answered them all,	=	John answered them,
"I baptize you with water;	=	"I baptize with water;
but he who is mightier than I is coming,	=	but among you stands one whom you do not know, even he who comes after me,
the thong of whose sandals I am not fit to untie"	=	the thong of whose sandal I am not worthy to untie"

The first four phrases of the Lukan version of John's proclamation thus occur in the same order as the four phrases found in
John 1:26-27 (a,b,c,d). On the other hand, the order for these
same four phrases in Mark 1:7-8 is a,c,d,b, with the Markan
wording being also somewhat different (e.g., Mark 1:7a has "and
he preached" in contrast to the Lukan, "John answered them
all"). Matthew's order for these same phrases (3:11) is somewhat closer (b,c,d) to Luke/John, although his introductory
phrase ("he said to them") comes earlier in his narrative (3:7b)
than it does in either Mark, Luke, or John.

(2) The Jews Question Jesus

Luke 22:67		John 10:24b-25b
And they said,	=	And said to him . . . ,
"If you are the Christ,	=	"If you are the Christ,
tell us."[115]	=	tell us plainly."
But he said to them,	=	Jesus answered them,
"If I tell you,	=	"I told you,
you will not believe."	·	and you do not believe."

Thus the four phrases found in Luke 22:67 occur in exactly the
same order as do the parallel phrases in John 10:24-25. The
first three of these phrases have a parallel in Matt 26:63-64a/
Mark 14:61-62a, but the wording of the next phrase in Matthew/
Mark[116] is quite different from the form found in Luke 22:67d/
John 10:25b. Luke 22:67b/John 10:24c also contain only a
single question concerning Jesus' messiahship in contrast to
Matthew 26:63c/Mark 14:61c. The seven words common to Luke
22:67b/John 10:24c ("If you are the Christ, tell us") also
occur in the same order in both gospels, while the response of
Jesus found in Luke 22:67d/John 10:25b has no parallel in
either Matthew or Mark.

(3)   The Arrival at Golgotha

Luke 23:33		John 19:17c-18
to the place which is called The Skull,	=	to the place called the place of a skull . . . .
there they crucified him,	=	There they crucified him,
and the criminals, one on the right and one on the left.	=	and with him two others, one on either side, and Jesus between them.

Thus in both Luke and John the identification of the site of
the crucifixion (Luke 23:33a/John 19:17c) is followed immediately by the statement that "there they crucified him" (Luke
23:33b/John 19:18a), and this latter reference in both gospels
immediately precedes an allusion to the "two others" who were
crucified with Jesus (Luke 23:33c/John 19:18b). Contrariwise,
in Matt 27:34/Mark 15:23 the claim that Jesus was offered
"wine mingled with gall/myrrh" to drink (a detail that is lacking in both Luke and John) is located between the identification of the site and the reference to his crucifixion (Matt
27:33-35/Mark 15:22-24) while the allusion to the "two robbers"
who were crucified with Jesus (Matt 27:38/Mark 15:27) does not
occur in Matthew/Mark until after both the casting of lots
(Matt 27:35/Mark 15:24) and the reference to the wording of
the inscription (Matt 27:37/Mark 15:26). The word order of
Luke 23:33a ("to the place which is called The Skull") would
also seem to be closer to the word order found in John 19:17b
("to the place called the place of a skull")[117] than Luke/
John are to either Matt 27:33 ("to a place called Golgotha")
or Mark 15:22 ("to the place called Golgotha").[118] Other
similar Lukan/Johannine verbal/phrasal sequential agreements
are to be found in such passages as Luke 22:50/John 18:10,
Luke 22:58/John 18:25, Luke 23:20-22/John 19:6, and Luke
24:36/John 20:19.

IV.   THE PASSION NARRATIVES OF LUKE AND JOHN

An examination of the Lukan Passion Narrative (22:1-24:53)
seemingly discloses that Luke's degree of verbal/factual/se-
quential agreement with Matthew/Mark is much lower in these
three chapters than it is in most other sections of his gospel.
Thus not only do less than 25% of the verses found in chs. 22-
24 of Luke have a real parallel in either Matthew or Mark, but
Luke's average percentage of verbal agreement with Matthew/
Mark in his Passion Narrative is only about half (22-26%) of
what it is in the earlier sections of his gospel (42-56%).
A further analysis of Luke 22:1-24:53 also discloses that
only two of the twenty-three pericopes that comprise th[e]
Passion Narrative (22:1-2,7-13) does Luke closely fol[low]
agree with) the form of the tradition found in Matth[ew/Mark]
with no major divergences from or additions to the [material]
found in the comparable Matthean/Markan pericope[s ...]
other twenty-one Lukan Passion pericopes eithe[r ...]
verbal/sequential departures from the compara[ble Matthean/]
Markan passages (cf. e.g., Luke 22:14-23,31[...]
54-62,63-65,66-71; 23:18-25,32-38,50-56; [...]
sess factual/conceptual material that [...]

242

Gospel (i.e., 22:15,24-27,31-32,35-38,43-44,51,66; 23:2,5-12, 27-31,34,39-43,48-49; 24:5-7,13-35,45-53). Yet Luke also exhibits parallels with Matthew/Mark throughout most of his Passion Narrative (cf. Luke 22:1-2,4-6,7-13,14,17-19,21-22, 34,39b-42,45-46,47,50,52-53a,54-55,56-57,59-60,61b-62,64,69-70a; 23:1,3,18b-19,21-22b,23-25,26,33,34b,35b,36-38,44-45, 47,50,51b-53b,54-55; 24:1b-2,9) and possesses a sizeable quantity of material that the third evangelist shares only with John (cf. esp. Luke 22:3,14a,26-27,33,39a,40a,50b,53b-54a,58,59b,66c-67,70b; 23:2a,2d,4,8c,9b,11b,14b,16,18,20-22a, 22c-23b,32-33,53b-54; 24:1a,1c,2-3,4b,8,12,22-24,30b,36,39a, 40-41,44).[121] Certainly, many differing source theories have been suggested for Luke's Passion Narrative (e.g., Luke's primary source was Proto-Luke,[122] Luke's primary source was a special non-Markan Passion Narrative,[123] Luke made use of at least one other rather continuous passion source in addition to Matthew/Mark in composing chs. 22-24,[124] Matthew/Mark was Luke's primary source[125]) and the question is still unresolved. Nevertheless there seems to exist a rather general consensus that in his Passion Narrative Luke is considerably less dependent upon Matthew/Mark than he is in the earlier chapters of his gospel,[126] and that Luke 22:1-24:53 contains a far greater number of verbal/factual agreements with John than is to be found in any other section of the Third Gospel.[127]

Similarly, an analysis of John's Passion/Resurrection Narrative (13:1-38; 18:1-20:31) discloses that in these chapters the Fourth Gospel seems to contain more parallels with the Synoptics than it does anywhere else. For example, while less than 7% of the verses in John 1:1-12:50 (39 vss. out of 574) have a parallel in any of the Synoptics, over 30% of the Johannine Passion/Resurrection Narrative (47 vss. out of 151) possess parallels with one or more of the Synoptic Gospels. John's passion/resurrection parallels with Luke would seem to be especially frequent, with over forty distinct Lukan/Johannine parallels having been isolated by recent writers in their comparative studies of these sections of the Third and Fourth

... an examination of these parallels that exist
... hn would seem to justify the following ob-

... hannine parallels are not confined to
... their Passion/Resurrection Narratives,
... irtually every pericope in which their
... itions overlap. The following chart
... this situation (in this chart the
... column will be to Luke and the
...).

... T IX

... URRECTION PARALLELS WITH JOHN

	Luke/John
57a	23:55c = 19:41c
..5	23:54a = 19:42a
..b	24:1a = 20:1a
..a	24:2 = 20:1c
	24:4b = 20:12a

Luke/John			Luke/John			Luke/John		
22:33a	=	13:37a	23:11b	=	19:2c	24:12a	=	20:3-4
22:34	=	13:38	23:14	=	19:4	24:12b	=	20:5a
22:39a	=	18:2c	23:18	=	18:40a	24:12c	=	20:6b-7
22:40a	=	18:2b	23:20b	=	19:12a	24:23b	=	20:12-13
22:50	=	18:10	23:21	=	19:6b	24:24a	=	20:3
22:53b	=	7:30	23:22a	=	19:6c	24:30b	=	21:13
22:54a	=	18:12-13a	23:22c	=	19:6d	24:36a	=	20:19c
22:55	=	18:18	23:23b	=	19:15a	24:36b	=	20:19d
22:58	=	18:25	23:32a	=	19:18b	24:39a	=	20:27c
22:59b	=	18:26c	23:33a	=	19:17b	24:40	=	20:20a
22:67a	=	10:24b	23:33b	=	19:18a	24:41a	=	20:20b
22:67b	=	10:25a	23:34b	=	19:24	24:44a	=	14:25
22:70b	=	18:37b	23:36	=	19:29	24:44b	=	1:45b
23:2a	=	18:29b-30	23:53b	=	19:41c	24:48	=	21:24a

An analysis of this chart discloses that only six of Luke's pas-
sion/resurrection pericopes (the plot to arrest Jesus, the
preparations for the Passover, the two swords, the daughters
of Jerusalem, the penitent criminal, the walk to Emmaus) lack
verbal agreements with John. On the other hand, Luke also
lacks parallels with Matthew/Mark in five of his pericopes in
these same chapters (the two swords, the daughters of Jerusalem, the penitent criminal, the walk to Emmaus, Jesus'
appearance to his disciples in Jerusalem) so that Luke's passion parallels with John (or vice versa) would seem to be
almost as extensive as are his parallels with Matthew/Mark in
22:1-24:53.

(B). Luke's Passion/Resurrection Narrative also contains
at least twelve pericopes (i.e., 22:3-6,31-34,47-53,54-62,
66-71; 23:1-5,16-19,20-25,32-33,50-56; 24:1-12,36-43) in which
the Third Gospel's verbal parallels with John would seem to be
especially quite close. Indeed, Luke's degree of verbal agreement with John in these passages would often seem to be quite
comparable to the degree of verbal agreement that exists
between Luke and Matthew/Mark in these same pericopes.[129] The
following chart will attempt to illustrate this situation by
using fractions to indicate the degree of agreement that
exists between Luke and his co-evangelists in comparable passages in these pericopes (e.g., the fraction 10/20 would mean
that Luke shares ten of twenty words in this particular passage with Mark or John).

CHART X

A COMPARISON OF LUKE'S PASSION PARALLELS WITH BOTH MARK AND JOHN

Lukan Pericope	Markan/Lukan Parallel[130]		Johannine/Lukan Parallel	
22:3-6	14:10/22:4	(6/12)	13:27a/22:3a	(5/8)
22:31-34	14:30/22:34	(8/15)	13:38b/22:34	(9/15)
22:47-53	14:47/22:50	(10/17)	18:10b/22:50	(11/17)
	14:49a/22:53a	(6/9)	7:30b/22:53b	(3/6)
22:54-62	14:53a/22:54a	(4/11)	18:12-13/22:54a	(5/11)
	14:67/22:56	(8/18)	18:25b/22:58b	(6/12)
22:66-71	14:62/22:69	(9/16)	10:24b/22:67a	(7/8)
	14:61b/22:70a	(5/10)	10:25a/22:67b	(5/9)
	14:63/22:71	(5/15)	18:37c/22:70b	(4/10)
23:1-5	15:2a/23:3a	(10/12)	18:33/23:3b	(9/12)
	15:2b/23:3b	(6/7)	18:38c/23:4	(10/17)

Lukan Pericope	Markan/Lukan Parallel	Johannine/Lukan Parallel
23:16-19	15:11/23:18 (4/11)	18:40/23:18 (6/11)
23:20-25	15:12a/23:20 (4/10)	19:12a/23:20 (5/10)
	15:13/23:21 (4/7)	19:6b/23:21 (4/7)
	15:14a/23:22a (7/11)	19:6d/23:22b (3/6)
23:32-33	15:22/23:33a (5/9)	19:17b/23:33a (4/9)
23:50-56	15:46b/23:53a (8/11)	19:41c/23:53c (4/6)
24:1-12	16:1b-2/24:1b (4/10)	20:1a/24:1a (5/5)
	16:3b/24:2 (4/8)	20:1c/24:2 (4/8)
	16:1a/24:10 (7/17)	20:3-7/24:12 (13/21)
24:36-43	-	20:19c/24:36b (7/10)

(C). A comparative study of the passion/resurrection narratives found in our four gospels also discloses that Luke 22:1-24:53 contains almost as many verbal parallels with John as it has with Matthew/Mark.[131] Contrariwise, such a study also demonstrates that John's passion/resurrection parallels with Luke are far more numerous than are his parallels with either Matthew or Mark in these same chapters. Chart XI will attempt to represent this situation.

CHART XI

A SUMMARY OF THE PASSION PARALLELS THAT EXIST BETWEEN OUR FOUR GOSPELS

Area of Comparison	Matthew	Mark	Luke	John
Number of Passion verses author shares with all three of his co-evangelists	5	5	5	5
Number of Passion verses evangelist shares with both Matthew and Mark	-	-	26	3
Number of Passion verses evangelist shares with both Matthew and Luke	-	25	-	1½
Number of Passion verses evangelist shares with both Mark and Luke	26	-	-	1½
Number of Passion verses evangelist shares with Matthew only	-	73	3	3½
Number of Passion verses evangelist shares with Mark only	74	-	12	2½
Number of Passion verses evangelist shares with Luke only	3	13	-	31
Number of Passion verses evangelist shares with John only	3½	3	33	-
Number of Passion verses that are peculiar to each evangelist	48	9	97	125

Chart XI thus illustrates the phenomenon that even though John shares relatively few of his passion verses (outside of the five verses common to all four gospels)[132] with either Matthew[133] or Mark,[134] the Fourth Gospel nevertheless does contain almost forty passion/resurrection verses that exhibit verbal agreements with the comparable pericopes in the Third Gospel.[135] Contrariwise, this chart also discloses that of the 180 verses

245

found in Luke 22:1-24:53, about forty-five of these Lukan
verses are found to contain verbal agreements with Matthew/
Mark[136] and about forty of these same Lukan verses are found
to contain verbal agreements with John.[137]

(D). An examination of the Passion/Resurrection Narratives of Luke and John similarly discloses that in these
chapters the Third and Fourth Gospels also share in a considerable number of factual traditions that are unique to
these gospels (cf. above, esp. Chart VI). And although these
Lukan/Johannine agreements occur in many of the seventeen
passion/resurrection pericopes that are common to these two
gospels, the Lukan factual agreements with John against
Matthew/Mark in 22:50-71, 23:1-25, and 24:1-40 would seem to
be especially noteworthy. For example, in Luke 23:1-25 there
exist at least eight factual agreements between Luke and John
against both Matthew and Mark (i.e., specific charges are
brought to Pilate against Jesus; Jesus is accused of making
himself a king; three affirmations by Pilate of Jesus' innocence; three cries by the Jews; the cry, "away with him;"
the double demand; two attempts by Pilate to release Jesus;
one final attempt by Pilate to release Jesus following his
third assertion of Jesus' innocence). Similarly, the Lukan
Resurrection Narrative also seems to contain at least eight
factual agreements with John 20:1-21:25 (or vice versa)
against Matthew 28:1-20/Mark 16:1-8 (i.e., Luke/John begin
their Resurrection Narratives with a reference to "the first
day of the week;" the women/Mary Magdalene see "two angels"
at the tomb; some/two of Jesus' disciples are also described
as going to the tomb; Jesus is described as "taking bread"
and "giving it" to some of his disciples; both describe a
Jerusalem appearance of Jesus to his disciples on the evening
of his resurrection; both mention "the hands" of Jesus;
Jesus' disciples/Thomas are invited to touch him; both gospels
refer to the "joy" of the disciples).[138]

(E). In certain instances in their Passion Narratives the
Lukan and the Johannine sequence of events would also seem to
be closer to each other than either is to the Matthean/Markan
order for these same events (cf. above, esp. chart VIII).
Thus the Lukan/Johannine sequential agreements against Matthew/
Mark in such pericopes as the last supper (Luke 22:14-38/John
13:1-38), the arrest (Luke 22:47-54/John 18:1-13), and the
Jewish trial of Jesus (Luke 22:66-71/John 10:24-36) would seem
to be especially quite close. However, the most remarkable of
these Lukan/Johannine sequential agreements would seem to
exist between their pericopes describing Jesus' trial before
Pilate and the road to Golgotha (Luke 23:1-33/John 18:28-19:18).
The following chart will attempt to illustrate this situation.

CHART XII

THE SEQUENCE OF EVENTS FOUND IN LUKE 23:1-33 AND JOHN 18:28-19:18

Luke 23:1-33	John 18:28-19:18
1. Jesus brought before Pilate (23:1)	Jesus brought before Pilate (18:28)
2. Accusations brought against Jesus (23:2)	Accusations brought against Jesus (18:29-32)

Luke 23:1-33	John 18:28-19:18
3. Pilate questions Jesus (23:3)	Pilate questions Jesus (18:33-38)
4. Pilate's first affirmation of Jesus' innocence (23:4)	Pilate's first affirmation of Jesus' innocence (18:38b)
5. A mocking of Jesus by Herod (23:6-12)	-
6. Pilate's second affirmation of Jesus' innocence (23:13-15)	-
7. Pilate offers to release Jesus (23:16)	Pilate offers to release Jesus (18:39)
8. The Jews cry out against Jesus (23:18a)	The Jews cry out against Jesus (18:40a)
9. The first mention of Barabbas (23:18b)	The first mention of Barabbas (18:40b)
10. The description of Barabbas (23:19)	The description of Barabbas (18:40c)
11. -	A mocking of Jesus by the Roman soldiers (19:1-3)
12. -	Pilate's second affirmation of Jesus' innocence (19:4)
13. Pilate addresses the Jews again (23:20)	Pilate addresses the Jews again (19:5)
14. The double cry, "Crucify, crucify him!" (23:21)	The double cry, "Crucify him, crucify him!" (19:6b)
15. Pilate's third affirmation of Jesus' innocence (23:22b)	Pilate's third affirmation of Jesus' innocence (19:6c)
16. Pilate again seeks to release Jesus (23:22c)	Pilate again seeks to release Jesus (19:10-12)
17. The Jews again demand that Jesus be crucified (23:23)	The Jews again demand that Jesus be crucified (19:15)
18. Pilate delivers Jesus to be crucified (23:24-25)	Pilate delivers Jesus to be crucified (19:16)
19. The road to Golgotha (23:26-32)	The road to Golgotha (19:17a)
20. The arrival at Golgotha (23:33a)	The arrival at Golgotha (19:17b)
21. There they crucified him (23:33b)	There they crucified him (19:18a)
22. A reference to the two who were crucified with him (23:33c)	A reference to the two who were crucified with him (19:18b)

Thus even though Luke placed a mocking of Jesus and Pilate's second affirmation of Jesus' innocence before the Barabbas' incident while John placed these two events right after his version of this incident, chart XII nevertheless demonstrates that rather extensive sequential agreements seem to exist between Luke 23:1-33 and John 18:28-19:18. Contrariwise, a quite different order for these events seemingly is to be found in both Matthew 27:1-33 and Mark 15:1-22. Thus if we ascribe the same numbers for the events listed in the above chart to the comparable events described in Matthew 27/Mark 15, then the Matthean/Markan order for these events would be as follows: #1, #3, #2, #10, #9, #7, #8, #13, #14, #4, #17, #18, #11, #19, #20, and #21. Even in small sub-sections of these pericopes the agreement in sequence between Luke and John is quite close (cf. above, esp. Sec. III-B).

(F). There also exist at least ten passion/resurrection pericopes common to Luke and John (i.e., Luke 22:31-34,47-54, 66-71; 23:1-5,13-19,20-25,32-33,50-55; 24:1-12,36-43; and parr.) that exhibit a number of various types of agreements (verbal/factual/conceptual/sequential) between these two evangelists. Let just three examples suffice to illustrate this situation.

(1). Peter's Three-Fold Denial Foretold

(Luke 22:31-34/John 13:36-38)

Luke 22:31-34 possesses verbal parallels with both Matt 26:30-55/Mark 14:26-31 and John 13:36-38, with Luke sharing eleven of his sixty-two words in this pericope with Matthew, twelve of these sixty-two words with Mark, and fifteen of these same words with John.[139] For example, even though Luke 22:34 contains a number of verbal agreements with all three of his co-evangelists (Matt 26:34/Mark 14:30/John 13:38), the main Lukan phrase in this verse (οὐ φωνήσει σήμερον ἀλέκτωρ ἕως τρίς με ἀπαρνήσῃ εἰδέναι) is "almost verbally identical" with the quite comparable phrase found in John 13:38b (οὐ μὴ ἀλέκτωρ φωνήσῃ ἕως οὗ ἀρνήσῃ με τρίς),[140] with seven of the nine Johannine words in this phrase having a parallel in Luke 22:34b. Contrariwise, just five of the eleven words found in Matt 26:34b and six of the fourteen words in Mark 14:30b have a parallel in Luke 22:34b. John A. Bailey has also observed that in this saying both Luke and John "have an οὐ . . . ἕως construction, whereas Matthew and Mark have a construction with πρίν which produces an entirely different sentence syntactically."[141]

Luke 22:31-34 and John 13:36-38 also share certain basic structural characteristics that are unique to these two gospels. Thus Luke (22:33) and John (13:37) agree against Matthew (26:35)/Mark (14:31) in placing Peter's claim that he was willing to die with (for) Jesus prior to the prophecy of the denial, and Luke/John also contain just this one assurance by Peter of his loyalty. Luke and John also agree in locating Jesus' prophecy of Peter's denial in the upper room prior to their departure for the Mount of Olives instead of afterwards as do both Matthew and Mark, and both evangelists also made this prophecy the concluding saying in their version of this incident (cf. Luke 22:34/John 13:38).

In this pericope Luke and John also exhibit virtually the same omissions of Matthean/Markan material. Thus Luke and John both lack Jesus' prediction that his disciples would "all fall away" as well as the allusion to Zech 13:27 that the shepherd would be struck down and all the sheep scattered (cf. Matt 26:31/Mark 14:27). Luke/John also lack Jesus' prediction that after his resurrection he would go before them to Galilee (cf. Matt 26:32/Mark 14:28) and Peter's assertion that "even though they all fall away, I will not" (cf. Matt 26:33/Mark 14:29). The Matthean (26:35)/Markan (14:31) description of Peter's vehement protest to Jesus' prophecy of his betrayal is also lacking in both Luke and John as well as certain individual phrases ("this very night," "before the cock crows," "and they all said the same") that are common to both Matthew and Mark. Thus Luke 22:31-34 and John 13:36-38 would seem to contain a number of verbal/sequential/factual traits that are lacking in Matthew and Mark.

(2). Pilate's Third Assertion of Jesus' Innocence
(Luke 23:20-23/John 19:6-15)

Luke 23:20-23 contains verbal parallels with both Matt 27:22-23/Mark 15:13-14 and John 19:6-15, with Luke sharing eleven of his fifty-one words in these verses with Matthew/Mark only, thirteen of his fifty-one words with John only, and seven additional words with both Matthew/Mark and John. Thus Luke is verbally close to Matthew/Mark in vss. 20a (five words out of six) and 22b (four words out of five) and to John in vss. 20b-21 (seven words out of eleven) and 22c (four words out of six).

Luke's opening phrase in vs. 20 ("Pilate addressed them once more") is verbally quite similar to the Markan phrase ("And Pilate again said to them") that introduces the final statement by Pilate in the Markan version of the Barabbas episode (15:12). Luke's second phrase in vs. 20 ("Pilate . . . , desiring to release Jesus") is, on the other hand, quite comparable to John 19:12a ("Pilate sought to release him"), and Luke agrees with John in placing such a statement subsequent to the Barabbas' incident (Luke 23:16-19/John 18:39-40). Luke 23:21 (οἱ δὲ ἐπεφώνουν λέγοντες Σταύρου, σταύρου αὐτόν), then agrees both verbally and conceptually with John 19:6b (οἱ ἀρχιερεῖς καὶ ... ἐκραύγασαν λέγοντες, Σταύρωσον σταύρωσον) by sharing four of its seven words with John, in containing the double cry ("Crucify, crucify him"), and in placing this double cry just prior to Pilate's third affirmation of Jesus' innocence (Luke 23:22/John 19:6c). Contrariwise, Matt 27:22-23/Mark 15:13-14 describe no further attempt by Pilate to release Jesus after the Barabbas' incident (Matt 27:15-21/Mark 15:6-11) and contain only the single cry, "Crucify him" (in Matt 27:22, the form used is "Let him be crucified").

Luke 23:22 and John 19:6c both also contain a description of Pilate's third affirmation, with Luke seemingly emphasizing this fact in vs. 22a ("A third time he said to them"). Luke's wording (23:22c) of this affirmation ("I have found in him no crime deserving death") would also seem to resemble the wording found in John 19:6c ("for I find no crime in him") except for the Lukan qualification θανάτου which is peculiar to the Third Gospel.[142] Luke 23:22d then agrees with John 19:10-12 (or vice versa) in portraying Pilate as making one more attempt to release Jesus after his third affirmation of Jesus' innocence. Luke/John also place the final cry of the Jews (Luke 23:23/John 19:15) right after Pilate's final attempt to release Jesus (Luke 23:22d/John 19:12) in contrast to Matthew (27:23b)/Mark (15:14b) who both portray the final cry of the Jews as occurring immediately after Pilate's sole assertion of Jesus' innocence (cf. Matt 27:23a/Mark 15:14a).

(3). Jesus' Appearance To His Disciples in Jerusalem

(Luke 24:36-43/John 20:19-29)

In this pericope Luke not only shares thirty-four of his 101 words with John (or vice versa), but Luke/John are also the only gospels that contain an account of a resurrection appearance of Jesus to his disciples in Jerusalem on that first Easter Sunday evening. Thus both Luke 24:36 and John 20:19 depict Jesus as suddenly appearing to his disciples in Jerusalem, and both contain the statement, "Jesus (himself) stood among them," in quite comparable language.143 Indeed, if the "so-called Western non-interpolations" in Luke 24:36b-40 should ever be found to be an authentic part of the Lukan narrative (as Aland, Jeremias, Snodgrass, the 26th Edition of the Nestle/Aland Greek New Testament, and the 2nd Edition of the UBS text have urged),144 then Luke 24:36-43 would exhibit a quite remarkable verbal/sequential parallelism to John 20:19-29. Yet even if vss. 36b and 40 of Luke 24 are not included in this comparison, there nevertheless exist several close verbal/conceptual agreements between the Lukan and the Johannine versions of this appearance.145 As J. N. Sanders has written:

> There are clear contacts here between the Lucan and Johannine traditions; cf. he stood among them (ἔστη εἰς τὸ μέσον) with 'he stood in the midst' (ἔστη ἐν μέσῳ αὐτῶν, Luke xxiv. 36) and then the disciples rejoiced (ἐχάρησαν) with 'they disbelieved for joy' (ἀπὸ τῆς χαρᾶς, Luke xxiv. 41), and especially he showed them his hands (τὰς χεῖρας) and his side with 'See my hands and my feet' (τὰς χεῖρας μου καὶ τοὺς πόδας μου, Luke xxiv. 39) - only here in the gospels is it implied that Jesus was nailed to the cross.146

Similarly, Luke 24:38a (καὶ εἶπεν αὐτοῖς) can seemingly be compared with John 20:21a (εἶπεν οὖν αὐτοῖς πάλιν), Luke 24:39a (ἴδετε τὰς χεῖρας μου) with John 20:27b (καὶ ἴδε τὰς χεῖράς μου), and Luke 24:39c (ψηλαφήσατέ με καὶ ἴδετε) with John 20:27a (φέρε τὸν δάκτυλόν σου ὧδε καὶ ἴδε).147

Thus the following verbal/factual/sequential agreements would seem to exist between the shorter text of Luke 24:36-43 and John 20:19-29: (1) In both Gospels the Jerusalem appearance of Jesus to his disciples follows right after a personal manifestation of Jesus to certain individuals (cf. Luke 24:13-35/John 20:11-18); (2) Both Gospels depict this appearance as taking place on the first Sunday evening (cf. Luke 24:29/John 20:19a) following his crucifixion; (3) In both Gospels Jesus is described as coming suddenly and "standing among them" (Luke 24:36a/John 20:19c); (4) Both also portray Jesus as saying, "See my hands" (Luke 24:39a/John 20:27b); (5) Both accounts depict Jesus as inviting his disciples to touch him (Luke 24:39b/John 20:27c); (6) Both Gospels emphasize the importance of "seeing" (Luke 24:39/John 20:27-29); (7) Both also refer to the "joy" of the disciples (Luke 24:41a/John

20:20b). It thus seems to us that whether one accepts vss. 36b and 40 of Luke 24 as authentic or not, Luke does exhibit a number of important agreements with John 20:19-29, with the material in these two Lukan verses in question merely increasing the number of verbal/factual/sequential contacts that seem to exist between the Lukan and the Johannine versions of Jesus' Jerusalem appearance to his disciples.

V. SUMMARY AND CONCLUSIONS

Our examination of the various agreements that exist between Luke and John have disclosed the existence of certain phenomena that seemingly could be summarized as follows.

* There not only exist some sixty/sixty-five verbal agreements between Luke and John, but these agreements are to be found in virtually every pericope in which the Lukan and the Johannine traditions overlap (cf. above, esp. chart IX).

* These parallels are especially frequent in their passion/resurrection narratives, with some twenty-five of these parallels exhibiting a verbal agreement rate of at least 50% (cf. above, esp. chart X).

* Many of these Lukan/Johannine parallels are quite close (cf. above, esp. chart I), with some seven/ten of these parallels exhibiting near verbatim agreement.[148]

* In individual verses the degree of agreement/disagreement that exists between Luke and John is sometimes quite comparable to the degree of agreement/disagreement that exists between a number of Luke's parallels with Matthew/Mark.

* Just as the highest degree of verbal agreement between Luke and Matthew/Mark often occurs in the "sayings" they have in common (cf. above, esp. n. 53), even so the highest degree of verbal agreement between Luke and John is often to be found in the "sayings" these two evangelists have in common (cf. e.g., Luke 3:16/John 1:26-27; Luke 4:22b/John 6:42a; Luke 19:38a/John 12:13b; Luke 22:34/John 13:38b; Luke 22:58b/John 18:25c; Luke 22:67/John 10:24b-25a; Luke 22:70b/John 18:37b; Luke 23:4b/John 18:38c; Luke 23:18/John 18:40; Luke 23:21/John 19:6b; Luke 24:36b/John 20:19d; Luke 24:40/John 20:20).

* Luke and John also share in a considerable number of factual agreements (e.g., a miraculous catch of fish, one feeding, Jesus is hailed as King, Judas' treachery is attributed to Satan, a servant's right ear is cut off, three assertions of Jesus' innocence, the double cry, two angels, a Jerusalem appearance of Jesus to his disciples) that are lacking in both Matthew and Mark.

* Luke and John contain some twelve pericopes (i.e., Luke 3:16; 19:37-40; 22:14-34,47-54,66-71; 23:1-5,13-19,20-25,32-33, 50-56; 24:1-11,36-43; and parr.) that exhibit sequential agreements that stand in contrast to a differing order for these same events that is to be found in Matthew/Mark (cf. above, esp. chart VIII).

* Luke and John also contain a number of names, terms, and phrases (e.g., "Annas," "Mary and Martha," "Lazarus," "another Judas," "the son of Joseph," "Saviour," "sons of light," "my

friends," "rulers," "saw his glory," "away with him,""and chose
from them twelve," "witness," "from the beginning") that are
peculiar to these two evangelists.

Our examination of the Gospels of Luke and John have thus
disclosed the existence of a number of areas where these two
Gospels seem to stand in quite close agreement. Thus a considerable number of verbal/factual/sequential/conceptual agreements would seem to exist between Luke and John, with some of
these agreements being "too precise to be accidental."[149] All
of the foregoing considerations would therefore seem to suggest
that the Lukan/Johannine question stands in need of careful re-
examination. Indeed it seems to this writer at the present
time that these various Lukan/Johannine agreements indicate
that some type of direct relationship (e.g., John may have
known some form of Luke, Luke may have known some early form
of John, both evangelists may have been influenced by some
other common source or sources) may possibly exist between
these two Gospels. At the least, these extensive Lukan/Johan-
nine agreements suggest that the question of dependence/inde-
pendence is an area of NT study that needs considerable study
and discussion.

252

FOOTNOTES

1. Cf. e.g., B. H. Streeter, The Four Gospels: A Study of Origins (London, 1924); J. H. Bernard, The Gospel According to St. John, ICC (Edinburgh, 1928) xciv-cii; W. F. Howard, "The Gospel According to St. John," IntB 8 (Nashville, 1952) 457-58; C. K. Barrett, The Gospel According to St. John (London, 1956) 14-34; John A. Bailey, The Traditions Common to the Gospels of Luke and John (Leiden, 1963), esp. 1-5; D. Moody Smith, Jr., "John 12:12ff. And the Question of John's Use of the Synoptics," JBL 82 (1963) 58-60.
2. Cf. esp. M. Goguel, Introduction au Nouveau Testament (Paris, 1923-24) 222; H. Windisch, Johannes und die Synoptiker (Leipzig, 1926) 41-43; A. Schlatter, Das Evangelium des Lukas (Stuttgart, 1931) 465; C. K. Barrett, The Gospel According to St. John, 96-97; E. K. Lee, "St. Mark and the Fourth Gospel," NTS 3 (1956-57) 50-58; S. Mendner, "Zum Problem ' Johannes und die Synoptiker,'" NTS 4 (1957-58) 282-307; Edwin D. Freed, "The Entry into Jerusalem in the Gospel of John," JBL 80 (1961) 329-38; A. Wikenhauser, New Testament Introduction (New York, 1958) 299-302.
3. Cf. esp. Raymond E. Brown, The Gospel According to John I-XII (AB 29; Garden City, NY, 1966) xliv; A. Wikenhauser, New Testament Introduction, 300-301; M. H. Shepherd, "The Gospel According to John," The Interpreter's One-Volume Commentary on the Bible (Nashville, 1971) 707.
4. Cf. e.g., J. H. Bernard, The Gospel According to St. John, xciv-xcvii.
5. Cf. esp. E. C. Hoskyns, The Fourth Gospel (London, 1947) 58-85.
6. Saint John and the Synoptic Gospels (Cambridge, 1938).
7. Cf. esp. R. H. Fuller, The New Testament in Current Study (New York, 1962) 111-12; C. H. Dodd, The Interpretation of the Fourth Gospel (Cambridge, 1953) 448-49; D. Moody Smith, Jr., "John 12:12ff. And the Question of John's Use of the Synoptics," 58-59; Raymond E. Brown, The Gospel According to John I-XII, xliv-xlv, 236-50.
8. Cf. E. R. Goodenough, "John a Primitive Gospel," JBL 64 (1945) 145-82; B. Noack, Zur johanneischen Tradition (Copen-hagen, 1954) 89-109; R. Bultmann, Das Evangelium des Johannes (Gottingen, 1957); E. Haenchen, "Johanneische Probleme," ZTK 56 (1959) 19-54; I. Buse, "St. John and 'The First Synoptic Pericope,'" NovT 3 (1959) 57-61; C. H. Dodd, Historical Tra-dition in the Fourth Gospel (Cambridge, 1963); B. M. F. van Iersel, "Tradition und Redaktion in John 1:19-36," NovT 5 (1962) 245-67; D. Moody Smith, Jr., "John 12:12ff. And the Question of John's Use of the Synoptics," 58-64; Frederick H. Borsch, The Son of Man in Myth and History (Philadelphia, 1967) 257-58; Raymond E. Brown, The Gospel According to John XIII-XXI (AB 29a; Garden City, NY, 1970) 787-91.
9. See our remarks on this question in "St. Luke and the Johannine Tradition," JBL 90 (1971) 424-26.
10. Cf. C. K. Barrett, The Gospel According to St. John, esp. 33-34; E. K. Lee, "St. Mark and the Fourth Gospel," 50-58; A. Mendner, "Zum Problem 'Johannes und die Synoptiker,'" 282-307; John A. Bailey, The Traditions Common to the Gospels of Luke and John, esp. 109-116; J. Blinzler, Johannes und die Synoptiker: Ein Forschungsbericht (Stuttgart, 1965) 31-33.

11. Cf. J. N. Sanders, A Commentary on the Gospel According
to John (Harper's New Testament Commentaries; New York, 1968)
8-12; R. Schnackenburg, The Gospel According to St. John, Vol.
I (Herder's Theological Commentary on the New Testament; New
York, 1968) 41-43; R. T. Fortna, The Gospel of Signs: A Recon-
struction of the Narrative Source Underlying the Fourth Gospel
(S.N.T.S. Monograph Series, 11; Cambridge, 1970) 8-11, 55-70;
L. Morris, The Gospel According to John (The New International
Commentary on the New Testament; Grand Rapids, Mich., 1971)
49-52; A. Wind, "Destination and Purpose of the Gospel of
John," Novum Testamentum XIV (1972) 26-69; Charles A. A.
Scobie, "The Origins and Development of Samaritan Christian-
ity," NTS 19 (1973) 406-408; James M. Robinson, "Trajectory
Theories" (Unpublished Paper presented to the Mark/John Group
at the 1977 SBL Meeting) 1-5.
12. Cf. e.g., D. Moody Smith, "Johannine Christianity:
Some Reflections on Its Character and Delineation, NTS 21
(1975) 227.
13. Cf. esp. J. H. Bernard, The Gospel According to St.
John, xciv-xcix; S. I. Buse, "St. John and the Passion Narratives of St. Matthew and St. Luke," NTS VII (1960) 65-76;
Raymond E. Brown, The Gospel According to John I-XII, xliv-
xlvii, 244; J. N. Sanders, The Gospel According to John, 10-12;
R. T. Fortna, The Gospel of Signs, 46-47.
14. See our study, "St. Luke and the Johannine Tradition,"
JBL 90 (1971) 424-26.
15. Thus D. Moody Smith ("John 12:12ff. and the Question of
John's Use of the Synoptics," 63) could write that "the vari-
ous lists of verbatim or nearly verbatim between John and the
Synoptics never turn out to be very long."
16. Cf. esp. O. Zurhellen, Die Heimat des vierten Evan-
geliums (Tubingen, 1909) 39; John A. Bailey, The Traditions
Common to the Gospels of Luke and John, 5; J. N. Sanders, The
Gospel According to John, 8; Raymond E. Brown, The Gospel
According to John XIII-XXI, 790, 816-17.
17. Cf. e.g., B. H. Streeter, The Four Gospels, 397-98;
J. H. Bernard, The Gospel According to St. John, xciv-xcviii;
C. K. Barrett, The Gospel According to St. John, 35-36; J. N.
Sanders, The Gospel According to St. John, 8-10.
18. See our study, "The Agreements That Exist Between Acts
and John" (Perspectives on Luke-Acts; Danville, Va., 1978) 40-
44.
19. "Les points de contact entre le récit de la passion
dans saint Luc et dans saint Jean," Mélanges J. Lebreton (ESR,
39, 1951) 146-54.
20. "Luke and the Fourth Evangelist," NTS IX (1962-63) 335.
21. The Gospel According to John I-XII, xlvi.
22. The Gospel According to John XIII-XXI, 791.
23. "Fortna's Signs-Source in John," JBL 94 (1975) 576-77.
24. Cf. esp. Luke 3:16d/John 1:27b; Luke 4:22b/John 6:42a;
Luke 7:44d/John 12:3c; Luke 19:38a/John 12:13b; Luke 22:3a/
John 13:27b; Luke 22:34/John 13:38b; Luke 22:50/John 18:10b;
Luke 22:67a/John 10:24c; Luke 23:4b/John 18:38c; Luke 23:53c/
John 19:41c; Luke 24:1a/John 20:1a; Luke 24:36/John 20:19c;
Luke 24:39a/John 20:27c; Luke 24:40/John 20:20.
25. I.e., Luke 3:15-16,21-22; 7:36-39; 9:10-17,18-20;
19:36-40,45-46; 22:3-6,14-23,31-34,39-46,47-53,54-62,63-65,
66-71; 23:1-5,6-12,13-19,20-25,32-33,34-38,44-49,50-56; 24:1-11.
26. Of the 143 verses found in the twenty-four pericopes
that Luke shares with all three of his co-evangelists, fifty-

nine of these Lukan verses (3:16,21-22; 5:10-11; 7:36b-37;
9:10a,12-13a,14,16-20; 19:36,38a,45-46; 22:1-2,4-6,9-13,16,
19,22,34,40b,42,45-47,50,52-53a,55b-56,59-60,62,69; 23:3,19,
22b,25-26,33b,35,37-38,44-45,47,50,51b-53a; 24:1b,7) are
found to contain verbal parallels with Matthew/Mark and fifty-
one of these same Lukan verses (3:15-16,22; 5:5a,6; 7:38;
9:11,14,20; 19:37b-38,45; 22:3,14a,23,33-34,39a,40a,50,53b-55a,
58,59a,60b,64b,66c-67,70b; 23:2a,2d,3a,4,8c,9b,11b,13,14c,16,
18,20b-22c,23a,33,34b,36,38,50a,52,53c,54a; 24:1a,2,4b,8,23b-
24) are also found to contain verbal parallels with John.
    27. Cf. our article, "A Study of the Contacts That Exist
Between St. Luke and St. John (SBL 1973 Seminar Papers, Vol.
2) 88-90.
    28. Cf. esp., "St. Luke and the Johannine Tradition,"
423-24.
    29. Thus Mark 1:6,9-10,14-15; 6:3; 8:1-10,27b; 11:10a; 14:2,
19,21b,27,28,31,32a,37b,44,45,50,56,58,60,61a,63,64a,64b,69a,
71; 15:1,4,8-9,11-12,19a,23,27a,29-30,34,35-36,46c; 16:5,7 (and
the parallels in Matthew) are lacking in both Luke and John.
    30. Cf. e.g., J. Jeremias, The Eucharistic Words of Jesus
(London, 1966) 97-99; V. Taylor, The Passion Narrative of St.
Luke (SNTS Monograph Series, No. 19; Cambridge, 1972) 122-25;
F. L. Cribbs, "A Study of the Contacts That Exist Between St.
Luke and St. John," 9-10.
    31. Cf. e.g., Raymond E. Brown, The Gospel According to John
XIII-XXI, 615; J. N. Sanders, The Gospel According to St. John,
318-19; A. Plummer, The Gospel According to St. Luke (ICC;
Edinburgh, 1922) 503; John A. Bailey, The Traditions Common to
the Gospels of Luke and John, 42-44; V. Taylor, The Passion
Narrative of St. Luke, 133-35; F. L. Cribbs, "St. Luke and the
Johannine Tradition," 444-45.
    32. Cf. e.g., J. C. Hawkins, "Three Limitations to St.
Luke's Use of St. Mark's Gospel," Oxford Studies in the Synoptic Problem (London, 1911) 81-84; V. Taylor, The Passion Narrative of St. Luke, 122-23; F. L. Cribbs, "A Study of the Contacts That Exist Between St. Luke and St. John," 68-73.
    33. The exact number of verbal parallels that exist between
Luke and John depends on whether one accepts vss. 12,36b, and
40 of Luke 24 as authentic or not. Thus if these "so-called
Western non-interpolations" should ever be found to be an
authentic part of the Lukan narrative (as the 26th edition of
the Nestle/Aland Greek NT and the 2nd edition of the UBS text
have urged, an argument that it supported by the witness of
P⁷⁵ to the longer text of Luke), then Luke 24 would not only
contain at least four more additional parallels to John 20,
but Luke 24:36-40 would then also exhibit a remarkable parallelism to John 20:19-27 (See also Raymond E. Brown, The Gospel
According to John XIII-XXI, 1928; Kurt Aland, "Neue neutestamentliche Papyri," NTS 12 (1965-66) 193-210; Klyne Snodgrass,
"Western Non-Interpolations," JBL 91 (1972) 369-79; J. N.
Sanders, The Gospel According to St. John, 430; I. H. Marshall,
The Gospel of Luke (New International Greek Testament Commentary; Grand Rapids, Mich., 1978) 901-902.
    34. Cf. Pierson Parker, "Luke and the Fourth Evangelist,"
335; F. L. Cribbs, "The Agreements that Exist Between John and
Acts," 48-54,60-61.
    35. See our concluding remarks in "A Study of the Contacts
that Exist Between St. Luke and St. John," 91-92.
    36. Cf. e.g., John A. Bailey, The Traditions Common to the
Gospels of Luke and John; C. K. Barrett, The Gospel According

to John, esp. 34-36; J. Blinzler, Johannes und die Synoptiker, 57-58; W. G. Kümmel, Introduction to the New Testament (Philadelphia, 1966) 142-54; William Barclay, Introduction to John and the Acts of the Apostles (Philadelphia, 1976) 176-78.

37. Cf. esp. E. Osty, "Les points de contact entre le récit de la passion dans saint Luc et dans saint Jean," 146-54; Pierson Parker, "Two Editions of John," JBL 75 (1956) 303-14; M. -E. Boismard, "Saint Luc et la rédaction du quatrième évangile," RB 69 (1962) 185-211.

38. Cf. esp. V. Taylor, Behind the Third Gospel (Oxford, 1926) 221-30; F. Rehkopf, Die lukanische Sonderquelle, Ihr Umfang und Sprachgebrauch (Tubingen, 1959) 275-84; S. I. Buse, "St. John and the Passion Narratives of St. Matthew and St. Luke," 65-76; Pierson Parker, "Luke and the Fourth Evangelist," 335-36; I. H. Marshall, The Gospel of Luke, 787-88, 853.

39. Cf. e.g., R. Dunkerly, "Lazarus," NTS 5 (1958-59) 321-27; Robert T. Fortna, The Gospel of Signs, 47, 124-29; Edwin D. Freed and Russell B. Hunt, "Fortna's Signs-Source in John," 574-79.

40. Cf. esp. E. Osty, "Les points de contact entre le récit de la passion dans saint Luc et dans saint Jean," 151-54; Raymond E. Brown, The Gospel According to John XIII-XXI, 791; V. Taylor, The Passion Narrative of St. Luke, 44, 87-90, 101; F. L. Cribbs, "A Study of the Contacts That Exist Between Luke and John," 8-9, 91-93.

41. See our concluding remarks in "St. Luke and the Johannine Tradition," 450.

42. See our study, "The Agreements That Exist Between John and Acts," 61.

43. Samuel Sandmel, "Parallelomania," JBL 81 (1962) 1-2.

44. J. C. Hawkins, Horae Synopticae (Oxford, 1909); B. S. Easton, The Gospel According to St. Luke (Edinburgh, 1926); B. H. Streeter, The Four Gospels; V. Taylor, The Passion Narrative of St. Luke, 30-34; P. Parker, The Gospel Before Mark (Chicago, 1953); A. M. Perry, "The Growth of the Gospels," IntB 7 (Nashville, 1951) 62-67; A. M. Honore, "A Statistical Study of the Synoptic Problem," NovT X (1968) 95-147; R. Morgenthaler, Statistische Synopse (Zurich, 1971) esp. 65-68.

45. Stephen Neill, The Interpretation of the New Testament 1861-1961 (London, 1964) 107.

46. Cf. Joseph B. Tyson, "Source Criticism of the Gospel of Luke," Perspectives on Luke-Acts (Danville, Va., 1978) 32-33; F. V. Filson, "The Literary Relations Among the Gospels," 1129-31; J. C. Hawkins, Studies in the Synoptic Problem (Oxford, 1911) 77-79; V. Taylor, The Passion Narrative of St. Luke, 30-32.

47. Cf. e.g., J. C. Hawkins, Horae Synopticae; B. S. Easton, The Gospel According to St. Luke, esp. xxvi-xxiv; A. M. Perry, "The Growth of the Gospels," 62-63; V. Taylor, The Passion Narrative of St. Luke, 30-32.

48. Cf. e.g., J. C. Hawkins, Studies in the Synoptic Problem, 78; A. M. Perry, "The Growth of the Gospels," 65; P. Winter, "The Treatment of His Sources by the Third Evangelist," Studia Theologicia VIII (1954) 138-72; V. Taylor, The Passion Narrative of St. Luke, 32-33.

49. Ibid.

50. Cf. e.g., A. M. Perry, "The Growth of the Gospels," 63; Joseph B. Tyson, "Source Criticism of Luke," 32; A. Wikenhauser, New Testament Introduction, 239-52.

51. Cf. esp. A. M. Honore, "A Statistical Study of the

Synoptic Problem," 142-47; Joseph B. Tyson, "Source Criticism of Luke," 33.

52. Ibid.

53. Cf. esp. R. Morgenthaler, Statistische Synopse, 82-83.

54. Cf. e.g., A. Wikenhauser, New Testament Introduction, 231-52; Stephen Neill, The Interpretation of the New Testament, 108-127; W. R. Farmer, The Synoptic Problem (New York, 1964) 118-52; E. P. Sanders, "The Overlaps of Mark and Q and the Synoptic Problems," NTS 19 (1973) 454-65.

55. See F. V. Filson, "The Literary Relations Among the Gospels," 1130.

56. Ibid., 1129-30.

57. Cf. esp. John 4:35,44; 5:8; 9:6,38; 10:15,36; 12:27,48; 13:16,20; 21:15; and parr.

58. Cf. John 1:27b; 6:42a; 12:13b; 13:38b; 18:10,33b; 19:6b; and parr.

59. Cf. e.g., D. Moody Smith, Jr. ("John 12:12ff. and the Question of John's Use of the Use of the Synoptics," 63), who observed that "the various lists of verbatim or nearly verbatim parallels between John and the Synoptics never turn out to be very long."

60. Cf. e.g., S. I. Buse, "St. John and the Passion Narratives of St. Matthew and St. Luke," 65-76; Raymond E. Brown, The Gospel According to John I-XII, 244; J. N. Sanders, The Gospel According to St. John, 8-11.

61. "St. John and the Passion Narratives of St. Matthew and St. Luke," esp. 74-76.

62. The Gospel According to St. John, 430.

63. Cf. e.g., E. Osty, "Les points de contact entre le récit de la passion dans saint Luc et dans saint Jean," 146-54; P. Parker, "Luke and the Fourth Evangelist," 322-23; F. Rehkopf, Die lukanische Sonderquelle; Raymond E. Brown, The Gospel According to John XIII-XXI, 791; I. H. Marshall, The Gospel of Luke, 853, 901-903; F. L. Cribbs, "The Contacts That Exist Between Luke and John," 49-86.

64. Thus John could have been influenced by some form of Luke, the third evangelist could have been influenced by some form of John, or both could have been influenced by some common source or sources.

65. In addition to the verbal parallels listed in chart I, the reader is referred to the following additional verbal agreements that also seemingly exist between Luke and John: Luke 5:5b/John 21:3b; Luke 5:6b/John 21:6d; Luke 6:13b/John 6:70b; Luke 7:2c/John 4:47c; Luke 7:3a/John 4:47a; Luke 7:3c/John 4:47b; Luke 7:38a/John 11:32-33a; Luke 7:46b/John 12:3b; Luke 9:14a/John 6:10c; Luke 9:20b/John 6:69c; Luke 16:8b/John 12:36b; Luke 22:14a/John 13:1b; Luke 22:26/John 13:14; Luke 22:33a/John 13:37a; Luke 22:39a/John 18:1a; Luke 22:40a/John 18:2a; Luke 22:54b/John 18:28a; Luke 22:59b/John 18:26c; Luke 23:2d/John 18:37a; Luke 23:3a/John 18:33b; Luke 23:8c/John 6:14a; Luke 23:9b/John 19:9c; Luke 23:16/John 18:39b; Luke 23:22a/John 19:6c; Luke 23:38/John 19:19 Luke 23:54a/John 19:42a; Luke 24:4b/John 20:12; Luke 24:22b/John 20:1b; Luke 24:24a/John 20:3b; Luke 24:41a/John 20:20b; Luke 24:43/John 21:24a.

66. Cf. e.g., John A. Bailey, The Traditions Common to the Gospels of Luke and John, 17; Robert T. Fortna, The Gospel of Signs, 46-47; I. H. Marshall, The Gospel of Luke, 278-80.

67. Interestingly, W. Wilkens (Die Entstehungsgeschichte des vierten Evangeliums; Zollikon, 1958) and Raymond E. Brown (The Gospel According to John I-XII, 118) have both assigned

the Johannine version of Jesus' cleansing of the temple to one of the later stages in the literary development of the Fourth Gospel.

68. See our study, "The Contacts That Exist Between Luke and John," 8.

69. Thus in these passages Luke may have used Mark, Mark may have used Luke, or both may have used some other common source.

70. Cf. Matt 27:11b/Mark 15:2a/Luke 23:3a/John 18:33b.

71. On the other hand, Acts 13:25d ("the sandal of whose feet I am not <u>worthy</u> to untie") agrees with John 1:27b over against all the Synoptics in its use of the singular form of "sandal" and in its use of "worthy" instead of "fit" (see our study, "The Agreements That Exist Between John and Acts," 48).

72. Cf. Raymond E. Brown, <u>The Gospel According to John I-XII</u>, 51-52.

73. Thus John A. Bailey (<u>The Traditions Common to the Gospels of Luke and John</u>, 22) has observed that in both Luke 19:38 and John 12:13 "Βασιλεύς, is part of the sentence following on the first εὐλογημένος , and Βασιλεύς is in apposition to ὁ ἐρχόμενος ."

74. Cf. esp. Raymond E. Brown, <u>The Gospel According to John</u> I-XII, 460.

75. John A. Bailey, <u>The Traditions Common to the Gospels of Luke and John</u>, 22.

76. Thus it can be noticed that not only is the Lukan word "all" (πᾶσιν) the sole word found in Luke 3:16a that has no parallel in John 1:26a, but that this is a term that occurs with considerable frequency in the Third Gospel (cf. e.g., Luke 4:14; 5:26; 6:10,30; 7:16,35; 8:37,52; 9:23,42; 11:4; 12:8,10; 18:43; 19:48; 20:45; 21:38; 22:70; 23:48).

77. Similarly, this same Lukan term ("all") is the only word found in Luke 6:10 that is lacking in its parallel in Mark 3:5.

78. Thus the familiar Johannine word "plainly" (cf. John 7:4,13:26; 10:24; 16:5,29; 18:20) is the only word found in John 10:24b that is lacking in Luke 22:67a (this term "plainly" is lacking in both the Matthean and the Lukan vocabularies). On the other hand Mark does use this term in 8:32 although it is lacking in both the Matthean (16"21-22) and the Lukan (9:21-23) parallels to Mark 8:31-32.

79. Thus Luke never uses this title ("the King of Israel") even though the Third Gospel contains passages (19:38; 23:37) that are parallel to Matthean/Markan and Johannine passages in which this title is used.

80. Similarly, Pierson Parker could write ("Luke and the Fourth Evangelist," 335) that "John agrees with Luke alone five times as often as with Matthew alone, or with the Second Gospel alone."

81. Thus John could have been influenced by Luke, Luke could have been influenced by John, or both could have been influenced by some other common source or tradition.

82. Cf. e.g., Robert T. Fortna, <u>The Gospel of Signs</u>, 173-74; J. H. Bernard, <u>The Gospel According to St. John</u>, 39-41; F. L. Cribbs, "St. Luke and the Johannine Tradition," 431-33.

83. If the Johannine expression ("Away with him") found in 19:15a is included in our comparison of Luke 23:18b with John 18:40b, then Luke shares seven of his eleven words in vs. 18b with this comparable section of the Johannine passion narrative.

258

84. Thus Luke 23:18a (ἀνέκραγον δὲ παμπληθεὶ λέγοντες) would seem to be somewhat comparable to John 18:40a (ἐκραύγασαν οὖν πάλιν λέγοντες).

85. Thus even though Luke places the Barabbas' incident after a mocking of Jesus and John places this incident just prior to a mocking, there nevertheless exist some remarkable sequential agreements between Luke 23:13-19 and John 18:38-40. Thus both Luke (23:18-19) and John (18:39-40) place the Barabbas' incident right after an assertion by Pilate of Jesus' innocence (cf. Luke 23:14-15; John 18:38) in contrast to Matthew (27:15-21) and Mark (15:6-11) who both place the Barabbas' incident before any assertion by Pilate of Jesus' innocence. Similarly, in both Luke and John, Pilate's first attempt to release Jesus (Luke 23:16; John 18:39) immediately follows this assertion of Jesus' innocence and immediately precedes the Barabbas' incident (see our study, "The Contacts That Exist Between Luke and John," 71).

86. In addition to the Lukan/Johannine verbal resemblances listed in chart V, the reader is referred to the following passages that also seem to contain resemblances between these two Gospels: Luke 4:30/John 10:39; Luke 4:31a/John 2:12a; Luke 10:22/John 10:15; Luke 11:28/John 13:17; Luke 16:31/John 5:47; Luke 20:19a/John 7:30b; Luke 22:53c/John 12:27; Luke 24:39b/John 6:20; Luke 24:43/John 21:13a.

87. Cf. also Robert T. Fortna, The Gospel of Signs, 84-85; J. N. Sanders, The Gospel According to John, 386-87; I. H. Marshall, The Gospel of Luke, 901-903.

88. Cf. e.g., Sherman E. Johnson, "The Gospel According to St. Matthew," IntB 7 (Nashville, 1951) 235-37; A. M. Perry, "The Growth of the Gospels," 62-65; F. V. Filson, "The Literary Relations Among the Gospels," 1129-30; V. Taylor, The Passion Narrative of St. Luke, 30-33, 125.

89. F. V. Filson, "The Literary Relations Among the Gospels," 1130.

90. Mark 1:21-28/Luke 4:31-37; Mark 1:35-38/Luke 4:42-43; Mark 4:1-25/Luke 8:16-18; Mark 9:38-41/Luke 9:49-50; Mark 11:18-19/Luke 19:47-48; Mark 12:41-44/Luke 21:1-4.

91. See above, esp. n. 59.

92. While Luke (22:50) uses οὖς for "ear" and Mark (14:47)/John (18:10) use ὠτάρίον in their versions of this saying, Luke (22:51) and John (18:26) both use ὠτίον in their second reference to the "ear" of the "servant of the high priest."

93. While Luke uses the term "two men" at 24:4, in his second reference to this incident at 24:23 he uses the word "angels" which would seemingly put Luke in quite close agreement with John 20:12. Contrariwise, Matthew 28:2-5 mentions only "an angel" and Mark 16:5, "a young man."

94. Thus both Luke 24:41a and John 20:20b refer to the "joy" (χαρᾶς) of the disciples (cf. J. H. Bernard, The Gospel According to St. John, 675; J. N. Sanders, The Gospel According to St. John, 430; I. H. Marshall, The Gospel of Luke, 902-903.

95. See our study, "St. Luke and the Johannine Tradition," 429-31.

96. The earlier Matthean (26:32)/Markan (14:28) reference to this event is also lacking in both Luke and John.

97. Cf. Pierson Parker, "Luke and the Fourth Evangelist," 321.

98. Ibid., 318. Cf. also Charles H. H. Scobie, "The Origins and Development of Samaritan Christianity," 403.

99. Pierson Parker, "Luke and the Fourth Evangelist," 318.

100. Ibid.

101. Ibid., 319.

102. Thus the Lukan and the Johannine writings are the only books of the NT that teach that Jesus had a number of disciples who had been with him "from the beginning" (cf. esp. J. H. Bernard, The Gospel According to St. John, 500; A. Plummer, The Gospel According to St. Luke, 4; Raymond E. Brown, The Gospel According to John XIII-XXI, 590; F. F. Bruce, Commentary on the Book of Acts (Grand Rapids, 1956) 50; F. L. Cribbs, "The Agreements That Exist Between John and Acts," 49-50).

103. Cf. Luke 1:2; 24:48; John 1:7,8,15,32,34; 3:11,26,28,32; 5:31,32,33,37,39; 8:13,14,18; 10:25; 15:26,27; 19:35; 21:24; Acts 1:8,22; 2:32; 3:15; 5:32; 7:44; 10:39,41,43; 13:31; 14:3, 17; 15:8; 22:15,20; 23:11; 26:16.

104. "Luke and the Fourth Evangelist," 335.

105. Cf. B. H. Streeter, The Four Gospels, 150-54; A. M. Perry, "The Growth of the Gospels," 61-63; E. P. Sanders, "The Argument from Order and the Relationship Between Matthew and Luke," NTS XV (1965) 249-61; J. Jeremias, The Eucharistic Words of Jesus, 97-99; A. Wikenhauser, New Testament Introduction, 229-48; V. Taylor, The Passion Narrative of St. Luke, 17-18, 125; F. V. Filson, "The Literary Relations Among the Gospels," 1130.

106. Cf. e.g., A. M. Perry, "The Growth of the Gospels," 62; Robert M. Grant, Historical Introduction to the New Testament (New York, 1963) 110-113; S. M. Gilmour, "St. Luke," IntB 8 (Nashville, 1952) 14-18; William R. Farmer, The Synoptic Problem (New York, 1964) esp. 210-12; F. V. Filson, "The Literary Relations Among the Gospels," 1130-33.

107. A. Wikenhauser, New Testament Introduction, 229.

108. Ibid., 234.

109. Cf. esp. B. H. Streeter, The Four Gospels, 151-52; J. Jeremias, The Eucharistic Words of Jesus, 98-99; V. Taylor, The Passion Narrative of St. Luke, 125; I. H. Marshall, The Gospel of Luke, 190.

110. Thus the order for these nineteen pericopes in Mark is 1:1-4,7-8,9-11,12-13,14-15,16-20,21-28,29-31,32-34,35-39,40-45; 2:1-12,13-17,18-20,21-22,23-28; 3:1-6,7-12,13-19 while the order for these same pericopes in Luke is 3:1-6,15-17,21-22; 4:14-15,31-37,38-39,40-41,42-44; 5:12-16,17-26,27-28,29-32,33-39; 6:1-5,6-11,17-19,12-16 (See our chart in "A Study of the Contacts That Exist Between Luke and John," 10).

111. Cf. Mark 1:21-28,29-31,32-34,40-45; 2:1-12; 3:1-6; 4:35-41; 5:1-20,24-34,35-43; 6:30-44; 9:14-29; 10:46-52/Luke 4:31-37,38-39,40-41; 5:12-16,17-26; 6:6-11; 8:22-25,26-39,42-48, 49-56; 9:10-17,37-43; 18:35-43.

112. J. C. Hawkins, "Three Limitations to St. Luke's Use of St. Mark's Gospel," 81-84; V. Taylor, The Passion Narrative of St. Luke, 122-23; J. Jeremias, The Eucharistic Words of Jesus, 97-99.

113. Pierson Parker, "Luke and the Fourth Evangelist," 322-23; J. A. Bailey, The Traditions Common to the Gospels of Luke and John, 42-43,78-80; Raymond E. Brown, The Gospel According to John XIII-XXI, 615, 817; J. N. Sanders, The Gospel According to St. John, 430-31; Edwin D. Freed and Russell B. Hunt,

260

"Fortna's Signs-Source in John," 576-77.

114. Cf. J. A. Bailey, The Traditions Common to the Gospels of Luke and John, 42.

115. See above, n. 78.

116. Thus Luke 22:67d ("If I tell you, you will not believe" and John 10:25b (" I told you, and you do not believe") are quite different from both Matt 26:64b ("You have said so") and Mark 14:62a ("I am").

117. This would seem to be especially true if the word order for John 19:17b found in P66 were to be used.

118. Thus John 19:17b gives the Greek and Hebrew words for the site of Jesus' crucifixion in the inverse order from that which is to be found in Matt 27:33/Mark 15:22, while Luke 23:33 contains only the Greek form of this place-name.

119. See above, esp. n. 48.

120. Cf. e.g., H. Schürmann, Der Paschamahlbericht (Munster, 1953) 75-104; T. Schramm, Der Markus-Stoff Bei Lukas (SNTSMS 14; Cambridge, 1971) 182-84; V. Taylor, The Passion Narrative of St. Luke, 42-46; I. H. Marshall, The Gospel of Luke, 785-92.

121. Cf. esp. E. Osty, "Les points de contact entre le récit de la passion dans saint Luc et dans saint Jean," 146-54; S. I. Buse, "St. John and the Passion Narratives of St. Matthew and St. Luke," 65-76; Raymond E. Brown, The Gospel According to John XIII-XXI, 790-91; F. L. Cribbs, "A Study of the Contacts That Exist Between St. Luke and St. John," 46-86.

122. Cf. esp. B. H. Streeter, The Four Gospels, 201-22; B. S. Easton, The Gospel According to St. Luke (Edinburgh, 1926) xxvii.-xxviii; V. Taylor, Behind the Third Gospel: A Study of the Proto-Luke hypothesis (Oxford, 1926); R. Rehkopf, Die lukanische Sonderquelle, esp. 31-84.

123. Cf. e.g., A. M. Perry, The Sources of Luke's Passion Narrative (Chicago, 1920); F. C. Burkitt, Gospel History and Its Transmission (Edinburgh, 1906) 130-41; J. Jeremias, The Eucharistic Words of Jesus, esp. 97-125; P. Benoit, The Passion and Resurrection of Jesus Christ (New York, 1969).

124. Cf. e.g., V. H. Stanton, The Gospels as Historical Documents (Cambridge, 1909) 210-229; H. Schürmann, Quellenkritische Untersuchung des lukanischen Abendmahlsberichtes Lk. xxii. 7-38 (Munster, 1953-7); P. Winter, "The Treatment of His Sources by the Third Evangelist," 138-72; G. Schneider, Verleugnung, Verpottung und Verhör Jesu nach Lukas 22, 54-71 (Munchen, 1969) 96-132; I. H. Marshall, The Gospel of Luke, esp. 818-19, 834.

125. Cf. esp. J. M. Creed, The Gospel According to St. Luke (London, 1930) 272-84; S. M. Gilmour, "The Gospel According to St. Luke," 16-18; W. G. Kümmel, Introduction to the New Testament, 92-95; E. E. Ellis, The Gospel of Luke (New Century Bible; London, 1966) esp. 26-27; E. Linnemann, Studien zur Passionsgeschichte (Gottingen, 1970) 34-40, 97-101.

126. Cf. esp. V. Taylor, The Passion Narrative of St. Luke, 32-33; A. M. Perry, "The Growth of the Gospels," 65.

127. Cf. esp. E. Osty, "Les points de contact entre le recit de la passion dans saint Luc et dans saint Jean," 73-76; C. H. Dodd, Historical Tradition in the Fourth Gospel, 27-28; Pierson Parker, "Luke and the Fourth Evangelist," 322-23; W. Grundmann, Das Evangelium nach Lukas (Berline, 1966) 426-27; I. H. Marshall, The Gospel of Luke, 787-88, 858; F. L. Cribbs, "St. Luke and the Johannine Tradition," 442-47.

128. See below, esp. chart IX.

129. Thus in these passages Luke possesses some twenty parallels with both Matthew/Mark and John that exhibit a verbal agreement rate in excess of 50%.

130. Most of these Markan/Lukan parallels also have a parallel in Matthew, with the rate of agreement that exists between Matthew and Luke being quite comparable in almost every instance to the rate of agreement that exists between Mark and Luke.

131. See above, esp. n. 26.

132. See John 13:38b; 18:10,33b; 19:6b,19; and parr.

133. Cf. Matt 26:21b/John 13:21b; Matt 26:23/John 13:26a; Matt 26:52a/John 18:11a; Matt 27:28b/John 19:2c; Matt 27:29a/ John 19:2a; Matt 27:29d/John 19:3b; Matt 27:43c/John 19:7c; Matt 27:50b/John 19:30c; Matt 27:57c/John 19:38b; Matt 27:60a/ John 19:41b; Matt 28:10b/John 20:17c; Matt 28:18a/John 20:19d.

134. Cf. Mark 14:18b/John 13:21b; Mark 14:20b/John 13:26a; Mark 14:54b/John 18:15c; Mark 14:54d/John 18:18d; Mark 15:9b/ John 18:39b; Mark 15:17a/John 19:2b; Mark 15:17b/John 19:2a; Mark 15:18b/John 19:3b; Mark 15:42b/John 19:42a; Mark 16:2a/ John 20:1b.

135. Cf. John 13:1b,2b,14,21b,26c,27a,37a,38; 18:1b,2a,2b, 10,12,13a,18a,23c,25,26c,28a,29b,33b,37,38b,39a,40; 19:2c,4b, 4d,6,9c,12a,14b,15a,17b,18,19,24b,29b,30c,41c,42a; 20:1a,1b,3b, 4a,5,6b,7b,11b,12a,19c,19d,20,21a,26c,27c; 21:5a,13,24a; and the parallels in Luke.

136. Cf. Luke 22:1-2,4-6,7,9-13,16,19,22,34,40b,42,45-47,50, 52-53a,55b-56,59-60,62,69,71; 23:3,19,22b,25-26,33a,33c,35,37-38,44-45,47,50,51b-53a; 24:1b,7; and the parallels in Matthew and Mark.

137. Cf. Luke 22:3,14a,21,33-34,39a,40a,50,53b-55a,58,59a, 60b,64b,66c,70b; 23:2a,2d,3a,4,8c,9b,11b,13,14c,16,18,20b-22c, 23a,33,34b,36,38,50a,52,53c,54a; 24:1a,2,4b,8,12,22b,23b,24a, 30b,36,39a,40,41a,44a,44b,48; and the parallels in John.

138. See above, esp. chart VI.

139. Although the word count is our own, any inaccuracies should not greatly alter the results we have attained.

140. Thus J. H. Bernard (The Gospel According to St. John, 529) could write that John 13:38b "is almost verbally identical with Lk 22:34, where the word σήμερον is added."

141. The Traditions Common to the Gospels of Luke and John, 37-38.

142. Luke 23:15,22; Acts 13:28.

143. Cf. esp. J. H. Bernard, The Gospel According to St. John, 673; J. N. Sanders, The Gospel According to St. John, 430; Raymond E. Brown, The Gospel According to John XIII-XXI, 1021; I. H. Marshall, The Gospel of Luke, 901.

144. Cf. esp. J. Jeremias, The Eucharistic Words of Jesus, 151; K. Aland, "Neue neutestamentliche Papyri," 206-208; K. Snodgrass, "Western Non-Interpolations," JBL 91 (1972) 369-79; B. M. Metzger, A Textual Commentary on the Greek New Testament (London, 1971) 186-87; I. H. Marshall, The Gospel of Luke, 901.

145. Cf. esp. V. Taylor, The Passion Narrative of St. Luke, 113; Raymond E. Brown, The Gospel According to John XIII-XXI, 1028-29; I. H. Marshall, The Gospel of Luke, 900-902.

146. The Gospel According to St. John, 430.

147. Cf. also Heb 12:18; I John 1:1.

148. Luke 3:16d/John 1:27b; Luke 4:22b/John 6:42a; Luke 19: 38a/John 12:13b; Luke 22:34b/John 13:38b; Luke 22:67/John 10: 24b; Luke 23:4b/John 18:38b; Luke 24:1a/John 20:1a; Luke 24:12/ John 20:3-7; Luke 24:36/John 20:19; Luke 24:40/John 20:20a.

149. Cf. esp. S. I. Buse, "St. John and the Passion Narratives of St. Matthew and St. John," 73-75; Raymond E. Brown, The Gospel According to John XIII-XXI, 791; V. Taylor, The Passion Narrative of St. Luke, 23.